Chuck Pennacchio
303-499-

5.00

APPROACHING VIETNAM

Other Books by Lloyd C. Gardner

Economic Aspects of New Deal Diplomacy
A Different Frontier (editor)
Architects of Illusion: Men and Ideas in American Foreign Policy 1941–1949
Creation of the American Empire (with Walter LaFeber and Thomas McCormick)
Looking Backward: A Reintroduction to American History (with William L. O'Neill)
Imperial America: American Foreign Policy since 1898
Wilson and Revolutions: 1913–1921
A Covenant with Power: America and World Order from Wilson to Reagan
Safe for Democracy: The Anglo-American Response to Revolution, 1913–1923
Redefining the Past: Essays in Honor of William Appleman Williams (editor)

APPROACHING VIETNAM

From World War II Through Dienbienphu

1941–1954

by

Lloyd C. Gardner

W. W. NORTON & COMPANY

NEW YORK LONDON

Published simultaneously in Canada by Penguin Books Canada Ltd., 2801 John Street, Markham, Ontario L3R 1B4.
Printed in the United States of America.

The text of this book is composed in Janson Alternate, with display type set in Rockwell Bold.
Composition and manufacturing by The Haddon Craftsmen, Inc.
Book design by Marie-Hélène Fredericks.

First published as a Norton paperback 1989.

Library of Congress Cataloging-in-Publication Data
Gardner, Lloyd C., 1934–
Approaching Vietnam: from World War II through Dienbienphu, 1941–1954 / by Lloyd C. Gardner.
p. cm.
Bibliography: p.
Includes index.
1. United States—Foreign relations—Vietnam. 2. Vietnam—Foreign relations—United States. I. Title.
E183.8.V5G36 1988
327.730597—dc 19 87–16616

ISBN 0-393-30578-3

W. W. Norton & Company, Inc., 500 Fifth Avenue, New York, N.Y. 10110
W. W. Norton & Company Ltd., 37 Great Russell Streeet, London WC1B 3NU

2 3 4 5 6 7 8 9 0

TO SANDY AND WALT LAFEBER

AND

BERYL AND CHRISTOPHER THORNE,

"FRIENDS FOR ALL SEASONS,"

AND

NANCY,

WHO GAVE IT A NAME

Contents

Acknowledgments

Many people have aided me at each step along the way. The staffs at the various presidential libraries, Roosevelt, Truman, Eisenhower, always provide the researcher with the constant nudges and hints necessary to relieve the anxious scholar's concern that he has "gotten everything." Like their colleagues at the Public Record Office in London, they are the historian's most important support system.

Extracts from Crown-copyright material in the Public Record Office appear by permission of the Controller of Her Majesty's Stationery Office. For offering advice, notes, and copies of pertinent material, thanks to Patrick Hearden of Purdue University and David Langbart of the National Archives, Washington, D.C. At Rutgers I am much indebted to Warren Kimball, who gets me back on the right track when necessary, and John Rossi, Jon Nashel, and Chris Jespersen, who all helped in different ways to make finishing the book a lot easier. George Herring of the University of Kentucky read a draft of the manuscript and made several key suggestions. I am grateful to all of these friends and colleagues.

Walter LaFeber and Christopher Thorne read the entire manuscript at an early stage, and have contributed so greatly to the final version that the dedication page, usually undecided till the last moment, was a foregone conclusion.

July 1985—October 1987
Winchester, England, and Dutch Neck, New Jersey.

Introduction: After the Fall

> Sometime or other, before the day is over, just as a matter of fact in straightening myself out, I'd like to try and find out just when it was, and why it was, that in Indochina we seemed to move from an idea which President Roosevelt had when he was alive that the French were not going to end up back in Indochina and then sometime or other in '45 they ended up. I don't know how they got there or what happened or what was done.
>
> DEAN ACHESON, May 15, 1954,
> one week "after the fall"
> of Dienbienphu[1]

To begin the story of America's "longest war" in the Johnson years—or even in the Kennedy Thousand Days—is like coming into a darkened theater in the middle of the picture. You can gather what has happened after a while, but the relationship between what you are seeing happen on the screen and what had gone before remains fuzzy. Yet the desire to find out "when" and "why" is today no less compelling than it was when Dean Acheson pondered the origins of an already troubling Vietnam experience. This we cannot do simply by writing about how the war ended—or how it brought to bay the imperial presidency.

Unfortunately, the narrow focus of books about the years when Vietnam was our overwhelming national concern inevitably detaches the war from its historical context. Something happened back then, these books suggest, then hurry on to the trauma of the first television war. At the famous National Teach-In in 1966, a leading historian with experience in the Kennedy White House told the audience that there was little to be gained by lengthy discussions of how America found itself entangled in the war; the pressing problem was to consider how to get out safely without endangering American credibility. A former Harvard colleague who heard this statement felt troubled, and rose to ask when history became irrelevant. Was it last week? Or 1964? A decade previous?

The point, obviously, was that the way in which one determines future options is largely based upon a body of knowledge gleaned from experience. Shortening the historical record to the immediate concerns of the day may be necessary for writers of National Security Council option papers (or to politicians looking over their shoulders at public opinion polls), but it reduces choices to the famous Goldilocks syndrome.

Going back to 1941 is a partial corrective. Historical myopia does not completely explain, however, the tendency to see Vietnam as somehow confirming American exceptionalism. Taking a cue from Lyndon Johnson's famous promise to give the Vietnamese a Mekong Valley replica of the TVA—if the North would only listen to reason—historians and others have talked about "welfare imperialism" and "sentimental imperialists," phrases that echo, however unintentionally, policymakers' justifications for the war. It is not a matter of hypocrisy or self-delusion, this belief in the uniqueness of the American "mission," but rather a process that began, in the case of Vietnam, with confident assertions in the Eisenhower years that the American record in the Philippines authorized, if indeed it did not command, the United States to undertake nation building in Southeast Asia. As the war darkened prospects for success, the process increasingly became one of setting up intellectual barricades against an encroachment as potentially devasting to policy foundations as the siege of Dienbienphu had been to French rule in Indochina.[2]

France lost a valuable colony. America was threatened with a much greater loss, as evidenced in post-Vietnam debates when critics sought to pinpoint blame, ironically, by focusing not on the original commitment to nation building but on what they mistakenly identified as a liberal obsession with transporting democracy over military victory. Exceptionalism thus comes full circle. The problem is to get outside the circle.

The early years of American involvement in Indochina, from 1941 to 1954, tell us much we need to know about the connections, the nature of the forces, and the policymakers who sought to control them that would later produce the most unsettling time in American history since the Civil War. Dean Acheson might ask to be briefed on details of how the French got back into Indochina, but he was well aware, from his own experiences as secretary of state, that for Americans the post–World War II colonial question had become a slippery banana peel. "When you step on a banana peel you have got to keep from falling on your tail, but you don't want to be lurching all over the place all the time."[3]

Efforts to keep from falling, or lurching around all over the place, gave way, of course, to the deadly serious matter of sustaining "credibility," the final argument for staying the course in Vietnam. The plethora of books that followed hard upon the appearance of various editions of the Pentagon Papers have documented the disintegration of policy into that fatal obsession, and have, incidentally, created a dangerous asymmetry in our historical consciousness: we know in great detail, repeated many times now, about how the war escalated (whatever we feel should have been done differently to either "win" the war or disengage with honor), but have forgotten about how we got in.

As in any historical account, there are major and minor themes to be considered. The major themes roll forward like a moving stream or river. Minor themes intrude in a variety of ways: some are like mountain freshets that tumble down into the stream, swelling the waters; others form natural dams that force the river to make a bend; still others are rocky-bottomed, shallow places that produce white-water rapids. All come together in the total reality as seen from either bank of the river, and at the delta.

Probably it is useful to introduce the major themes by first saying what the book does not claim to be. It is not about Vietnamese politics, but rather about the way American policymakers perceived Vietnam within the outlines of a global vision. They knew very little about Vietnamese politics, as evidenced, for example, by Franklin Roosevelt's explaining to Stalin at one point that the Indochinese were a small, passive people, or Dwight Eisenhower's commenting ruefully in 1954 that Ho Chi Minh would win 80 percent of the vote if an election were held at that moment.

Neither is it a book about French colonial policies. It is very much concerned, nevertheless, with Washington's interpretation of those policies, and how to deal with them. Nor does it profess to answer all the questions about the origins of American involvement. Some questions are not discussed, and some remain unanswerable. Would, for example, Secretary of State John Foster Dulles have pushed Korean matters to some sort of showdown with China in

1953 if President Eisenhower had given him a green light? Or would Eisenhower have intervened in Indochina during the Dienbienphu crisis if his conditions had been met?

But it is possible to identify the major themes and tendencies in American policy. These are discussed briefly here so that when they appear at various points in the narrative, it will not be necessary to point them out:

1. *The Cold War.* Early in 1945, advisers to President Roosevelt, including Harry Hopkins, urged him to rethink his "plan" for placing French Indochina under trusteeship in the light of American requirements in Europe in the postwar era. They put the case simply: the United States would need France in any conflict with the Soviet Union. These views predated, of course, the "outbreak" of Cold War, generally dated from the "Iron Curtain" speech by Winston Churchill a year later in 1946. But the Cold War produced, especially after the Communist triumph in China in 1949, a preoccupation with "drawing the line" in Southeast Asia, though it also confused exactly what the line was being drawn against. Containment, the Cold War policy in Europe, really did not fit the situations in Asia. But the difficulties with containment were not yet so apparent as they would become. It sufficed for the moment that George Frost Kennan, serving a brief term as ambassador to the Soviet Union, and the "father" of the containment policy, would note in a 1952 letter to President Truman that the Russians hoped to take advantage of "economic difficulties and break-up of colonial relationships."[4]

2. *Liberation.* The 1952 Republican election battle cry was "Liberation!" Like "drawing the line," however, liberation turned out to be difficult to define or implement. Although the term originally referred to Eastern Europe, it soon became apparent that the Eisenhower administration had little inclination to disturb the status quo there. As events unfolded, indeed, liberation better defined the administration's attitude toward Asia: not going north to liberate the North Koreans, but liberating American foreign policy from the colonial "taint" that clung to it and, it was feared, ruined chances for an anti-Communist nationalism to become the wave of the future across Asia.

"Colonialism is on the way out as a relationship among peoples," Eisenhower wrote Prime Minister Winston Churchill in midsummer 1954. "The sole question is one of time and method. I think we should handle it so as to win adherents to Western aims."[5] Ike had hoped to persuade his old wartime colleague to deliver a speech in this vein, specifying places and times for the further voluntary dismantling of empire. Churchill replied that he had read all that the president had said about "what is called Colonialism," but added, "I was brought up to feel proud of much that we had done. . . . I am a bit skeptical about universal suffrage for the Hottentots even if refined by proportional representation. . . . I shall certainly have to choose another topic for my swan song: I think I will stick to the old one 'The unity of the English-speaking peoples.' With that all will work out well."[6]

Eisenhower had grave doubts. More likely, Churchill's swan song would drift out over the Pacific, an ugly reminder to Asian nationalists of Western rule, and rebound as distorted accusation in the blare of loudspeakers exhorting enraged mobs to action. Yet, try as they might, Eisenhower and his advisers could devise no plan for "united action" in Southeast Asia that could be implemented without the British and French. They were, as Christopher Thorne has so eloquently put it, "allies of a kind," with all that phrase implied.[7]

Dulles, especially, felt encumbered by this heritage, and by the dilemmas liberation posed. They put an extra burden on American policy that, he believed, muffled the spirit of American "liberalism" abroad. In a speech delivered on May 21, 1954, Dulles paused to consider why it had come about that the United States found itself too often unlistened to, both in Europe and in the "newest" worlds of Asia and Africa. In its youth, he said, America had not only had economic prestige, but intellectual and spiritual eminence as well. "We had an environment around us of friendly and admiring countries who were very eager to take guidance from the United States."[8]

Dulles puzzled long and hard about how to recapture that admiration in Vietnam, for he and others believed in an ideological domino theory that was not limited geographically to Southeast Asia. Yet, in the end, the course he chose only further undermined the possibility of recapturing the original place America had held in the world's imagination.

3. *Holding the center.* From the beginning, Vietnam figured in the plans of policymakers to reconstruct the old prewar order into a liberal capitalist system that would insure prosperity and peace. It was the British, however, who called attention to the specific role

Southeast Asia would have to play in the proposed world political economy. By 1950, however, the Japanese trade issue had become key. If Japan were to emerge from the years of occupation a full-fledged citizen of the free world, it had to have export outlets. Dulles put it well at a cabinet meeting on August 6, 1954:

> Southeast Asia is one of the markets Japan must have. But until Southeast Asia markets can be opened up, as an interim measure we must permit Japan to enter into the open world competitive market with us, the British and Germany. The question of Japanese trade is one of great difficulty.
>
> I would like to remind you of one of the last things Stalin wrote before he died. He said that the Red world did not need to go to war to win the world. He said that the free world would find itself in a position where it could not absorb the industrial capacities of Japan and Germany; that the free world would try to set up trade barriers between Germany and Japan and would fall apart eventually on this question, and all the Reds would have to do then would be to pick up the pieces.[9]

Policymakers and diplomatic historians often have difficulty coming to terms with the ambiguities of the relationship between ideas and self-interest in American foreign policy and particularly, as well, the sources of that self-interest. Expounding on the American Revolution after a diplomatic dinner, Dean Acheson once explained (perhaps more fully than he thought) how specific factors such as Dulles mentioned get generalized into universalisms. "The whole mercantile system was irritating," he began,

> whereby trade had to go through the center at London and could not take place directly between the colonies and other trading points. . . . At every point they were met by restrictions imposed on the ruling, powerful, directing groups by a government which was far away and, most important of all, had shown its inability to govern. . . .
>
> What happens when people who want to resist want support? They generalize their position. They don't ask support to fight against timber restrictions. They talk about taxation without representation, and each generalization leads to broader generalizations. Until finally they get to the broadest generalization; which is that all men are created equal.[10]

It was not such a great leap, given Acheson's interpretation of American history, from devising the proper language for the Declaration of Independence to helping Japan gain needed markets in Southeast Asia, though the objectives spanned nearly two hundred years. The trick was to find the broadest generalization, whether it was the Cold War, or drawing the line, or spreading democracy, that would incorporate both strategic concerns and the minor themes of policy.

Secretary Dulles essayed such a generalization with his "Uniting for Action" speech in March 1954. But it was soon coupled with the speculation that Washington intended to use atomic weapons in Indochina. The threat proved to be a double-edged sword. It may have given the Chinese pause, and the Russians a powerful reason for urging Ho Chi Minh to moderate his demands at Geneva, but it also inhibited American policy, making it more, not less, likely that the British and French would resist calls for united action to save Vietnam intact.

Domestic opinion and politics further hampered the administration's efforts, often working in opposite ways in regard to Vietnam policy. Yet after the Geneva Conference in 1954, Dulles benefited from an "odd-couple" alliance of conservative "China lobby" Republicans and liberal Democrats in his fight to protect the new American-sponsored Diem regime in South Vietnam from critics at home and abroad.

A full study has yet to be written of the Dulles/Eisenhower relationship, but when it is, we will have before us the beginnings of the complicated executive maneuvers that came to dominate later White House "insider" politics. At the height of the foreign policy crisis of the Reagan administration, Secretary of State George Shultz, testifying about the sale of arms to Iran, said that "nothing ever gets settled in this town. It's not like running a company, or even a university. It's—it's a seething debating society in which the debate never stops, in which people never give up, including me. And so that's the atmosphere in which you administer. And what I try to do is stay as close to the President as I can, and I feel very close to him."[11]

Shultz had to deal with a whole set of agencies and individuals who claimed "a piece of the action" in foreign policy, a pattern that could already be seen, however dimly, emerging in the Eisenhower years. Suddenly prominent in the Reagan years was Lieutenant Colonel Oliver North, a second-level figure in the National Security

Council, who proudly took credit for devising the "neat" scheme of transferring funds from the clandestine sale of arms to Iran to rebels fighting the leftist regime in Nicaragua. He should have mentioned a predecessor, however, in his recounting of the origins of the stratagem for getting around a congressional ban on aid to the "contras": the legendary Colonel Edward G. Lansdale.

Called to the White House at the outset of the Reagan administration to advise on ways to implement covert aid schemes, Lansdale, now in his seventies, impressed North with tales of his own scheme for extracting money from American businessmen in the Philippines in the early 1950s to fund the presidential campaign of Washington's favorite son candidate in the islands. Lansdale headed counterinsurgency efforts in the Philippines, then moved on to Vietnam at the behest of the Eisenhower administration, to play kingmaker for Ngo Dinh Diem.[12]

Lansdale approached his assignment as a problem in mechanics, while superiors set the overall goals of policy. What follows is an account of such interactions, among other things, and an effort to suggest how it was that choice and circumstance placed the colonel in such a pivotal role with ramifications far beyond the immediate events surrounding the French defeat in Indochina.

APPROACHING VIETNAM

CHAPTER ONE

Roosevelt's Dream

> These Americans represent the new Roman Empire and we Britons, like the Greeks of old, must teach them how to make it go.
>
> Attributed to HAROLD MACMILLAN[1]

"DID I ever tell you the story of French Indochina?" asked the president. It was March of 1944, the eve of the Allied invasion of Europe, a moment when all things seemed possible—or, maybe, simply inevitable. Either way Franklin Roosevelt liked to muse aloud about postwar changes. "A year or so ago when Churchill was over here," the president told Vice-President Henry A. Wallace, "I called his attention to the fact that the French had renounced their claims to Indochina in favor of the Japs six months before the United States was attacked by the Japs."[2]

For three presidents—Roosevelt, Truman, Eisenhower—that was the most obvious fact about colonialism. It was on its way out. By their inability to defend Indochina, contended Roosevelt, the French had forfeited any claims to sovereignty there. Now it was up to America—up to Roosevelt—to oversee the transition to colonial independence. American leaders felt enthusiastic about the challenge, and confident they could take the lead in such a vast endeavor, in part because after World War II there would be no one else to do it, and in part because they all believed the United States could count on the goodwill of Asian and African peoples.

Of course there were risks involved. If things went wrong, really wrong, Washington could alienate its erstwhile European friends without satisfying the nascent "new nations." During the war such gloomy thoughts were banned. Words like those spoken by Dean Acheson about the American "mission" during the Truman years would have horrified Roosevelt stalwarts, not because of the priority he gave to world order, but because of the pessimism they revealed. "I sought to meet the Soviet menace and help create some order out of the chaos of the world," he would write in retirement. "I was seeking stability and never had much use for revolution."[3]

In Roosevelt's day, policymakers had the same priority, but were not yet looking over their shoulders at what Moscow had planned for the "third world." The Soviet menace played some part in official thinking, especially, of course, as the war came to an end in Europe. Pre–Cold War concern not to alienate a potential ally while relations with Russia remained a question mark would later develop into a fixation, but it was secondary to the threat of postwar chaos caused by inept attempts to retake the colonies by shortsighted European leaders seeking a lost glory.

However presumptuous such a perspective seems today, it was the basis for FDR's various suggestions for dealing with problem areas like Indochina. Some critics would say Mr. Roosevelt took too much to heart the quip about small minds and a foolish consistency. FDR had no fear of hobgoblins, so he was as inconsistent as he liked. After all, he could hardly predict what the situation would be at war's end, what could be done immediately and what would simply have to be anticipated without a precise plan. So he *was* fuzzy-minded. He might, as he told Wallace he had, try to line up China and Russia against Churchill on taking Indochina away from France. And he might, as he did on occasion, make public promises that France would be restored to all its greatness after the war, which meant retaining its overseas territory. There was no telling what he might say.

Beneath this free-floating style was a firm commitment to an American role expanded far beyond past definitions of national security. The biggest change from prewar years was not that FDR or his aides might juggle hard-nosed strategic concerns with self-flattering moral pronouncements about the evils of colonialism—all nations and leaders entertain themselves that way—but that they vowed not to be denied a voice, the major voice, in the settlement of any issue of concern.

Indochina claimed less attention than most other wartime issues. But it seemed obvious to Roosevelt and other policymakers that the French colony could not be left alone to fend for itself. It had to be part of something bigger. The only question was what.

When he first shocked Prime Minister Winston Churchill with his proposal to place the colony under a trusteeship, adding that he had already consulted Russia and China without telling Churchill, he got the negative reaction he expected. "Well," he remembered telling the nettled British leader, "we are three to one against you on this. You had better come across and we will make it unanimous." When the prime minister still demurred, saying he had to consult the cabinet, Roosevelt chided: "The trouble with you is that you are thinking that Burma might want to be independent, that the Straits Settlements might want to be independent, or the Dutch East Indies might want to be independent after they have gone through an apprenticeship under a trusteeship."[4]

Roosevelt seemed to relish such encounters, more, perhaps, in the retelling, when they became embellished into morality plays. This behavior confirmed a vision of America's benevolent postwar role, of the United States as history's agent, endowed not only with a superior political and economic system, but also with a superior moral system. Whatever Americans did, therefore, whether they talked about transforming the war into a crusade against colonialism, or only about defeating the Axis, it could hardly be surprising that America's European allies believed, as one British observer put it, that America was "on the verge of a great expansionist movement," without having thought through very carefully where it wanted to go.

The problem for the prewar colonial powers thus became how to manage Roosevelt's dream so that the least damage was done to British and French interests, while obtaining the most from America's postwar position as a superpower. "Our main reason for favoring the restoration of Indo-China to France," read a British Foreign Office conclusion near the end of the war, "is that we see danger to our own Far Eastern colonies in President Roosevelt's idea that restoration depends upon the United Nations (or rather the United States) satisfying themselves that the French record in Indo-China justifies the restoration of French authority."[5]

Fear that the Americans wanted to make the peace settlement something of a "final judgment" on colonialism was an ever-present concern for the British and French during the war. Whether the expansionist thrust would "take the form of imperialism à la Henry Luce or even à la Wallace" was open to question, added the Foreign Office seers, but not that it would occur. The two Henrys, Luce and Wallace, were aptly chosen symbols. They represented not only the traditional American consensus on the evils of colonialism, but the ambiguity, once one got past the Rooseveltian aura (admittedly a hard thing to do during the war), of where American "ideals" would lead when translated into politics and policy.

Henry Luce, head of the vast Time-Life publishing empire, represented an older version of an ongoing manifest destiny, defined for a contemporary audience in his already famous piece "The American Century" as follows: "to accept wholeheartedly our duty and our opportunity as the most powerful and vital nation in the world and in consequence to exert upon the world the full impact of our influence, for such purposes as we see fit and by such means as we see fit."[6]

Vice-President Wallace, on the other hand, was the stereotypical New Deal liberal, while also a true believer in a special kind of manifest destiny, something he liked to call "The Century of the Common Man." No less grandiose in scale than Henry Luce's vision, Wallace's international program projected American interests to the ends of the earth: "The nation must not be subjected to an economic Munich or Dunkerque [after the war]. . . . with me . . . there would be a continuous campaign for maximum production, maximum sales, maximum exports and imports."[7]

Colonial empires were regarded, in both of these versions, as highly suspect. Both literally and symbolically, they encouraged the view that positions in the world economy were forever "fixed," the strategic lines drawn, aspirations limited. Not a few people in leadership positions believed, indeed, that America would not have been called upon to oppose Germany and Japan were it not for the mistakes (both real and imagined) of the colonial powers.

Thus Hitler's demand for the return of Germany's African colonies suggested both that unfulfilled colonial ambitions would always be a cause for "secret diplomacy" and war and, on the other side, that appeasement stemmed from a craven attempt, mixed with a guilty conscience, perhaps, to buy off the dictator with Eastern Europe instead so as to protect the empire as a way of life. Even stronger was the conviction that London had refused to stand up to Japanese ambitions on the Asian mainland during the 1931 Manchurian crisis in a forlorn hope of diverting Tokyo's ambitions out of the areas under British suzerainty.

Against this specific list of grievances charged to colonial policies pursued by European metropolitan powers in the prewar decade, the desire to give colonial peoples a stake in the new order was little more than an abstraction. It could hardly be otherwise. Information about nationalist movements in colonized lands was sparse. And it was simply taken for granted that what Washington decided on their behalf would be better than a return to their prewar condition.

French Indochina proved a good example of the moral concern Americans felt about colonialism's heritage, while at the same time illustrating the largely abstract nature of thinking about colonial issues in general. "Indo-China should not go back to France," Roosevelt admonished Secretary of State Cordell Hull in mid-October 1944. "France has had the country—thirty million inhabitants—for nearly one hundred years, and the people are worse off than they were at the beginning. . . . The people of Indo-China are entitled to something better than that."[8]

Even as he himself reexamined the issue, Roosevelt continued to criticize any subordinate's views that appeared a little too accommodating toward the colonial powers. Under Secretary of State Sumner Welles, on the other hand, was an eloquent spokesman for the president in postwar planning committees. He often talked about the rising power of nationalism, and the dangerous futility of trying to suppress Asian peoples demanding independence. "In various parts of the world," he said in explanation of the White House interest in a trusteeship plan, "there are many peoples who are clamoring for freedom from the colonial powers. Unless some system can be worked out to help these peoples, we shall be encountering trouble. It would be like failing to install a safety valve and then waiting for the boiler to blow up."[9]

Colonialism touched upon everything else. Indeed, if the later domino theory ever had any validity, it was probably during World War II.[10] World War II was no sooner begun than its protagonists realized that in truth they were fighting many overlapping wars; traditional struggles raged in the same geographic areas where shadowy wars of national independence were being fought out, and ideology permeated the thinking of many in the anti-Fascist grand alliance, just as it did on another level in the villages of Southeast Asia. Above all, there was the sense that this time the victors, as well as the vanquished, would be held accountable before the world. The feeling was present everywhere, from the street corner to the summit.

When Churchill traveled to Washington shortly after Pearl Harbor to coordinate wartime strategy, the colonial issue came up briefly, a foreshadowing of future disagreements. The prime minister wanted to put off facing an issue that, he knew in his heart, could only be decided one way, while Roosevelt was already leaping ahead to a better world.

The question at the moment was the public relations issue of whether India should sign the Declaration of the United Nations on war aims. As the Anglo-Americans maneuvered for position, however, Russian diplomats brought in for the final drafting of the language in the declaration sought to amend the document by substituting a phrase about the general struggle against Hitlerism. The proposed change troubled at least one American policymaker, who warned that the Russian amendment might be a sly reference "to a forthcoming world revolution."[11]

Far from expanding Marxist horizons in the postwar world, the Russian purpose was diplomacy. The Soviets were not at war with Japan.[12] On the other hand, Roosevelt experienced no shivers at words that might refer to a revolution. He expected his policy to succeed, ill-defined as it was (and remained) throughout the war. America would not fail in its second chance at world leadership.[13]

Even in the wake of the shocking Japanese success at Pearl Harbor, and the string of military reverses in Asia and Europe that followed, American policymakers felt confident about the ultimate outcome of the war, an inner surety about their purpose that many had not felt since the early days of the New Deal. Roosevelt's domestic program had enabled the nation and its institutions to weather the long strain of the depression decade; but after 1937, especially, the New Dealers had gone on the defensive. What had been exciting now seemed unnaturally confining, a bit like the harrowing experience in those days of digging a long tunnel under rushing waters above, always tense, always fearful the next foot would bring disaster.

Compared with the depression, even the terrible difficulties of throwing back the Axis powers and winning the peace afterward appeared straightforward tasks. The nation was united politically as it had not been since the beginning of Roosevelt's second term. In early 1942, moreover, there was as yet no visible conflict between American idealism and the nation's strategic interests. Everything was as clear-cut as Norman Rockwell's square-jawed, eyes-lifted, wartime illustrations for *Collier's* or *Saturday Evening Post.*

1.

> I can't believe that we can fight a war against fascist slavery and at the same time not work to free people all over the world from a colonial policy.
>
> FRANKLIN D. ROOSEVELT, August 1941[14]

In his first instructions to his "watchdog" ambassador to the Vichy French government, a regime all the world knew existed only at German sufferance, and that he particularly despised, Roosevelt had ordered Admiral William D. Leahy to convey to "all and sundry that an Axis victory would mean the dismemberment of the French Empire."[15] Despite his best efforts, the leaders of the "spineless Vichy Government," as Leahy called Marshal Henri Petain and his aides, yielded to Japanese demands for military bases in Indochina. The admiral then delivered a fateful new message from Washington. If Japan won the war, "the Japanese would take over French Indo-China; and if the Allies won, *we* would take it."[16]

It did not help matters at all, moreover, when, in response to Leahy's threats, Vichy officials explained that granting Japan military bases was the lesser choice of evils. This way, an already suspicious Leahy was told, Tokyo would "respect French sovereignty and . . . withdraw when the emergency no longer existed." If anything, such statements only confirmed Leahy's views—and what he thought Washington would do. "The whole affair had but one meaning in my mind—the end of the French colonies in Asia."[17]

Leahy's superiors were not so blunt, but the threat was there. "In its relations with the French Government at Vichy and with the local French authorities in French territories," read one policy guideline, "the United States will be governed by the manifest effectiveness with which those authorities endeavor to protect these territories from domination and control by those powers which are seeking to extend their rule by force and conquest, or by the threat thereof."[18]

The affair, however, was already a bit more complicated than Leahy's conveying of Washington's indignation and dislike for "imperialist" deals would imply. Seeds were being planted that would yield a bitter harvest in Franco-American relations many years later. As the Japanese-American crisis deepened in late 1940 and on into the summer of 1941, Washington responded negatively to Vichy French efforts to involve the United States directly in the immediate fate of Indochina. There was some truth, for example, to French complaints that the United States, by turning its back on suggestions for American trade negotiations with Indochina, offered no alternative to an overall French bargain with Japan.[19]

Roosevelt's response to Japanese pressure, in fact, was to offer his own "deal" to Tokyo. If Japan would refrain from sending its forces into Indochina, he, in turn, would seek to bring about the "international neutralization" of the French colony—and also the neighboring independent country of Thailand. The kernel of Roosevelt's idea for a postwar trusteeship thus appeared first as a scheme for big-power management of a potential crisis point, not in response to revolutionary nationalism. Around that determination to take affairs out of the hands of those who could not control a strategic situation, moreover, a pattern was established. It would repeat itself again and again in the postwar era, most dramatically, of course, in 1954, when French appeals for American aid, were met with counterdemands that Paris turn over the management of the final stages of the first Indochina war against the Vietminh to Washington's direction.

Meanwhile, policymakers in prewar Washington continued to search for a method to check Japan's drive into Southeast Asia before it hindered the war effort against Germany by slicing across Great Britain's lifelines to the Orient. Japan's threat to Indochina, read a State Department press release, also posed "vital problems" to national security, including the loss of "essential materials . . . [such] as tin and rubber which are necessary for the normal economy of this country and the consummation of our defense program."[20]

American concerns about Indochina would never be limited to one particular problem, or to any specific point on a priority list of factors—economic, political, or strategic. Roosevelt's offer to "neutralize" Indochina was accompanied by an order freezing Japanese assets in the United States. Under these conditions, a favorable response was most unlikely. But it is quite remarkable, nonetheless, that the American president already felt, months before Pearl Harbor, that the United States could speak for all the interested parties in dealing with Japan—or disposing of territory.[21]

When Tokyo responded to the president's gambit with a set of unacceptable counterdemands, no one was very much surprised. In the interim, Roosevelt and Churchill had met off the coast of Newfoundland. In this, the first of their many wartime conferences, the subject of maintaining the status quo in the Pacific claimed much attention. The president explained it was his intention to negotiate about Japan's counteroffer without easing economic measures against Germany's Axis partner, expecting only to secure a few weeks' delay in the outbreak of hostilities.[22]

As the pressing problem was to gain enough time to get ready to fight in two oceans, Indochina quickly faded into the background. But Roosevelt had put a marker on that file, labeling it unfinished business. The two leaders then turned to other questions, including the problem of military aid to the Soviet Union in its struggle to turn back the German onslaught. But there was something else to talk about, however unrelated to immediate difficulties it might at first appear. Out of this momentous meeting, Roosevelt had urged, should come a preliminary statement of war aims.

Looking back after the war, Churchill took great pleasure in pointing out to readers of his memoirs that he, and not Roosevelt, had produced the first draft of what was to become famous as the Atlantic Charter. "Considering all the tales of my reactionary, Old-World outlook, and the pain this is said to have caused the President, I am glad it should be on record that the substance and spirit of what came to be called the 'Atlantic Charter' was in its first draft a British production cast in my own words."[23]

Roosevelt and his entourage were seeking a commitment to certain goals. If they got the substance, they thought, the spirit would take care of itself. After several language changes, this first Allied statement of war aims contained eight "common principles," which, it declared, summed up "their hopes for a better future for the world." Point three declared their commitment to "respect the right of all peoples to choose the form of government under which they will live; and . . . [the Allies'] wish to see sovereign rights and self-government restored to those who have been forcibly denied them."

Both men were thinking first of Europe, of course, thinking of ways to encourage peoples in lands overrun by Nazi Germany. When it appeared that others read the charter to include everyone else "forcibly denied . . . sovereign rights and self-government," Churchill tried to put the lid back on as quickly as he could. But too late. Labour party leader and Deputy Prime Minister Clement Attlee told an audience of West African students in London that the charter applied to "all the races of mankind." The prime minister's protestations that he and the president had confined their promises to the "national life of the states and nations now under the Nazi yoke" only called attention to the issue of war aims, and, as it developed, gave the president even more leverage in their complex personal and national relations.[24]

Roosevelt was not displeased, then, by the way in which the Atlantic Charter provided a raft on which he could store a number of related high-policy matters, dealing with each as circumstances permitted. Always a careful swimmer in political currents, the president could leave the raft and return to the safety of the shore whenever he needed. The raft served as an international liberal "party platform" from which he could retrieve reasons for what he already intended to do to accomplish American purposes. "The Atlantic Charter is a beautiful idea," Roosevelt said near the end of the war.[25]

2.

> I . . . have already made it perfectly clear that we believed that the Atlantic Charter applied to all humanity. I think that's a matter of record.
>
> FRANKLIN D. ROOSEVELT,
> October 1942

Throughout the war Roosevelt dealt with French Indochina through several "screens." He seldom talked directly with French authorities, but instead preferred to send "messages," as Admiral Leahy had done during his tenure as ambassador to Vichy. This situation did not change when the Free French put forward their appeals for recognition as the rightful government of France and ruler of the French empire. Roosevelt simply turned Free French entreaties aside as premature. He always spoke as if the real obstacle to his program for Indochina were the British. French views simply didn't count. Repeating his Indochina "story" to another group of advisers, the president explained how he had assured Churchill that China had no designs to succeed the French. He wanted to encourage the prime minister to believe that Big Four management could work, but, Roosevelt added, "we are still going to have a tough time with the British on this issue."[26]

There were places in the world, Roosevelt told British chargé Sir Ronald Campbell, who came to see him at Hyde Park in early August of 1942, such as Korea, Malaya, and the Dutch East Indies, where the people "were simply not ready to manage their own affairs." For Korea the trustees might be China, the United States, and Russia. In any event, Korea could not be left to itself, nor to Russia and China alone.

As for Malaya, the trustees might be China, the United States, and Great Britain. The Netherlands would have to be included for the East Indies, he supposed. "The poor dears thought they should have them back for themselves in the same conditions as before, but he doubted whether this was possible." As he envisioned the post-war situation, the trusteeship would be on the lines of ordinary trusteeships in private life, with a stipulated term, say ten years, and with provisions for a further extension of ten years.

When Campbell asked about details of this machinery, the president "waved my question aside." At that point Sir Ronald thought it best to say nothing more and seek guidance from London.[27] Additional Roosevelt musings convinced the Foreign Office that the president was off on a tear, stimulating his advisers to say outrageous things that would store up trouble for the future. Campbell reported that the president had also told him about racial theories being examined by American experts that explained "the nefariousness of the Japanese." Sir Ronald gathered that the president believed it was necessary to drive the Japanese back to their home islands, and apply the trusteeship system so as to encourage good "racial crossings." "As far as I could make it out, the line of the President's thought is that an Indo-Asian or Eurasian or (better) Eurindasian race, could be developed which would be good and produce a good civilization and 'order,' to the exclusion of the Japanese, languishing in Coventry within their original islands."[28]

Dismissing FDR's eugenics lecture, the Foreign Office took under consideration what he had said substantively about Far Eastern territories. The Korean solution was perhaps feasible, but as for the rest, even leaving aside the presumption of deciding empire questions over tea at Hyde Park, the president seemed to be forgetting that what he was proposing would very likely "contribute forcefully to the disillusionment of Europe and to the strengthening of the many potential anti Anglo-Saxon forces in Europe. This concerns us more closely than it does the USA and it will therefore be our job to convince the US Govt. of this danger."[29]

The first to undertake this mission was Richard Law, parliamentary under secretary and later minister of state at the Foreign Office. After several conversations in Washington, Law reported back that it was essential to understand that American attitudes were a "blend of fierce dogmatism . . . and bland ignorance, freely confessed, and, indeed almost gloried in." But it would be a very bad mistake to dismiss American views because they were, paradoxically, in a way, "very practical." You could not say to Americans, he went on, that the United States had not managed its own racial problems. They would only reply that you were absolutely right. "The [N]egro problem should never have arisen, reflects very badly upon us and is probably quite insoluble. But we have a very much more practical interest in, say, India or Malaya than you have in Harlem or Alabama." Further, whatever happened to the American blacks, British interests would hardly be touched, but "we have a deep interest in India for we share the defense of India with you."[30]

Law also learned that American policymakers were deeply concerned with bringing China "into the mainstream," that the background of their Asian policy, and especially the trusteeship proposals, displayed a deep concern about "a militant China leading a militant Asia against the West." All very well, but what would happen if FDR lost control of this juggling act? With so many things in the air already, one had to be very careful to avoid everything crashing in a heap, especially when the juggler was tossing your valuables up alongside his own pretensions.

A perfect example was Wendell Willkie's famous 1942 world tour. Fitted out in an army transport plane, the Willkie entourage included its own grandstand of press representatives and Office of War Information publicists. Roosevelt had given his former opponent in the 1940 campaign a rousing send-off for this expedition, flinging him up there with all the rest. Arriving in Moscow at the climax of the journey, Willkie issued his own war bulletins, pronouncements that made it appear he agreed with every criticism uttered by Stalin or Chiang Kai-shek—especially those directed at Great Britain for "stealing Lend-Lease" or "delaying the Second Front" in Europe.[31]

The Republican leader decided he had a duty, also, to bring the British ambassador, Sir Archibald Clark Kerr, up to date on what Roosevelt thought. Assuring Clark Kerr that he and the president were of one mind, he let it be known that they had agreed that British imperialism had a bad record to overcome. Willkie felt sure, however, that in the future, British policy would be "liberal." If it was, he would use all his efforts to swing American public opinion around to a favorable appreciation of British efforts.

"If, however, he were not convinced he must tell me frankly

that he would be obliged to come out against us. He begged me to understand that what he had now said was in no sense a threat. It was straight from his heart."[32] Now, what could be done, Willkie asked rhetorically? An "immense step," he suggested to Clark Kerr, would be for the prime minister to give a speech "showing that in respect of dependencies the 'old imperialism' was as dead as he believed it to be, and that subject races could look to the future with new confidence." Willkie liked the idea so much that he decided to deliver the speech himself, and then to write a book, *One World* (1943), expanding his views for the benefit of the broadest possible audience, and probably for a new try at the presidency. "We believe this war must mean an end to the empire of nations over other nations. . . . And we must say so now, not after the war. We believe it is the world's job to find some system for helping colonial peoples who join the United Nations' cause to become free and independent nations."[33]

Roosevelt had been somewhat annoyed at Willkie's Moscow comments on war strategy, but when asked about the Republican leader's views on the future of imperialism, the president beamed his famous smile and quipped, "[There] is not a controversy in a carload of speeches."[34] "Not a cough in a carton," proclaimed a popular cigarette ad of the day. FDR's takeoff was also an advertising triumph, especially as it came just before he promised the French at the end of 1942 that "French sovereignty will be re-established as soon as possible throughout all the territory, metropolitan or colonial, over which flew the French flag in 1939."[35]

Roosevelt had acted to soothe Vichy throats on the eve of the Anglo-American invasion of Morocco and Algeria to free North Africa of German forces. It was a spoonful of sugar to make the medicine go down. Churchill, however, was not willing to let Willkie's presumptions pass unnoticed. "Let me . . . make this clear," he boomed out, "in case there should be any mistake about it in any quarter. We mean to hold our own. I have not become the King's First Minister in order to preside over the liquidation of the British Empire."[36]

Churchill's reaction to Willkie's challenge stood out, as he undoubtedly meant it to, in contrast to other expressions inside Britain that the Americans were close to the mark, that "the imperial game is up," and that the situation mandated Anglo-American cooperation in a united effort to implement a genuine decolonization policy.[37] But the Foreign Office, while it winced at the tone if not the substance of the prime minister's bulldog defense of Britain's position, certainly felt that Roosevelt was on the verge of Wilsonian "megalomania."[38]

Worrisome evidence about how far the president's mind had slipped into that dangerous state would soon appear at the Casablanca Conference, where Anglo-American talks were to be held on the next stage of the war against Germany.

3.

> We front on both of the world's two great oceans; the Atlantic and the Pacific. We stand midway between the developed European continent and the underdeveloped continent of Asia. Apart, you and we can turn into bitter rivals! Together, you and we, with our manufactures and our exports and our investments, can be the world's mightiest force toward lifting all the world's regions toward a higher and higher level.
>
> ERIC JOHNSTON, president of the United States Chamber of Commerce, in a London speech, 1943[39]

Roosevelt arrived at Casablanca at the end of January 1943, ready to celebrate the Anglo-American victory in North Africa. The first awkward corner of the war had been turned. German armies had been beaten; Hitler's mythical supermen, who devastated enemies with their blitzkrieg, were exposed as ordinary humans who bled and died.

The president had invited Stalin to be present, indeed, had importuned him to come, so that together they might do battle with Churchill's advisers on military strategy. FDR did not want to be trapped in a Mediterranean imbroglio, where, it could be charged, America's future role was to help John Bull regain his imperial territories and prestige. It was time to start thinking in earnest about the postwar "facts of life."

Without Stalin's presence, FDR would lose this battle. Whether the Russian's vote would have made any difference may be doubted, but the next campaign, it was decided, should be the invasion of Sicily, then Italy. To compensate for the loss, and out of concern for Stalin's reaction to the decision, Roosevelt summoned newspaper reporters to tell them "unconditional surrender" on all fronts was the Allied aim, not the particular interests of any one of them.

Searching for ways to make the point clear, Roosevelt settled on a familiar topic: the end of empire. Empire was not on the agenda at Casablanca, but in peripheral discussions, at dinner, for example, with the sultan of Morocco, Roosevelt entertained those present by disparaging colonial regimes. On other occasions, he belittled Free French leader Charles de Gaulle's pretensions, and stripped France of nearly all its prewar possessions to provide for setting up an Anglo-American police force at strategic points around the world.

Roosevelt thus picked up where he had left off in Washington at the beginning of 1942. If he wanted to draw Churchill into a debate on colonialism, he was to be disappointed; the prime minister knew better than to fight on the grounds Roosevelt chose. A British observer recorded that at the outset of the Casablanca Conference, he had privately "christened the two personalities the Emperor of the East and the Emperor of the West, and indeed it was rather like a meeting of the later period of the Roman Empire."[40]

Surrounding the Emperor of the West in his villa were military advisers—who had always had their own suspicions of British political "imperial" motives in urging the North African campaign. To them, the president stated that he did not feel bound by any promises made to the French. Looking mildly reproachful, he told his diplomatic representative in the area, Robert Murphy, that he, Murphy, had overdone things a bit in promises to guarantee France the return of "every part of her empire." "That was the first indication to me," recalled the ambassador, "that Roosevelt was planning to encourage extensive reductions in the French empire, but it was apparent at Casablanca that this project was much on his mind."[41]

Roosevelt was to meet Charles de Gaulle at this conference, an assignment necessary to unite Free French forces—but not one he looked forward to with much relish. He prepared for this confrontation by scarcely disguised attempts to put de Gaulle on notice that the Emperor of the West, and not the Emperor of the East, called the shots. This piece of diplomatic business was accomplished at a dinner with the sultan of Morocco, then a protectorate of the French. With Churchill seated nearby, Roosevelt launched into a discussion of his sympathy for colonial aspirations for independence, and suggested to the sultan that he hoped to see postwar economic cooperation between the United States and Morocco.[42]

This table talk was reported, of course, to de Gaulle, who had been summoned to appear at the conference against his will, under actual threat of Allied abandonment. In sharp contrast to his wooing of the sultan, Roosevelt would not recognize General de Gaulle as the leader of a provisional French government in exile. The president had made it plain he regarded France as having ceased to exist, and until the liberation of metropolitan France no French authority could be recognized. Harold Macmillan, Churchill's chief diplomatic adviser in North Africa, who was also present at the dinner for the sultan, concluded that the prime minister had ample reason for his "sulkiness" beyond the absence of his usual liquid refreshments. "The President talked a great deal about colonial aspirations towards independence and the approaching end of 'imperialism'. All this was equally embarrassing to the British and to the French."[43]

More was to come. In de Gaulle's presence, Roosevelt described France's present state as like a "child" in need of trustees. And without Churchill's knowledge, the president attempted to promote de Gaulle's chief rival, General Henri Giraud, to a superior position in the Free French movement. He did this, it has been convincingly argued, because de Gaulle had served notice he would not accept "a secondary role for France after the war."[44]

Returning to Washington, Roosevelt unveiled his personal sketches for the United Nations. Once again, France was left out. The postwar security organization was to consist of three bodies: a general assembly of all members, an executive committee of the Big Four, and an advisory council elected on a regional basis to meet from time to time with the Big Four to resolve crisis issues. The assembly, suggested Roosevelt, would meet once a year to let "the smaller powers . . . blow off steam." The executive committee, on the other hand, would "take all the more important decisions and wield police powers of the United Nations."

Within this framework he imagined that some mechanism—still undefined—could be devised to solve the colonial problem. The Big Four executive committee that Roosevelt had put at the center, for example, he often spoke about as having special regional responsibilities. Sometimes he called them the Four Policemen. But if that were so, how would the demands of the the colonial areas for genuine independence fare against what was shaping up as a traditional spheres of influence arrangement?

Russia had already indicated it wanted no one bothering too

much about what it did in the Baltic states. And China was known to have its own ambitions, especially in regard to Hong Kong and Indochina, which it wanted to classify as "lost territories." Roosevelt professed not to be troubled in conversations with the British ambassador, Lord Halifax, who had been invited to the unveiling.

As Halifax watched in astonishment, Roosevelt redrew prewar maps, not as Wilson had done in Europe, but all around the globe. French Indochina would be placed under trusteeship, he said. When the ambassador asked who would administer the former colony, FDR ignored the question, and continued scratching out other pieces of the French empire, including the Marquesas and Tuamotu Islands—to be used as United Nations bases, he said—and strong points in North and West Africa, Dakar and Bizerta.

He had decided, Roosevelt at last explained, that the United States should "act as policeman" for the United Nations at Dakar, and Great Britain likewise at Bizerta. In reply to this breathtaking recital, Halifax could only manage to wonder if perhaps the president was not being "very hard on the French." Yes, that was so, admitted Roosevelt, but then "France would no doubt require assistance for which consideration might be the placing of certain parts of her territory at the disposal of the United Nations."[45]

When Halifax went off to ponder the consequences of this latest presidential effusion, Roosevelt turned the page to China. Ah, there was a real trouble spot. When the war began, Roosevelt had in mind something like what Henry Kissinger would one day call the "structure of peace." He had got as far as naming it the Big Four. The idea held little appeal for either Churchill or Stalin, however, both of whom suspected—with some reason—that FDR had it in mind to get them over the barrel with China's vote whenever he determined it was in America's interest to inject himself into disputes within their areas of "responsibility." But for Roosevelt, the idea seemed to suggest a solution to the various possibilities for China's entrance onto the world scene as a major power.

Certainly he did not want Chiang Kai-shek going off alone, thinking he might replace the French in Indochina. It troubled the British, however, when FDR sometimes talked about throwing Hong Kong to Chiang as a kind of consolation prize.[46] From the spotty reports coming out of occupied Indochina, and from the more easily available Chinese press reports, it appeared that Roosevelt was indeed right to be concerned about a Kuomintang forward movement after the war. It was not entirely clear what the Chinese were doing, but that they were doing "something" could not be doubted. The arrest of an "unidentified Annamite" (Ho Chi Minh) in Chungking was reported at the end of 1942, along with other information about Chinese involvement with a so-called provisional government for the French colony.[47]

Over the next twelve months, much harder evidence was available to Washington that China was behind certain "Annamite activities." In early 1944, Ambassador Clarence Gauss reported from Chungking:

> Chinese policy in regard to Indochina is ill-defined. It appears to rest, as do so many other Chinese policy questions, on a shifting basis of political opportunism, international and domestic. . . . One of the principal aims of present Chinese policy is, understandably, the recovery of "lost territories", and Chinese national opinion (insofar as it exists in China) is therefore in an expansionist mood. It may accordingly be expected that action based on the premise that such areas as Indochina and Burma are "lost territories" might be considered if thought expedient by the leaders of the Kuomintang and the Government. In other words, judging from the present temper of China, it is probable that no opportunity will be lost to establish and increase Chinese influence and control in Indochina to as great a degree as circumstances render practicable.[48]

As this evidence mounted, State Department planners worried that the absence of a settled policy on Indochina left both the colonial powers and the Asian colonial peoples with the strong impression China was in fact being encouraged to become involved in the French colony.[49] But Roosevelt had not been idle all this time. In conversations with British policymakers he continued to stress the need to accommodate postwar China—or face very unpleasant consequences. To Roosevelt's repeated suggestions that the British return Hong Kong to Chinese sovereignty as a goodwill gesture, Foreign Secretary Anthony Eden inquired drily what gestures he had in mind for America to make.[50]

At the Cairo and Teheran conferences, the president discussed Indochina with Chiang and Premier Joseph Stalin. In the first conference, Roosevelt continued his efforts, without much consultation of the British, to insure that China received its full due. The communiqué from Cairo stressed that China must have all its lost territories restored. It did not, however, mention the territories Japan had taken from the Western powers.[51] Instead, FDR proposed to "negotiate" about those. According to the Chinese record of his conversation with Chiang, Roosevelt began with an invitation, readily accepted, for China to "participate on an equal footing in the machinery of the Big Four Group and in all its decisions." Then he proposed that China and the United States "should reach a mutual understanding on the future status of Korea, Indo-China and other colonial areas as well as Thailand." Chiang replied that the two nations should help Indochina achieve independence. "The President expressed his agreement."[52]

His initial meeting with Stalin a few days later at Teheran began on the same plane, with outstretched hands of greetings for the first nation to be invited to join the Grand Alliance chartered by Roosevelt and Churchill. "I am glad to see you. I have tried for a long time to bring this about." In this case, however, it was the Russian who first brought up Indochina, saying that he did not propose to shed Allied blood to restore French rule. FDR said he was in "100%" agreement. France had had the colony for a hundred years, and the inhabitants were worse off than they had been. Chiang Kai-shek had assured him, he went on, that China harbored no designs on Indochina. But the generalissimo had also said that the people there were not ready for independence. Roosevelt also agreed with that, suggesting a parallel with the Philippines. The best solution, Roosevelt and Stalin concluded, would be for an international trusteeship.[53]

They did not tell Prime Minister Churchill what had been "decided" about Indochina at this intimate little session, but from Stalin's jibes at France, he may have suspected the worst. At dinner, the Soviet ruler declared the entire French ruling class was rotten to the core, and that it would be not only "unjust but dangerous to leave in French hands any important strategic points after the war," or indeed to restore its empire. Roosevelt chimed in. He "agreed in part," he began, with the marshal's opinion, and mentioned Dakar and New Caledonia as vital strong points. The latter he now identified as a threat to Australia and New Zealand.

Churchill responded in remarkably subdued tones, not to the accusations against France, but only to say that his country had no desire for new territory. Since the Big Four would have to be responsible for the future peace of the world, he conceded that it was obvious that certain strategic points would have to be under their control.[54]

At dinner alone with Churchill, Roosevelt tried to reassure the prime minister that whatever harsh things were said about France and the colonial issue could be, should be, interpreted as crisis management. The French, he now added, must not be allowed to let the world down a second time. "Therefore Indo-China should *not* be returned to them; Dakar (in French West Africa) should be under American protection; Bizerta under British, and so on. There is no need to abolish French sovereignty in these places; the French flag can fly, 'But if Great Britain and America are to police the world, they must have the right to select the police stations. Dakar can be a French-owned station, with an American sergeant; Bizerta the same.' "[55]

4.

If you Britishers don't come up to scratch—toe the mark—then we will let all the world know!

ROOSEVELT, repeating to black publishers what he had said to Prime Minister Churchill recently about Africa, press conference, February 5, 1944[56]

Although Roosevelt once claimed to have spoken to Churchill at least twenty-five times about Indochina—and the prime minister confirmed, if not the exact number, then the frequency of these expressions—both men preferred to save their most dramatic statements for third parties.[57] Immediately following the Cairo and Teheran meetings, Roosevelt received a group of diplomats, including representatives from Turkey, Egypt, Persia (Iran), China, the Soviet Union, and Great Britain. To London's dismay, the president went on record before this group of outsiders—in effect telling all the world—to say that he had been "working very hard" to prevent Indochina's return to France. "At recent meetings it has been decided," he went on in a reference to his discussions with Churchill and Stalin, "that peace must be kept by force. There was no other way and world policemen would be necessary who would need certain places from which to exercise their function without bringing up [the] question of changes in sovereignty."[58]

Taking a cue from the second statement, and Roosevelt's other pronouncements, the British began thinking along the lines of persuading the French to grant the United Nations (or the United States as a likely surrogate) military bases at various key points within their empire.[59] That way, presumably, the French could demonstrate their ability to act responsibly in the postwar era, and thus deflect American criticism about their past record. But first it was thought necessary to get the Free French military forces properly involved in the Southeast Asian Command (SEAC).

Roosevelt had deliberately designed the war theaters precisely to prevent such a maneuver. Not surprisingly, then, a debate developed over the "boundaries" of SEAC, formed under the command of Lord Louis Mountbatten, and the China-Burma-India Theater (CBI) under Chiang and General "Vinegar Joe" Stilwell. Like so many other key parts of the Indochina puzzle, however, it soon proved difficult to keep a grip on the SEAC boundary issue. Around the time of the Cairo and Teheran conferences, Mountbatten had gone to China to negotiate his own arrangement with Chiang, who was apparently unsure about the boundaries himself. Their understanding provided that Mountbatten was to have "full and independent right to operate freely in those two countries (Thailand and Indochina) and furthermore that areas conquered would automatically form part of the South East Asia theatre."[60]

The boundary dispute would resurface later. Meanwhile, Mountbatten reported that the president's semipublic declarations already threatened his plans to use covert Free French agents in preliminary operations for retaking Indochina. Mountbatten never questioned that defeat of Japan was only a step toward the restoration of that colony to France, or Burma to England. But there was something more. To use French agents if the goal was not to restore "would be regarded as treachery by all Frenchmen and would . . . be dangerous to us."[61]

But all private efforts to get Roosevelt to pull in his horns only brought more oaths. Warned by Lord Halifax that his words were sure to get back to the French, the president quipped, "I hope they will." And when the ambassador tried to draw him into a discussion of long-range French policy, and the dangers of starting off the postwar era by giving that country a "slap in the face," Roosevelt shifted back to talk of Anglo-American relations. "Well tell Winston I gained or got three votes to his own one as we stand today." It was all "very good tempered," noted Halifax, "but I am left feeling that he has got this idea in his mind a bit more than is likely to be quite wholesome."[62]

Churchill thought it best not to press Roosevelt. "Do you really want to go and stir all this up at such a time as this?" he asked of his advisers. Securing a "legitimate" French position at SEAC headquarters could wait. "It is erroneous to suppose that one must always be doing something."[63] But even Churchill could not hold back the progress of events. In mid-summer 1944 de Gaulle journeyed to Washington. The confrontation did not throw off as many sparks as some thought it might, but Roosevelt made it clear that while he was ready to recognize the general's committee as a temporary authority, France was still excluded from the Big Four, and would still have to yield up portions of the empire for use as military bases according to the needs of the United Nations.[64]

"I have heard rumors," Lord Mountbatten then wrote Eden about the de Gaulle pilgrimage. What these rumors implied was that the United States had done a complete about-face in regard to the Free French, and was now "embarking on a kind of competition with us to secure the good graces of the French for after the war." In exchange for a "few bases," it was said that the United States intended to offer the liberation of French Indochina under "purely American auspices." If these suppositions had any truth to them, it was all the more important that Free French representatives and military forces be accredited to Mountbatten's command. That action would serve two purposes: it would finally clear up the vagueness of the boundary issue in SEAC's favor, and it would reengage any loose ties in the Anglo-French connection.[65]

Little wonder Mountbatten was concerned about the spreading confusion he saw enveloping SEAC. Someone had to respond to French demands for a share in the Far Eastern war, Mountbatten had said, and even if America was not bidding up the stakes, or—more likely—did not know what its different hands were doing, postponement would almost surely damage British interests beyond repair. A mission under General R. C. Blaizot, to be followed by a body of troops, the Corps Leger d'Intervention, was primed for the task. Mountbatten urged that the best way to accomplish his "mission" would be to allow these officers and men to filter into SEAC, "thus eventually presenting Washington with a *fait accompli.*"[66]

London preferred a different route. On August 4, 1944, a formal request was put through from the British Chiefs of Staff to their counterparts in Washington asking for recognition of the Blaizot mission at SEAC headquarters, and of a French training post for the Corps Leger in India. The American chiefs had no objection, but the White House did. Meanwhile, on August 24, Anthony Eden met with the Free French foreign minister, René Massigli, to discuss the delay. They also discussed the possibility of a Japanese move to unseat the Vichy authorities and rule directly themselves. Here Sir Maurice Peterson, a Foreign Office adviser to Eden, interjected that "a Japanese *coup de main* in Indo-China might not, on a long view, be a bad thing, to the end of preserving the French title to French Indo-China."

The minutes of the discussion continue, "M. Massigli took this point, with special reference to the effect on the United States." Vichy's bad record could be erased. And if the French also saw things clearly, they would on their own initiative propose granting United Nations bases. Eden sealed his counsel with his comment that "in his opinion, the Americans had not really made up their minds . . . though President Roosevelt was inclined to throw out ideas from time to time."[67]

Mountbatten's continued warnings sounded a new note of urgency. The tempo of the war against Japan was picking up, he advised London at the end of September 1944. And when it ended, the real contest would be with the United States: "That being so these interminable delays will, if they result in General Stilwell obtaining concentrated control of Indo-China, have a disastrous effect not only on [the] future of operational principals of [t]his command, but on the whole British position in the Far East."[68]

The truth was, the president had gone on the defensive. His hopes for China were dimming. It now appeared that Chiang would not be able to hold things together after the war.[69] Curiously, however, it was at this moment that Vice-President Wallace, who had gone to China with an offer from Roosevelt to mediate Kuomintang—Communist differences, picked up Willkie's mantle in a series of interviews and speeches that left British policymakers flabbergasted. His roseate vision of postwar Asian economic developments—and American interests therein—was not surprising, nor, probably, his Rooseveltian formulas for international levels of solution for colonial problems. But Wallace also suggested the Chinese "should have some special relationship towards neighboring areas in their progress toward self-government."[70]

Out in the shadowy corners where SEAC and CBI met, however, the very thing that British policymakers most feared about the

Roosevelt version of Wilsonian rhetoric—that somewhere somebody would take it all very seriously—was about to happen. A new American initiative was getting under way, a "low policy" connection between Office of Strategic Services (OSS) intelligence agents and that mysterious "Annamite leader," Ho Chi Minh. Details are lost, but it appears the connection was first suggested by Chinese Communist representatives stationed in Chungking during the brief united front truce in that country's civil war. If the OSS could negotiate Ho's release from a Kuomintang prison, they said, he could be seduced into serving the Allied cause. As it happened, Kuomintang leaders had something of the same idea—to draft Ho for a Chinese-sponsored Vietnamese liberation front.[71]

Ho Chi Minh was freed, only to be dropped by the Kuomintang in favor of a more amenable group of puppets. Left to his own devices, Ho saw the OSS as a possible vehicle for promoting Vietnamese nationalism, a view that happily coincided with certain American intelligence interests. But not with those of American diplomatic representatives, such as consul William Langdon at Kunming, China, who could not convince themselves that liberating Indochina from France would mean anything more than setting China loose in Southeast Asia. Presented with a petition drafted with the aid of OSS agents, urging that their independence league be permitted to secure American help in its struggles for freedom, and, of course, to fight Japan, Langdon told a group of Vietnamese in his office, "It would not make sense . . . if America with one hand at great expenditures of life and treasure rescued and delivered France from German slavery and with the other hand undermined her Empire."[72]

If London officials shuddered at Wallace's Sinophile ramblings, there were by now a growing number in Washington who also cringed. State Department officers in the capital felt much the same way as Langdon did. It was not that they suspected British and French ambitions any less than Roosevelt, but that they feared Chinese aspirations more. Where FDR felt chagrin that Chiang had not been able to unite China, State Department warning flags were going up signaling the danger of Kuomintang imperialism. Of course, Roosevelt had from the beginning expressed concern about such a development, and tried to balance his options, but a China that no longer qualified for Big Four status was a severe blow to his Asian policy.

Abbot Low Moffat of the Philippine and Southeast Asian Division ably summarized the difficulties in a memo written the same day Eden assured René Massigli that FDR had not made up his mind. Put simply, if Americans continued to delay, they would wind up having to find solutions in Asia all alone, for they would have alienated their European allies while China could do no more than thrash about. "The Chinese will not be strong enough," Moffat wrote (using the views of Ambassador Gauss as a guide), "to give us effective support, and, indeed, will take advantage of our altruism to advance their economic and political interests in Indochina, Thailand and Malaya."[73]

Still, Roosevelt was not yet ready to approve the Blaizot mission.[74] On September 4, 1944, Harry Hopkins told China expert John Paton Davies that Roosevelt remained interested in the trusteeship plan, but was now absorbed in European problems. The presidential adviser also let it slip that he, personally, had less hope for China then than at the time of the Cairo Conference. When Davies agreed China was in trouble, Hopkins "wryly observed that this did not seem to give much scope for the rosy plans which were being drawn up for expansive post-war economic development of China by the United States."[75]

The China options were rapidly disappearing. A rueful awakening to the real prospects for Asia began to take their place. If China "survived" intact without a civil war, that would be a miracle, and at that maybe even a wicked miracle. But whatever shape the country took after the war would not fit Roosevelt's original blueprint. American influence could better be used elsewhere; for example, to make sure that French promises to end its empire commercial monopolies were kept, and Indochina was integrated into the world market. So wrote senior State Department officials Joseph Grew and James Clement Dunn in a memorandum to Roosevelt in early September 1944:

> These areas [of Southeast Asia] are sources of products essential to both our wartime and peacetime economy. They are potentially important markets for American exports. They lie athwart the southwestern approaches to the Pacific Ocean and have an important bearing on our security and the security of the Philippines. Their economy and political stability will be an important factor in the maintenance of peace in Asia.[76]

Economic planning for the peace, a component Roosevelt had considered only very generally in devising the trusteeship plan, now made its way to the forefront. How would American interests be better off, asked the State Department planners, with Indochina under French rule with promises of an end to past discriminations, or under a China ambitious but torn by civil war? The answer seemed plain.

Yet Roosevelt still deferred a decision: "In regard to this Indochina matter," he instructed Cordell Hull, "it is my judgment that we should do nothing in regard to resistance groups or in any other way in relation to Indochina. You might bring it up to me a little later when things are a little clearer."[77]

They never were.

5.

> I asked the President if he had changed his ideas on French Indochina. . . . He said no. . . . The President hesitated a moment and then said—well if we can get the proper pledge from France to assume for herself the obligations of a trustee, then I would agree to France retaining these colonies with the proviso that independence was the ultimate goal.
>
> Memo of a talk with Roosevelt,
> March 15, 1945[78]

With both Churchill and Roosevelt willing to wait until things were a "little clearer," their advisers had no alternative but to sit tight and hope for the best.[79] One of the most difficult assessments to make, in this regard, concerns the shifting domestic political climates within the two leading Western powers. Roosevelt's New Deal coalition held firm for electoral occasions through 1944, but the influx of the famous "dollar-a-year men" into key policy-making positions altered the tone and some of the substance of internal debates. The presence of many such new faces in the wartime Roosevelt administration probably gave encouragement to the more conservative voices in foreign policy making, such as Secretaries of State Hull and Stettinius. But it is difficult to say that the influx of conservatives really tipped the balance, when one finds Harry Hopkins arguing for full reintegration of France, with all that implied for FDR's trusteeship plan, early in 1945.

There is also other evidence to consider. Roosevelt's antipathies toward France, perhaps as much as any other factor, account for the harsh tones he used about French colonialism. These reached their highest levels in the general time frame of the Casablanca Conference. Yet an old diplomat with long-standing access to the White House, Norman Davis, reported to a postwar planning committee that the president was changing his mind about certain ideas such as his view that France should be disarmed. After Casablanca, the president had "received a thesis concerning what would happen if Russia was not fully cooperative and France and Germany were both disarmed. Europe in this case would be impotent against aggression. It was thus necessary to have France a strong power as part of our own security."[80]

Combined with other factors, this concern no doubt began to weigh on FDR in the last months of 1944 and early 1945. In the Far East there was China's "decline"; in Europe, the growing evidence of a postwar contest for political control of the liberated nations. In the SEAC area itself, the Anglo-American "Cold War" went on unabated. Mountbatten no longer had to contend with the Anglophobe "Vinegar Joe" Stilwell. Instead, the American commander in the CBI was his former deputy in SEAC, General Albert Wedemeyer. If anything, however, Wedemeyer was more determined than his predecessor. He put forward new claims for the CBI in Indochina, and laced them with personal opinions to the effect that "there would not be a British empire after the war." British officials complained in return of "American imperialists in the armed forces, backed by [the] ubiquitous businessman in uniform . . . determined to do what they please in the Far East . . . without any regard to any other interests concerned."[81]

At the end of 1944, frustration and division characterized the various echelons of policy-making in the State Department and the Foreign Office. But still no word came from on high in either capital. M. E. Dening, Mountbatten's political adviser, issued a dark prophecy that the unrest evident in liberated Europe would soon spread to Asia. "On our side there is a sense of frustration and resentment, and on the American a spirit of ruthless go-getting, coupled with a conviction of our Far Eastern bankruptcy." If the "problems of empire" he saw looming over the horizon were not solved "before the reaction and ill temper following upon a long and strenuous war begin to manifest themselves . . . all discontents will come to the surface . . . and hostile elements will not be lacking beyond our borders who will seek to take advantage of the situation to undermine our whole position in the Far East."[82]

Had Dening sat in unobserved in a corner somewhere at Washington policy sessions, on the other hand, he would have been surprised at the disarray reigning there as well. State Department policymakers were sharply divided, more sharply than ever, between WE (Western European experts) and SEA (Asian specialists) over what to do about dependent territories in Asia. Those who worked closely with Southeast Asian problems warned that American troops would be largely responsible for driving out the Japanese, and Washington would, therefore, be held largely responsible also "for the postwar treatment accorded those areas." It was easy enough to stand back and criticize the European empires, but how would Americans react to the assignment of providing even temporary civil government for peoples of different races? The American experience in the Caribbean area offered little comfort to those worried about getting off to a good start in postwar Asia.

The Japanese introduction of pseudo-independence in some countries could very well stimulate "a future Pan-Asiatic movement directed against the Occident." Hence the need to obtain "explicit commitments" from the British, the French, and the Dutch about what they planned to do to meet colonial peoples' demands.[83]

When told of British requests for decisions in the disputes raging in SEAC, Roosevelt only grumbled that his ambassador to China, Patrick Hurley, and military authorities were sending him reports of British and French efforts to "undermine our whole policy in regard to China." His concern was that the colonial powers still clung to "white supremacy," and believed it would last. But those days were over. Despite its temporary weakness, China would one day "assume the leadership in that area which the Japanese had attempted to seize." The matter of Indochina needed further discussion.[84]

The longer he delayed, the less likely Roosevelt would have any options. The president was under seige, whether from SEAC or the more obscure offices of the State Department. His personal strength rapidly failing after nearly twelve momentous years in the White House, FDR could concentrate on only the biggest issues. Meanwhile his chief adviser at the forthcoming Yalta Conference, Harry Hopkins, was telling Secretary of State Edward R. Stettinius, Secretary of War Henry L. Stimson, and Secretary of the Navy

James V. Forrestal that a review of "our entire French approach" was overdue. In certain instances, Hopkins went on, "we had held back," only to change our position in the end anyway under British pressure. "This had resulted in the French feeling that we were opposing their regrowth." The group nodded their agreement: "With the British position what it is . . . our policy of deferring a decision on Indo-China until some general peace settlement would probably be doomed."[85]

When Roosevelt met with Ambassador Halifax, the change was apparent. If it was absolutely necessary to use some Frenchmen for "sabotage work" to disrupt Japanese communications, "we had better tell Mountbatten to do it and ask no questions." One reason for the secrecy, he warned Halifax, nevertheless, was that "he did not want to appear to be committed to anything that would seem to prejudice political decisions about Indo-China in a sense favorable to restoration of French status quo ante." If he were quoted, FDR added, he would disown everything. This was most unsatisfactory, concluded the ambassador, because while it seemed to permit Mountbatten to go ahead, it did not settle the main question. Most important, it did not permit him to get the word to American military commanders. It was indeed most unsatisfactory, almost a trap.[86]

Roosevelt had his own ideas about what to do next. At Yalta he let his advisers in on part of the secret, without implying he had approved any British schemes. Any action that damaged the Japanese in Indochina was "satisfactory to him." "He had no objection to any *U.S. action* [emphasis added] which it was considered desirable to take in Indochina as long as it did not involve any alignments with the French."[87] But there was no meeting with Churchill about the disputes between Mountbatten and Wedemeyer—neither man wanted it.[88] Instead, FDR took his case to Stalin privately, and in a curiously nostalgic session linked his original 1942 plan for a three-power (Russia, China, the United States) Korean trusteeship with his continuing interest in seeing Indochina put under international control. The British did not approve, he said, because of the danger to Burma. Stalin agreed that Indochina "was a very important area."

Encouraged once more, the president told the Russian leader that the Indochinese were people of "small stature . . . and were not warlike." General de Gaulle had asked for ships to transport his troops to Indochina, said Roosevelt. When Stalin asked where the general would get the troops, he answered that de Gaulle "said he was going to find the troops when the President could find the ships, but the President added that up to the present he had been unable to find the ships."[89]

It may be that Roosevelt imagined that he had disarmed Stalin, and enlisted him in a stabilizing effort for postwar Asia. The president had seen his hopes for China go aglimmering, and in fact confided during this tête-à-tête that he had for some time "been trying to keep China alive."[90] His references to the Indochinese people—with their suggestions that he understood them best, à la Woodrow Wilson's old view of Mexico—coupled with his self-assumed role as China's spokesman at Yalta, and the offer of a share of responsibility in Korea, point to a gambler's inclination to envision Russia as a potential ally, a silent backer as it were, in a chancy, last-ditch scheme to keep France from sneaking back into Indochina.

If so, it was a piece of self-deception. He could no longer maneuver effectively between the various rocks and shoals that confronted him on this final journey to secure a postwar settlement among the great powers. The trusteeship plan as finally presented at Yalta, the day after his private talk with Stalin, provided for placing under the United Nations only those territories taken from the defeated Axis powers, or those "voluntarily" put under international control by the colonial powers.[91] Though the plan involved only pinpoints of territory, Roosevelt had another reason to alter his original ideas for a trusteeship system—the U.S. Navy's insistence that nothing hamper its administration of former Japanese mandated islands in the Pacific. Pinpoints of territory, it developed, could move tons of principle, with the right leverage.[92]

At Yalta, Admiral Leahy, now Roosevelt's chief of staff, sensed perfectly what had happened. He had heard the president talk about his interest in having Hong Kong returned to Chinese sovereignty during preparations for the Yalta meeting. At the conference, however, Roosevelt proceeded to agree to a Russian demand that another nominally Chinese port be opened to them. Leahy recalled that he leaned over and said, "Mr. President, you are going to lose out on Hong Kong if you agree to give the Russians half of Dairen." Roosevelt shook his head. "Well, Bill, I can't help it."[93]

After Yalta the president told reporters that the French had talked about recapturing Indochina, "but they haven't got any shipping to do it with." Still, plans for a trusteeship would only "make the British mad. Better to keep quiet just now."[94] If Roosevelt's post-Yalta silence was maddening to American policymakers, it was downright ominous to the British. Since the spring and summer of 1944, London had been trying unsuccessfully to get American approval for French participation in SEAC. Churchill had refused to confront Roosevelt directly, and the latter had talked to just about everyone about his "ideas" without making any commitments. On his own, Mountbatten had been making more and more use of the French, but the heavily charged atmosphere in SEAC threatened to explode at almost any moment.

While Roosevelt had been disposing of Chinese assets and diminishing China's power in the Manchurian area at Yalta in the hope of achieving Russian aid against Japan and, more problematically, a postwar Sino-Russian settlement, General Wedemeyer was laying claim to Indochina on Chiang's behalf—at least so far as military operations were concerned. "Indications are reaching us here," M. E. Dening warned London, "that Americans are proposing to equip and train Chinese forces for an attack on Indo-China." Confronting Washington without more proof was impossible, but this would be the most "lamentable" of all developments in the Far Eastern war.[95]

When the Japanese "overthrew" the Vichy regime in Indochina on March 9, 1945, bringing to an end the facade of French rule, London was perplexed by the resulting situation. "In the long run it may turn out to French advantage," suggested L. H. Foulds, another Foreign Office adviser, as it would erase the last vestige of taint from the Free French cause. Then again, it might not. So thought Sir Ronald Campbell, who had heard Roosevelt on the subject of Indochina many times. "I myself believe High Authority in the U.S.A. hopes for a useful morsel of Chinese aggression."[96]

After two prodding memos from Anthony Eden, Churchill finally addressed a full-scale appeal to Roosevelt in mid-March calling for an effort to clear up the disagreement between Wedemeyer and Mountbatten that would leave SEAC free to operate throughout Indochina. The president's reply suggested that all operations be "coordinated" through Wedemeyer, "at least until any adjustment of theater boundaries is made in connection with an advance by Mountbatten's forces into Indo China from the south."[97]

It was hardly the sort of answer to remove suspicion. General Wedemeyer might have drafted it himself, noted the Foreign Office's J. C. Sterndale-Bennett. But word arrived from Washington that orders had been given to fly in supplies to French detachments operating in Indochina. Then came the news that Wedemeyer and Mountbatten had worked out a temporary *modus operandi.* With skies clearing in SEAC, British officials pressed the prime minister to renew an appeal for employing the whole Corps Leger. Again, after prodding, he did so, cabling the president on April 11, 1945, that it would "look very bad in history" if the United States and Britain failed to associate the French "with our operations into their country."[98]

Roosevelt died on April 12, 1945, leaving it for history to decide what his answer would have been. A week earlier, however, he had met for a final time with newspaper reporters. Questions were asked about the Japanese mandated islands in the Pacific. What would happen to them, who would exercise the mandate after the war? The United States? Roosevelt replied, "I would say the United Nations. Or—it might be called—the world, which has been much abused now, will have a chance to prevent any more abuse." But he also said, "It seems obvious that we will be more or less responsible for security in all the Pacific waters."[99]

Roosevelt was a powerful conjurer. Long after he had left the stage, the impression lingered that he had never abandoned his determination to liberate colonial peoples, but had been outmaneuvered by the wily Europeans. Sometimes, unfortunately, this made self-deception all the easier. Roosevelt may not have believed in the dream—or all of it, anyway—but his curious discussion with Stalin at Yalta, when he might have said nothing and let the issue drop, suggested that even when none of the pieces had fallen into place, he still held out a hope that an atmosphere could be created that would help move things along to a more decent world order than had prevailed before the war.

Confidence had given way to ambiguity. Roosevelt had "dreamed up" a magical trusteeship system that would at one and the same time protect and advance American interests, remove the onus of colonialism from the Allied cause, maintain big-power unity in keeping the peace, adjust legitimate demands for independence, yet avoid the chaos of violent revolution. In a sudden gust at Roosevelt's death, the pieces all flew apart. What survived out of the confused ending to World War II colonial policy could not have been foreseen by Roosevelt; nor could it be said that he would have disavowed what his successors did in his name.

The complexity of Roosevelt's heritage, and of the issues that will confront us in succeeding chapters, is well illustrated, however, by noting remarks John Foster Dulles made at another crucial turning point in the Vietnam tragedy. Dulles, who was ready to blame FDR's successors for all that went wrong with American foreign policy after the war, invoked the lost dream as the basis for his own determination to replace European colonialism with an anti-Communist policy that would enlist the support of Asian nationalists.

In 1954, as Americans watched the final agony of the French effort to recapture Indochina from its people, Secretary of State Dulles recast the first act of the drama as one of avoidable error: "The fundamental blunder . . . was made after 1945. . . . The question then was whether or not the United States . . . would use its power to put the French back into Indochina. Originally, President Roosevelt was against this on the ground that France did not have a good record as a colonial power and its return would not be accepted by the people. Nevertheless, our Government allowed itself to be persuaded in this matter by the French and the British and we acted to restore France's colonial position in Indochina."[100]

Dulles' cautionary tale warned against the intrigues of the declining empires, his own preoccupation during and after the Dienbienphu crisis. But Roosevelt had not been pushed off the colonial issue. In the end he had backed off, avoiding a confrontation that involved too many uncertainties. During the war it had been easy to believe, as he once told an ambassador, he could change "all that" by turning over his hand. By the time he discovered that was not so, and that it was not at all certain *anything* America could do would headoff the incipient armed struggles in colonial areas, Roosevelt had no time left. Nevertheless, Roosevelt's dream had great mythic power. John Foster Dulles, for one, believed he knew how it could be realized.

CHAPTER TWO

A Crowded Boat

> Key our position is our awareness that in respect developments affecting position Western democratic powers in southern Asia, we essentially in same boat as French, also as British and Dutch. . . . We consider as best safeguard . . . a continued close association between newly-autonomous peoples and powers which have long been responsible for their welfare.
>
> Secretary of State GEORGE C. MARSHALL to the American ambassador in France, May 13, 1947[1]

WHEN Harry Truman recovered from the shock of finding himself president of the United States, he was appalled at the disorder he found in the Oval Office. The dead president's desk was cluttered with half-finished projects. Somewhere in the pile were Roosevelt's musings on the colonial question, pieces of a policy that came unstuck as soon as Truman held them up to the light of postwar reality. Always keenly aware, as he stood there surveying his mixed legacy, that FDR had "won the war," leaving him the much harder task of securing the peace, Truman had every right to feel some resentment that things were not as he had imagined. What was more, it now fell to Truman to reorder FDR's files without letting on that there were any difficulties in the way of fulfilling American war aims as set forth in Roosevelt's speeches from Pearl Harbor to Yalta.

In many ways, nevertheless, Truman was the perfect executive to preside over the transition from Grand Alliance to Cold War. Vice-president only for a matter of months—weeks, really—Truman had made no impression on the national consciousness. He had to prove himself, but no one could in fairness expect him to produce the sort of miracles FDR had (apparently) wrought. He could, for a time at least, compromise with Roosevelt's declared positions, while leaving them inscribed on the imagination, like the sayings surrounding Lincoln in Henry Bacon's Greek temple a few blocks from the White House.

A few disgruntled New Dealers thought they espied in Truman and his entourage a deliberate attempt to undo all of Roosevelt's works in both domestic and foreign policy. They were mistaken, although the atmosphere changed. No doubt about that. Had Lincoln lived to face the postwar traumas of the Reconstruction Era, it might have taken even longer for Congress to get around to commissioning a memorial, delayed as it was for forty years and more. Truman was determined to avoid Andrew Johnson's fate in this new reconstruction era.

Until near the end of the war, Roosevelt had the powerful adhesive of total war to hold things together. Then it failed. Signs that the glue was drying out were evident at Yalta, when Prime Minister Churchill thought he discovered a plot against the British Empire in a reference to the Atlantic Charter in the draft proposal the president had submitted for a Big Three Declaration on Liberated Europe. Knowing Roosevelt's penchant for discovering new meanings in their wartime communiqués, the prime minister excitedly explained how he had long since refuted Wendell Willkie's assertions that the charter had anything to do with the British Empire. Roosevelt quipped, "Was that what killed him?" Laughter went round the table. But the joke came back to him with a different face, a staring grimace of past promises demanding satisfaction, for he had to decide—and soon—how to reconcile that document, and other war aims statements, with the work the Big Three had undertaken together to fashion a workable peace.[2]

With all his talents (and failings), FDR could postpone the time of reckoning for only so long. And for every petition he granted, others were denied. It was better all around that Roosevelt did not have to face that reckoning; better for the country and better for FDR's image—itself a not inconsiderable political advantage for a successor needing to rally a postwar coalition around evolving Cold War policy necessities.

Finally, as Truman knew, Roosevelt's method of decision-making had worked only for Roosevelt. It could not be transferred, even in part, to his successors. Only FDR had had the prestige to overcome obstacles to the consolidation of the wartime alliance, and only Roosevelt could have used it to slip safely through the narrowing passages to postwar consensus at home and world recovery. For Truman to attempt such a feat with those methods was simply impossible. In a pointed reference to the changes—and his role—Truman told Stalin at their first meeting, according to Charles Bohlen's sketchy notes, that he was "here to—be yr friend—deal directly yes—or no—no diplomat."[3]

At his leisure, when he had time to review the events of the early Cold War years, Truman wrote in his memoirs about one of the most bedeviling problems of his entire presidency—what to do about China. A bigger issue than Indochina, or all the colonial problems put together, it still had the same dominant elements, the same hard and soft pieces to reconcile, and, it is possible to argue, it marks the initiation of the containment policy in Asia even before it was applied in Europe.

"We in America always think of China as a nation," Truman thus commented on China. "But the truth is that in 1945 China was only a geographical expression." At war's end, Chiang Kai-shek's authority extended only over the southwest corner, while the Japanese occupied the south and southwest, and north China was controlled by Communist forces and Manchuria by the Russians. "The task of creating a new nation was colossal. President Roosevelt had built up the idea that China was a great power because he looked to the future and wanted to encourage the Chinese people."

But in reality, Chiang could reoccupy even south China only with great difficulty. It was perfectly clear to him, Truman added, that if American commanders ordered the Japanese to lay down their arms and march to the seaboard, the Communists would take over the whole country: "So the Japanese were instructed to hold their places and maintain order. In due course [American-airlifted] Chinese troops under Chiang Kai-shek would appear, the Japanese would surrender to them, march to the seaports, and we would send them back to Japan. This operation of using the Japanese to hold off the Communists was a joint decision of the State and Defense Departments which I approved."[4]

Although Truman's memoirs make no note of it, the position was much the same in Indochina. Certainly that was the way the British, who arrived there soon after Japan's surrender, saw things, and even more so the French, who came back ready to challenge Ho Chi Minh's revolution.

Secretary of State Dean Acheson, never an admirer of FDR's organizational principles (or much else about him), later wrote that the new president's task was "reminiscent of that in the first chapter of Genesis—to help the free world emerge from chaos without blowing the whole world apart in the process."[5] To this awesome assignment, Acheson continued, Truman brought "unusual qualities," not least that he "looked principally to the Department of State in determining foreign policy."[6] Truman liked to say that "the buck" stopped in the Oval Office, but that was only after it had passed through the hands of the National Security Council (NSC), the Central Intelligence Agency, and the Departments of Defense and State.

Thus prepared, decisions were set in place almost as easily as a White House gardener might add a new planting in the rose garden outside the president's windows, and in the time it took Truman to read an NSC policy memorandum. Questions were fewer, and directed at narrower problems; for example, not whether France should return to Indochina, only whether it was capable of playing a proper role.

Soon, Indochina appeared in policy papers on China, as a matter related to the precedent set in the containment policy devised for China. By 1947 it was widely assumed that the initial dangers of the transition period had been surmounted. The new structure was considered complete with the Truman Doctrine and the Marshall Plan in place. Both posited, as Secretary of State Marshall said, that the European nations would continue to enjoy close relations with their colonies and the nations emerging from colonial rule. When the Truman Doctrine proposal was discussed in executive session by the Senate Foreign Relations Committee, Senator Alexander Wiley summed up what had taken place in the two years since the defeat of Nazi Germany and Japan. "My America is stepping out into a new field, reaching out and, yes, without mincing words, assuming the function of the British Empire, which she so gallantly handled in the century that is past."[7]

But Wiley and his colleagues, however confidently they would vote later on the Senate floor, were not altogether convinced that Truman really was, as he insisted, "fully aware of the broad implications involved" in the new departures, a commitment to aid all nations resisting "attempted subjugation by armed minorities or by outside pressures."[8] Wiley confessed he was "in doubt as to which way to go," while Senator Walter F. George pondered the implications of leaving the United Nations on the sidelines in favor of unilateral action: "I do not see how we are going to escape going into Manchuria, North China, and Korea and doing things in that area of the world. . . . we have got the right to exercise commonsense. But I know that when we make a policy of this kind we are irrevocably committing ourselves to a course of action, and there is no way to get out of it next week or next year. You go down to the end of the road."[9]

No one really imagined at this time, despite George's eerily prophetic words, that the road would wind dangerously from the rocky hills of Korea through labyrinthine jungle paths to a dead end in Southeast Asia.

1.

> As I told Mr. Hopkins when he was here, we do not understand your policy. What are you driving at? Do you want us to become, for example, one of the federated states under the Russian aegis? . . . If the public here comes to realize that you are against us in Indochina there will be terrific disappointment and nobody knows to what this will lead.
>
> CHARLES DE GAULLE,
> March 13, 1945[10]

General de Gaulle's fears were shared in Washington. On April 23, 1945, the day of Truman's famous "debate" with Soviet foreign minister V. M. Molotov over Poland's future—a harbinger of future encounters on the bleak landscape of Cold War diplomacy—James Clement Dunn, a senior State Department officer, wrote to Secretary of State Stettinius, "We have no right to dictate to France nor to take away her territory. We can only use our influence . . . to improve the Government of Indochina and conditions there, but we should not interfere."[11]

Now was the time, Dunn went on, to draw close to Great Britain and France. Obstacles to wholehearted cooperation must be gotten out of the way. And, in this regard, he wished to call the secretary's attention to recent conversations with Georges Bidault, de Gaulle's foreign policy spokesman, "in which the latter stressed his fears for western civilization as a result of the dominance of Russia in Europe."[12]

Stettinius took the point. At the San Francisco United Nations

Conference a few weeks later he told Bidault that the American "record is entirely innocent of any official statement of this government questioning, even by implication, French Sovereignty over Indo-China." It was true that "certain elements of American public opinion" had condemned past French policies and practices, but, Stettinius repeated, he was now able to offer "renewed assurances of our recognition of French sovereignty over that area."[13]

While Stettinius reassured Bidault, moreover, another State Department official at San Francisco, John Hickerson, confided to a British diplomat that the "American proposal at Yalta" in regard to United Nations trusteeships had been deliberately phrased by the department in order to "permit of a climb-down from the position that President Roosevelt had taken in conversations as regards Indo-China." Category C of that proposal would enable an Allied power to put a given territory under trusteeship "voluntarily," but would not compel it to do so. "He made it clear that the State Department felt that President Roosevelt had gone too far, and that Category C was a useful face-saver."[14] "It was important to United States policy that France should be an effective 'outpost' of Western influence," Dunn told Lord Halifax.[15]

Out in Asia, rumors of impending policy changes had a very different effect. General Patrick Hurley, ambassador to China, felt he had been kept in the dark too long. On May 29, 1945, he demanded an explanation of the apparent undoing of Roosevelt's plans. "There is a growing opinion throughout Asia that America favors imperialism rather than democracy. . . . The move of the imperialist powers to use American resources to enable them to move into Indochina is not for the purpose of participating in the main battle against Japan . . . [but for] the reestablishment of . . . imperialism in Indochina."[16]

Told there had been "no basic change," only a decision to "preclude" the forced establishment of a trusteeship over Indochina, and that it remained Washington's intention to ask for some "positive indication" of French policy on civil liberties and "increasing measures of self-government," Hurley was invited, politely, to shut up.[17] The ambassador, a Republican of the sort later to be known as "Asia-firsters," a group that hated European imperialism as much as they did Communism, did not take kindly to such treatment.

If Hurley was not deceived, neither was consul William Langdon in Kunming China, who wanted solid directives to continue his dealings with OSS operatives and other interested parties. His previous orders, straight from President Roosevelt in late 1944, had been to keep the French at arm's length. Following those instructions, no help had been given to the French when the Japanese turned on them in March 1945; but now not only were the local French, who had lived side by side with the Japanese for five years, being recognized at SEAC combat command, they were being outfitted there! "Could I . . . be informed as to what our policy toward Indochina now is? Whether the late President froze it into mañana status or whether the living are doing something about it?"[18]

In the Berlin suburb of Potsdam, meanwhile, the Big Three gathered at the end of July to consider the first postwar agenda. At Teheran and Yalta, Roosevelt had pulled Stalin aside to talk about Indochina. The only brief exchange Truman had with Stalin here over trusteeships, recorded in an adviser's cryptic notes, was Stalin's bid, later expanded at tripartite sessions, for a share in the Italian colonies in Africa. The Russians conceded, perhaps surprisingly, that the "trusteeship system" had been settled in principle at San Francisco.

Perhaps it was not surprising. Aside from brief references to Korea, Stalin and Molotov concentrated on the Italian colonies, implying a willingness (even eagerness?) to forget about Roosevelt's musings about far-off places, in favor of taking a simple slice of pie. And why not? If they could get the Italian colonies, they were perfectly willing to be spared the embarrassment of refusing to participate in any American-devised schemes for Big Four overlordship of the colonial issue—and free to pursue an independent course when opportunity offered.

Some of those in the American delegation at Potsdam thought that was the Russian purpose, to be realized sooner than might be expected. A comment that Secretary of War Henry L. Stimson recorded in his diary on July 23, 1945, catches perfectly the dawning of the postwar era. He noted that Averell Harriman, still ambassador to the Soviet Union, took Stalin's remarks to mean that the Russians "are now apparently seeking to branch in all directions." "The British and French are refusing to consider a trusteeship on Hong Kong and Indo China, and I foresee that if . . . [the British and French position is upheld] the Russians will probably drop their proposal for trusteeship of Korea and ask for solitary control of it."[19]

Here was a choice, so it seemed, between hoping to put a check on independent Russian action and alienating Allies in already visible disputes with Moscow. Put another way, it came down to a dead president's bravado against living reality. So it was really no choice. A Russian bid for control of strategic points in the Mediterranean or in Korea, even raised as a matter of equity with other Allied claims, took on sinister implications. Truman said later he wanted to insure Russian entry into the Far Eastern war. From Harry Hopkins' reports on conversations with Stalin, however, and from military intelligence reports of the Russian buildup, he knew that the Soviets would not ignore their "pledge."[20]

"Anxious as we were to have Russia in the war," Truman explained to readers of his memoirs, he had made up his mind by the end of the Potsdam Conference "that I would not allow the Russians any part in the control of Japan."[21] Any diversion, for any reason, into the military or political jungles of Indochina might slow down the American approach to Tokyo. Berlin had fallen to the Russians. That "mistake" must not be repeated in Asia.[22]

Where Stalin had feared that the West would delay sending military forces into Europe until it was possible for them to rush across the continent to Berlin, in northern Asia the situation was reversed. Washington feared that Russia would reap unreasonable benefits from the hard-fought Pacific campaigns after American forces had carried the burden of the war. Getting the war over as quickly as possible might not circumvent presumed Russian ambitions, but it would help.[23]

But if strategic considerations pushed old SEAC issues onto a remote siding where, it was fervently hoped, yesterday's notions could rust in secluded silence, events conspired to bring them back again. First there was the "bomb." It upset all timetables. Instead of holding back the Russians, the bomb came too soon, before the French were ready to occupy Indochina—and too soon for the OSS in Indochina to be reoriented. During the Potsdam Conference, it had been decided that Mountbatten would conduct operations below the sixteenth parallel in Indochina for the time being and that at a later date the remainder of that country might be placed within his command.[24]

This was the green light London had been waiting for for so long. Almost at once, however, Truman found that he was enmeshed in a dispute between the British and Chiang Kai-shek over the future of Hong Kong, and London's attempt to preempt Chinese interference in Indochina. "We trust," the Foreign Office instructed its ambassador in Chungking, "that Chiang Kai-shek will agree that our common object should thereafter be to restore the

French administration of Indo-China and to introduce French forces and administrators for this purpose as soon as they are available."[25] Chiang objected—and strongly. His appeal to Truman produced a nettling series of exchanges. In the end, the president shrugged it off. Chiang could not get to Hong Kong, he wrote, any more than he could reach "North China and Manchuria without aid from us. . . . Much as I deplored this friction between two of our allies, there seemed to be little else that could be done by us."[26]

The Chinese could get to Indochina, however, and there join the melee that commenced at the end of the Pacific war.

2.

> I have a government that is organized and ready to go. Your statesmen make eloquent speeches about helping those with self-determination. We are self-determined. Why not help us? Am I any different from Nehru, Quezon—even your George Washington? I, too, want to set my people free.
>
> HO CHI MINH, in a discussion with an OSS agent, summer 1945[27]

For twenty-five years and more Ho Chi Minh had hoped for American support in his struggles with the French. On June 18, 1919, Ho, whose name then was Nguyen Ai Quoc, rented a tuxedo and a bowler hat to wear on a visit to the American delegation at the Paris Peace Conference. "While waiting for the principle of national self-determination to pass from ideal to reality," began the petition he carried, a "Group of Annamite Patriots" wished to present "the following humble claims." There followed a list of desired reforms, including limited representation for "native people" in the French Parliament.[28]

By 1945 Ho could wait no longer. He continued to believe, however, that by the circumstances of its birth, the United States had a special understanding of the "colonial problem" that other nations lacked—even the Soviet Union. From his experiences in Europe and America he wondered if the unfulfilled promises of the Fourteen Points and the Atlantic Charter had more to do with race than politics.[29]

Nguyen Ai Quoc disappeared in Moscow after he became a founding member of the French Communist party in 1920, and the first Vietnamese Communist, to reappear under various aliases at different places in Asia on special instructions from the Comintern [Communist International in Moscow]. Inside Vietnam, meanwhile, there appeared the Viet Nam Nationalist party (VNQDD), which preferred the radical nationalism of a Kemal Attaturk to the Marxist precepts of Lenin.[30]

The Great Depression that swept across Europe and America at the end of the 1920s also struck hard at colonial areas, bringing in its wake strikes and protests that eventually developed into the Nghe-Tinh movement (named after the provinces where it originated), which was finally suppressed by the French, but not before desperate officials had resorted, unforgettably, to indiscriminatory air strikes against peasant strongholds. As it happened, Ho opposed the uprising, voting as a minority of one in Communist party councils against attempting to make it into a general revolutionary uprising.[31]

The party's role in the Nghe-Tinh events and eventual debacle was an ambiguous one, hardly an example of inspired leadership or even minimum control of the rapidly changing scene. Arrested nevertheless for the party's activities in the Nghe-Tinh affair, Ho disappeared once again, this time behind prison walls. After his still-unexplained "escape" from a Hong Kong cell, he was spirited out of China and returned to Russia. In early 1940, with Chiang forced by the Japanese invasion into an uneasy *modus operandi* with his hated Communist rivals, Ho turned up in southern China near the Indochinese border, indoctrinating Kuomintang troops in methods of guerrilla warfare![32]

It was there that he was able to meet ICP (Indochinese Communist party) leaders Pham Van Dong and Vo Nguyen Giap, and mold the team that would enter Hanoi at the head of the revolutionary junta in September 1945.[33] For this task, the man who had once sought to present Woodrow Wilson with a petition containing "humble claims" on the French adopted the name Ho Chi Minh, "He Who Enlightens." Once again, however, his career was interrupted, this time by Chiang's agents; and rumors of his death in prison were not completely dispelled until his appearance in Hanoi.

Like so much else about Ho's life, this second imprisonment and subsequent release in 1943 is shrouded in mystery. The local Kuomintang commander, a warlord named Chang Fa-kwei, had visions of leading a Chinese-leaning Vietnamese nationalist movement. Before his release, Ho informed Chang that he was ready to cooperate with the Kuomintang "liberation" league. With Chang's aid, ironically, the Communist-led League for Vietnamese Independence (Vietminh) joined forces with the Kuomintang-sponsored Revolutionary League of Vietnam. He was paid handsomely for this work, at the rate of $100,000 a month.[34]

A planned crackdown by French authorities against the Vietminh in March 1945 never took place. Instead, the French were themselves imprisoned by their Japanese overlords, who, witnessing the approach of American power in the Philippines, decided to rule directly in Indochina. In fact, however, they ruled hardly at all except to continue exacting rice quotas from an already starving peasant population. So the Vietminh, unhindered, built an army of ten thousand in the northern provinces of Vietnam. Aided, however unwittingly, by ambitious men, first the Chinese and then the Japanese, the Vietminh sought to bring other outsiders into play to gain independence: the Americans.[35]

An OSS contingent that arrived by parachute at Ho's jungle headquarters on July 16, 1945, found the Vietminh leader "shaking like a leaf and obviously running a high fever." For some months prior the OSS and the Vietminh had been "collaborating." In exchange for small amounts of aid, the Vietminh supplied intelligence information and assistance in rescuing downed airmen. A shared dislike for the French strengthened the bond and projected the half-conscious "alliance" into postwar political matters. So it was with genuine concern that the newly arrived OSS group's medic exclaimed, "This man doesn't have long for this world." American quinine and sulfa, according to yet another legend, saved Ho's life.

The OSS also brought rifles, mortars, machine guns, grenades, and bazookas. They even held training sessions for Giap's elite guerrilla forces, though one wonders who was instructing whom—and in what arts.[36] However that may be, the OSS team stayed on and accompanied Ho Chi Minh to Hanoi, where, on September 2, 1945, he proclaimed the establishment of the Democratic Republic of Vietnam, using these words: "All men are created equal. The creator has given us certain inviolable Rights; the right to Life, the right to be Free, and the right to achieve happiness."[37]

The remainder of his speech also read like Jefferson's original indictment of colonialism and the sins of George III in stultifying the political, economic, and moral growth of the thirteen colonies. When he asked that day, "Do you hear me distinctly?" Ho was also addressing an audience in the land that had sent its air and sea armada to conquer the Japanese. The night before, the Vietminh leader had invited two members of the OSS team to dinner. As he poured coffee, Ho said he wished to thank the government of the United States for the aid the Vietminh had received, and spoke of the hope for "fraternal collaboration" in the future.

Then a comrade spoke up—and the reason for the invitation became clear. Why, asked the Vietnamese, had the "real" issue of Indochina not been raised at San Francisco? Of all peoples, the Americans should understand what the Vietminh desired, and should be able to sympathize. After his colleagues reviled the French colonial system, Ho took up the charge that the Vietminh was an extension of the "Moscow apparatus in Southeast Asia." His American guests, he began, were well-placed to see through this colonialist subterfuge. Yes, the Communists were a leading element in the movement, but its members were "nationalist first and party members second."[38]

There followed an appeal for American aid and capitalist investment in Vietnam, as Ho's associates regaled their guests with visions of what would be once the French were gone. But what did Ho really think the future held? Long practiced in political disguises, the Vietminh leader might have seen himself as Sun Yat-sen, bargaining with opposites just as the Kuomintang founder had done in the 1920s with the Soviet Union and the reactionary Japanese to gain support against the warlords and their foreign backers.

Indeed, Ho confided to Bao Dai—the Indochinese counterpart to those warlords—that the Americans were "only interested in replacing the French. . . . They want to reorganize our country in order to control it. They are capitalists to the core. All that counts for them is business."[39] Bao Dai, "emperor" of Vietnam under the French and, since the March coup, "ruler" of "independent" Vietnam under the Japanese, had recently abdicated and accepted Ho's invitation to join his government as supreme political adviser.[40]

More bargaining, more jockeying, twists and turns, anything to get a little more space for the new Democratic Republic of Vietnam. That was Ho's strategy, and he would stick to it through the coming months of political struggle and, indeed, through the years of war with the French to the time of Dienbienphu. He wrote letters to Washington assuring President Truman of Vietnamese goodwill, announcing the formation of his government, asking for a place on the occupation council for Japan, asking to send Vietnamese students to America, and explaining that his government had its origins in the promises of the Atlantic Charter. "As a matter of fact," he summed up boldly on October 22, 1945, "the carrying out of the Atlantic Charter and San Francisco Charter implies the eradication of imperialism and all forms of colonial oppression."[41]

Ho's persistence in this regard, long after it was apparent that Truman had no intention of answering these letters, argues against simple posturing as an explanation of his behavior. To end the Chinese occupation of Hanoi and North Vietnam, he also behaved circumspectly by entering into the prolonged negotiations of 1946 with Paris for a limited "independence" that displeased Vietminh comrades, justifying his action by appealing to history: "You fools! Don't you realize what it means if the Chinese remain? Don't you remember your history? The last time the Chinese came, they stayed a thousand years. The French are foreigners. They are weak. Colonialism is dying. The white man is finished in Asia. But if the Chinese stay now, they will never go. As for me, I prefer to sniff French shit for five years than eat Chinese shit for the rest of my life."[42]

A man of many faces and talents, "Uncle" Ho proved a more formidable and durable enemy than anyone imagined at the end of the war.

3.

> The solution which would bring these two policies most completely into accord would be a Far East progressively developing into a group of self-governing states—independent or with Dominion status—which would cooperate with each other and with the Western powers on a basis of mutual self-respect and friendship. The interests of the United States and of its Allies require that the Far East be removed as a source of colonial rivalry and conflict not only between the Great Powers, but between the Great Powers and the peoples of Asia.
>
> George Atcheson to
> General Douglas MacArthur,
> September 26, 1945[43]

MacArthur's political adviser had a good idea, but he was away in Japan. Major General Douglas D. Gracey of the British army and his senior staff arrived at Tan Son Nhut airport near Saigon on September 13, 1945. There to greet him was a contingent of senior

Japanese officers. Off to one side was a small group of Vietnamese. "We didn't know who they were," recalled Gracey's second in command, "they were just a little group which turned out to be Viet Minh." When they started forward to greet Gracey, however, it quickly occurred to the major general who they were—and what he must do. Waving them aside, Gracey strode toward the bowing Japanese and asked to be taken to General Terauchi's headquarters to complete the transfer of power.[44]

The "wonderful" old Chrysler convertible that carried Gracey to his rendezvous with the Japanese commander passed along roads lined with Union Jacks and cheering French nationals. Saigon looked for all the world to be a "liberated" city in the European fashion. Gracey had expected such a welcome. He was also confident that, as he said upon leaving India for his new assignment, "civil and military control by the French is only a question of weeks."[45]

Appearances deceived. The Democratic Republic of Vietnam had been proclaimed in Hanoi, but while nationwide uprisings placed the Vietminh in nominal control, the true state of affairs was that Ho's government was only one of several simultaneous anti-French "revolutions." In Saigon, for example, the insurgents were led by a Trotskyist faction that favored arming the populace for immediate action against the French. And where the events in Hanoi on Independence Sunday had been peaceful, those in Saigon were marked by violence, which continued to seethe as both sides, Vietnamese and French, anxiously awaited the arrival of the British to accept Terauchi's surrender.[46]

Ho's ability to control the revolution was further limited, moreover, by the appearance of Chinese troops in northern Vietnam. According to the Potsdam decisions, the Chinese were to accept the Japanese surrender in this region. The troops that poured into northern Indochina were undisciplined looters and scavengers.[47] To whom, then, should the Vietnamese appeal for independence? Quite apart from Ho's warnings to the French not to attempt to return as conquerors, Bao Dai had also sent admonitions, both to General de Gaulle and to President Truman. Asking that de Gaulle hear him as a "friend," rather than as Vietnamese head of state (Bao Dai had not yet abdicated the first time), the emperor wrote:

> You would understand better if you could see what is happening here, if you could sense the desire for independence which runs

> to the bottom of every heart and which no human force can curb. Even if you should manage to reestablish a French administration here, it would no longer be obeyed; each village would become a nest of resistance, each former collaborator an enemy and your officials and your colonials themselves would demand to leave this asphyxiating atmosphere.[48]

To Truman he added:

> The colonial regime no longer conforms to the present course of history. A people such as the Vietnamese people who have a two-thousand year old history and a glorious past cannot accept remaining under the domination of another people.
>
> The French people must yield to the principle of equity which the powerful American nation has proclaimed and defends. France must recognize this with good grace in order to avoid the disaster of a war breaking out on the territory of our country.[49]

Bao Dai's eloquently phrased appeals suggest that he was prepared to lead a non-Communist, independent Vietnam, if that option was made available. It was not, of course, and his later performance as a figurehead in the French scheme of things does nothing to encourage a belief that he could have succeeded even had there been no Ho Chi Minh to lead the revolution. But that is not the same as saying there could have been no other history of the Vietnamese War of Independence.

French strategy to regain control of Vietnam, meanwhile, centered upon holding the area around Saigon, the heart of the highly profitable prewar rubber plantation economy, and limiting the Vietminh to a "role" in governing northern sectors of the country. The original French scheme for Indochina had also followed a classic divide-and-rule outline. Sparsely populated Cambodia and Laos were maintained as separate states, while Vietnam had been repartitioned into three "states," Tonkin in the north, Annam in the central regions, and Cochin China in the south. As amended to conform with postwar sensibilities, French plans for a loose counterpart to the British Commonwealth of Nations called for linking Tonkin, Annam, and Cochin China under the rubric of an Indochinese Federation within the "French Union."

By this means ultimate authority over the economic and political direction of the area would remain in Paris, but, it was hoped, the heavy hand of "imperialism" would remain as hidden as that which directed affairs in Adam Smith's magical marketplace. A layered citizenship for the Indochinese would make residents of the three states citizens of the Indochinese Federation, as well as citizens of the French Union. The federation would be presided over by a governor-general with broad powers. General de Gaulle put it this way in March 1945: "Le Gouvernor général sera, dans l'intérêt de chacun, l'arbitre de tous." Inside Indochina, the Vietminh were to be compensated by a carefully circumscribed role in ruling Tonkin, while, it was expected, Ho Chi Minh's control over his coalition would further weaken as various members opted for a share in the new order.[50]

Though there was a much friendlier attitude toward the French in Washington in these days than had been the case earlier, the State Department—especially Asian desk officers—never felt entirely comfortable with what it gleaned of Paris' plans for Indochina. And though the recommendations of the pro-trusteeship bloc in the department had been shunted aside by WE and higher levels, the objectives and fears expressed in memoranda by the former still framed the broad outlines of policy goals. "The economic interests of the United States," read one of these, "a non-imperialist nation, demand not only free access and trade in Southeast Asia, but also a rising standard of living there. This would increase the market for our products in the area, and markets are one of our primary interests in the postwar world."[51]

Markets were not America's only interest. Continued access to supplies of tin and rubber, continued the memorandum, required careful attention to the area. "We must make sure that these countries will be strong enough, internally and externally, to resist domination or conquest by a hostile or potentially hostile power." To this end, and to insure the future balance of power in the world, it would be to America's advantage to encourage a "defense chain of democracies in the Far East." Otherwise, it was argued here, "Russia may well pre-empt the kind of good-will we have had until the present in the Orient." In sum, supporting the colonial powers was a dangerous game, probably a no-win situation: "We are the 'last best hope' of democracy in the colonial areas. If we do not act to fulfill this hope, the Russian system and Russia may well become the 'new hope.' "[52]

Yet the dominant Washington view also held that the best

opportunity to insure internal strength in the area rested in supporting French efforts, while keeping an eye on the colonies' progress. Roosevelt's shade may well have chuckled over this predicament. But any other course risked chaos in both France and Indochina, insisted the forerunners of the NSC policy paper authors. Why, it was asked by those cutting their teeth on postwar Southeast Asia, should the Vietminh be considered any different from the Italian partisans or the Greek ELAS? From this point of view, the Vietminh were not mere bandits, they were every bit as dangerous as European leftist cadres.

De Gaulle's aides were eager to reassure Washington that the world could count on a French Enlightenment to match that of Voltaire's day. Younger men had replaced the "Rudyard Kiplings," Georges Peter of the Colonial Ministry told a State Department official in early September 1945. French laws, Peter continued, would have only limited application in Indochina. If the Metropole should nationalize mines, utilities, and heavy industries, it would have no bearing upon freedom of enterprise and ownership in Indochina. Nor would any new tax laws apply. "It is apparently the purpose," recorded the official, "to make Indo-China a haven for private enterprise."

Peter wanted to emphasize, moreover, that the Indochinese tariff would be low, and would apply equally to all. Ultimately, all foreign investors would be treated the same way. The only restriction contemplated was that foreign companies must allow for a 51 percent voting stock share for French interests. "It is clear that a new policy is being proposed," the State Department's representative said, summarizing the talk, "that Indo-China is to be given a large degree of economic autonomy and thrown open to the world for trade and development; and that the interest of the U.S. Government and U.S. private enterprise is warmly solicited."[53]

In Indochina itself, Jean Sainteny, who was appointed to negotiate the French scheme with Ho Chi Minh, blurted out to an OSS agent that he was empowered to extend a credit of five billion French francs "to Americans only, to invest in Indochina, and I [Sainteny] would like to know the right person to contact on this matter and to start negotiations."[54] Sainteny's listener, Archimedes L. Patti, was stunned. For a moment he remained silent. "I felt anger, contempt, and personal insult." Patti believed he was being offered a private bribe, but the French diplomat went on to say that he was anxious to spread the word of the new policy promising "greater freedom for Annamese and French alike."[55] For his part, Sainteny saw Patti and the whole OSS mission as blinded by their "infantile anti-colonialism." As such, however, they were more dangerous to French plans than the Vietminh. He was "face to face," he reported, "with a deliberate Allied maneuver to evict the French from Indochina." For proof, British and French authorities cited OSS refusal to suppress Ho's Radio Hanoi.[56]

Such tales continued to poison Franco-American discussions about Indochina for years to come, right down to Dienbienphu. To a certain extent, moreover, they obscured a fascinating clash on a higher level. With all Europe moving leftward after World War II, the French persisted in trying to separate economic policy at home from colonial policy, which, they tried to assure the anticolonial Americans, would be conducted according to nineteenth-century liberal precepts.

"As for the Americans," mused Chester Cooper from the perspective of twenty-five years, "they hung around for a while and then quietly left. Nothing more was to be heard in Washington pronouncements about independence or trusteeship. Our official interest was manifested by the presence in Saigon and Hanoi of a few junior Foreign Service officers."[57] That was not quite the whole story, even on the lower levels of policy-making, as the Americans had raised quite a ruckus, if short-lived, with General Gracey over his determination to "restore order" in the countryside. On September 25, 1945, Gracey ordered all Allied officers, including the small contingent of Americans (regulars and OSS alike) to fire upon any Vietnamese seen carrying firearms. "This had the effect of definitely bringing the Americans into the picture." One American, fighting with a company of British, was shot in the neck and abdomen. Gracey also ordered the Americans not to fly their flag on U.S. vehicles, a ploy intended to erase whatever distinctions the OSS contingent still hoped to maintain between Americans and other white men in Indochina.[58]

Peter Dewey, who was to be the first American casualty in Vietnam, made himself a particular thorn in Gracey's side by challenging his every move. Eventually Gracey ordered him to leave. An intelligence report on Dewey's death identified his killers as Vietnamese, but also printed a Hanoi radio message asserting that the Vietminh stood to gain nothing from "creating unpleasant incidents with the Americans, who are very much in favor of our independence." The report recommended no further American personnel be sent to Indochina "until adequate measures are taken by the British to insure their protection."[59]

Taken together, the items in the intelligence report on Dewey's death pointed an accusing finger at the British for putting American military men in such an ambiguous position. It was a forecast, in miniature, of later complaints about the "taint" of colonialism that hampered American efforts to save Vietnam from the Communists.

In a final report of his own, prepared as a valediction for the OSS mission, Dewey wrote: "Cochinchina is burning, the French and British are finished here, and we [the United States] ought to clear out of Southeast Asia."[60]

4.

If those gooks want a fight, they'll get it.

GENERAL ETIENNE VALLUY,
December 17, 1946[61]

Resentment at local American interference no doubt colored General Gracey's attitude, and that of the French who followed closely behind, as they went about pacifying southern Indochina. If Washington no longer wished to be involved, neither did it appear able to disengage smoothly. Whether traces of that resentment can be seen in the harsh measures of repression against the Vietnamese cannot be known. Fear was an important element; so, too, once the cycle of violence began, was revenge and traditional attitudes toward "natives." Years afterward in Paris, however, as the struggle demanded more and more of the French in blood and treasure, the aid Ho received from the OSS became part of the dark legend of the war's origins. "*If* the Americans had not interfered . . . ," the retelling of a "tragedy" would begin—then trail off vaguely, usually ending in a confusion of assertions.

The violence of those early weeks after Gracey's landing is also sometimes blamed on a reactionary general for exceeding his orders, overstepping geographic and political limits on his mission of disarming the Japanese. In fact, however, the election of a Labour government in Britain changed London's policy not so much as a word or a comma. On the eve of Gracey's arrival in Saigon, Sir Esler Dening warned that the French would try to blame all subversive elements, i.e., the Democratic Republic of Vietnam, on the Japanese. This was not true. And the planned use of British troops posed a delicate problem: how to avoid laying His Majesty's government open to the accusation that here was a case of the West suppressing the East yet again. The new foreign secretary, Ernest Bevin, minuted on Dening's cable, "I regard this as an important point to watch."[62]

Within days, however, in a first meeting with Chinese special envoy T. V. Soong, Bevin went out of his way in response to a query to say, "We naturally assumed that Indo-China would return to France. . . . I got the impression," Bevin went on, nailing down the point in his record of the conversation, "that he would have welcomed a less unequivocal assertion of our support of French rights in regard to Indo-China."[63]

Two overriding considerations remained foremost in London, as they had all through the war. First, as a colonial power, it was in Britain's interest to see that "revolutionary outbreaks" did not have "an unsettling effect on the native populations of our own territories in South East Asia." There was full realization that steps toward self-government in the dependent areas would have to be speeded up. But "we cannot, in the name of liberty, allow territories which we control to fall into chaos and general unrest, nor into such weakness and instability as to create political danger-spots."[64]

The second consideration was that nothing should be done that would even appear to confirm ancient French notions about supposed British desires to undermine their empire. The only way out of this touchy predicament, concluded the Foreign Office, was to get "white" French troops in large numbers into Indochina as soon as possible. Meanwhile, it might be wise forGracey to state that he "cannot tolerate activities of any political groups which did not serve to contribute to the orderly administration of the country pending the resumption of control by the French." In the final draft, this last was amended to read, "He cannot tolerate any activities or agitation which may be detrimental to the security and orderly administration of the country and thus prejudicial to the fulfillment of his task."[65]

What proved more difficult, however, was getting enough French troops into Indochina. Attempts by Admiral Mountbatten to have General Philippe Leclerc, the French commander, take over responsibility for disarming the Japanese and maintaining order only brought the horrified response that that "would be [the] surest way to invite civil strife and bloodshed." The British could not evade their "responsibilities," Leclerc charged, "and leave European population at the mercy of a native rising."[66]

There it was: stay and be faced with accusations of neocolonialism or get out and be damned by the French for shirking responsibilities to the European population. The alternative—the only alternative, it appeared—was for the British to commit a full division to Indochina for at least three months. That meant using Indian troops, a political danger, and delaying the return home of thousands of additional soldiers from other dominion countries as well.

When London sent Lord Killearn as special commissioner to Southeast Asia, Mountbatten told him that the area was indeed of great strategic value—a bastion. "In the background, of course, was the Soviet Union," Killearn said of his discussions with SEAC personnel, "but it was agreed that there was no evidence of direct Soviet activities (as distinct from local Communist tendencies) within the area at present."[67]

Sainteny was the one, however, who would have to negotiate with the local "tendencies," communist or not, in Indochina. His impressions of Ho Chi Minh were that the Vietminh leader "had aspirations . . . of becoming the Gandhi of Indochina."[68] Sainteny felt more at ease once the OSS departed, but now he was to be undermined by the recently appointed high commissioner, Admiral Thierry d'Argenlieu, who had a narrowly Gaullist vision of France's undying and undiminished imperial role.

Nevertheless, by mid-February 1946 Ho had signaled his willingness to negotiate on the basis of membership in the French Union. Paris replied to this overture by stipulating two conditions: the autonomous Vietnamese government must welcome French troops when they arrived to take over from the Chinese, and Cochin China's future was to be decided by referendum. Faced with the dual dangers of a prolonged Chinese occupation and a Sino-French deal over his head, Ho accepted the proffered terms on March 6, 1946.[69]

Neither Admiral d'Argenlieu nor his superiors in Paris ever imagined any outcome in Cochin China but French control. The area surrounding Saigon was the rice granary and rubber center of Indochina. With Cochin China securely French, moreover, Cambodia and Laos could also be kept under control. From Ho's perspective as well, Cochin China stood at the center of things. No promise of even an autonomous, much less fully independent, Vietnam meant anything unless it included the Saigon area.[70]

As Ho boarded an airplane for Paris to negotiate a variety of issues left vague in the March 6 agreement, the French suddenly announced that they were recognizing the "free republic" of Cochin China. Admiral d'Argenlieu promptly sent a representative of the Cochin Chinese "republic" to take part in the Paris talks. What did that do to promises of a referendum? Little wonder that the Fontainebleau discussions began with accusations of bad faith.[71]

More than that, however, d'Argenlieu behaved as if the talks had absolutely nothing to do with the program he was putting in place, an Indochinese federation incorporating the "states" of Laos, Cambodia, and Cochin China. All the while, moreover, fighting continued in the background between Vietminh forces and French troops. With negotiations thus rendered meaningless—there was no thought on the French side of holding the referendum pledged in the March 6 agreement—the Vietnamese delegation left Paris. All except Ho himself, who stayed behind to sign a *modus vivendi* that gave the French practically everything. "I have just signed my death warrant," Ho remarked of his efforts to avoid a break with France.[72]

On his return to Hanoi, Ho did indeed face tremendous criticism; but he had considerable experience at slipping through nooses, and did so once again. Both he and d'Argenlieu knew full well their assigned roles in the Indochina drama. Neither expected the *modus vivendi* to last. D'Argenlieu had no intention of waiting for Ho to solidify his position for an attack on Cochin China. Probably it would not require a frontal attack; Cochin China could never become a viable state if things remained as they were.

The inevitable "incident" took place on November 23, 1946, when the French bombarded the port city of Haiphong in retaliation for a series of Vietnamese provocations as an excuse to occupy Tonkin and crush the Vietminh once and for all. Some six thousand Vietnamese were killed. In the weeks that followed, French troops landed, ostensibly to protect French property in the area. On December 19, 1946, Vietnamese militia forces launched their own attack, and the Franco-Vietnamese War had begun.[73]

Despite Ho's protests that he wanted no "catastrophic" war with France, and Paris' repeated assertions that it recognized the "independence" of Vietnam, it was hard to see how either side could settle for anything less than victory in the field. So long as Ho's Republic of Vietnam existed, its claim to be the only legitimate government throughout Indochina would undermine France's future in Southeast Asia.

Ho and his key leadership group vanished into the countryside, there to map out a "long and difficult" campaign of guerrilla war. In Paris, Socialist premier Leon Blum proclaimed French actions defensive. "Before all," he told the Assembly, "order must be reestablished, peaceful order which is necessarily the basis for the execution of contracts." Blum wanted General Leclerc as French high commissioner to replace the controversial d'Argenlieu. But the general had little confidence in the war he saw developing, whether conceived in Gaullist or Socialist imagination. "Anti-Communism will be a lever without a fulcrum so long as the national problem remains unresolved."[74]

5.

> In brief, with inadequate forces, with public opinion sharply at odds, with a government rendered largely ineffective through internal division, the French have tried to accomplish in Indochina what a strong and united Britain has found it unwise to attempt in Burma. Given the present elements in the situation, guerrilla warfare may continue indefinitely.
>
> Memorandum by JOHN CARTER VINCENT,
> December 23, 1946[75]

The outbreak of serious hostilities in Vietnam brought varied reactions. In Paris, the left-wing parties, including the Communists, spoke of the need to protect the interests of the French Union. It was said that the Communists expected to take power soon, hence their concern was a very "special" one; nevertheless, while entering various demurs about d'Argenlieu's methods, they expressed themselves very clearly against a scuttle and run policy in the Far East.[76]

French policy, as it then developed, centered on finding a way of promoting "other elements," eventually the former emperor Bao Dai, with whom it could negotiate a satisfactory settlement. The terms of that settlement, as before, would preserve a dominating French presence in Cochin China. The American consul in Saigon reported that the French were using various means, petitions, manifestos, declarations, etc., to build up a following for Bao Dai. "While French publicize their dislike [for] treat[ing] with Ho because of Communist danger and their duty [to] protect interests [of] other peoples FIC, little doubt they have eye to their own interests and future, hence divide and rule."[77]

The State Department was deeply worried, at the same time, that a failure in Indochina might well have such severe repercussions in France that it would insure the Communists' coming to power. For that reason recommendations that the United States step in with mediation offers were soft-pedaled in talks with French officials. And, for the first time, concern about Russian influence in the area became of itself a major consideration—with profound implications. No one could escape the fact that colonial empires were a thing of the past, new Secretary of State George C. Marshall explained to the American ambassador in Paris, but equally so, no one in Washington wanted to see those regimes replaced by "organizations emanating from and controlled by Kremlin. . . . Frankly we have no solution of problem to suggest."[78]

In less than two years since the end of World War II, the Cold War and the containment policy had replaced the Grand Alliance and anticolonialism as ruling metaphors in American policy. The Cold War reified revolutions into subversive thrusts against Western civilization, and stigmatized all revolutionary leaders as mindless robots carrying out the Kremlin's will. That Stalin had tried to dissuade the Chinese Communists from making a bid for power, and himself preferred "good fences" or iron curtains to revolutions not sponsored by the Red Army, does not mean, of course, that he wished France and its friends well. It also does not mean that he was unhappy to see his most dangerous enemy, the United States, getting embroiled in a war that was sure to alienate either Washington's allies or large numbers of the Asian masses.[79]

In a somewhat confused fashion—purposely so—the Bao Dai "movement" gained momentum in 1947. The French saw him as the vehicle by which they could remain in Vietnam, while some of those who pushed the former emperor forward as the solution apparently had in mind a mediatory role, a temporary position that would improve chances for a truly independent Vietnam. Among the latter group was Ngo Dinh Diem, a prominent Catholic nationalist, who argued that Bao Dai could produce independence without the "Red terror." Other groups had their reasons as well. And in October of that year, Bao Dai gave an "acceptance speech" of sorts: "I want first of all to get independence and unity for you. . . . Then I shall exert the full weight of my authority to mediate in the conflict which has put you one against the other."[80]

It proved difficult to accomplish his reaccession to the throne, however; and it was not until March 1949 that Vincent Auriol, president of France, and Bao Dai exchanged the letters that became known as the Elysée Agreements. As in 1946, Vietnam was given its "independence"; and as in 1946, the terms negated any common definition of that word.[81] By that time, moreover, a new menace, the threat of a Communist China had appeared. The gloomy prospect of a linkup between Ho and Mao Tse-tung chilled hopes of an early victory over the Vietminh.

Still, there was a silver lining, even to this cloud. Communist control of Beijing might well put such a fright into the guardians of the American treasury that they would dispense with further questions and produce ample funds for fighting the war. That proved to be the case. Whatever lingering doubts or fleeting thoughts of encouraging Ho's flirtation with "Titoism" still held up a final commitment were blasted away by Cold War winds roaring in from Asia.[82]

It was never a simple matter of drawing the line against Communism in Asia—at least not of drawing a *single line.* If the American-led world system was to succeed in the face of the Communist victory in China's civil war, many connecting lines had to be attached. Trade lines that ran from Japan to South-east Asia were required for certain, as well as ties between Southeast Asian countries and, eventually, military sinews to bind the United States to an Asian "defense perimeter." The economic strands that once looped around the world from European metropolises to colonial areas would have to be retied, but made secure in ways that promised to improve political life and standards of living for both ends. All these would be needed, plus adequate political wiring to keep the connections alive between Western Europe, Southeast Asia, and the United States.

Looked at from this perspective, the world Washington imagined lit up like a chart of night sky constellations, dots and lines against a dark background of unknown depths. The British Foreign Office assessed the American mood this way: "To some extent, they are influenced by the desire to try to perpetuate the sort of world in which American individualism, almost isolated, can hold its own against State trading policies of other countries; but they do desire world trading arrangements for their own sake as a means of knitting the world together into an orderly whole."[83]

Where Communist/Nationalist uprisings in Southeast Asia posed only an indirect danger to the United States, they posed an immediate threat to European economic recovery, a matter the

British Foreign Office felt did not receive enough attention in Washington. Thus in early 1947, Foreign Secretary Ernest Bevin sent an alarmed memorandum to Prime Minister Clement Attlee about the situation developing throughout Southeast Asia, from which, he reminded the prime minister, three-fourths of the world's supply of rice was drawn. Communist troubles in Burma and Siam and civil war in Indochina threatened that supply. "The outcome of the Indo-China situation is difficult to foresee, but we are unlikely to be able effectively to influence it."[84]

A few months later, in the midst of the famous dollar-pound convertibility crisis brought on by the terms of the 1945 Anglo-American loan agreement, Bevin had some other thoughts about the relationship of colonial and former colonial territories to European economic recovery. In the summer of 1947 he was constantly having to fend off attacks at home from Labour backbenchers about Britain's subservience to American policies in the emerging Cold War. And at the same time, he was asking old friends in the coal miners's union for an extra hundred-weight on the day so as to turn things around: "I get accused of tying Great Britain up to America. My God! I am here this morning to appeal to you to fight for our independence in the workshop, in the mine, in the field. It is a very ignoble thing for any Foreign Secretary to have to deal with anybody upon whom you are dependent."[85]

Bevin had a plan for confounding his critics, however, that promised better times for the British workingman. He had been looking ahead, he wrote Prime Minister Attlee on July 7, 1947, to see how future foreign exchange crises could be avoided, and how "to prevent a deteriorating standard of life in this country." Over the years, he went on, he had become a "strong advocate of colonial development, which I regard as more vital than ever now." He was having a survey made of all the essential raw materials that were in short supply in the United States. Priority should be given to the production and export of such goods. Then this statement from the Labour party's spokesman on foreign policy echoed words from the days of Joseph Chamberlain's reign at the Colonial Office in Queen Victoria's time:

> What I am afraid of is that, if we have to go on pushing goods into the hard currency areas, in a short time we may find ourselves in another form of collapse, because the rest of the world and ourselves will not be consuming our goods, and the areas in

which we are trying to sell them will become a bottleneck. Some of the weight therefore of this foreign exchange position should, in my view, be taken on to raw materials from the Empire and not rest solely on manufactured goods.

Attlee was intrigued. "I agree with your general proposition," he minuted the next day.[86] Meeting with French foreign secretary Georges Bidault at the end of another failed foreign ministers' conference as Soviet-American disagreements deepened into Cold War, Bevin agreed that there was little use in trying to appease the Russians. But there was also a peril in remaining dependent on Washington. And in that regard, continued Bevin, Western Europe had great resources in Africa. "If properly developed, these resources amounted to more than either the Soviet Union or the United States could muster, and should enable Western European powers to be independent of either."[87] What needed to be discussed, therefore, was "how to develop the colonies in harmony." As it happened, American policymakers were thinking along similar lines, at least to the extent that the British should be encouraged to develop a leadership role that would integrate Western European policies. In a review of current policies during February 1948, the Policy Planning Staff of the Department of State concluded that it would be unwise to locate Great Britain and Canada within the "American system." That would leave the continent more vulnerable, it was suggested, to Russian pressures.

On the other hand, Europe by itself could not resolve its economic problems. A union of Western European nations would have to agree on a program of "economic development and exploitation of the colonial and dependent areas of the African continent." "The African Continent is relatively little exposed to Communist pressures; and most of it is not today a subject of great power rivalries. . . . Its resources are still relatively undeveloped. It could absorb great numbers of people and a great deal of Europe's surplus technical and administrative energy."[88]

But it was Asia where the greatest danger emerged.

6.

The extension of communist authority in China represents a grievous political defeat for us; if southeast Asia also is swept by communism we shall have suffered a major political rout the

> repercussions of which will be felt throughout the rest of the world.
>
> NATIONAL SECURITY COUNCIL, NSC/48, December 23, 1949[89]

Communist China quickly became a conduit for Russian arms to Ho Chi Minh, and a sanctuary for his soldiers, but these were at best only slivers sticking out of the "bamboo curtain." The French had gotten themselves painfully impaled, a nasty situation, but what disturbed American planners most now was that a Japan isolated from the Asian continent would be drawn closer and closer economically to the Sino-Soviet bloc.

NSC/48 revealed Washington's uncertainty about Japan's predicament, but affirmed it to be a potentially disastrous calamity. To avoid a decline in its living standards, and a subsequent threat to its political stability, Japan might soon face a crucial choice: increasing "dependence" on China, or additional sources of raw materials and outlets in Southeast Asia, "in which its natural markets lie."[90]

Privately, American leaders spoke frankly (and more and more frequently) of the necessity of, in George F. Kennan's words, reopening for Japan "some sort of empire toward the south." Or as Senator Elbert Thomas put it during hearings on aid to Korea and Nationalist China: "If the United States is going to allow the disintegration of what was the Japanese Empire, to such an extent that we allow it entirely to go to Russia, then it makes it all the harder for us to maintain ourselves in Japan, because, despite what anybody says, Japan is the most democratic of all of the countries there and the one country where you must realize Communism can go faster than any other country if it starts moving."[91]

Secretary of State Dean Acheson explained all this in great detail to a dubious President Quirino of the Philippines early in 1950:

> So far as the economic future of Japan was concerned, Japan in the past had been dependent to a large extent for raw materials and minerals from Manchuria. . . . [A] very important objective of policy was to enable Japan to substitute for this excessive reliance on China trade relations with the non-communist world. If this could be done, not only would Japan's ability to withstand communist pressure be increased but Japan's interest in doing so and in maintaining its connection with the non-communist world would also be increased.[92]

One difficulty with this solution—and there were obviously several other obstacles, not least the still-fresh memories of what Japanese overlordship had meant in World War II—was that it set the projected empire "of sorts" (for Japan) against the "commonwealth-style" empire (for the Europeans) in a potentially self-defeating fashion. NSC/48 expressed a hope that through the good offices of the United States the colonial/nationalist conflict could be resolved, and the still-important ties between Europe and the old empires could be revitalized. As the authors put it: "If members of the British Commonwealth, particularly India, Pakistan, Australia and New Zealand, can be persuaded to join with the United Kingdom and the United States in carrying out constructive measures of economic, political and cultural cooperation, the results will certainly be in our interest."[93]

Given the multiracial nature of the British Commonwealth, and the advanced policies London had followed, such cooperation would "arrest any potential dangers of the growth of a white-colored polarization." Meanwhile, the United States could best assist economic development of the area by increasing its purchases of strategic materials, providing "an important source of dollars for use by Asian countries in and outside the sterling area in meeting their current and capital needs."

British policymakers fully agreed with American hopes for a strong defense line in Southeast Asia, and with the notion of commonwealth leadership. A Foreign Office committee headed by Sir William Strang had already concluded that there was a real danger that the whole of Asia would come under Russian suzerainty unless Britain made use of its special position there to bring about a close relationship between East and West. The trouble was that while most Asians no longer regarded Britain as a power to be reckoned with, the hoped-for welding of Western technology and Eastern manpower would raise cries of neo-imperialism. Russia's main advantage in this regard was that most Asians knew little of Soviet methods of overlordship.[94]

London and Washington actually exchanged policy papers on the subject of regional defense, London sending a sanitized version of Strang's report to Washington in return for one written by George Kennan. When Foreign Office experts studied the two, what stood out, in their minds, was the heavily ideological tone to the American product.[95] As events would soon demonstrate, the ideological current in American policy ran two ways. Thus when

Ernest Bevin talked with Dean Acheson in September 1949 about the altered situation in the area created by the Chinese Communist victory, the American secretary of state raised the issue of India's taking the lead in such an endeavor. Clearly, Acheson said, the way to counter Communism's appeal was with nationalism, but that was liable to bring the United States into conflict with the French and Dutch. Bevin made the interesting point in reply that the smaller nations of the area also feared Indian domination. And then he said that Pandit Nehru had warned him against a Western stand against Communism as such. It would be better to stress the expansionist tendencies of Moscow, the Indian leader had told him.[96]

The principal subject of their discussion on this occasion had been the question of diplomatic recognition of Communist China. It was already an issue that divided London and Washington. Acheson said he opposed "premature recognition," but gave his colleague no reason to believe that the United States was frozen into this position. Bevin replied in kind with a statement that His Majesty's government "were in no hurry to recognize," but there was a risk that if they waited too long, China would be lost to Russia for certain.[97]

And that would mean a China lost to Japan as well. Although traditional British trade was an important factor in the subsequent decision by London to extend recognition, as was concern about the fate of Hong Kong, there is considerable evidence to suggest that British policy was also influenced by developments in Southeast Asia. Despite the pleas of the British high commissioner in Southeast Asia, Malcolm MacDonald, that recognition would mean accepting dangerous subversives disguised as diplomats in countries with large overseas Chinese populations, the Foreign Office felt that a hostile attitude would only increase the danger. It would also create the additional problem, thought many in the Foreign Office, of a split with India.[98]

No one in London doubted the dangers of promoting Japanese-Chinese trade, either, but there was considerable feeling that while Asian stability depended upon a revived Japan, pushing Japan toward Southeast Asia as a substitute for Chinese outlets was a poor way to do it, especially from a British point of view.[99] In making the decision to recognize Communist China in early 1950, moreover, British policymakers set aside French and Dutch objections as well. Paris was generally upset about the Chinese Communists, but a letter of greeting that Mao sent Ho Chi Minh brought an impassioned plea for British nonrecognition. Sir Esler Dening, formerly Mountbatten's political adviser in SEAC, dismissed this plea with a harsh comment that "France would have a better case if she would do anything at all to try to safeguard her own position in Indo-China."[100]

The agreements the French government signed with Bao Dai in March 1949, giving Vietnam "associate state" status in the French Union, satisfied no one. And months later they remained unratified by the French Assembly. Little wonder that Dening despaired of the Bao Dai "experiment." Yet despite Britain's determination to recognize the new regime in China and, more remarkably, its ever deepening skepticism about French policies in Indochina, Bevin and his colleagues began a full-scale campaign to encourage a strong American policy in Southeast Asia—a task that the foreign secretary thought would be "long and difficult." It proved not to be.

Thus British policy was motivated by several concerns, among them a longtime concern about Japanese competition in empire and commonwealth markets. But there was also a fear that the insurgency in Indochina would spread to Malaya, where the British had spent eighty-five million pounds in the postwar period to stimulate the production of tin and rubber. Malaya was a crucial source of badly needed dollars, even more so in the postwar period than in the 1930s when America bought more from Malaya than from any other single country. The insurgency that began in the colony in 1948 added another complication for the British in formulating an Asian policy to meet all needs.

It was hardly enough, by itself, to persuade American policymakers of the wisdom of supporting Bao Dai. Nor should the British be given "credit" for the decision to aid the French in Indochina. Britain played a most important educational role, nevertheless, in formulating the problem in terms of the requirements of world leadership political economy.[101] At the highest level of sophistication, British policy endeavored to engage the United States in Southeast Asia in order to make it possible for Britain eventually to regain its "independence" of action. This had been Bevin's goal since 1947. "What I intend to do," he had told Prime Minister Clement Attlee then, "in order that we can develop an independent position with the United States instead of being supplicants, is to have a policy which, in addition to fueling our own industries adequately here will give a priority to developments which will produce the raw materials in short supply in the United States and enable us to ship them there."[102]

He needed time, he had also said, to get things going. British reconstruction—and world reconstruction—had taken longer than anyone had supposed at war's end. Time was short. The Communist victory in China demonstrated just how little there was left. For several months, until the end of 1949, American policy had also been one of playing for time to "allow the dust to settle." Dean Acheson's frequent assertions to Bevin and others that he wanted to get the China question out of domestic politics indicated that recognition was nowhere ruled out, as soon as things calmed down.

Southeast Asian concerns impinged on the China question for a variety of reasons, some of which we have examined above. The important point to remember is that these came to policymakers' attention as factors separate and distinct from domestic political questions. If, for example, Acheson and Truman could speak of the "Tito option" for dealing with China as a real possibility as late as November 1949, "to attempt to detach it [China] from subservience to Moscow and over a period of time encourage those vigorous influences which might modify it [the Communist regime]," the reasons why this option was not pursued cannot be found simply in Republican outcries or even in nascent McCarthyism. Acheson, far less than many who occupied his post, cared little for public opinion, and was hard at work preparing the ground through publication of the famous China White Paper in 1949 for some sort of accommodation.[103]

What interrupted the process, then, was not public opinion, nor the hard-liners in the State Department such as Dean Rusk, but the overall picture.[104] At the same time that Bevin was informing French leaders in mid-December of the decision to recognize Communist China, while also reassuring them that Southeast Asia was of great importance to both their countries and pledging qualified support to Bao Dai, Dean Acheson was telling the British ambassador in Washington that the United States government had changed its mind about China, as well as about the Bao Dai experiment.

China was now regarded as inherently expansionist and dangerous, while the Bao Dai experiment was considered not nearly so hopeless as previously thought. "At this point," noted Sir Oliver Franks, "Acheson interpolated a paean of praise about French achievements in Indo-China. They had done far more than they had ever let on. Bao Dai had a good chance and the thing to do was to press early recognition on the French. The American Government in distinction from its earlier views would be ready to recognize and help Indo-China as soon as the French had acted."[105]

French ratification of the agreement signed with Bao Dai came on February 2, 1950. What made it easier for the United States to act, however, was the recognition Communist China gave Ho Chi Minh on January 18, 1950, with Russia following on January 30, 1950. Whether or not either Moscow or Washington wanted it to be so, Indochina was now part of the Cold War. Acheson offered several reasons to Truman for taking this action, including giving encouragement to nationalist aspirations "under non Communist leadership," supporting a NATO ally, and demonstrating "displeasure with Communist tactics which are obviously aimed at eventual domination of Asia, working under the guise of indigenous nationalism."[106]

Diplomatic recognition was accorded Bao Dai's government on February 3, 1950. A few weeks earlier, Sir Oliver Franks had asked Acheson for an appointment to discuss a topic very familiar to them both: "the problem of sterling balances." They met at the Washington home of Hume Wrong, the Canadian ambassador. Franks plunged in "by referring to Great Britain's position during the 19th century, emphasizing the close relationship between Britain's position as a world banker and her position as a strong military and political force. He stressed the importance which capital investment had played in Britain's key position in the world." Of course, everyone knew that London could not play such a role in the post–World War II era. But perhaps the United States, Britain, and Canada could do it as a "joint arrangement." Acheson noted of the British diplomat's presentation, "The general conclusion which Sir Oliver apparently sought to draw was that the main hope of maintaining a strong democratic force in South and Southeast Asia would be for the US not only to inject some dollars into that area but to maintain both a military and political interest as well."

When confronted with this conclusion, however, Franks demurred. "The Secretary asked whether or not Sir Oliver was suggesting that we should 'use the marines' in connection with overseas investments. The Ambassador replied in the negative."[107] Recognition of Bao Dai's government was not an excuse for sending in the marines to help out the French, but the general problems of Southeast Asian security were closely tied to the successful functioning of the world system still under construction. Acheson's question was not an idle one.

Whatever contradictions or loose ends remained to be dealt with, the United States had taken the first long steps toward involvement with wide open eyes. In the long term, British policymakers forgot their role in educating Americans to the intricacies of political economy, and bemoaned the awful outcome of Washington's decision not to recognize Communist China. But the Korean War a few months later dominated everything. America began footing the economic costs of the war in Indochina as a result, and it also began to take a harsher view of French policies—now not only for failing to understand nationalism, but for weakening a vital flank on the battlefront with world Communism.

CHAPTER THREE

The Korean Rescue Mission

> When the North Koreans invaded South Korea last June, Mr. Acheson said, it seemed to the President and to his advisers that it was a deliberate, calculated thrust. It was done to shake the confidence of the people in Asia in the progress the free nations had been making. In Japan, there had been very real progress. There had been progress in the Republic of Korea. The French had been making fine progress in Indo-China. The Philippines had been doing well and so had Indonesia. The attack in Korea in June was an effort by the communists to break up all the progress that was being made in the Far East.
>
> Briefing for French premier René Pleven in the White House, January 29, 1951[1]

EXPLANATIONS of the Korean War soon went beyond Truman's original assertions that the Russians had been probing for soft spots, testing American reactions, either to lop off another piece of the free world, or as a feint preparatory to a strike somewhere else—in a truly strategic area. No one ever pretended that Korea was of great military value to either side. From the first assault by North Korean troops across the thirty-eighth parallel on June 25, 1950, to the prolonged and agonizing "truce talks" that were to last for nearly two years from 1951 into 1953, the Korean War was different from any other war America had fought.

Traditional concepts of "winning" or "losing" had to be revised. At times the war itself became almost incidental to what was said about the stakes involved. If a good case could be made for repulsing Kim Il-sung's initial attack, framed around the dangers of allowing violent acts to once again become the denominator of political change, what was to be said about the hazard of attempting to reunify Korea under a United Nations banner? Taking risks to block the North Korean assault commanded a large measure of world support, chasing down the retreating invaders less so, especially after the Chinese intervened to halt the northward march short of the Yalu River border with Manchuria.

Outside the Cold War framework, it made no sense to send American soldiers to advance the fortunes of Syngman Rhee's South Korean regime. No sense whatever. Across the thirty-eighth parallel, Korea became a different war. It required a deft hand, therefore, to get the emphasis right so as to illustrate to a variety of audiences what the stakes really were.

At the outset, Korea demonstrated, said Truman, that the Communists were ready to resort to war to advance their purposes. The president told a Boy Scout jamboree at Valley forge, Pennsylvania, only five days after the North Korean assault that what was happening in Communist countries had happened before, "back in the days of Hitler and Mussolini. Today, the young people of Communist dominated countries are being mobilized and marched, in the same fashion, under the hammer and sickle. . . . They are being made into tools of power politics, and their masters will not hesitate to sacrifice their lives if that will advance the cause of Communist imperialism."[2]

Acheson's explanation to René Pleven, while certainly not incompatible with the strong statement Truman made to the Boy Scouts, put greater emphasis on the regional objectives of the Soviets. More commonly, however, Acheson "used" Korea in a European context. Pointing to Korea as an example of Communist willingness to employ armed cadres to achieve their goals, American officials had at last gotten the Europeans to talk seriously about rearmament. Acheson wanted to keep that gain, and expand upon it. In American eyes, the major difficulty in meeting the Soviet threat before Korea had been the reluctance of Western European nations, most especially France, to reorient their thinking.

Building the North Atlantic Treaty Organization into a real deterrent force, policymakers believed, required German participation. Even more did Western Europe need German industrial prowess if a "liberated" capitalist system was to succeed. Before June 25, 1950, Acheson had strained mightily at the oars, trying, alas, to row a boat away from shore that was still tied to the dock.

Korea cut the knot. Whatever happened on those hills in a far-off corner of Asia, Europe had been rescued from the Soviets—and its tragic history.

Later commentators, however, saw the Korean War as "the decisive event" that converted the measured response the administration had made to the Soviet challenge, the Truman Doctrine and the Marshall Plan, into an overexpanded (ideologically as well as militarily) world crusade.[3] American foreign policy then commenced its dangerous wanderings throughout the forbidding terrain of the Asian continent, crippled to boot, as a result of the self-destructive McCarthyite "attack of the primitives" on the few guides, the silenced State Department China experts, who might have brought the nation through safely.

Little wonder that the meaning of the Chinese Revolution got lost in the midst of war, and little wonder, also, that events in Indochina became so distorted. There is an alternative way of viewing the Korean War, however, that suggests instead the following sequence. In the wake of the Chinese Revolution, the Russian A-bomb test, and Ho Chi Minh's increasing success against the French, Korea had to be fought to keep Cold War unities intact; this also meant going above the thirty-eighth parallel.

The Korean War, stripped of its superpower rivalry, was simply another example of a generally muddled state of affairs throughout the Far East. In country after country civil war(s), in various manifestations accompanied the decolonization process. Korea, after all, had been part of the Japanese empire for forty years, 1905–1945. The prewar political economy of Asia, badly fractured in numerous places, had not mended well at all. If energies currently being wasted on such internal disputes were not refocused on a common enemy, the outlook for a decent world order was grim indeed.

There was a "very strong belief," Acheson recalled later of conditions in postwar Europe, that economic recovery was tied to progress "in the security field."[4] NATO had resulted from such thinking. Where was its Asian counterpart? The United States had much more to do to fulfill its role as world leader; it could not long rest secure with only Europe sheltered from aggression or subversion.[5]

Put another way, the Korean War had many European ramifications, and was sometimes seen as almost exclusively European in long-term consequences. But what exactly were to be its "Asian" aspects? Asian policy was in chaos before Korea. The bipartisan consensus on foreign policy at home had broken down, said Republican senator Robert A. Taft, because Truman was "departing from the policy pursued by us in every other part of the world" by refusing to declare his intention to defend Formosa.[6]

Formosa became a rallying cry for Republican critics, but whatever domestic political pressures were mounting inside the country before Korea, the administration remained puzzled about what to do. It still mused on an eventual accommodation with the new regime in China, an approach the British clearly desired. Such thoughts had to be postponed until "the dust settled." How long that would take no one ventured to say. Great Britain's declared intention of pursuing a "two-Chinas" policy did not help American policymakers resolve the larger issues posed by Formosa. London hoped to couple diplomatic recognition of the People's Republic while encouraging a military alliance against purported Chinese Communist expansionism, a policy also adopted by the French somewhat later in an effort to "buy off" Chinese support for Ho.[7] To Truman and his aides, as well as to their critics, however, this European stance suggested a "two-Americas" strategy in the making that had to be scotched. If the nation's allies wanted aid for protecting their interests in Southeast Asia, they would have to stop expecting to succeed with a two-Americas policy: to wit, invoking an American military involvement while courting Communist China even after the Korean War began.[8]

And if Truman once harbored any hidden thoughts of his own about having the Chinese Communists "rub out" Nationalist leader Chiang Kai-shek, thereby eliminating his political problems at home, once the Korean War began, he and his advisers had—with few regrets—put aside the complicated suggestion that Ho Chi Minh might become, or might be lured into becoming, an Asian "Tito." As already noted, the French were in a crucial position to block German reintegration, so it was hardly the time to raise that possibility in Paris. Second, talk of an Asian "Tito" undermined a basic premise of the Cold War that posited a single source of Communist evil, located in Moscow, whence came all orders to make war or carry out subversive activities.[9]

While one Tito's defection offered an opportunity to use Yugoslavia to expose the Kremlin's hypocrisy, and its ruthless determination to dictate to its "comrades" abroad, what would many "Titos" imply? Certainly not the Cold War partitioning of the world both sides found so useful in maintaining their fragile, Orwellian grip on East bloc and West bloc. Moscow, of course, wanted no more Titos. But neither did Washington. Korea rescued the Cold War from deconstruction.

Arising out of Korea, finally and more fatefully, was a "new" Cold War. Only partly understood at the time, this new struggle resulted from the deadlock on the battlefield. Had there been a clear-cut victory in Korea, rethinking the situation elsewhere, even in neighboring areas, *might* have had some chance. But that was not to be. What good would it do to accept a truce anywhere short of the Yalu if the Communists then "bulged out" again in Indochina? By its own statements, Washington had declared that Communist momentum was the issue—not the sere woods and bomb-pocked hills of Korea. Deadlock meant American soldiers could not go home—they still have not. Victory would have meant, on the other hand (if only to Americans), that "Communism" could be defeated—and the possibility of separating out Soviet-sponsored aggression from colonial wars. As things stood, Korea was impossible to win, making it impossible to accept "defeat" in Indochina.

1.

> The choice confronting the United States is to support the French in Indochina or face the extension of Communism over the remainder of the continental area of Southeast Asia and, possibly, farther westward. We then would be obliged to make staggering investments in those areas and in that part of Southeast Asia remaining outside Communist domination or withdraw to a much-contracted Pacific line. It would seem a case of "Penny wise, Pound foolish" to deny support to the French in Indochina.
>
> State Department, "Problem Paper," February 1, 1950[10]

Discussions of a possible military pact to defend Asia against Communism something on the pattern of the North Atlantic Treaty Organization had not gotten very far before Korea. Along with other distractions there was the size of the defense budget, which before Korea Truman wanted to hold under $15 billion. New alliance commitments had to be measured against that standard with great care so as not to strain financial limits. But more than any other single item was the fear policymakers had of attempting to replace colonialism with a military pact that would offend the newly independent nations.

In a widely publicized speech on January 12, 1950, to the National Press Club, Secretary of State Dean Acheson attempted to discuss U.S. Far Eastern policy, rocked back on its heels by the Chinese Revolution, by cautioning that "even the most utter charlatan" would not assert a belief that there could be a single "uniform policy" for Asia. Here was grist for the relentless mills of the "China lobby." Remembered ever after as the speech which invited the Russians to send their puppet forces against South Korea, Acheson defended himself in his memoirs, describing his remarks instead as "another effort to get the self-styled formulators of public opinion to think before they wrote."

It would probably not be a mistake to read into these words hints of a sophisticated two-Chinas policy, cut off, unfortunately, by domestic politics and the Korean War. It probably would be a mistake, on the other hand, to take the hints too seriously.[11] The secretary's lengthy address—delivered almost extemporaneously from a page or two of notes—dealt first with "the matters Asia has in common."[12]

First and foremost, he said, Asia was in revolt everywhere against accepting misery and poverty as normal conditions of life, and just as firmly against any sort of foreign domination. "Whether that foreign domination takes the form of colonialism or whether it takes the form of imperialism, they are through with it." Russia, he went on, was using Communism as an imperialist weapon in an attempt to dominate China.

For Americans, therefore, the great rule of conduct must be to do nothing that would deflect Chinese wrath away from the Soviets and onto themselves. The only way that could happen, he continued, was to breach that rule by engaging in the "folly of ill-conceived adventures. . . . we must not seize the unenviable position which the Russians have carved out for themselves. We must not undertake to deflect from the Russians to ourselves the righteous anger, and the wrath, and the hatred of the Chinese people which must develop."

Turning to military security issues, the secretary drew an imaginary perimeter that excluded South Korea—as it did Southeast Asia. Peoples in those areas would have to repel any attacks, initially, on their own. But they could rely ultimately on "the commitments of the entire civilized world under the Charter of the United Nations." Extending these remarks, Acheson added that the United States could not "furnish loyalty of a people to its government." If loyalty and will and determination were there, "American help can be effective and it can lead to an accomplishment which could otherwise not be achieved."

In his memoirs, Acheson admitted, "It was a supercharged moment to be speaking on Asian matters."[13] If Acheson wished his audience in 1950 or, even more so, readers of his memoirs to believe that he was thinking about splitting China, one should keep in mind what he had to say about Indochina. Indochina came in for very brief mention, but what he said contradicted other parts of the speech, unless Communism was indeed a monolithic entity. "Progress is being made in Indochina where the French, although moving slowly, are moving." He knew full well the burden the foreign minister of France was shouldering, he concluded, and "I would not want one word I say to add a feather to the burden that he carries."

A two-Chinas policy would add enormously to such a burden, reducing the French actions to those of an outraged colonial ruler seeking to regain his lost treasure. When either the French or Republican critics tried to pin him down to a unified military policy in Asia, however, Acheson demurred. To operate effectively, a defense pact would have to be based on relations between Asian leaders. "He had in mind the complete distrust which Nehru has for Chiang Kai-shek. He also mentioned the fact that Baodai *(sic)* was not respected by other heads of Asian countries."[14]

Late in March, Congressman Christian Herter returned to the charge, asserting that American energies were divided between trying to balance the budget and meeting both domestic and foreign commitments. As a result, the security position vis-à-vis the Soviet Union was deteriorating. Acheson agreed that Americans had a false sense of well-being, "and do not realize that the world situation, which is called a cold war, is in fact a real war and that the Soviet Union has one purpose and that is world domination." But except for the "loss of China which was expected," no serious deterioration had taken place. Yet Acheson immediately qualified that statement: "There has been a trend against us which, if allowed to continue, would lead to a considerable deterioration in our position."

The Soviets schemed, he went on, to isolate the United States from its allies. Hence Herter's proposal to break off diplomatic relations with the Soviet Union as a means of alerting the American people might backfire. A good chance existed, however, that the Russians would do something soon to set off alarm bells around the world. It might come in Berlin, Acheson observed, or in Austria. "Finally, I referred to the possibility of an overall attack on Formosa from the mainland of China where we understand air strips are being built, Soviet planes are being furnished, and Soviet crews are training Chinese crews."[15]

These last comments offer additional proof that the administration, even without Republican pressure against the idea, could never have adopted a two-Chinas policy. The fact was it was simply too dangerous to attempt to do anything to support the French unless China was included as part of Russia, for political purposes, on strategic maps of the area. When Acheson talked about the Chinese buildup opposite Formosa, therefore, he was saying his prayers out loud. Ironically, what made it possible for Washington to (at last) put Roosevelt's doubts aside became, in a few years, a source of trouble for the French as they sought to cling to their hold on Indochina by dealing directly with Beijing.

Acheson had another immediate problem to deal with, however. Truman had ruled out "military aid or advice to Chinese forces on Formosa." Suppose an attack came and internal divisions over China policy prevented an effective response? That would be the worst imaginable scenario. But it might happen, for Congress, piqued over the administration's refusal to commit the United States to defend Chiang's bastion, Formosa, had rejected proposals for aid to South Korea. In a public letter to the president, Acheson warned: "It has been fundamental to our policy that in those areas where a reasonable amount of American aid can make the difference between the maintenance of national independence and its collapse under totalitarian pressure, we should extend such aid within a prudent assessment of our capabilities."[16]

The immediate damage was repaired with the passage of a new bill, but these protracted struggles with Congress threatened to hamstring the nation's foreign policy. Clearly, some Russian initiative was needed to bring policy back into gear.[17]

Acheson's favorite Republican, Senator Arthur Vandenberg, advised the secretary that the only way to restore bipartisan cooperation would be to bring John Foster Dulles into the State Department. Dulles, adviser to two-time presidential candidate Thomas Dewey, would be given the tough assignment of writing the peace treaty with Japan.[18] No one believed more firmly then, or later when he became secretary of state in the Eisenhower years, in the absolutely essential task of keeping open Southeast Asian markets for Japan than did John Foster Dulles.

That mission would ultimately require a military pact, but before that could come about—before anything could be done—Dulles lectured his new employers, the United States would have to restore its credibility in Asia, and the Truman administration resolve its conflicts with congressional critics. "There should be some early affirmative action in the field of foreign affairs," Dulles told Truman on April 28, 1950, some action that "would restore the confidence of the American people that the Government had a capacity to deal with the Communists."[19]

In a private note to himself, Dulles wrote that the loss of China had meant a dramatic shift in the balance of power. Whether it could ever be righted again depended on standing firm in the immediate future. If the nation kept falling back, the situation in Japan and the Philippines might become untenable, the rich resources of Indonesia lost, and oil supplies in the Middle East placed in jeopardy. "This series of disasters can probably be prevented if at some doubtful point we quickly take a dramatic and strong stand that shows our confidence and resolution. Probably, this series of disasters cannot be prevented in any other way."[20]

The South Korean ambassador to the United States, John Chang Myun, recalled that President Syngman Rhee had sent him on a mission to Australia, New Zealand, and the Philippines in search of a military treaty like NATO for the Far East. But before he could do that he learned that Dulles was making a preliminary tour of the Far East on his way to Japan. Ambassador Myun waited to see Dulles first. The American emissary brought good news. He had drafted a statement, Dulles told him, declaring that if Korea fights it would not be alone. And Acheson had approved it.[21]

On the eve of the Korean War, plans had been drawn for a Pacific Pact to complement a speedily negotiated and lenient peace treaty with Japan.[22] Yet even as tensions rose in Korea, the Joint Chiefs of Staff had not withdrawn their 1948 warning that the United States should not become "so irrevocably involved in the Korean situation that an action taken by any faction in Korea *or by any other power in Korea* could be considered a casus belli for the United States."[23]

When the North Korean attack came in the early morning

hours of June 25, 1950, Korean time, the administration hesitated not at all. Truman's statement to the nation two days later said that the attack made it plain that "communism has passed beyond the use of subversion to conquer independent nations and will now use armed invasion and war." In Korea, theoretical foundations found their reality, a reality Truman and his advisers had been seeking for a new Asian and European policy.

Aid would be sent to Korea, of course, but in addition the Seventh Fleet would stand by in the Formosan Straits to prevent the war from spreading there. Military assistance to the Philippines was to be accelerated. "I have similarly directed acceleration in the furnishing of military assistance to the forces of France and the Associated States in Indochina and the dispatch of a military mission to provide close working relations with those forces."[24]

Several things stand out here. By unmasking Communism as the enemy, not Russia, China, or even North Korea, Truman slipped around an awkward corner. He also expanded the field for American policy, both geographically and temporally, far beyond the Korean peninsula and for long after the fighting ended there.[25] With the indispensable help of the North Koreans and the Russians, the United States had "come to terms" with a world situation and, as it were, put Indochina into its proper niche. Acheson had warned against "the folly of ill-conceived adventures." Truman now felt perfectly safe in recommending a "military mission" for Indochina, to protect a valuable Cold War investment. In National Security Council discussions at the White House on June 29, 1950, Acheson relieved everyone's mind on the one remaining question. All indications were that the Soviet Union did not intend to commit its forces in Korea. The gauntlet flung down by the North Koreans fit a child's hand, if one that could cause a good deal of trouble. But when Truman displayed it for Americans to see, it grew larger, enough to fit a ghostly giant's hand.[26]

2.

> Indo-China is the highway to the rest of South East Asia, easier than Burma. If Indo-China falls Siam would be easier to pick up. Siam wouldn't resist at all, although they would like to. If deprived of rice by the fall of Burma and Siam, you would have to have an air lift into Malaya in order to maintain defense.

> Indo-China is the place where Communists, we should think, would want to conquer in their plans for South East Asia. If Indo-China holds, all holds.
>
> MALCOLM MACDONALD,
> British high commissioner,
> in a briefing for American
> officials, August 8, 1950[27]

Five days after the North Korean attack, Norwegian ambassador Wilhelm Munthe de Morgenstierne congratulated Dean Acheson on the stand the American government had taken. "The smaller nations of Europe were much heartened, he said, feeling that if the US is capable of meeting a situation in Korea so firmly, it will certainly not falter in its commitments in the NAT[O] area." He had personally never doubted American fortitude, but there had been skeptics. "This action will sweep away the skepticism."

That had indeed been a major consideration for American leaders: a demonstration to Europe. It was too soon to tell, replied the secretary, how the situation would develop. But he appreciated the sentiment. De Morgenstierne went on: "If the communists had been allowed to get away with their Korean aggression other areas would certainly have followed—Formosa, Indo-China and others." Acheson agreed. Then he put the point he had been arguing for some time: "This situation has pulled us together. I observed that the present situation is completely different from the previous situation in which it had been urged that we intervene in Formosa. I said that the communist intention to take Formosa and Indo-China had been evident . . . if Korea had been allowed to pass . . . Asia would have fallen apart."

De Morgenstierne concluded by saying it was "a great moment in history." Acheson went further: "I said I thought it was a turning point in world history."[28] Sir Oliver Franks, the British ambassador, was as elated as his Norwegian colleague, reporting to London that the American government and people had "instinctively followed their high destiny in the world." And adding that that was "a very great thing for all of us."[29]

Franks recommended that London offer ground troops as soon as possible. There were several reasons why it would be to Britain's advantage to do so; but the most important of these was the chance of once again assuming great-power status—as an equal to the United States and the Soviet Union. "Now with new strength and vitality in our association with the Commonwealth, a reviving more flexible and much stronger domestic economy, and a great improvement in our overseas payments, we are effectively out of the queue, one of two world powers outside Russia."[30]

Some second thoughts began to surface, however, once the initial excitement wore off. Despite Truman's public assurances that the U.S. Seventh Fleet would remain in the Formosan Straits only for the duration of the Korean War, Foreign Secretary Ernest Bevin had become concerned about a Sino-American confrontation. Already complaints from Beijing about American "armed aggression" had produced growing fears that in a showdown Asian members of the commonwealth might support China's position. In that case a split within the commonwealth was almost unavoidable, and hopes for great power status would go aglimmering. Worse still, Minister of State Kenneth Younger wrote Bevin, when that happened the Korean War would be transformed from an act of collective security into "an act of imperialism by white troops."[31]

At the end of August 1950, Bevin advised his cabinet colleagues of these dangerous undercurrents beneath the surface in Asia. British policy under Labour, he claimed (with a wee bit too much confidence), had been to encourage nationalist alternatives—as in Indochina—as the most effective counter to Communist subversion. Thus there was a strong reservoir of goodwill toward Britain throughout the area. But the war had weakened Britain's position, opening the way to American domination, with less than happy results. Until 1949, south and Southeast Asia had been British interests, but with Washington's concern growing about the Communist threat, and the United States supplying economic and military aid, all that had changed. The Americans had become, for better or worse, "a law unto themselves."[32]

Unless American policy took more account of Asian susceptibilities, the foreign secretary concluded, the result would be alienation and a drift toward Russia. As events unfolded in the summer and fall of 1950, the British found themselves in an awkward spot. On one level it appeared that they might have to choose between Hong Kong and Malaya. If the United States pushed too far onto the Asian continent, Hong Kong could be put at risk. If, on the other hand, the Americans backed off, what would happen to Malaya with its valuable dollar exports of tin and rubber, or to Thailand's crucial rice crop next to Indochina?

Britain's military leaders had advised the Foreign Office, to make matters more difficult, that if the French could not contain the Vietminh, there would be the gravest consequences ahead in Malaya and elsewhere. That side of British policy was relieved, then, when Acheson told his British and French colleagues in mid-September that aid to Indochina had been given the highest priority.[33] Pulled along by American boldness—although it did not take much tugging at all—after MacArthur's landing at Inchon, and the ensuing sweep north across the thirty-eighth parallel, the British sought to minimize the risk of a Sino-American confrontation by working with India's Pandit Nehru to assure the Chinese that no threat was intended to their security. Bevin also told Acheson that the United Kingdom would vote for China's admission to the United Nations if the issue could be separated from Korea.[34]

Separateness of that sort was exactly what Americans did not want at this time. The Korean War had severed the link between nationalism and Communism, argued Special Ambassador John Foster Dulles, and revealed the Soviets for the blatant imperialists they were. "What is going on in Asia is little more than a recrudescence in a new guise of the aggressive ambitions of the Czars. Our present policy of attacking communism and not attacking Russia seems to me doomed to failure. There is no particular opposition to communism among the peoples of Asia, indeed it has quite an appeal. . . . What they will fight for is their national independence from whatever quarter it is threatened."[35]

Dulles was not alone, obviously, in believing that the Korean War put the Cold War in Asia within a new framework. Others had anticipated his recommendation. Korea thus flattened out the political landscape, and cleared away the remnants of World War II ideology. What was true for the West, however, was also true for the "other side." Indeed, it could be argued that Korea helped Ho Chi Minh get around a potentially difficult political quandary within his movement—and for precisely the reasons given by John Foster Dulles in his prescription for fighting the Cold War.

The triumph of the Chinese Communists was reason for celebration in North Vietnam. Ho's military commander, the former schoolmaster Vo Nguyen Giap, wrote later: "Viet Nam was no longer in the grip of enemy encirclement, and was henceforth geographically linked to the socialist bloc."[36] The impact on the war with the French was felt almost immediately, as southern China became a sanctuary and training base for Ho's troops. Yet there were adjustments that had to be made. The Chinese were particularly interested in seeing Ho give the "party" a larger role, and in labeling the struggle a fight against feudalism. Perhaps Ho was ready in any event to put socialism at the forefront of the effort, but Beijing wanted it spelled out. In fact, Ho was now faced with what would become a permanent task of balancing off the views of Moscow and Beijing. And it would require, at times, some pretty nifty footwork.[37]

Having taken the position that real and potential disputes in the Communist world did not exist, American policymakers solved one problem at the cost of creating for themselves a future nightmare. Ho's problems were not resolved either. Chinese aid was neither cost free nor limitless. With the outbreak of the war in Korea, Ho could, however, both justify past compromises and set foot upon a new road of world Communist unity, marching together with the two great revolutions in Russia and China toward socialism.[38]

Korea, by bringing the United States directly onto the Asian scene, also meant an opportunity to justify the "tightening up" of party discipline—actually the reformation of the Indochinese Communist party into the Vietnam Workers' party—and the abandonment of popular front tactics. The fight against the French became, for the first time really, a struggle to overcome world capitalism—led by the United States.

For some time after 1945, Ho Chi Minh had continued to soft-pedal Washington's support for the French, perhaps because he was not sure which way the Americans would finally jump. On July 25, 1950, Ho Chi Minh answered written "press" queries about "U.S. imperialists" with the flat statement that "they have become the dangerous enemy of the Indochinese people." And then this revealing comment: "The deeper their interference the more powerful are our solidarity and our struggle."[39]

Where Truman had spoken of youth forced to march under the hammer and sickle, Ho talked about the disruption of local Vietnamese culture and economics by American lust for markets and the contamination of Vietnamese youth by America's "pornographic culture."[40] Clearly, John Foster Dulles had identified the key theme—but for both sides—of the Cold War in Asia.

3.

Once Tonkin has been lost, there is no barrier to Communism before Suez. . . . Hanoi is the Berlin of Southeast Asia. . . . We have given our shirts; now we are giving our blood. What more do you expect of us?

GENERAL DE LATTRE DE TASSIGNY, speech to the National Press Club, Washington, September 20, 1951[41]

General de Lattre's question was a good one. What *did* the Americans expect? Before Korea the answer was: a successful political response to Vietnamese nationalism that would undermine Ho's appeal. After Korea the answer was more complicated: military victory, for which Washington was willing to put up a considerable stake in money and arms, but combined with what Washington was now calling an "evolutionary statement" pledging eventual full independence.[42]*

No one in Washington believed that Indochina could be made militarily secure, let alone achieve long-term political stability, without French recognition of nationalist aspirations. But at the same time, no one believed any longer that Indochina could be made politically secure without military victory. And therein lay the dilemma. In the fall of 1950, alas, the French were in retreat on both fronts.

On the battlefield General Giap had struck a blow at an isolated fortress in the province of Cao Bang that reverberated loudly in Paris. More than 2,500 French troops were killed or taken prisoner by the enemy. Called by many the worst military disaster in French colonial history, the defeat in Cao Bang produced a divisive debate

*The post-Vietnam debate that arose over the issue of "nation building" usually begins with a discussion of the Kennedy-Johnson "liberal" insistence on putting South Vietnam on a democratic basis while attempting to fight a war at the same time. The argument is that the goals were not compatible, and that ideology was allowed to determine military strategy. To be properly understood, however, the question needs to be taken back at least to 1950 (if not before), and American pressure on the French to counter Ho's nationalist credentials. For critiques of nation building that influence current policy assumptions, see Harry G. Summers, Jr., *On Strategy* (San Francisco: Presidio Press, 1982), p. 105, and Maxwell D. Taylor, *Swords and Plowshares* (New York: Norton, 1972), pp. 339–40. For a critique of nation building with a very different emphasis, one that *does not* influence current policy, see George Ball, *The Past Has Another Pattern: Memoirs* (New York: Norton, 1982).

in the National Assembly that brought out the first impassioned demands for negotiations from Pierre Mendès-France, and vehement rejoinders from the right that "there can be no question of our abandoning the struggle."[43] American observers watched this debate with anxious eyes. While they agreed with the rightist position in the Assembly that proposals for taking the issue to the United Nations would only increase Ho's international prestige, they disagreed that U.N. intervention was the only way to "internationalize" the war.[44]

How to accomplish internationalization was the trick. Washington's plans for a regional defense organization, modeled loosely on NATO, to cover Southeast Asia had been shelved temporarily, in large part because no one had yet thought how to break the membership "barrier." It would be disastrous to make it a sahib's club, whites only, but how could the colonial powers be excluded if it was to have the wherewithal to cope with the Communist challenge? Anything that smacked of neocolonialism was sure to be rejected by the Nehrus and U Nus, while America could not go it alone without the Europeans. Such obstacles stymied immediate American action on an area defense pact.[45]

As the debate in the French National Assembly reached its climax, however, Truman's advisers agreed that the military situation in Indochina was "so grave as to require the very highest priority by the United States." Aircraft deliveries of fighter planes and bombers were speeded up, as were deliveries of transportation equipment and bulldozers. At the same time, however, American policymakers continued to urge that Paris give equal attention to the political problem, now focused on the matter of creating a Vietnamese national army.[46]

Ambassador David Bruce offered a sympathetic view of the French predicament as seen from embassy windows. While it was true that an "evolutionary statement" might win support from India's Nehru, for example, it would also jeopardize Premier René Pleven's government, already battered by the Cao Bang disaster. Consideration had to be given to Pleven's "oft-expressed" concern about the morale of French troops and the public's reaction to the expenditure of lives and money "solely to insure Vietnam independence and French withdrawal." Besides, said Bruce, if such a statement were made at this time it would appear to have been from "weakness" rather than "strength."[47]

Acheson may have smiled to have one of his favorite phrases

tossed back in this fashion. As the originator and advocate of the phrase "negotiation from strength," the secretary had set the tone for Cold War diplomacy (or the lack thereof), but the general feeling in Washington was that the French were actually forfeiting the contest on the political front by their dilatory attitudes.

A joint State-Defense committee that traveled to Southeast Asia reported its view that the area could be held, given responsible policies adopted in Paris and other capitals. "We are equally persuaded that American interests dictate the accession of the area to the American camp if it is within our capability to bring this about." The two policies advocated in the report were by now familiar subjects: regional organization and proper use of "native troops." In regard to the latter, there was always a danger that a trained force might be "turned against us." But that had to be weighed against the prospects of ultimate defeat if things continued as they were. "The former is a risk, the latter well-nigh a certainty. . . . Much of the stigma of colonialism can be removed if, where necessary, yellow men will be killed by yellow men rather than by white men alone."[48]

John F. Melby, who chaired the committee, wrote in its final conclusion, "America without Asia will have been reduced to the Western Hemisphere and a precarious foothold on the western fringe of the Eurasian continent. Success will vindicate and give added meaning to America and the American way of life."[49] As it happened, the committee's report was being read in Washington alongside urgent cables from Korea and General MacArthur's headquarters in Japan in late November and December, detailing in grim figures the scope of the Chinese intervention in Korea.

As the stunned U.N. forces retreated south before the blue-quilted Chinese army, almost certain victory turned to disaster. MacArthur called it a new war and demanded to be given the weapons, and the opportunity, to carry it to the enemy's "sanctuaries." Washington faulted the general's intelligence and strategy. Apportioning blame could not ease the pain, nor prevent America's position in Korea from being reduced perhaps to a "precarious foothold"—or even to no foothold at all. Within weeks China had risen to the rank of major world power, the *first* Communist power to defeat a Western army, and U.S. power was pushed back to the very edge of the Asian continent.[50]

In retrospect, political and military commentators, nearly everyone, in fact, rued the decision to cross the thirty-eighth parallel and the attempt to "reunify" Korea. But while the decision turned out to be based on faulty military calculations, what had made it so tempting were the same political calculations that went into the original decision to repulse the North Korean attack, among them the consequences for the situation in Indochina. The administration had not taken Chinese warnings seriously, in large part because it wanted not to, was predisposed not to do so by other imperatives, and wanted to believe that its assurances to Beijing (coupled, of course, with American military might) provided the Chinese leadership with sufficient reason to allow the Korean War to end on American terms.[51]

Now the piper must be paid. Up until the Chinese intervention, Washington had had it both ways. Korea was a "limited war" on the battlefield, and a global conflict for other purposes. Both campaigns had been successful. Now both looked to be routs. If the United States faced a Dunkirk ending for its expeditionary force in Korea, boatloads of soldiers fleeing the beaches for Japan, what outlook was there for the French in Indochina?

It was perhaps absurd, but still true, that the most powerful nation the world had ever seen could not supply troops for Indochina. U.S. military strength was based on atomic strategy and power. But if the Americans could not hold on in Korea without using the "bomb," on the other hand, did that not mean that accepting American aid meant accepting the possibility the bomb would be used as well? If, as a result of Communist successes in Korea, Secretary of State Dean Acheson told British prime minister Clement Attlee, the French pulled out of Indochina, it was doubtful that "any one of the President's advisers would urge him to intervene."[52]

Attlee had made a hurried trip to Washington to seek assurances that President Truman would never allow MacArthur authority to use atomic bombs in Korea, and would never use them himself except after full consultation with Her Majesty's government. The war in Indochina hardly came into these discussions at all, except for Acheson's brief comments. Indirectly, however, Acheson and other State Department officials felt the British were arguing for a "deal" with China that would undercut American policy.

Acheson told his colleagues that he had tried to point out to the British delegation that "the consequences to their proposal was greater than they thought. . . . you can not, as the British seem to want to do, make a distinction between little aggressions and big aggressions." To bail out of Korea because the Chinese had come in would concede to Russia and China the position of top dog in Asia, "and as a result of that all Asians would hurry to make the best deals they could with them."[53]

Truman refused to satisfy Attlee's specific requests for written guarantees, but however great the temptation of recent days to use the bomb to extricate American forces, the military had long ago concluded that using atomic weapons in Korea, under any circumstances, would be the wrong move. Western Europeans would see it not as a demonstration of power, but an admission of weakness that would threaten retaliation against them. Asian nationalists, who had generally applauded the decision to resist the North Korean attack, would now listen to Communist propaganda exploiting use of the bomb for its own purposes. Military Intelligence, G-2, summed it up this way:

> Use of atom bombs at this stage of the conflict [July 1950] would probably be interpreted as an indication of the ruthlessness of U.S. policy and a disregard for the lives of the Asiatic peoples, or as a "desperation measure" which would signify U.S. weaknesses and consequent inability to really help Asia, except by means of mass destruction and slaughter. In this respect, the resulting decrease of support by our Asiatic allies might well off-set the military advantages of such use.[54]

The only thing that had changed since mid-July was the military position of U.S. forces; otherwise, the G-2 estimate remained valid. When Premier René Pleven arrived in Washington for talks with Truman at the end of January 1951, the immediate danger that American forces would be driven out of Korea had passed. Pleven responded to Truman's invitation to discuss the Far East as the first item on their agenda with assurances of French determination to cooperate in a unified Western policy, and appeals for increased American aid. But the premier also hinted strongly at a desire to negotiate with China. "France did not want to settle anything by herself. His Government wanted to do it with their friends."[55]

Truman replied, with his usual Missouri frankness, "Since you have been talking about Chinese communists, I'd like to state our attitude on China so that you will know just where we stand." Ticking off American grievances against China, Truman worked himself into a high dudgeon that concluded with the words "We believe in calling an aggressor an aggressor." Still wound up, the president went on to declare that America would not falter. Formosa would be held. "We have been furnishing a great many supplies to you in Indo-china to fight these Chinese communists," he practically admonished Pleven, "and we will continue to do that too." Calming a bit, the president asked Acheson to elucidate details of American policy, only to interrupt again. "As Mr. Acheson began to speak, the President broke in and added, 'I made this clear to Mr. Attlee, too.' "[56]

Very well, said Pleven, in that case he needed at least $60 million in additional funds to create what the Americans said they wanted to see, a large Vietnamese army, and what General de Lattre de Tassigny's strategic plan for halting the Vietminh advance required. He also asked that a three-power consultative body, the United States, France, and Great Britain, be set up to deal with the whole problem of Communism in Asia. Truman and Acheson proved somewhat reluctant to commit themselves to either proposition, if still anxious to meet all "reasonable" French requests for aid.[57]

When the National Security Council reported on progress in implementing a decision to extend aid to the French in Indochina, the reasons for this reluctance became clearer. Too much of the world still saw the struggle as a colonial war. One arm was already tied down, the right one needed to fling atomic bombs; now the French lilliputians wanted to secure the left to an Allied consultative body, a dead weight that would pull down American support to the level of French political aims in Indochina.[58]

The continuing lack of success in getting other Asian countries to recognize the governments of the Associated States of Indochina as legitimate and autonomous regimes only pointed up the difficulty facing Washington policymakers. Qualms about being tied to French colonialism, under whatever guise, were only partially alleviated by progress on the military front.[59] General de Lattre stemmed the tide of Vietminh advances in 1951, yet Franco-American tensions actually increased in this period.

Appointed in the aftermath of the Cao Bang reverse, de Lattre promised an aggressive military strategy and a conciliatory political approach. On arriving in Vietnam, the general had said, "I have come here to complete your independence, not to limit it."[60] Over the next several months certain powers were, in fact, transferred, but overall French control remained intact. Even the small, symbolic gestures Americans had hoped would give the trappings of independence were denied the Vietnamese. American officials in Saigon had hoped, for example, that de Lattre would allow Bao Dai to occupy the palace that had traditionally belonged to the emperor until it was taken over by the French high commissioner. General de Lattre was adamantly opposed to this "Anglo-Saxon" idea, and told Ambassador Bruce that he hoped his relations with the American Legation would not be clouded by a return to this question "on which his mind was made up." "We have graver issues to discuss," he said, and dismissed the subject.[61]

As many Americans feared might happen, the influx of U.S. aid, though below the levels Paris desired, and the deceptive string of military victories allowed de Lattre to eschew any real compromises. Yet they prompted the French commander to complain about the increasing number of Americans present in Vietnam, spending too much money, making themselves too visible. The American aid program, he complained, was making France "look like a poor cousin in Vietnamese eyes," while the Americans themselves in their destructive innocence fanned "the flames of extreme nationalism."[62]

Accused of promoting French puppets by Asian countries, American policymakers found themselves under attack both in Indochina and France for seeking to dominate the war.[63] De Lattre's behavior they put down to egotism with a budding Napoleonic tinge, deepened by "his own enthusiasm following a somewhat unexpected success. It is our hope that the General will soon come back to earth."[64]

4.

> We believe that there is a big market for Japanese industrial output in Southeast Asia. Things like locomotives, tractors, rails, irrigation equipment and the like can be a very profitable mutual exchange of capital goods from Japan to underdeveloped areas which can, in turn, give Japan food and raw materials.
>
> JOHN FOSTER DULLES,
> memorandum for press conference, September 1950[65]

At best, Americans believed that General de Lattre's military campaigns held out prospects for a stalemate. Meanwhile, public attention in the United States was focused on another apparent stalemate: Korea. The MacArthur hearings in Congress had commenced, and were in the process of becoming something of a court-martial, with the administration in the defendant's box. Removed from command by President Truman, the famous "I shall return" hero of World War II played out the final scenes of his military career before a joint committee, one of whose members asked if he also thought that the use of Chinese Nationalist troops from Formosa might not "help with the situation in Indochina." The general assured them that they would, and that anything that caused the Chinese to disperse their forces over several fronts would help in the struggle against Communism.[66]

Secretary of Defense George C. Marshall, another war hero, responded for the administration by saying that the Korean War should not be considered a stalemate at all. Positive things had resulted from Korea. It had provided "sorely needed time and impetus to accelerate the building of our defenses and those of our allies against the threatened onslaught of Soviet imperialism."[67]

Neither MacArthur in his accusations, however, nor Marshall for the defense touched upon a tricky issue that involved Japan's future and linked it with Indochina. Before Korea, policymakers had debated the question of Sino-Japanese trade, coming to the tentative conclusion in May 1949 that efforts to prevent that natural connection would only delay further Japan's economic recovery, cost American taxpayers large sums, and quite probably "produce profound Japanese hostility" to the United States.[68]

Policymakers were uneasy with this conclusion, however, for all the obvious reasons: the political climate in the United States, the risks of encouraging Sino-Japanese cooperation in the creation of another Communist power, and so on. Korea had temporarily freed Washington from these complications, and insured Japan's economic recovery—for the immediate future. "Procurement contracts pumped millions into Japanese industry, and production, previously stalled at low levels, surged ahead." But with Japan now a staging area for the Korean War, the issue of "commitment" in the Cold War raised questions about the long-range future of the island country located off the Asian mainland. An Asian containment policy required a healthy Japan, and a healthy Japan required Asian markets; if not in China, then elsewhere.[69]

To this set of problems John Foster Dulles, who had been charged with negotiating and drafting the peace treaty with Japan, now turned his attention. Japanese security, policymakers recognized, required two major components: a horizontal economic "lifeline" and a vertical military "backbone." Dulles had to devise a system that would guarantee Japan both—yet not alienate either the new Asian nations or old European allies.

Whenever Dulles opened his briefcase full of policy papers and treaty drafts, everyone knew what he had to offer. And it was no easy sell in postwar Asia. Even Japanese emperor Hirohito was skeptical. How could Philippine anger be assuaged? he asked Dulles at one point. Well, replied the American negotiator, perhaps something could be worked out whereby Philippine raw materials could be finished, at Japanese expense, into manufactures. The emperor liked the idea, but Filipinos did not.[70]

Philippine president Carlos P. Romulo actually accused Dulles of caring more about Japan's welfare, an enemy country, than he did about the welfare of an ally, the Philippines. Hardly surprising, said the American ambassador in the Philippines, that he should feel this way. "To Phil[ippines], as to other Asians, status of raw materials suppliers connotes colonial subservience. Any western tendency to discourage indigenous industrial development therefore automatically suspect as ruse to retain dominance economically despite relinquishment polit[ical] control."[71]

Dulles dismissed the complaint. Large-scale reparations from Japan such as the Filipinos demanded were simply out of the question. And Dulles remained convinced, as he told Prime Minister Yoshida, that Japan ought to consider offering to fabricate "reparations goods from raw materials" in "countries which had been occupied by Japan and with which Japan normally traded." The gesture could "facilitate the reopening of former channels of trade. . . . It might be good business."[72]

Other Southeast Asian countries were not so adamant as the Philippines about reparations, nor yet in a position to be heard about their fears of being saddled with a neocolonial relationship, though Indonesia and Burma both expressed doubts about the Dulles scheme at various times. London and Paris were aghast. Unable to brush off their complaints with the same ease as he did Philippine protests about reparations, Dulles hewed to a strong line and, when necessary, acted unilaterally.

The British, Dulles argued in notes he wrote to himself, were primarily concerned with the "impact of Japanese commercial competition."[73] The ensuing struggle over which "China," the People's Republic or Chiang's Nationalist regime on Formosa, should sign the peace treaty brought out these concerns—as well as other British fears about the proposed peace treaty. In late October 1950, Dulles took his brief to the Council on Foreign Relations in New York. One night over dinner a council of elders met as a grand jury to consider the problems that faced American policymakers as they devised a method for containing Communism in Asia.

Among their number were those who had been concerned with Japan, and how to fit it into a liberal capitalist world system, since before World War II, well before, in fact. The chairman, Everett Case, opened the proceedings: "One of the greatest tragedies of the twentieth century has been the failure of Germany and Japan to become respected members of the comity of nations." A nodding of heads. A brief exchange followed over whether the goal should be to make Japan "democratic," in the American sense, or only to insure that whatever government emerged remained tied to the United States. No general agreement was reached before dinner.

After dinner Dulles addressed them. Japan could not be "coerced" into the West, he began. Again a nodding of heads. It could be frightened out of the free world, however, and would have been were it not for American military resistance to Communism. The Korean War had to be fought, if for no other reason than to preserve Japan's morale. Korea may have frustrated a major Soviet aim of gaining control of Japan, but the future presented still more difficult problems of bringing Japan under the Western security umbrella, and integrating the Japanese into the world economy. The treaty could make a provision for American garrisons, and thereby offer both security to Japan and guarantees to countries like Australia and New Zealand that feared a resurgent Japan, but the treaty could only do some things about the second problem. It should impose no reparations burden or restrictions on Japanese rearmament. Japan's new constitution forbade rearmament, but Dulles believed a solution could be worked out. "To fulfill its obligations it could ask us to retain our forces there." He also had in mind some sort of arrangement for a Pacific security treaty, vague as yet, that would include Japan in some capacity.

Then there was the economic issue to consider: Japan had to be made able to get along without China. "The solution lies partly in the development of the Japanese capital goods industry and in enlarging markets for such products in the underdeveloped areas of Southeast Asia." At that point the group began asking questions. Friendly relations with the future Japan, Dulles averred, would turn on this question. Comparisons were made with West Germany, whose need for outlets in the free world was as obvious as that of Japan. But where were Germany and Japan to trade? "In so far as the United States feels it necessary to inhibit the trade of these countries with certain areas," said one discussant, Percy Bidwell, "it has a positive responsibility to assist them in the development of trade relations in other directions." Others agreed: Japan was the natural "workshop" for Southeast Asia. The jury was in.[74]

"The U.K. attitude is worrying," Dulles wrote to General MacArthur several months later. But well armed with the sentiments of a broad consensus of American thinkers and doers, the special ambassador knew what to do: "The United States and Japan are the only significant sources of power in the Pacific, we actual, they potential. If we can work in accord, the lesser Pacific powers will get security and will sooner or later, formally or informally, endorse that accord. If the United States and Japan fall apart, the situation in the West Pacific is grave for a long time."[75]

British efforts to include the People's Republic at the Japanese Peace Conference to be held in San Francisco in September 1951, their continuing objections to granting Japan trade equality with other nations, and their refusal to consider a Pacific security treaty that would bring together Japan and any Southeast Asian nations were all put down in American minds to part of a traditional pattern of attempting to deflect Japanese expansion northward and away from imperial interests.

The French also protested against allowing Japan trade equality, asserting that it would hold back economic integration in Europe. French labor costs, it was argued, would mean that France could not compete with Japan in North Africa and Indochina, and if it could not do that, the economic situation would become more difficult within Europe. Barriers against Japan would inevitably become fences against others as well.[76]

These Allied complaints only deepened the American impression, on the other hand, that France's fight in Indochina was not yet America's, that there were definite limits on what Washington could or, more important, should do to support Paris. It was a terrible dilemma, because the choice between a Communist Indochina, tied to Russia and China, and a colonial Indochina, serving only narrow French ends, was not simply unpalatable, it was unimaginable in terms of the Cold War.

To satisfy the more reasonable security complaints of Australia and New Zealand, Dulles had also negotiated a treaty, the ANZUS Pact, already signed at the time the Japanese peace treaty was being discussed. Ostensibly designed to guard against a reborn Japanese menace, ANZUS was something of a breakthrough as it was the first alliance against Asian Communism.[77] London did not really like ANZUS all that much, an inner grouping within the commonwealth through which the United States now enjoyed special leverage, however limited, but neither Labour nor the Conservatives, who returned to power in the general elections of the fall of 1951, knew exactly what to do about the situation.

Behind the scenes, meanwhile, Dulles was involved in a semiprivate wrestling match with British diplomats to gain Prime Minister Yoshida's signature on a letter setting forth Japan's determination not to recognize the People's Republic. The British managed to hold open the theoretical possibility of Japan's recognition of the Communist government after the treaty came into force, in part because they were still able to use the sterling bloc to threaten trade retaliation, but Dulles had applied a hammerlock in the form of Senate ratification procedures.[78]

When he appeared as the administration's chief witness on behalf of the Japanese peace treaty before the Senate Foreign Relations Committee, Dulles described it as an "act of faith" in Asia's future. It was full of hope for all Asia, because it symbolized America's positive determination. "We must adopt these positive policies," he said, "and get away from the idea that this overrunning of China by Soviet communism is a final last word as to what is going to happen to China. There have never been those final last words as regards China in the past, and I do not think it is so now."[79]

Dulles' testimony bristled with sharp references to Communist China, making him look like a bespectacled porcupine. It is hard to weigh the factors here. Dulles had a genuine concern that over the long run it would be impossible for Japan to survive without access to China, and yet he combined that with a suggestion that the only alternative to a generous Western economic policy toward Japan was a war of liberation against Communist China. He also had a good idea what Congress wanted to hear. So he launched a broadside at Russia. The Cold War matched two historic enemies, he said, beginning in the early nineteenth century:

> When this country was formed and organized the world was ruled by despots. It so happened that the leader of those despots was Czar Alexander of Russia, who organized the Holy Alliance, exercising the rule of despotism over a large part of the world. It was largely inspiration that stemmed from this Nation that rolled back that tide of despotism. Never before in our history have we adopted a defeatist attitude toward despotism and I can see no reason why we should do so now. I believe that if we can inspire the free peoples of Asia, those who are still free, with this spirit, and if they know that that is our spirit, it will completely revolutionize the whole situation in Asia and the people who still love freedom will find ways to make that effective.[80]

5.

> Granted the inability of the native governments to assure the territorial integrity of the area for the foreseeable future without outside help and the unlikelihood that other friendly nations than France are able or willing to participate in the defense of the area, individually or collectively, we are obliged to support the only practicable means available to us, which in this case is the French.
>
> State Department memorandum,
> May 7, 1952[81]

With the Korean War all but stalemated—and reminiscent of the bogged down western front in World War I, with all that meant for the prospects of revolution in Russia and Germany—American policymakers became increasingly apprehensive of a "breakthrough" in Indochina. This could occur in several ways, all but one of which, victory over the Vietminh, would be disadvantageous to American interests. By far the most likely possibility was Chinese intervention, but there were others: French weariness and withdrawal, and even an unwelcome political initiative to put Indochina within the framework of an overall settlement with the Soviet Union along lines of spheres of influence.

A settlement in Korea, where truce talks now mimicked Orwellian dialogues, was both wished for and dreaded. Wished for, for obvious reasons; dreaded, out of fear that the unity of Cold War purpose—whether in Asia or Europe (or America)—would dissipate once the guns fell silent. Histories of past wars, especially those in the twentieth century, suggested that pattern was the common one. "Since the national interest requires it," wrote a Far Eastern expert in the State Department, "we must keep on keeping on in Indochina, until the Viet Minh is liquidated and therefore, no longer an effective instrument of the Kremlin and Peiping, or until events elsewhere in the world relieve, in whole or in part, the burden now borne by anti-communist forces in this theater of action."[82]

This global vision of the war in Indochina had come into being as a result of the Korean War or, perhaps better said, had *become accepted* as a corollary of that conflict. It had replaced the colonial vision, so fraught with difficulties for French and other Western policymakers. Inside Indochina, unfortunately, the colonial vision persisted, and not only persisted, dominated. The global vision failed not because it assigned Southeast Asia to a "theater of action," but because instead of engaging outside forces to defend their interests, Western powers reified the Vietnamese, reducing them to the status of occupants of a territory where valuable raw materials and resources were at risk. They counted otherwise only as numbers in a zero-sum game, in which, at the end of each Cold War campaign, each superpower totaled winnings and losses, hoping that the balance of power had been tilted in its direction.

Inside Stalin's "empire" there was no room for nationalist revolutions, but Vietnam was a lever against the West. Maybe it kept alive the long-lost revolutionary energy of 1917, kept it alive in a safe place, far away from Moscow. Yet the Russians could not control what Ho Chi Minh thought about Marxism-Leninism, nor what he planned to do about it on behalf of his own vision of Vietnam's destiny. The Americans were similarly trapped with a problematical counterrevolution on their hands.

Emperor Bao Dai, a reluctant ruler to begin with, saw clearly where things were headed. It was time, he told American ambassador Donald Heath on January 20, 1952, that the French said what their real aims were. Heath replied that Paris had made no secret of its desire that the nascent French Union would offer the metropolis "some economic assurances and preferences along line of Brit[ish] imperial preferences." There was also a "legitimate desire" to maintain "a certain currency of Fr[ench] language and culture in Indochina."

To that Bao Dai responded that it was time for Paris to get off the plane of sentiment and come to an appreciation of Indochinese reality. French prestige and pride was a matter for the French to take up in other surroundings. Perhaps it would not be "utterly tragic," he went on, if the Chinese did invade. At least then he could found and lead an effective resistance to"the hated traditional enemy." Heath was stunned. When he recovered, he could only reply that with "Commie ruthlessness and efficiency," the Chinese would do away with all resistance leaders. "At present time only Fr[ench] Union forces kept Vietnam from becoming Chi[nese] Colony."[83]

Bao Dai's oblique bid, made through Ambassador Heath, to become in fact as well as in name Vietnam's ruler was presumably well placed, for the United States had already bought into the war to the extent of $500 million, and was now paying one-third of its annual cost. Yet even if the French had been willing to turn over management of the struggle with Ho, which they were not, even if the Korean War came to a speedy end, freeing men and resources, which it would not, and even if Washington had more confidence in Bao Dai's qualifications for such a role than it did, American policymakers had no intention of putting ground forces in Vietnam.[84]

In preparation for a visit from Prime Minister Winston Churchill in early 1952, once again in office as a result of the recent Conservative victory, policy planners reviewed the general outlook in both Europe and Asia. The greatest differences were likely to arise over policy toward Communist China. While Churchill was presumably, as a Conservative, more inclined toward the American position, there were long-term British interests in China trade and the protection of Hong Kong that made full agreement difficult.

Even more important in this regard, the British were now in the position of having to accommodate Indian opinion. Once the keystone of British power and prestige in Asia, India retained that position in certain respects. Only now London could not afford to get in a contest for commonwealth leadership with a nation that asserted a claim, however dubious it might be, to speak for all Asia. And India's views were increasingly at odds with those of the United States concerning China.

It was suggested by the briefing paper authors that the president should try to counter this tendency in British policy by focusing on the likelihood of Chinese intervention in the Indochinese war. "There are definite signs that an armistice [in Korea] will increase the danger of communist aggression in other places in the Far East, particularly in Indochina." An armistice, therefore, should be no reason to modify current policies, or in any way to let down the West's guard on the China coastline.[85]

Anticipating as well a possible suggestion from Churchill for a global settlement with the Soviet Union, these planners listed all the reasons why that could not be done. "The international Communist movement can and would continue to work for the extension of Soviet control," it was asserted, "without attaching any responsibility to the Soviet Government. The same opportunities are not available to us."[86] No better statement of the imperfections of both the colonial vision and the global vision exists, or of the advantages accruing to the "other side" in a conflict pitting dynamic forces against static positions. The French conception of strategic strong points in Indochina to hold back an enemy that swept past them in the night perfectly mirrored in life the abstractions in official policy papers.

In short, these were status quo outlooks. They were containment images where containment had only counterrevolutionary definitions. In the Truman-Churchill talks, Secretary Acheson said as much. The greatest danger from the Soviets, he opined, lay not in the constantly feared mass attack on Europe, "but rather in creeping actions taken through satellites in parts of the world which would exhaust the Western powers, such as was now taking place in Indochina."[87]

Such statements doubly reified Indochina, treating it as important only for its impact on Europe. Throughout the briefing papers for these talks ran the theme that Korea had allowed the West to regain the initiative. And Churchill confirmed this was still the British view in his first exchange with Truman.[88] But where did one go from there? Americans really had no idea except, as the State Department asserted, "to keep on keeping on." They were not even sure what the response should be if China did come into Indochina with both feet. Again, Acheson made no secret of the American indecision. Staff talks with the British and French were scheduled for the near future. But beyond that was unchartered territory: "The West is indeed faced with a dilemma: if we do nothing it would be most unfortunate yet it is most difficult to see how we can do something effective. In any event the western powers must work closely together."[89]

Churchill and Foreign Secretary Anthony Eden had no answers for Acheson, only more questions. The prime minister pointed out that the war in Indochina drained the French, and made it more difficult for Paris to produce a decent fighting force for use in Europe. Eden said it was hard to see what the French could do if China continued to reinforce the Vietminh, yet the prospect of withdrawal, with its threat to Malaya, could be very injurious to the British economy. The discussions, as all such Far Eastern talks tended to do in this period, wound down in desultory fashion until the president suggested they adjourn.[90]

Over the next several months the sense of frustration these talks conveyed further deepened, especially as new French requests for increased aid arrived in Washington. "I was left with the impression," one American official reported of a conversation with Jean Monnet, that if the latter had his way, he "would liquidate whatever now remains of French interests in Indochina."[91] The French, stalemated (if not actually in a worse position) in Indochina, enjoyed a curiously strong position vis-à-vis Washington. They knew the United States was determined to "have it all." The United States desired French acquiesence, indeed support for German rearmament, and at the same time wanted France to go on fighting in Southeast Asia. It abhorred the thought of having to make a choice between these objectives, and was willing to give the French whatever financial aid was necessary to secure their realization. But it did not want to stake this higher wager on a foredoomed enterprise.[92]

Told by French foreign secretary Maurice Schumann that the French public was "weary and tired of the Indo-China war," and reminded that the proposed European Defense Community (EDC) plan would, so long as Germany did not have to divert its military resources to places like Indochina, result in a military disequilibrium, Acheson offered more aid for building up native armed forces, and a new proposal for issuing an Anglo-French-American warning of some sort to China not to intervene.[93]

The French ignored Acheson's comments on native armed forces, but took up the idea of a joint warning to make a different point. True, such a warning might stop one war, but it also might "start or extend the war." Had the United States and United Kingdom "considered whether negotiations might possibly end the war"?[94] Once this forbidden subject had been put on the table, it became a central concern in American thinking. Attempts to find out exactly what French policy was were now colored by a determination to head off any negotiations that would deliver Indochina over to Communist hands.

This was made more difficult, obviously, by the ongoing "negotiations" in Korea, however unproductive they might be at the moment. Why was it right for the Americans to settle their affairs with the Communists in one "theater of action," and not for the French to avail themselves of a similar opportunity, if it came along? It was hard to give a reason why, especially since it had been the Americans who, unwilling to fight a colonial war, insisted upon the global vision with its necessary identification of a single source of mischief: the Kremlin.

As it happened, the French really were thinking of a deal with Communist China over Ho Chi Minh's head, a bargain that would salvage something (perhaps a great deal) out of Indochina. They did not want, therefore, to take American money to build up the Indochinese army; neither, however, did they want to agree to a joint warning to Beijing that would rule out independent diplomacy. When Dean Acheson and Truman met with President-elect Dwight D. Eisenhower in mid-November, the secretary of state explained that the "real" problem for the incoming administration would be the "French will to carry on the . . . war." Admiral Arthur W. Radford, soon to be Eisenhower's chief military adviser, put it more bluntly after a visit to the "front." "What seemed most needed in Indochina, and what the United States could not offer under our MDAP [Mutual Defense Assistance Program], was guts."[95]

Secretary of State John Foster Dulles soon demanded something else from the French, however: the courage to turn over the war to Washington.

CHAPTER FOUR

True Liberation

> We shall again make liberty into a beacon light of hope that will penetrate the dark places. It will mark the end of the negative, futile and immoral policy of "containment" which abandons countless human beings to a despotic and godless terrorism, which in Korea enables the rulers to forge the captives into a weapon of our destruction. . . .
>
> The policies we espouse will revive the contagious, liberating influences which are inherent in freedom. They will inevitably set up strains and stresses within the captive world which will make the rulers impotent to continue in their monstrous ways and marks the beginning of the end.
>
> Draft for Republican
> party platform, 1952,
> by JOHN FOSTER DULLES[1]

EISENHOWER's inaugural speech resonated with all the now familiar Cold War themes. "Here, then, is joined no argument between slightly differing philosophies," he intoned. "Freedom is pitted against slavery; lightness against the dark. The faith we hold belongs not to us alone but to the free of all the world." An unexceptional recitation, but Eisenhower added a further note: "It confers a common dignity upon the French soldier who dies in Indo-China, the British soldier killed in Malaya, the American life given in Korea."[2]

Such a linkage *was* exceptional. In fact, it was alien to the thinking of the new administration. Eisenhower wanted to fight the Cold War on terms different from those of his predecessors. He had many reasons, some of them contradictory, for seeking to change foreign policy and Cold War strategy. His party, of course, had kept

Korea uppermost in the voter's mind. Throughout the 1952 electoral campaign the Republicans had promised to reverse the defeatist containment policy pursued by the Democrats, which had, they insisted, resulted in the "loss" of China and the Korean War. America would take the offensive. No more stalemated wars. No more imaginary lines. No more Communist sanctuaries. No more retreats—anywhere. General Eisenhower, hero of America's "crusade in Europe," had come forward to lead the nation once again. He would return America to its true mission: liberation.

"We will have a dynamic policy of liberation which will develop a resistance spirit within the captive peoples," John Foster Dulles wrote in a speech draft. "This is the only effective check on aggressive despotism short of general war."[3] Eisenhower winced during the campaign, however, when Dulles got carried away with the liberation theme, and called him on the telephone to remind him that they had agreed to talk about liberation "by all peaceful means."[4]

Eisenhower's main concerns were not Eastern Europe at all, but the global interconnections he had observed from World War II days and through his experiences at NATO. Defending Western Europe, he had decided, was worth it for geopolitical and economic reasons, "because only Western Europe and its colonies, possessions and related allies in the Eastern Hemisphere can furnish the things we need, and Western Europe is the cradle of our civilization. If it goes India will follow soon, for example, and where will we get our manganese?"

Similarly, Eisenhower supported the original decision to defend South Korea. He had early recognized there could be "no satisfactory conclusion" to the Korean situation. On the other hand, he wrote in his diary, had the United States allowed South Korea to go under, "we would have by this time [January 1952] been kicked out of Southeast Asia completely, and it would be touch and go as to whether India would still be outside the iron curtain." Ike always displayed a keen appreciation of the economic dimensions of the Cold War. "If we had lost those areas," he wrote in the same entry, "I do not know exactly how we would obtain some of the raw materials we now import from those regions."[5] But he was as frustrated about Korea as the man in the street, declaring that the Soviets had us bogged down—and were enjoying every minute of it. "Let's get out of the swamp we are in, whoever put us there."

A newspaper columnist present when Ike sounded off wrote, "He would get out of Korea and defend our Pacific outposts in the midst of a 'friendly people,' the Japanese."[6]

"Consequently I feel that we should figure out our strengths," Eisenhower once wrote Bernard Baruch, "and push toward them steadily, but always having in mind that we must retain a strong and solvent economy."[7] Yet he had doubts of another kind, about how long the United States could continue with a containment policy before something snapped. The H-bomb, he wrote Dulles on September 8, 1953, changed everything. The costs of maintaining a deterrent, in a permanent state of war readiness, "would either drive us to war—or into some form of dictatorial government. In such circumstances, we would be forced to consider whether or not our duty to future generations did not require us to *initiate* war at the most propitious moment that we could designate."[8]

Eisenhower's moods alternated perhaps more than other presidents', swinging from glowing optimism to gloomy assessments like the one above. But one thing he never doubted: the costs of containment were becoming too great.[9] How to reconcile the nation's strategic and economic requirements was further complicated by the lopsided burden of colonialism. The United States needed, as Eisenhower wrote, access to raw materials, but it also needed access to the minds of the areas emerging from European rule. Here was indeed the core difficulty, for the Soviets had launched a major Cold War campaign on that front, skillfully probing the weakest spot in Western ideological defenses: colonialism.

Thus, as Eisenhower commented on one of Dulles' memos on foreign policy in the early summer of 1952, "The minimum requirement of these programs [defense and foreign policy] is that we are able to trade freely, in spite of anything Russia may do, with those areas from which we obtain the raw materials that are vital to our country. Since it is just as tragic for us to lose one of those areas to Communism by political action as by marching armies, our programs will not satisfy our minimum requirement unless they protect us and the areas in which we are concerned from both kinds of aggression—that is, military and political."[10]

This lopsided burden of European colonialism had weighed heavily on American policymakers since World War II ended, and despite what Ike now said about the "common dignity" of the Cold War struggle, the new administration wanted to be rid of the millstone before it finally dragged the American cause under along with the tattered and worn-out defenders of no-longer-glorious empires. He did not want the third world thinking, despite what he said in his inaugural address, that American purposes in South Korea were the same as the British in Malaya or the French in Indochina.

It was hard to find the proper means to make the distinctions clear, given all the other requirements of a sound strategy. Outgoing Secretary of State Dean Acheson, as usual, had many pertinent comments on the problem, if no solutions to offer. "I don't believe that the current view that there's a great competition between the communists and the west for this whole [colonial] area," he predicted, "is really the authentic and true picture of it. It is mostly that things are going on in that part of the world which are of importance, and their importance from the point of view of the diplomacy of the United States comes from the terrific potentialities of trouble which they have between us and our allies."[11]

The colonial problem was like stepping on a "banana peel." "You have got to keep from falling on your tail, but you don't want to be lurching all over the place all the time."[12] When Truman and Acheson met with Eisenhower and his aides on November 18, 1952, however, the secretary warned that there was a strong body of opinion in France that regarded Indochina as a lost cause. That was reflected, to some degree, in the lack of military aggressiveness shown by the French in Indochina. "The central problem," he went on, "was the fence-sitting by the population. They would never come down on one side or another until they had a reasonable assurance of who would be the victor and that they had some interest in the victor." The United States was already paying half of the financial burden, but military discussions with England, France, Australia, and New Zealand had not produced a program for a military solution. "The French now sought political discussions," he concluded this gloomy briefing, with the enemy.[13]

A spokesman for the new administration saw things differently. Our image around the world, lamented United Nations ambassador Henry Cabot Lodge, who held a post where the millstone collar of perceived colonialism would rub especially hard on American initiatives, is getting to be that of "supporting outgoing regimes—the Colonel Blimps." Like it or not, he went on, the colonial powers had to be pressured to promise dependencies full freedom. It was for their own good. Besides, they "really have nowhere else to go."[14]

Stalin's death, only a short time after Ike stepped across the

White House threshold, prompted some of his advisers to talk about the prospects of an American "peace offensive." Not, however, John Foster Dulles. "As Stalin dies," read the new secretary of state's Delphic proclamation, "General Eisenhower, the man who liberated Western Europe, has become President of our Great Republic, with a prestige unmatched in history."[15] For a decade Stalin's malignant shadow had dominated the world scene. But now the evil colossus was gone, and there was no one to replace him; no one, Dulles meant, who could hold the Soviet empire together. "The Eisenhower era begins as the Stalin era ends." A Christian lay leader, as well as a highly successful international lawyer, Dulles had impressed Eisenhower with his concern about the "lack of morality" in contemporary politics.[16]

Dulles' stern code struck other observers as arrogant religiosity. "He wore God as his boutonniere," quipped a State Department professional.[17] He did, in fact, suffer from a missionary's narrow zeal, but that bias also sharpened his awareness of Communism's appeal in underdeveloped areas. Stalin's death might offer a chance to take the offensive, not in Eastern Europe (he agreed with Eisenhower on this point) but in reordering the Western alliance around new ideals in place of the static containment paradigm, which, among other things, did nothing to address the issue of Asia and Africa.

Dulles' thoughts on this general issue began with certain assumptions about economic growth and development. "This country was largely developed by capital in Europe," he reminded everyone periodically, "private capital . . . and the business of Government is primarily to help create an investment climate such that private capital does the job."[18] But that did not mean you could return to nineteenth-century laissez-faire methods—or colonialism—to find answers for current problems. "You know, it's like getting a bunch of people who are suffering from malnutrition, rickets, all sorts of congenital ailments—who are weak—and saying, 'What you ought to do is play rugby football. Come on, get in there, out in the field. Tackle each other. Be rough and tough.' . . . Well," he went on, "you know this is madness. But after all you say to them, 'Have a free competitive system.' And they say, 'Good God, there must be a better way of doing things.' Furthermore, you say, 'The way to build up your industry is to save, become capitalists, invest—and so on.' But they want a steel mill over night. They want public utilities. They want everything."

How was one to combat Communist promises that they *could* have everything in far less time than it took the capitalists to provide decent living standards—and without going through the further agonies and sufferings of a capitalist industrial revolution? "This is a tremendous difficulty in trying to save souls for political freedom, when the devil has so much on his side."[19]

Liberation has been dismissed in recent years as simply an electioneering slogan, quickly abandoned for a return to containment. The only thing Dulles ever did in the name of liberation, the argument runs, was to fire George Frost Kennan, the author of the famous "X" article, "The Sources of Soviet Conduct," from which the then-despised term "containment" had arisen.[20] Having banished Kennan in unseemly fashion to the wilderness, Dulles ceased his dreaming (if he ever really did) and set about pursuing a workaday foreign policy that differed hardly an iota from previous Cold War policy. "Dulles had to sack Kennan," suggested an insider, "in order to be free to pursue a Kennan policy."[21] Where was there any evidence of a desire to arouse the captive peoples? Not in Eastern Europe. Dulles had indeed talked about the "rollback" of Soviet power during the election campaign, but Eisenhower made it clear he wanted no part of any such adventure in Russia's front yard—a point brought home almost immediately when the United States did nothing about exploiting food riots in East Berlin during the summer of 1953, nor, indeed, anything to help the Hungarian "Freedom Fighters" three years later.[22]

Korea was a question mark. Dulles would dearly have loved to press that matter, but while Eisenhower speculated about using the bomb to bring about a peace settlement, he was thinking about last-resort measures to achieve an early end to the fighting, not about driving the Communists out of North Korea so that Syngman Rhee could achieve his life's ambition to rule over a unified Republic of Korea.[23]

No president has benefited more from revisionist interpretations than Eisenhower.[24] In post-Vietnam America, Eisenhower's stature has grown steadily. Where Eisenhower the "captive hero" once stood, imprisoned in bronze on the White House putting green, we now have before us another Eisenhower, the restrained seeker after peace, and author of the second most famous farewell address in the nation's history. Only Jefferson's warning against entangling alliances is more familiar, perhaps, than Ike's famous admonition about the growth of the military-industrial complex.

Yet it is Jefferson's caveat that provides a clue in reconciling the liberation theme with the realities of Eisenhower's foreign policy. Containment might have worked in Europe, where the Soviet military presence was the dominant feature of the political and geographical landscape. But it would never work in Asia, where ideology and cultural affinities—especially Chinese influence—predominated.[25] An effective fight against Communism could be waged, therefore, only by aligning the United States on the "dynamic" side of world movements.

Liberation would embarrass the Soviets in Europe, call world attention to their repressive policies, and generally put them on the defensive ideologically; it would also put America's allies in an awkward position, prompting them, it was hoped, to speed up the dismantling of empire. However maddening the Korean War had become, it still had a place in this scheme, if only because the abrupt abandonment of Syngman Rhee would send the wrong signals—to Europe, to Asia, and to America. If Korea could not be won, damage control was an absolute necessity, or liberation would never get off the ground.*

True liberation, then, became Dulles' efforts to free America from the "tyranny of the weak," the drowning man's death grip on the living, the colonialist's wasteful misuse of resources. These were the parsimonious requirements, as well, of Eisenhower's projected foreign policy to replace Truman's costly war of containment. It was not a perfect fit, but close enough.

1.

The Secretary said that it is extremely difficult to find precisely the right course, for the dilemma confronting us is that of allies

*Hard for contemporaries to pin down, liberation is no less difficult for historians. An intriguing comparison can be made, however, between Jimmy Carter's human rights campaign and the Dulles/Eisenhower liberation policy. Both came at the end of stalemated wars that left Americans in doubt about the soundness of their nation's foreign policy. Both were originally aimed at getting votes for the national ticket; but both also became integral to the foreign policy concepts of the administration. Carter hoped, like Dulles and Eisenhower, to launch new foreign policy initiatives. He felt the challenge of Euro-Communism had to be met by something more than détente, which had a bad name as a negative status quo policy; while Eisenhower and Dulles were convinced, similarly, that containment had little to offer the precursors of the revolution of rising expectations. And, finally, both found their ideas turned against them in a succeeding presidential campaign.

> in Europe who are, in a sense, old, tired, worn out, and almost willing to buy peace in order to have a few years more of rest. The leadership of the world has passed to us, and the free world will only be saved if it gets out of us what is lacking in the rest of the world.
>
> JOHN FOSTER DULLES before the Senate Foreign Relations Committee in executive session, February 13, 1953[26]

Dulles never wearied of quoting Stalin on the colonial issue. He did this in private and in public, paying the Russian tyrant the compliment of taking him and Communist ideology (as it found expression in Stalin's writings) seriously. The Soviet "theft" of the Chinese Revolution haunted the secretary to the end of his life. It was essential to find out what had made this possible. In Stalin's *Problems of Leninism,* Dulles' favorite text next to the Bible, the secretary found what he was looking for—and what made American liberation from European policies essential.

Stalin envisioned there, Dulles observed, taking advantage of the colonial issue to implement a two-stage plan to transform the dependent areas from "a reserve of the imperialist bourgeoisies into a reserve of the revolutionary proletariat." In the first stage, the Russians would support national independence movements, thereby "mortally weakening the West by an Asiatic policy which will not only deprive the western powers of their colonies, but bleed them in a futile effort to hold them."[27] Actual amalgamation into the Soviet Union would take place in the second stage, when Moscow replaced the leaders of the national revolutions with their own puppets. "Events suggest, and the facts when known may prove, that, for China, the independence phase has passed and the second phase has begun, when China is amalgamated in the Soviet Communist 'reserve.' " It was America's task to expose this "vast scheme of imperialism lurking behind an outer mask of benevolence toward the national aspirations of the people."[28]

Simply exposing it would not be enough. To turn the tide in the Cold War, the United States would have to interrupt the Russian amalgamation process, and reverse it by first demonstrating that the Soviets could not protect the former colonies, i.e., they could not replace the metropolitan powers' traditional role of providing the military or economic aid needed by new nations; and second, by accepting that responsibility itself.

"I would have a policy," the Republican policy spokesman told questioners on "Meet the Press" early in 1952, "which is designed to make the going so tough for the present regime in China that it's going to change in some way. I wouldn't be sure in advance what way it was going to be changed. It may be changed through the Chinese people putting in a totally different form of government. It may be changed with a break with Moscow. The essential thing is to have action which will bring about a change."[29]

Dulles offered these conclusions, in slightly different form, at a meeting with Eisenhower and his future colleagues in the cabinet in mid-December 1952. The Soviet "program" was to exhaust American resources in a series of local actions around the world at times and places of their choosing. Korea, Indochina, and Morocco were "present illustrations." America must respond in kind. "We are like a boxer who abides by the Marquess of Queensbury rules until our opponent strikes foul blows." Now it was time to beat the enemy at his own game.

Actually, the enemy was extremely vulnerable to any initiatives "that we could mount by civil and revolutionary tactics." Dulles closed this presentation with a classic warning. The Republican administration was supposed to be tougher. "If it is not tougher, they will enlarge their estimate of what they can get away with. Our future plight will be worse than our past." There were risks, but these were less likely than the almost certain "disaster" that would result from a perpetuation of present policy.[30]

Or, again, as Dulles told the Senate Foreign Relations Committee in his first appearance before them in 1953, "The free world will only be saved if it gets out of us what is lacking in the rest of the world." In these last passages can be found the rationale for a grand *re*design of Cold War policies, although certainly it was one as yet untempered by real experience. The Republican party, to start with, was hardly the vehicle for the bold experimentation that this vision of liberation would demand. Its powerful isolationist wing remained obdurate against interventionism. Yet the Asian emphasis in Dulles' worldview pleased many diehard isolationists—who at heart were really Asia-firsters—at the outset.

The famous China lobby and its various adherents had made life miserable for the Truman administration from before the Korean War. It is always difficult to gauge the impact of domestic politics on any foreign policy issue. Certainly the "outs" can be expected to take advantage of any opening to improve their position at the next election. Senator Joseph McCarthy's venomous accusations carried partisan politics about as far as the system could tolerate. But Eisenhower also faced unrelenting pressure from the Bill Knowlands and Walter Judds of his party, who fell into a special category of "true believers" on the China question. At times, especially whenever Knowland, who succeeded Robert Taft as Republican leader in the Senate, suspected that Ike was listening too much to British appeasers or any other "softies" from the liberal East Coast, relations between the White House and Capitol Hill were strained. It was on those occasions that the president would question Knowland's good sense. "It's a pity that his wisdom, his judgment, his tact, and his sense of humor lag so far behind his ambition."[31]

When the subject became Indochina itself, however, there eventually emerged a different coalition, a complex of China lobby Republicans and liberal Democrats. This compact solidified around the person of Ngo Dinh Diem, the champion Americans thought they had found to enter the lists against Ho Chi Minh. The important contributions of this Capitol Hill alliance came later, however; it had not come into being at the time of the Dienbienphu crisis in April 1954, nor did it determine American policy in the aftermath. The basic decisions on all these questions were made in the National Security Council and the executive offices of its members.

The first of these decisions was Eisenhower's surprise announcement in his first State of the Union message on February 3, 1953, that he was "issuing instructions that the Seventh Fleet no longer be employed to shield Communist China." The order to withdraw from the Formosan Straits implied "no aggressive intent on our part. But we certainly have no obligation to protect a nation fighting us in Korea."[32] Dismissed by some critics as a sop to Asia-first congressional leaders, and elevated by others to a dangerous sign of the unilateralist tendencies that would ultimately produce the Suez and U-2 debacles, the decision was a first effort at interrupting the Russian amalgamation process. No doubt Ike knew it would be popular with the China lobby people in his party, but that was not the reason he did it. Eisenhower said later, long after he left office, that "unleashing Chiang Kai-shek" was intended to "worry" the mainland Chinese. It was a sign that Washington had its own two-Chinas policy, allowing the Chinese émigrés, who were spread all through Southeast Asia, to look someplace else besides Beijing.

"He [Chiang Kai-shek] was a sort of a symbol, and if he were gone we thought it would have a very bad effect all over Southeast Asia."[33]

Eisenhower's estimate of Chiang's symbolic reputation in Southeast Asia may have been off 180 degrees, but not his recollection of the reasons for moving the Seventh Fleet out of the Formosan Straits. This was confirmed at the time by discussions Dulles had with British diplomat Selwyn Lloyd and with Canada's Lester Pearson. Lloyd had expressed his concern over the deteriorating situation in Indochina to Dulles at the end of December 1952. He was thinking about it, too, replied the secretary of state designate, and he "felt that the Asian situation might have to be considered as a whole with some deterrent power created at the center to avoid increasing pressure on the two flanks of Korea and Indochina. He said in this connection that President Eisenhower might modify the present instructions to the 7th Fleet so that our Fleet would not, in effect, serve as an adjunct to Chinese Communist forces protecting their center."[34]

Dulles had convinced himself, and thought his conclusions warranted the attention of Charles Wilson, Eisenhower's choice for secretary of defense. So he sent him a memorandum of the conversation. Dulles may well have hoped to plant the idea that events should be encouraged, after the Seventh Fleet had been withdrawn, so that they would crest in an offensive of some sort against the "center." The West could not go on "sitting back" while the Communists caused trouble in the free world, he told Lester Pearson. "The free world must take positive action and retaliate by causing trouble in Communist territory."

Pressed by Pearson for examples of such action, Dulles appeared stumped, mentioning only "political warfare." What alarmed the Canadian most, however, was that he heard no assurances that the allies would be consulted. Indochina was much on Dulles' mind. What happened there, he prophesied, was even more important than what happened in Korea: "If the whole of Korea were to go it would be a set-back of the first magnitude. Nevertheless, the results would not be fatal, whereas the consequences of a collapse in Indo-China could be incalculable."[35]

Dulles also liked to think out problems en route from one Cold War command post to another. On one flying trip through Asia he drew a diagram for an assistant on the back of an envelope displaying arrows for a "three-front war against China" emanating from

Formosa, Korea, and Indochina.[36] Such were the fantasies he indulged in at twenty thousand feet. It was by no means certain, as he well knew, that the West could even hold Indochina. But the diagram revealed his intense feelings about finding a way to interrupt the Soviet Union's dreadful amalgamation process operating through "Red" China to absorb all of Asia.

When these feelings surfaced in diplomatic conversations, they scared the dickens out of the European allies.[37] Recognizing signs of alarm in his listeners, or sometimes preparing himself for a meeting with skeptics, Dulles would advance what might be called the "wedge" theory, that through maximum pressure on China, he was actually forcing a sliver in between Moscow and Peking—something that would irritate immediately, and just might grow into the means of splitting the Communist giants apart. If Moscow found the demands of its partner too much of a strain, economically or politically, the theory proposed, then the process of de-amalgamation might begin. Eisenhower always held out the possibility that China might, on the other hand, make itself eligible for American diplomatic recognition by abandoning its dangerous pretensions.[38]

There was a time and place for all theories of future Sino-Russian and Sino-American relations, each suited to a particular purpose. Eisenhower had a contingency plan for atomic warfare against China, for example, if the Korean War could not be settled on reasonable terms fairly quickly. But the contingencies to bring it into operation were so many that it is hard to call it a strategy at all. What the wedge theory did not cover (and does not when used by historians to explain Dulles' China policy) was the risk of unwanted "Titos" or, in the immediate circumstances, the one "Tito" candidate in Asia, Ho Chi Minh.

Dulles believed he had only months, or just possibly a year or two in Indochina, not long enough to pry open a split between Russia and China. Unlike Europe, where, whatever political capital could be made out of containment, the deterioration had stopped, in Southeast Asia decolonization and revolution ran together in a tide that already rose above flood level, and swirled throughout the countryside. White armies operating out of the cities could not stem it by piling sandbags around the old governor's palace. While he knew that, he did believe that a combination of American strategic power and regional pacts operating together offered some chance of success.

If China could be held at bay with threats, the regional alliances, uniting peoples with natural affinities, could provide a buffer so that new government buildings with secure foundations could be constructed to replace the crumbling colonial era structures. In the event, Washington exaggerated the Chinese military presence in other Asian revolutions, misled in part by Korea, which, it turned out, was a special case, and in part by a combination of ideological propositions necessary to perceived Cold War verities. It was America's allies, the colonial powers, who pursued the wedge theory, based on a more traditional interpretation of what could be expected from China among the great powers.

Dulles underestimated, on the other hand, the fear that he would inspire in the allies by threats against China, and the adverse reaction to American policy among the very peoples and nations he wanted to influence. Thus the insights he had into the need for a different policy in Asia to overcome the corroded and corroding heritage of colonialism were blunted at the outset by an urge to telescope short-term and long-range problems, and to mix New Look military solutions with political remedies. If sandbags would not hold back the flood, neither would bombing threats. But Dulles, a prudent lawyer for private clients, thought America's future was being held at gunpoint by Marxist cadres. He must get them to drop their guns, then history could work itself out.

Asked at his first press conference as secretary of state to explain the significance of Eisenhower's decision on the Seventh Fleet, Dulles responded with a short lecture. America's purpose, he began, making a now common linkage, was to "try to bring to an end the fighting in Korea and Indochina on acceptable terms." "One of the ways in which that perhaps can be done is to shift the burden of the land fighting at least more and more to the indigenous forces, thereby permitting the engagement in Asia of the land forces of the western powers to be brought to an end."[39]

In an Illinois campaign speech a few months earlier, Eisenhower had even applied that caveat to the possible continuation of the Korean War. The first thing to do there, he said, was to make it possible for Koreans to defend themselves, and to stop Americans from being killed and wounded. To that appeal to voters anxious to end the war, the candidate added this liberation twist. "We don't want Asia to feel that the white man of the West is his enemy. If there must be a war, let it be Asians against Asians, with our support on the side for freedom."[40]

"All this is very bad for us," wrote a worried commentator,

Roger Makins, the British ambassador in Washington.[41] Part of the problem, he reported home, was that we, the British, looked upon Korea as the "type of action we took in nineteenth century, e.g., on the northwest frontier." But Americans lacked the patience or inclination for that sort of role. Hence the administration felt the need for a dramatic gesture. "Unilateral action by the United States would be very popular."[42] When Foreign Secretary Anthony Eden then queried President Eisenhower, the latter assured him that there would indeed be consultation "before any major step was taken."[43]

But doubts lingered.

2.

> The free world's hope of defeating the Communist aims does not include objecting to national aspirations. We must show the wickedness of purpose in the Communist promises, and convince dependent peoples that their only hope of maintaining independence, once attained, is through cooperation with the free world.
>
> Dwight D. Eisenhower, diary record of a conversation with Winston Churchill, January 6, 1953[44]

Poor Winston, thought Ike, his last years were being spent clinging to power, dreaming of the World War II days. Churchill had idealized those times, imagining that he and Roosevelt sat together "on some rather Olympian platform with respect to the rest of the world." Even if that picture were accurate, noted Eisenhower, it would have no relevance to current problems. But it was only partially true, even then, "as many of us who, in various corners of the world, had to work out the solutions for nasty local problems are well aware."[45]

For his part, Churchill spotted Dulles right away as an enemy, while the prime minister's entourage at least agreed that he was the brains of the outfit. The future secretary of state kept talking about the dangers of seeming "collusion," interlarding remarks on that subject with his favorite references to the need for the new administration to get off to a good start. If the American people lost faith in it, "who could say what might happen."[46]

Do nothing for four months, countered Churchill, that was the best thing. They grated on one another, Churchill and Dulles. Everything the secretary of state said, Churchill took amiss. In private the prime minister threw up his hands, he would have no more to do with him, that man whose "great slab of a face" he disliked and distrusted.[47] How much emphasis should be put on the growing animosity between Dulles and Churchill can be debated, but it soon focused on questions outside Europe, Egypt and Indochina in particular.

Personality differences can account for only so much, especially when there were so many other factors contributing to Anglo-American friction. Actually, Dulles' relations with Foreign Secretary Anthony Eden had started off well enough. Soon after the American election the two had met to talk over things, with the conversation coming around to "non-Western problems." Eden had readily assented to a proposition that it was of the "utmost importance" that the United States, France, and the United Kingdom "create a united position because our policies, when contradictory, are almost sure to fail, and only our enemies profit."[48] When Eisenhower ordered the Seventh Fleet out of the Formosan Straits, however, it appeared that the "unified position" meant unquestioning acceptance of American initiatives. Reassurances that the administration did not intend to provoke war with China eased this early strain, but this incident was often referred to in retrospect as signaling Washington's disregard for allied sensibilities.[49]

What Dulles foresaw, however, with truly mixed feelings, was an early French decision to turn over Indochina in similar fashion to what happened in 1947 when the British found they could no longer go it alone in Greece and Turkey. In that instance there had been a sense of relief on both sides. London was more than happy to relinquish the burden; and in Washington there was relief that the other shoe had dropped, ending an awkward transition from Grand Alliance to Cold War. So, Dulles hoped, it would go in Asia.

Not that he wanted a mud-filled French shoe in his lap. Consideration had been given to sending two divisions to Greece in support of the Truman Doctrine. Dulles hardly envied that option in Indochina. Talking with Congressman Walter Judd—who agreed with his every word—Dulles ventured the opinion that the Communists were readying themselves for an offensive in Southeast Asia. "It would not be surprising if, at any moment, the French said to us, regarding Indochina, exactly what the British did in January and

February of 1947 regarding Greece; namely, that they are pulling out and it's our baby."[50]

But not too fast, of course. The trick was to manage the succession without losing the game. And without losing France. Interested in securing France's support for German rearmament, which required among other things a confident government, not one humiliated by a defeat in Indochina, Washington had to swallow hard and do what it could to humor French sensibilities. Worse, said Ambassador David Bruce to Henry Cabot Lodge, who was Eisenhower's liaison officer with the Truman administration, there was widespread fear in the State Department that unless the United States increased its aid, "the fall of Indochina would have a devastating effect on France, opening her up to being overwhelmed by a communist sweep."[51]

Over the course of the next year and a half, the primary object of the Eisenhower administration became the prevention of Indochina's fall to the Vietminh and, at the same time, the prevention of "political discussions" by the French in an effort to appease China and Russia. For their part, French leaders cited Eisenhower's willingness to complete the armistice negotiations in Korea as a precedent for their own efforts to settle with China.

Dulles did not want simply to keep the French going. Aside from the obvious lack of a military "line" in Indochina that could be reasonably defended, as in Korea, a holding action meant to him only defeat. He well understood the principle that would plague all future American efforts in Indochina: the guerrilla wins if he does not lose. He wanted to win the Cold War in Asia, and had convinced himself it could be done. But he also knew that, as Acheson warned, the French were seeking political talks. Indeed, when Eisenhower prepared to leave for Korea, as he had promised he would do during the election, French representatives asked his associates if he could not also go to Indochina. Dulles wanted no part of that, fully aware as he was that Ike was predisposed to a quickly negotiated end of the Korean War.[52]

Speaking to the French National Political Science Institute in May of 1952, Dulles sympathized with the burden France had borne in Indochina. That led him to this conclusion, however: "You are there paying a heavy cost, in lives and money. I am glad that the United States is now helping substantially. *I should personally be glad to see us do more, for you have really been left too much alone to discharge a task which is vital to us all.*"[53]

There were also fresh military opinions inside the new administration, generally associated with the "New Look" strategies but whose origins had much deeper roots, and which had a special tactical application to Southeast Asia. In general, these jibed with Dulles' proposals for hitting the Communists where they were most vulnerable—something the French could never manage to do on their own with their colonialist strategic conceptions, and their basic military weaknesses as compared with the United States. In his speech to the Political Science Institute, Dulles again zeroed in on the "vulnerability" of the Communists to American air and sea power. Especially in Asia, the West could never meet Communist aggression on a man-for-man basis. Prospects for victory depended upon striking with overwhelming power, "at times and places of our choosing." "Siberia and much of China, notably Manchuria, are vulnerable from the standpoint of transport and communication. There are ports and lines of communication which, if destroyed, would paralyze Soviet strength in Asia." And since every despotic police state depended upon highly centralized controls, such attacks would spell its defeat.[54]

Early critics of the Eisenhower administration perceived a deep yearning between the lines of such remarks for the verities of yesterday, and the freedom of action promised (but not delivered) by the bomb, in short, a "New Isolationism."[55] Dulles anticipated the accusation. Look at it this way, he told members of the Eisenhower cabinet, the analogy is with the states of the union. Citizens of one state did not consider themselves vulnerable because the nation's military power was located outside their borders in some other state. If the United States did not succeed in selling this idea, he admitted, "we can anticipate that the governments and peoples of the free world will dismiss our proposed new policy as simply camouflaged isolation."[56]

Vice-President Richard Nixon elaborated on Dulles' original point. The idea of Fortress America, he said, originated in the prewar era. "At that time it meant to its exponents that America could be defended, but Europe could not. We now believe, however, that we can defend all vital parts of the free world by applying the principle of conservation of forces. This, insisted the Vice-President, was *not* the Fortress America of the past."[57] In theory it was not. But strategically the U.S. position relied upon dubious propositions such as the notion that the situation in Indochina could be attributed to the threat of the "mighty land power of the Communist world."[58] It is easy, therefore, to fault Dulles for a woeful lack of understanding of revolutionary nationalism in imagining that it could be overcome in such a manner, by some military strike at China or Russia. It was maddeningly true that since the fall of the Chinese national government in 1949 and the outbreak of the Korean War, Ho's forces had been able to draw heavily upon China for both matériel and moral support.[59]

The beguiling sanctuaries controversy carried over from Korea, where it made some sense, to Indochina, where it made no sense at all. America supplied much more aid to the French than China or Russia gave the Vietminh, but it was, for a variety of reasons, not being effectively used. Marshaling world opinion against outright aggression, Dulles lamented on one occasion, was easy, "but it is quite another matter to fight against internal changes in one country." "We are confronted by an unfortunate fact—most of the countries of the world do not share our view that Communist control of any government anywhere is in itself a danger and a threat."[60]

What was needed, Dulles never tired of saying, was a proper strategy. And that was not a matter of placing wedges between Russia and China. Whatever authority succeeded France in Vietnam (and that was a given) would have to solve the problem of Chinese support for the guerrillas. Without some means of intimidating China and discrediting Communist pretensions, how could the West gain time for any non-Communist government to succeed? It was a depressing truth that French strategy in Indochina had been based upon a fort system associated with a colonial military mentality, limited by a corresponding reluctance and/or inability to build a Vietnamese army capable of taking the offensive, and hampered by a divided nation at home.

Coming in at this point in the struggle, it was all the more important for the new administration to adopt a strategy to change the attitude inside Indochina. If American policymakers still lacked an overall plan for defeating revolutionary nationalism, they were close to the mark in their assessment of French weaknesses and the implications that flowed from that evaluation.

Admiral Arthur W. Radford, appointed chairman of the Joint Chiefs of Staff by Eisenhower, was a strong partisan of the New Look. He believed with Dulles that air and sea power was the right approach to the Asian crisis, and also, as did Dulles, looked with baleful eyes on the struggling French military dragging along to defeat, chained to the corpse of colonialism.[61] Flying over the fortress system the French had devised, Radford concluded they were relics of a prewar era. "They reminded me of the Foreign Legion outposts in North Africa in the movie *Beau Geste.*"[62] Reporting later to State Department officers, the admiral added that he had sent a highly qualified marine colonel, a graduate of French military schools as well, to evaluate the situation. The colonel had reconfirmed his opinion that what was needed was a change in attitude. "Two good American divisions with the normal American aggressive spirit could clean up the situation in the Tonkin Delta in 10 months."[63]

3.

> The U.S. must try a policy which will ease the French out in a couple of years in order to develop indigenous forces as in Korea. The approach to the French should be a global one. We should help to ease their prestige problem.
>
> GEORGE F. KENNAN, "Solarium" recommendations to National Security Council, June 26, 1953[64]

At meetings with his advisers on February 11 and 12, 1953, Eisenhower broached the possibility of employing tactical atomic weapons in Korea if the armistice negotiations—then stalled over the vexing issue of forcible repatriation of prisoners of war—should break down. The president said that he wanted to increase the psychological pressure on China by letting them know "discreetly" that unless progress was made, the United States would move decisively, and move without any inhibitions about its choice of weapons. "We would not be limited by any world-wide gentleman's agreement."[65]

Korea was the pressing issue, but the president's words echoed those Dulles had used in his presentation at the pre-inaugural meeting in December. There would be no "world-wide gentleman's agreement," and no abiding by "Marquess of Queensbury rules." Perhaps the main thing that troubled Dulles about Stalin's death was the president's inclination to deliver a "peace speech" before the Korean issue had been settled. When Eisenhower instructed speech writers to prepare him such a message, Dulles demurred. "I don't think we can get much out of a Korean settlement," he told the speech drafters, "until we have shown—before all Asia—our clear superiority by giving the Chinese one hell of a licking."[66]

Eisenhower overruled his secretary of state on this occasion, and an appeal was made to the new Soviet leaders. Entitled "The Chance for Peace," it was delivered on April 16, 1953. The major ingredient was an offer to exchange arms negotiations for specific deeds, including the conclusion of an "honorable armistice" in Korea, Indochina, and Malaya. The president, according to his biographer, knew full well that his demands for proof were unacceptable, and that the Soviets might not even be able to shut down the guerrilla wars in Southeast Asia. Much of the appeal was a simple restatement of Cold War positions, though its warnings about the cost of the arms race brought Eisenhower worldwide applause.[67]

Meanwhile plans went ahead for stepping up American aid to the French in Indochina. The aim should be, Dulles advised the American ambassador in Paris, "liquidation of principal regular enemy forces within period of say, twenty-four months."[68] When French officials visited Washington, he added, they should be ready to talk about the general question of a free world policy in the Far East to discourage "further Chinese Communist aggression." Dulles also prepared some ground with Eisenhower, advising him that Indochina should claim "the top priority" in foreign policy. Aid would have to be increased, but also there would have to be steps taken to deter China before its forces were sent into Vietnam.[69]

Dulles was obsessed with the thought that Communist policy was indeed coordinated on a worldwide basis to such an extent that a truce in Korea would release thousands of troops for Vietnam. Premier René Mayer and his colleagues arrived in Washington at the end of March, prepared and anxious to talk about increased American aid, and also about a general Far Eastern policy. French policymakers saw the agenda somewhat differently, however. American criticisms that not enough was being done to turn over power to the Bao Dai government, or to build up the Vietnamese army (and its fighting spirit), only aroused French suspicions.[70] "Relevant officials in Paris knew very well that the transfer of power which mattered was not that from France to the Bao Dai-ists," concludes a recent historical survey of decolonization, "but that from France to the United States."[71] Mayer was in Washington to begin negotiations to get the best terms he could for that transfer, or, alternatively, to impress upon his listeners that American efforts for a truce in Korea—by their own definitions of the Cold War—required taking up Indochina as well. The object was to preserve as much for France as could be secured either through fighting or negotiations with the Russians and Chinese.

The principal hypothesis French leaders shared with their American counterparts was that there were two wars going on in Indochina: the internal struggle for power, and the great game of *Weltpolitik.* The French believed these could be sorted out and dealt with individually; the Americans thought not. For the time being this fundamental divergence was obscured.

Dulles even imagined that René Mayer was well-disposed to hearing arguments for taking the offensive in Indochina, probably more so than any of his possible successors, especially in the context of increased American aid that would "substantially reduce the strain on French human and material resources."[72] That could not be accomplished, of course, without a transfer of substantial proportions. When the formal discussions began, French officials asked bluntly if the United States had a plan to repel a massive Chinese intervention when the fighting ended in Korea.[73]

On one level this was merely a query from one ally to another. But Mayer and his aides were not really talking about military plans. France did not have the retaliatory power to strike at China, but it did not want, either, for the United States to do so. It was anxious to avoid a Sino-American war fought out in Indochina. That was the real meaning of the question, a complicated bid for peace talks. The secretary replied with an equally sophisticated negative directed at both possibilities. Chinese intervention with a large army was unlikely, he said—regardless of what he believed—because while China could not be invaded, "the vista of trouble through sea and air attack would be [a] strong deterrent to them."

Both sides danced around the central issue, with Dulles throwing out cautious hints that the French could rely upon the United States as Great Britain had in 1947, and the French not revealing the real reasons why they had brought up the China peril. The communiqué issued at the end of these talks represented something of a triumph for Dulles. It reported that military plans were being studied with a view to achieving success in Indochina and that the Chinese would face "the most serious consequences" should they try to take advantage of a Korean armistice to shift their forces to Indochina, and linked Korea to the struggle in Indochina without suggesting that diplomatic efforts should include efforts at a broad settlement.[74]

Having gotten the language he wanted in the communiqué, the secretary sought to convince his colleagues on the National Security Council that this represented a real breakthrough by putting the Chinese on notice that they could not transgress with impunity. "We must hold the present outpost position. There is no place around the orbit of the Soviet world which we can now afford to lose. . . . We should subject the presently over-extended Soviet orbit to strains incident to stimulating the spirit of nationalism and subjecting the rulers to the taking of hard decisions."[75]

Within a few days, however, the French interpretation of the communiqué revealed subtle differences of the sort Dulles feared most. René Mayer, in commenting on a draft of the president's "Chance for Peace" speech, pointed out that while the president had called upon the Soviet Union to bring to an end direct and indirect attacks on the peoples of Indochina, there was no specific statement about peace negotiations or terms. He hoped the president could strengthen that part of the speech by calling for a settlement "simultaneous with or immediately following a Korean settlement."[76]

This caveat, gently phrased as it was, hinted at the choices Americans would soon have to consider. Either Washington would put pressure on China (and on itself) to include the war in Indochina in broad negotiations, or it would have to permit the French to use the Korean precedent (without recrimination) in opening bilateral negotiations on its own. Politically, the latter might be the best way out for a French government to exit Vietnam, yet maintain peace at home. Obviously, if American policymakers felt they must handle the Indochina question carefully in dealings with Paris for fear of repercussions on other issues, so the French declined to challenge Washington frontally, out of concern—to take but one example—of irking the Americans into unilaterally rearming the Germans.

French defense minister René Pleven met with the Senate Foreign Relations Committee on April 13, 1953, and, behind the cover of an innocent inquiry about whether the U.S. government could accept a peace in Korea without getting peace in Indochina at the same time, raised the possibility of an overall settlement. In exchange for a "real stoppage of war" in both places, China would be admitted to the United Nations.[77]

The French had lacked any real idea of how to approach Beijing with such an offer on their own, and had had only the vaguest notion of satisfactory terms. Dulles had unwittingly supplied the French both with something to barter and possible terms. If China was interested in Ho primarily as a "buffer" against American power, and not as an agent of world revolution, then specifics might be worked out. France could, if things broke right, play its "American card." It was a form of diplomatic ju-jitsu, in other words, whereby Paris could finesse American power against itself, and shoulder-toss all its opponents, one by one, into a heap on the mat—if things broke right, a big question, for Dulles was alert to the danger.

Whether he suspected something or not, Dulles fretted about a precedent in Korea producing a partition plan for Indochina. New Franco-American talks on Indochina coincided with Dulles' efforts to get Eisenhower to take another look at the military situation in Korea, in the hope that the impasse at Panmunjon negotiations had exhausted Ike's patience. Dulles wanted the president to demand a final truce line considerably to the north of the thirty-eighth parallel, thereby depriving North Korea of its capital city, its population, and its viability. That would be a partition he could live with, the only one, a division guaranteed not to appeal to Ho (or the French) as a precedent.

In view of "our much greater power and the Soviet Union's much greater weakness currently," he argued, the United Nations ought to be able to get a much better armistice.[78] Eisenhower brought Dulles up short, however, with a comment that it would be impossible to call off the armistice and go to war again in Korea. "The American people would never stand for such a move."[79] Maybe not. But John Foster Dulles still believed the president's mind could be changed.

Returning to his office, Dulles instructed members of the department's Policy Planning Staff to draft their papers on the premise that military victory in Korea was important—and obtainable by threatening to strike at China from the sea and the air. "If we are able, ready and willing to exploit this situation that may cave in their negotiating position." More than that, and going back to his fundamental approach, such attacks would place a great strain on both China and Russia. "This would give us the best chance of securing our objectives either with fighting or without fighting."[80]

The secretary's maneuvers pose several difficulties for historians. The long scholarly argument over whether the United States actually threatened the use of A-bombs in Korea is a case in point. In focusing on Eisenhower, the controversy over whether he did or did not threaten to use the "ultimate weapon" obscures the possibility that there were really two different threats under consideration, or, at least, two different purposes. An explicit threat was never made. Yet Eisenhower had given instructions that the Chinese should be informed that if the negotiations broke down over the prisoner of war issue, the United States would feel no constraints on its choice of weapons or where they would be applied.

"The President did not have to deliver an ultimatum," concludes the latest survey of the Korean War, "peace or atomic bombs—because they understood he was thinking along these lines anyway."[81] Eisenhower simply sat tight and waited. Dulles never sat tight. He had to be moving all the time, anticipating the adversary's next move, preparing his own counterstroke. To the secretary, the danger of a partitioned Korea could be at least partly compensated for if, at some later date, Washington could "leak" the information that A-bomb threats had made China climb down on some issue of substance.

Blocked by Eisenhower from "reopening" the Korean boundary issue, Dulles looked around for means to use the bomb to chill any Beijing interest in intervening in Indochina. Thus he was delighted to carry the message to Pandit Nehru of India that if no armistice occurred, "hostilities might become more intense." When the Indian leader pressed Dulles to say precisely what he meant by "more intense," the secretary declined. "I made no comment and allowed the topic to drop," he reported to Eisenhower, thereby satisfying both the president and himself that he had acted sagaciously.[82]

When the "leak" occurred, Nehru later denied that he had conveyed any warning about an atomic threat to Beijing. Eisenhower insisted in his recollections, however, that he had sent the warnings by several messengers. Further clouding the issue, China's position on prisoners of war, the supposed reason for such warnings, had already begun to change, though it was impossible to tell if that presaged final agreement.

Dulles wanted to bare some teeth, but while he had talked about pushing the North Koreans up against the Yalu, his real objects were to scare China away from Southeast Asia, to boost French morale, to forestall a diplomatic settlement of the Indochina war, and, above all, to come out of the Korean negotiations with a forward momentum.[83] Like Blake, he had seen a fearful symmetry burning in the forest in the night, but he did not need to know what hand had fashioned it.

4.

> In response to an invitation from the French Prime Minister when he visited Washington last March, a U.S. military mission headed by Lt. Gen. John W. O'Daniel, present commander U.S. Army Pacific, will arrive at Saigon on June 20. . . . It is believed essential to insure an increasingly close integration of U.S. assistance with the plans developed by the authorities of France and of the Associated States.
>
> State Department press release, June 20, 1953[84]

On June 4, 1953, the North Koreans and Chinese finally accepted the essentials of the American position on prisoners of war—no forcible repatriation. Eisenhower's ability to fulfill his election pledges now depended on reconciling South Korean president Syngman Rhee, who was as intractable as the Communists, to the truce terms. Rhee held out until it was made clear the United States would sign a separate agreement, if necessary, to get peace. Even under this threat, however, Rhee extracted concessions from Washington, including a mutual defense treaty. And he never forgave Eisenhower.[85]

It was precisely the sort of thing Dulles had anticipated would happen. A very bad beginning, this, if one was trying to impress other Asian peoples to remain steadfast before the common enemy. Fighting went on—some of the bitterest in the war—almost until the day that the armistice was signed, July 27, 1953. No great celebration of "V-K Day" took place in American cities and towns, because there had been no victory, only an agreement to end the killing. Korea was to remain divided at a line very little different from where the boundary had stood in 1950.

Not pleased with these terms, Dulles had nevertheless worked hard to convince Rhee there was no alternative left for him except to go along—and get what assurances he could.[86] On the political front at home, however, Dulles was satisfied that congressional leaders had impressed on the president their unwillingness to allow

America's European allies to use the Korean truce as an excuse for permitting "Red China" to enter the United Nations.[87]

Keeping China ostracized obviously minimized the danger that the Korean negotiations would become a precedent for Indochina. At the same time, however, the president suggested that Rhee ought to be told that his persistent obstinacy in refusing to accept the truce threatened America's ability to carry out its general foreign policies, and, therefore, actually hampered any future peaceful efforts toward Korean unification.[88]

The threat that political negotiations, called for in the truce agreement, might be expanded to include not only Indochina but general discussions of the Cold War itself thus remained a live issue. Chiang Kai-shek, almost forgotten since the early days of the administration when Eisenhower removed the Seventh Fleet from the Formosan Straits, hastened to point out to the president the difficulty that now faced American planners. If they agreed to general discussions, he wrote Eisenhower, what could be kept out, including the fate of Formosa? Dulles prepared a draft answer for Eisenhower to sign, reassuring Chiang that the proposed talks would not "become a forum" to take up the integrity and safety of the Republic of China.[89] But here was another unhappy consequence of the Korean truce.

Despite bickering and acrimony, in the end, Rhee and Chiang could be dealt with; but Dulles had much less confidence about keeping the French on board. A critical moment was arriving, he informed the ambassador in Paris, when important decisions had to be made, and the United States, because of its large share of the burden in Indochina, was now entitled to have its views heard and heeded as well. American influence should be brought to bear in such a manner, continued the secretary, so that the "French themselves will come up with and implement needed decisions in military, political and economic fields." And there was more: "We should also help dispel any French illusion as to possibility a solution in Indochina may effortlessly and painlessly flow from some 'general settlement in Far East.' "[90]

Dulles ended with an admonition. For the French to withdraw under present conditions would be a dishonorable thing, and would set off a chain reaction that would "destroy France's position as a world power."[91] But what if the Vietnam War devoured France itself? Did Dulles have instructions to cover that possibility? Meanwhile, an unexpected complication had arisen concerning the proposal for rearming West Germany within the framework of the European Defense Community (EDC). No issue could divide Frenchmen more. Eisenhower's "Chance for Peace" speech had called upon the Soviets to demonstrate their desire for a new beginning by performing several specific acts. Among these was establishing a Korean truce. However hard Dulles had worked to limit the impact of the truce, and, as we have seen, to demonstrate that it had come about only as a result of military threats, American policymakers could not really avoid responding to French insistence that another attempt be made to broaden negotiations to include Indochina and Germany.

In May 1953, furthermore, Prime Minister Winston Churchill had issued a call for a summit meeting that elicited from post-Stalin Moscow suggestions and specific proposals for "neutralizing" a reunited Germany. Churchill fumed at American fixations on the Far East, complaining that they were becoming a major obstruction to a global settlement. Neither was he bothered when Vietminh forces invaded Laos that spring. He had lived all his life without hearing about such places, Churchill told associates, and now they came to "tease" him in his old age. "They have never worried me, and I haven't worried them."[92]

But they worried policymakers in Washington. Amid these mounting difficulties with London, Paris added to American woes with a note to Dulles in July, informing him that so long as any prospect existed for an agreement with Moscow, the Assembly would not ratify the EDC.[93] To make matters still worse, General de Lattre was gone, dead of cancer, and since his death the military in Vietnam had seemed to lose all heart.

Taking Vietnam to the United Nations was not an option acceptable to the French, who feared the growing number of Arab countries in that organization would prevent "fair treatment" "There would be a demand," said Georges Bidault, "that Ho Chi Minh be heard and made a party to the dispute which would increase his stature and diminish that of France."[94] Eisenhower offered increased military aid, while at the same time appealing to Paris to make absolutely firm guarantees of Indochinese independence at the end of the war, and urging the appointment of a "*forceful and inspirational leader.*"[95]

Deep down Eisenhower doubted such measures were anything more than anodyne remedies. In a draft letter to an old friend that he discarded because it rambled on and "gets too involved," the president thought on paper about what faced him in the future: "The tricky problem that is posed these days is this: if firm opposition to the spread of Communism requires fighting, as in Korea and Indo China, how can the free world turn its attention to the solution of these great humanitarian problems which must be tackled in order to eliminate conditions that promote Communism?"[96]

The succeeding months offered no answer to this question, except that the United States must work harder in the first instance to achieve "liberation" from French mistakes.

CHAPTER FIVE

The French Defense

> Local defense will always be important. But there is no local defense which alone will contain the mighty landpower of the Communist world. Local defenses must be reinforced by the further deterrent of massive retaliatory power. A potential aggressor must know that he cannot always prescribe battle conditions that suit him. Otherwise, for example, a potential aggressor, who is glutted with manpower, might be tempted to attack in places where his superiority was decisive.
>
> JOHN FOSTER DULLES,
> January 12, 1954[1]

"THE concept of this sturdy defence is to set the course and avoid unfamiliar lines," reads a standard work on chess openings, "and to build an impregnable wall of pawns against which the opponent's impetuous, premature onslaughts will be shattered." But the French defense also poses theoretical problems. "On the minus side, it is naturally defensive, it cedes the center temporarily. . . . Indeed, White does achieve a center bind, more mobility, and a quick, sharp King's side attack. But these theoretical considerations are not conclusive in practice."[2]

Just so did General Henri Navarre construct the French defense at the northwest border of Vietnam and Laos. Here, at a provincial administrative center, Dienbienphu, Navarre ordered a fortress to be built. Against this castle, with its "impregnable wall of pawns," the Vietminh would be lured into a premature attack; and against it, the enemy would smash itself to pieces on the battlements. Then it would become a matter of cleaning up the isolated cadres of guerrillas roaming central Vietnam.

Applauded as the first French commander willing to take the

offensive since General de Lattre de Tassigny's untimely death in January of 1952, Navarre vowed to achieve what had eluded de Lattre—final victory. In his memoirs, Eisenhower recalled that at the Bermuda Conference in December 1953, French foreign minister Georges Bidault "expounded at length" on the plan for victory. "While he did not mean that they were really hopeful of securing an early and decisive military victory," noted the president, "he did mean that for the first time they were thinking of winning eventually."[3]

Welcome news, indeed! These assurances bespoke a new firmness that Americans had thought beyond French mental and military capacities. Writing to a close personal friend, Ike had despaired of seeing anything positive come out of Paris. Riven by debilitating political disputes, he said, France had failed to help the "vast center group" of nations unite against the common enemy. The Bermuda conversations, whatever Bidault promised, Eisenhower went on, were not especially productive, because everyone knew Premier Joseph Laniel headed a caretaker government.[4]

Laniel has had few admirers. Described by a harsh critic of French military policy as "neither somebody nor something, but utter nothingness," and by an American correspondent as a "stocky, fat, red-faced character of medium height, who looks like a big Normandy butter-and-egg man . . . and talks like one," Laniel was indisposed with pneumonia and a fever most of the time during the Bermuda talks.[5] Yet he did not lack a certain shrewdness. It appeared, for example, in his explanation of the gap in the French budget. Eisenhower had complained that "there was evidence that the French had more equipment than they could use effectively" in Indochina.[6] Laniel used the promise of the Navarre Plan to get more. While the general was personally optimistic, Laniel lamented to American diplomats, he needed resources that unfortunately could not be given him. Of his own situation, the premier made weakness a virtue: "We hope you can help me for after me comes Mendès-France."[7]

Here was the ultimate threat. The very mention of Pierre Mendès-France's name, a radical socialist, was enough to spring open the vaults of the American Treasury. Inside of a week the National Security Council, with Eisenhower presiding, agreed to provide an additional $400 million. And so it went for a time. Laniel did not even have to conjure up Mendès-France; all he had to do was to say that he was asking Navarre to prepare contingency plans for withdrawal in the event no new funds became available.[8]

Whether Laniel was playing a double game, assuring Americans he planned to stay while actually seeking only an honorable out, and misleading Navarre in the process, has been debated in memoirs and accounts of the tragedy at Dienbienphu.[9] At the time, however, Americans believed that the British held the key to French policy in both Asia and Europe. Eisenhower had gone to Bermuda in December 1953 with one purpose in mind. He wanted to block Churchill's initiative for a Big Four summit conference.[10]

While the British prime minister stood squarely behind the EDC, and was, if anything, more ready to threaten France with an independent Anglo-American policy toward German rearmament than the president himself, Churchill's renewed pleas for a summit conference struck American policymakers as a ready-made out for Germanophobic Frenchmen united against the EDC. Anything that opened the door even a crack might well provide Laniel, or a successor, with an excuse to start dividing Cold War issues, anathema to Americans, whether it concerned the EDC or Indochina. Having "settled" in Korea, the new administration had good reason to fear such consequences, since it had set the precedent.

Bermuda proved to be a contentious meeting, the least satisfactory of any Western get-together in the middle years of the Cold War. The three appeared to be chasing one another around in a circle. Dulles made an attempt to cut through that fruitless pursuit on January 12, 1954, by waving the sword of massive retaliation. Threatening nuclear war had several political uses. First, of course, the "Massive Retaliation" speech was directed at Russia and China. But Dulles' insistence that "no local defense" could match Russian power was a reference not only to military events in one place, Central Europe or Indochina, but to individual efforts to negotiate the Cold War, either at the center (where Churchill saw visions) or on the periphery (where the French were tempted). Massive retaliation, finally, was another way of saying that there were no local issues in the Cold War and that, in the case of Indochina, it meant internationalizing the war. How far, indeed, Dulles ever planned to carry out the logic of massive retaliation militarily, with an attack on Russia to "save" Indochina, may be questioned. The conditions Washington finally set in March 1954, when the French appealed for aid to relieve the besieged fortress, already collapsing before a "quick, sharp King's side attack," did not include an agreement to bomb the Communist superpowers, but did include political concessions to Vietnamese nationalism.

1.

> "General, you must take care, for the Vietminh is organizing its big units and giving them a European character," said Lt. General Raoul Salan.
>
> "In that case, it's done for," replied Navarre.[11]

The best way to use massive retaliation, it turned out, was to say its threat ended the Korean War. That was a safe bet. Since only the United States could launch an atomic war, the threat showed the French, presumably, that they were dependent on Washington's lead. Put another way, America could end the Korean War with honor because it had threatened the atomic bomb; France could not end the Indochinese war that way because it could not so threaten.

It had been policy throughout the first year of the Eisenhower administration to encourage Navarre as against a supposedly weak-kneed set of French politicians. American military observers reported favorably on General Navarre's impact on esprit de corps, a bigger factor, they agreed, than any brilliant strategy he brought with him. Supporting Navarre, reported Lieutenant John W. O'-Daniel and political officers from Saigon, would discourage wishful thinking about a negotiated settlement.[12]

With French political leaders continually throwing up the precedent of the Korean armistice negotiations, Navarre's attitude was doubly welcome. Secretary Dulles had remonstrated with Georges Bidault, for example, who had raised doubts about the sufficiency of the Navarre "solution," using for the first time the new legend of how the Korean fighting had been brought to an end. It had come about, Dulles insisted, not because "we merely wished it to end," but because the United States had been prepared to use alternative measures. "We developed, and perhaps this came to the knowledge of the enemy, the measures which we are disposed to take."[13] This explanation was not yet the full-blown assertion that atomic threats had brought China to accept U.N. views at the negotiating table, but it was evidence of the special use Dulles had planned for "atomic diplomacy," to persuade flagging allies to stay the course; in this instance, to get behind Navarre and stop thinking that America's policy in Korea was a precedent except as regards the effectiveness of military force.

Dulles also insisted that the French *start* thinking about the independence of the Associated States of Indochina. He even held a showcase "consultation" with Bidault and representatives of Vietnam, Laos, and Cambodia, as if the Associated States were already in charge of their own affairs.[14] The American take-charge attitude alarmed French figures at almost every point on the political continuum from right to left. Where the right now said what was the use of fighting if America was the main beneficiary, the left argued that without French control of the war, a reactionary American-sponsored regime would come to power in Vietnam.

In the middle was Jean-Jacques Servan-Schreiber, who summed up the mounting fears in *Le Monde.* American aid, he said, made it more difficult to end the war. "With the arrival of every American bomber in Indochina, France's control of the war is reduced and her sacrifices in it are increased."[15] Laniel was not listening. Swayed for the moment by the prospect of full-scale American support for a military victory, the premier upped the stakes of the Navarre Plan. "Laniel said . . . that he felt that the Viet Minh were now at the peak of their power and on the way down," reported Ambassador Douglas Dillon after a meeting with the premier. "He was confident of victory in a fairly short period of time if the funds were available. France must end her commitments in Indochina very soon and the Navarre Plan was the only way to do this with honor."[16]

Awarding the French yet more money, $385 million, on September 9, 1953, Washington demanded that the Navarre Plan for victory be carried out as Laniel now envisioned it. The Eisenhower administration also proclaimed its belief in Vietnam's independence—a fiction that lasted about a month until the Vietnamese National Congress demanded it be allowed to leave the French Union, and was told to shut up.[17]

The chairman of the Joint Chiefs, Admiral Radford, meanwhile, had decided that the only way to see that American money was well spent was to send General O'Daniel "out to buck up Navarre in going through with his plans."[18] It was hard to get a fix on Henri Navarre. He was a quiet man, whose actions, said his admirers, spoke for him. But Navarre spoke at least one time too many, predicting victory: "Now we can see it clearly—like light at the end of the tunnel."[19] Even when first spoken of in 1953, the light at the end of the tunnel brought derisive hoots from listeners. In recent campaigns the Vietminh had extended its control over large areas of the north, and when Navarre opened a staff meeting with the words "Gentlemen, in order to win this war . . . ," he was greeted with mocking smiles. But he had a plan, he explained to the doubters: first, he would harass the enemy, preempt his likely moves, disrupt his supply system.[20] The second stage needed Paris' support. So Navarre returned to the capital briefly at the end of July 1953 to explain the next—and most fateful—step he had in mind, an "air-land" base at Dienbienphu guarding the gate to Laos.

The Committee of National Defense debated Navarre's proposal, praised its author's ingenuity, and advised him to go ahead, but only if it could be done with the means already at his disposal. Jules Roy, the chronicler of the Dienbienphu debacle, concludes that Navarre could not have misconstrued these instructions. Far from expressing approval, they were, in fact, adds Roy, a warning the Laniel government planned to seek negotiations with China. Navarre's mission was to improve the French bargaining position. Only that, and nothing more.[21] Now, also, there were direct hints reaching Paris from Moscow and Beijing that the Communist powers were ready to sit down and talk about stopping the fighting in Indochina.[22]

American documentation on the inducements offered to Laniel, and the encouragement given to Navarre by American military officers, was not available to Roy when he wrote his account of the political aspects of the background to the battle. It is entirely possible that General Navarre believed his real support would come from Washington, which would undertake the job of bucking up Laniel and the timid civilians. All that can be said is that Washington's involvement at this stage of the war, and the debate in Paris, appeared to open up French military options, when in fact they continued to narrow.

With all that military aid, France could not claim publicly only to be fighting a holding action, pending negotiations. Nor, no matter what Navarre told the politicians or they told him in Paris, could France really do it privately either. This was a trap deeper than the Vietminh had dug. General Navarre did not want American soldiers in Indochina, but he did want an all-out commitment to get the war over quickly, and, like the politicians in Paris, he wanted an end to criticism of French colonialism. Dienbienphu, then, would not only force General Giap's hand, but everyone else's as well.

So Navarre went ahead with his preparations despite a second warning that he would receive no reinforcements from France.[23] When the first three thousand troops were parachuted into the valley at Dienbienphu on November 20, 1953, the huddled peasants in the village near where they landed were not the only ones surprised. Paris was. And so were the Americans. That was what Navarre had hoped. Now he would have to be supported. The general boasted to Ambassador Donald Heath in Saigon that he had secured the vital base necessary to begin "positive and offensive operations."

American military observers were also caught off guard. None of them saw the events of this day as beginning the climactic phase of the French struggle for Vietnam. Army intelligence considered the Dienbienphu operation a ploy to keep the enemy off balance, in preparation for larger strikes in the Red River Delta.[24] The audacity of the deed caught the world's attention, as intended, then elevated it with a romantic aura of brave men standing guard on the borders of the free world. Navarre was proved right. Criticism was replaced by admiration. A carefully chaperoned parade of experts visited the fortress, coming away, as expected, with stirring tales of the exploits of the heroes of Dienbienphu.

There was even a heroine to celebrate, a Florence Nightingale figure, nurse Geneviève de Galard-Terraube, who stayed with the last defenders and treated their wounds to the end, to make the picture complete to the last detail. The list of distinguished visitors included not only military figures, but also the English author Graham Greene, who, not surprisingly, remained skeptical. But he was an exception. Military VIPs fell over one another in pronouncing the Dienbienphu fortress a military marvel.

All this was capped by the man Navarre named to command the outpost, Colonel Christian Marie Ferdinand de la Croix de Castries. Here was an instant legend. "He was meant to be a medieval knight," proclaimed the *Washington Post* even after the fall of Dienbienphu, "a cavalier in mail and armor."[25] Flamboyant as Navarre was taciturn, Colonel de Castries had spurned the easy way to the top in the French military, disdaining aristocratic privileges by coming up through the ranks. Other colonels had declined the honor of command at Dienbienphu; but a man whose ancestors had served France with the sword since the Crusades could not find a more suitable place. De Castries was a daredevil in everything he did, riding, flying, gambling, lovemaking, and as such was as irresistible to the press as he had been to the denizens, especially the females, of prewar French high society.[26]

Wounded twice in World War II, de Castries had served several tours in Indochina since 1946. Wounded again, he now walked with a cane, which, along with his bright red *Spahi* cap and scarf, held together a noble image from head to toe. His ducal mien (highlighted, of course, by a properly sculpted aquiline nose) created in real life a photographer's model of a "modern major general."[27] De Castries never "sat-agee" on his rounds outside the fortress wall, but strode along to where French troops were completing the modern warrior's lifeline, an airstrip that was to keep Dienbienphu's defenders supplied until the Vietminh rushed the fort for the last time, futilely pitching forward to death as in the days of Gunga Din and Beau Geste, and that was to prove so vulnerable to Vietminh artillery bombardment.

What a contrast de Castries was to the enemy commander, General Giap! Son of a peasant, Vo Nguyen Giap had been first arrested at fourteen for participating in public protests. For a time thereafter he had eked out a living as a schoolteacher and private tutor. Military history was his favorite subject, especially Napoleon's campaigns.[28] At the time the siege of Dienbienphu began, Giap commanded the Vietminh army. His recent studies of Chinese "human-wave" tactics in Korea would be put to use in the final stages of the battle. In the meantime, however, his force of Vietnamese in woven helmets and rubber-tire sandals were busy bringing up heavy artillery supplied by China from Russian stocks, and captured American weapons from Korea, to install in the densely covered hills looking down on Dienbienphu.

Giap may also have wondered a little at French insouciance, that they should challenge him thus. Or was there nothing in their training to compare with the advice of a classical era Chinese military manual? "Never fight on a terrain which looks like a tortoise turned upside down. Never camp there for long."[29]

The building of the fortress went on, and as it neared completion, the parade of military experts continued to express their admiration for French ingenuity.[30] It was considered a very good sign, too, that Ho Chi Minh was now talking peace. A Swedish newspaper published an interview at the end of November 1953, during which, among other things, the Vietminh founder said he was ready to end the war "by peaceful means." The impetus for this gesture apparently came from Russia and China. Russia was interested because, in the wake of the Korean armistice, it wanted to settle the German question, or muddy the waters, before France accepted the EDC. China was also interested because of the Korean armistice, but Beijing was concerned about forestalling an American front on its borders in Indochina.[31]

The French government did not answer diplomatic notes placed in the want ads, said the Foreign Office.[32] Inside the cabinet, however, Ho's overture sparked a debate. Foreign Minister Georges Bidault, once a skeptic of the Navarre Plan, insisted to a wavering Laniel on the eve of the Bermuda talks that "Ho Chi Minh is on the point of capitulating: we are going to beat him. Do not strengthen his position by a contact of this sort."[33]

At Bermuda, Bidault remained optimistic. "We have no intention of negotiating directly with Ho Chi Minh," he told Dulles. Dienbienphu, beyond all reason, had come to symbolize France's honor, tarnished in World War II by appeasement and Vichy, and would justify its reentry into the ranks of world power. Surrender was inconceivable now. Though they might later wish it otherwise and agonize over how to save Dienbienphu, American leaders were just as caught up in the drama as their emotion-flushed allies.

2.

> The Bermuda Conference was held without an agenda. It grew out of the inspiration which Sir Winston Churchill had one night, where he sent a message to the President, and his own advisers knew nothing about it, and it all happened like topsy-turvy and ostensibly it had no purpose, except to enable the great men to get together and wander along the beach and pick up shells, and so forth. It did not do much more than that.
>
> JOHN FOSTER DULLES, remarks in secret to Senate Foreign Relations Committee, January 7, 1954[34]

That was the way Dulles had wanted Bermuda to come out, with the most serious business conducted being the gathering of seashells. Eisenhower went to Bermuda in early December of 1953 for four days of talks, preoccupied with the final draft of his "Atoms for Peace" speech, which he was to deliver at the United Nations immediately following the talks. He gave a very good impression of a man considerably annoyed at being interrupted by these tripartite promenades on the beach.[35]

France was included out of concern for the fate of the EDC, so as not to give Paris any cause for offense until the scheme for European rearmament had been approved, but Americans also hoped that France's presence would dilute Churchill's strong penchant for talking summitry. More subtly, Bidault and Laniel would stand on an equal footing with Great Britain, an equal distance, therefore, below superpower level. Indochina discussions, as such, were really peripheral to the main purpose. But Bermuda would have a profound impact on the way others, particularly the British, responded to the Dienbienphu crisis and its aftermath.[36]

Eisenhower's opening revelation that he would address the United Nations just as soon as the Bermuda talks were concluded caught Churchill and Eden off balance. If the speech was as important as the president said, the offer of a brief opportunity to go over the draft hardly came under the category of consultation. It was more like a summons to assemble and hear the king's wishes. Upstaged, the prime minister and his aides, some of whom were themselves dubious about the old lion's "dying wish" to play peacemaker, resented what they saw as a ploy, a dramatic gesture and nothing more, that, in all likelihood, would preempt serious diplomacy in order to showcase Ike's popular appeal. Churchill did not regard the United Nations as a proper arena for serious diplomacy. To his mind it was too public for the serious business of survival in the atomic era. Whatever the original intention, the U.N. now served the Great Powers as a courtroom for prosecuting the Cold War.

Churchill expressed doubts about the wisdom of the U.N. speech, but he was clearly on the defensive, being forced to use his few opportunities alone with the president to seek modifications in the language Ike planned to use. Secretary Dulles had warned the president to beware of the prime minister's burning desire to play the role of "mediator," and to keep the discussion confined to a few general topics. The president should seek agreement on the "U.S. line of action in the Far East, particularly Korea," because disagreement there could lead to the "beginning of disintegration of NATO."[37]

Eisenhower also anticipated, correctly, that his old comrade in arms would seek to persuade him to go a bit slower in colonial and dependent areas. American policy in Iran was a sore spot of recent years, and Dulles' courting of Egyptian nationalists had become downright "unfriendly." Hardly surprising, then, that the British took offense at Eisenhower's pointed reference in the speech draft to America's clean record in support of decolonization. If not Eisenhower, Dulles certainly associated appeasement in the 1930s, on the other hand, with Neville Chamberlain's foolish attempt to ward off threats to the empire.

Here was a forgetful old man, Dulles surmised, believing he could appease Russia and thereby preserve what was left of the empire. Churchill's "Iron Curtain" speech had struck many Americans in 1946, including, oddly enough, Richard Nixon, as too melodramatic about Russian intentions; now his faith in face-to-face meetings with Stalin's successors appeared to a greater number, including, not at all oddly, many liberals, as too naive. If a supernatural force guided Churchill, however, it was most likely not the dour shade of Neville Chamberlain, but the blithe spirit of David Lloyd George, Churchill's first political mentor.[38]

David Lloyd George had first sought to crush the Bolsheviks after World War I, then to absorb them into the postwar economy. It was this pattern Churchill seemed to be following. But just as Lloyd George had found Woodrow Wilson unsympathetic to his plan, so Eisenhower proved to be thirty-five years later. From across the Atlantic, American policymakers could only see that Churchill was now waving something that looked to them very much like Chamberlain's umbrella.

Only recently recovered from a stroke, Churchill was too old and too tired to continue long in power. But at Bermuda Eisenhower encountered a man, who while obviously unable to summon up all the faculties he had once possessed in abundance, nevertheless was steering a straight course. At times Churchill would wander, Eisenhower now noticed, but there was a pattern, and it occurred to the president that this might be at least partly a deliberately adopted mannerism. "At least it seemed to come over him only when the subject under discussion or the argument presented was distasteful to him."[39]

Churchill found two topics especially distasteful at Bermuda: Eisenhower's talk about speeding up decolonization and his insistence that atomic weapons be considered "conventional," which latter point arose in the context of the danger of renewed war in Korea. In the prime minister's yet active mind, atomic weapons and decolonization had got all wrapped up in a dangerous American obsession with winning the Cold War in Asia. Decolonization, for that matter, was a part of the delusion as well. Eisenhower's America, like Wilson's, had gotten itself into a predicament by believing in the nation's special mission, and forsaking old friends. "It's Germany, not Korea, that matters," protested the British leader. Korea had served its one good purpose, by stimulating American rearmament. But now it was an obstruction. "Indo-China, too, does not really matter. We gave up India. Why shouldn't France give up Indo-China?"[40]

The death of Stalin and the Korean armistice had convinced him that the Cold War could be ended—if only people like John Foster Dulles did not insist upon pursuing a chimerical beast across the mountains and through the jungle undergrowth of Southeast Asia. "This fellow preaches like a Methodist Minister," Churchill growled to his personal physician at Bermuda, "and his bloody text is always the same: That nothing but evil can come out of a meeting with [Georgi] Malenkov [Stalin's successor]."[41]

Eisenhower's planned "Atoms for Peace" speech was itself a scheme for using atomic diplomacy to avoid East-West discussions. Eden's private secretary, himself friendly to the American position, commented in his diary, "The speech is not very clever, pretends willingness to internationalize atomic weapons, coupled with the threat to use them."[42] The threat was in regard to Korea. The president explained that while he wanted to give the world some hope for the future, if the Korean War reopened with a massive attack from the north the United States would not shrink from using atomic weapons. The American public no longer distinguished between atomic and other weapons, said Ike, nor was there any reason why it should. "Why should they [the Americans] confine themselves to high explosives requiring thousands of aircraft in attacking China's bases when they can do it more cheaply and easily with atoms?"[43]

Of course, on the British side, such comments fed the belief that America was spoiling for war with China; and if not over Korea, then, a few months later, over Indochina. Anthony Eden came away from this session in a deep gloom, saying to his colleagues that the "prospects are too horrible for the human mind to contemplate."[44]

Still, Eisenhower insisted, it was his objective to counter the hysteria surrounding atomic weapons with proposals for realizing the constructive capabilities of atomic energy.[45] American and British accounts differ, however, as to what Ike said when the prime minister tried to lead him away from the American atomic stockpile up the path to the summit. According to the American minutes, Ike resisted this tug at his sleeve with the fairly moderate demurrer that Stalin's death had not changed Soviet objectives, the destruction of the "capitalist free world by all means, by force, by deceit or by lies."[46]

British records have Ike responding to Churchill's suggestion that they "infiltrate" Russia through trade and other contacts "in the coarsest terms": the president "said that as regards the P.M.'s belief that there was a New Look in Soviet Policy, Russia was a woman of the streets and whether her dress was new, or just the old one patched, it was certainly the same whore underneath. America intended to drive her off her present 'beat' into the back streets."[47] When Ike finished there were pained looks and silence. Finally Anthony Eden asked when the next meeting would be. The president replied, "I don't know. Mine is with a whisky and soda."[48]

Subsequent discussions at Bermuda, whenever the topic was anything besides the EDC, found the British probing for assurances that their American allies were not just itching to prove their determination to use the bomb. The short note that John Foster Dulles made of a dinner conversation on December 5, for example, records British fears that the United States might take action "morally repugnant to most of the world."[49] Anthony Eden's minutes are more detailed about what the president said to produce such a remark. Eisenhower had begun talking about the growing power of the United States, noted Eden. "Nobody could say that even the hydrogen bomb, terrible as its explosive power was, would be the end. More discoveries were probable. Meanwhile all the three Services in the U.S. were being equipped with atomic weapons. If war came or if there were to be a serious breach of the armistice in Korea, the people of the United States would never understand it if the weapons were not used."[50]

Eisenhower's willingness to show the British and French the draft of his planned speech only intensified Churchill's concern. If the Americans detected an unseemly appease and preserve note in the prime minister's recitations, when the British read Ike's words they found an unhealthy pairing of tough nuclear talk and self-righteous posturing about the "obsolete Colonial mold." It was almost as if the Americans felt they had a special right to define the conditions for atomic warfare by virtue of their supposedly clean record on the colonial issue.[51]

It was easy for Churchill to "forget" how similarly he himself had treated the atomic question in his "Iron Curtain" speech of March 5, 1946, asserting "God has willed" that a monopoly of "these dread agencies" should be in American hands at that moment in history.[52] Reminded of those words, he might have replied, "Well, you see, the moment has passed!" In response to British suggestions Eisenhower did agree to modify his phrasing on atomic freedom of action, and to delete the offending reference to colonialism. But Churchill's aides were still worried that having seen the speech, and having had their objections acted upon favorably, they would become "accessories before the act."[53]

Dulles was barely able to repress his obvious delight at having so skillfully thwarted Sir Winston's effort to maneuver Ike to the summit table. As the secretary explained to the Senate Foreign Relations Committee in secret session, the president did not want to deliver the "Atoms for Peace" speech without having consulted the British, "because they do have a position in this field of atomic weapons." There was quite a prolonged exchange, continued Dulles, as it took some time to change Churchill's original negative attitude. About the speech and about use of atomic weapons in general, said Dulles, there had been an "educational exchange of views." He left it to the senators to divine who he meant was being educated.[54]

Indochina was discussed at length only one time at Bermuda, on the last day when Foreign Minister Bidault briefed the conference on prospects for the success of the Navarre Plan and encouraging developments in the political situation. In the course of a ritual denunciation of direct negotiations with Ho Chi Minh or China, however, Bidault made what Eisenhower noted at once was a "cryptic allusion" to a Five Power meeting. The idea of a meeting that included Communist China, the president said, had "very unpleasant connotations and we were likely to study this with a jaundiced eye."[55]

Bidault hastened to clarify his allusion, but not to withdraw its substance. What he meant, he said, was a Five Power meeting on one subject, a meeting where the Associated States of Indochina would also be present. "He hoped that this would exorcise in the eyes of the President the evil influence of the figure five."[56] Bidault was not, in fact, being inconsistent. Conservative French politicians abhorred the idea of dealing directly with Ho, however much they realized the war had to be brought to an end. When Bidault assured Dulles that Paris would not sit down at the bargaining table with the Vietminh leader, he did not exclude the possibility of a deal with China (and probably Russia) over Ho's head—at a level that would not humiliate the French.

The Laniel government, now on the way out (slowly), had ordered General Navarre to do what he could to improve the negotiating position. He had other plans. Either way the idea was to convince the Chinese that they, and presumably the Russians, had something to gain by pressuring the Vietminh into peace talks. What puzzled and chagrined Americans at these sessions were French remarks proclaiming Dienbienphu to be the cornerstone of a winning strategy, followed closely by comments injecting the idea of negotiations into the conversation.

Churchill did not get his summit; but French pressure after Bermuda for a Big Four conference could not be resisted. It was unfortunate, but Paris held the EDC hostage, and there was no adequate response to the argument that the French government had to demonstrate there was no other option. But that meant Indochina would be on the table as well. Dulles had assured Chiang and Rhee that China would not succeed in turning Korean talks into a forum on Asia's future. But now the French had invited the Russians to have their say.

With chips on both shoulders, the EDC and Indochina, Dulles grumbled all the way to Berlin, where the Big Four conference was held in January 1954. In his *Memoirs,* Eisenhower observed that Bermuda "had no purpose that could be translated into terms of hoped-for agreements among the three participating nations." Its sole purpose was to allow the leaders to get to know one another better.[57]

Unhappily for allied cooperation in Indochina, the conference proved that to know all was not to explain anything, either in personal relations or statecraft. America's allies had good reason to feel that the president's views on renewed warfare in Korea reflected a determination not to lose another half a country in Indochina, no matter the cost. Localized defense and conventional warfare had failed. Washington would now show them how it should really be done.

3.

Ho Chi Minh took off his sun helmet. "He turned this upside down on the table and felt around in the bottom of it, and he said, 'Dien Bien Phu is a valley, and it's completely surrounded by mountains. The cream of the French expeditionary corps are down there, and we (feeling the brim of his helmet) are around the mountains. And they'll never get out.' "

Conversation with
Wilfred Burchett,
early 1954[58]

Had Laniel and Churchill heard Vice-President Richard Nixon's report on his fact-finding mission to Southeast Asia, their fears about American winner-take-all attitudes would have abated, but not by much. Nixon offered his impressions to the National Security Council on December 23, 1953. "About Indochina we must talk optimistically; we have put good money in, and we must stick by it. However, the pessimistic side will be spoken here." In lucid fashion Nixon then went on to detail the problems. Even if the French achieved a military victory by spring, he said, that was absolutely no guarantee that the Vietminh or some other group would not rise again. The core issue was China.

Without Chinese backing, he continued, the local Vietminh forces could be defeated within three months. But that was not likely to be the case ever. The Navarre Plan was an improvement, yes, but the same sticking point as before was there: French reluctance to train local forces. In addition, the French military in Indochina believed that the war would be settled in Paris by negotiations. And this was harming morale.

Bao Dai, on the other hand, had told Nixon that he realized early negotiations would turn Vietnam over to the Communists. In these circumstances, the only option was to play for time, and meanwhile attempt to build up the "power and leadership" of Vietnam. This would require delicate maneuvering, of course, not least about the China question.

There were some Asians, he said, who argued for a plan to overthrow China militarily, or to force a breakdown internally by practicing a "containment" blockade. While he held out little hope for the success of either plan, Nixon did not want to go to the other "extreme," diplomatic recognition and an offer of U.N. membership. The question, then, was how to hold matters in check, and especially how to resist allied pressure to deal with Mao's regime. The only way, he concluded, was to stop opposing the China trade, an inevitability anyway, and in that way damp down other issues.[59]

Trade did not require diplomatic recognition by the United States, would remove irritations America's allies complained about, and thus strengthen Washington's hand. It might also create a stake for China in what, many years later, Nixon would call the "structure of peace." With the siege of Dienbienphu under way, and with Dulles fearing allied pressure to include China in any peace talks on Indochina, Nixon's "escape" route held little appeal in Washington. He himself would take a very different tack a few weeks later, urging, or appearing to urge, intervention with ground forces.

It is sometimes overlooked that the ultimate victors at Dienbienphu, the Vietminh, had placed their cause in the hands of fate just as surely as had the French. For all the retrospective confidence expressed in Vietminh accounts about the clear-sighted decision of the party to accept Navarre's challenge, General Giap's being the best known, the battle was a great gamble for the Vietminh. And in some ways it was a forced decision. As Giap put it, "Dien Bien Phu being the keystone of the Navarre Plan, we considered that it should be wiped out if the Franco-American plot of protracting and expanding the war was to be smashed."[60] What Giap stressed, therefore, was that Dienbienphu was not militarily decisive, but politically decisive. If the French strong point held for even a few months more, time would become a coconspirator in the "Franco-American plot."

A protracted struggle would see Kronos shift his loyalties to the other side, allowing the Americans to make their weight felt with more and more equipment, and more and more influence. The danger of an expanded war might also discourage the Vietminh's allies.[61] Giap had no sure way of knowing how susceptible Moscow might be to proposals for a trade-off, or how anxious China might be for offers of trade.

As a student of modern history, Giap certainly knew, for example, how the revolutionary wars of the Russian Revolution were followed by Lenin's New Economic Policy. If the West did not choose to take advantage of the opportunities Lenin had offered them, that was no reason to believe a similar move—either by China or the capitalist nations—was not being contemplated. He would not, of course, have known about Richard Nixon's speculative musings in the National Security Council. But one or two harbingers called attention to the precarious position the Vietminh occupied.

For instance, the new Soviet premier, Georgi Malenkov, had used his New Year's message to respond to Eisenhower's "Atoms for Peace" speech, calling for a ban on all atomic weapons. However unlikely the United States would surrender its best weapon, even under a nuclear-clouded sky there were lighter days when it appeared the sun might break through. Fallout from a relaxed nuclear atmosphere might include a Soviet-American deal on Indochina. There were also indications that both Great Britain and Japan were pressuring the United States to abandon its economic "blockade" of China.

Britain had traditionally wanted to divert Japanese trade from commonwealth and empire markets to China.[62] The speed with which Japan was being reintegrated into the Western political system demonstrated, on the other hand, that the fiercest and most intense ideological disputes, like thunderstorms, were often of short duration. If those who had been shooting one another in Korea and reviling one another everywhere else could also find common ground, the Vietminh would be left to fend for itself. Indeed China was soon sounding out the Indian government for a rapprochement that led in 1955 to the first Third World Congress at Bandung, Indonesia.[63]

If those portents posed imponderable questions, they nevertheless called attention to the unpredictable course of relations among allies, even revolutionary allies. At the moment a surge of zeal ran through the Vietminh ranks, but how long could such dedication be sustained, especially if the struggle dragged on and the Vietminh were abandoned by their allies? Would Vietnam become another Greece? As events unfolded at the Geneva Conference, any fears Giap might have had on this score would prove well-founded. Vietnam was not to become another Greece, but both Russia and China proved to be very interested in negotiating over Vietminh heads, or, more cynically, over Vietminh bodies at Dienbienphu.

At the very least, the longer the war went on, the more indebted Ho and his followers would become to those "comrades," and the greater the chance as well that the war would be decided in Moscow or Beijing or, as it was, at Geneva. As the siege of Dienbienphu deepened, both the French and the Vietminh had reason to speculate about the ultimate outcome of the forces they had set in motion in this remote corner of Southeast Asia.

The French still showed confidence under Colonel de Castries, with Dienbienphu described in one account as looking like a Boy Scout jamboree, pup tents everywhere and hundreds of little fires warming the night. De Castries' expert in artillery warfare, Colonel Charles Piroth, assured the commander that the Vietminh would never succeed in getting heavy artillery in place in the jungle hills around Dienbienphu, and even if they should somehow accomplish that feat, "we'll smash them." So confident was Piroth, in fact, that he turned down American offers of additional firepower.[64]

Confidence began to ebb, however, as French air power proved unable to interdict Vietminh supply lines. Soon, also, ground patrols outside the fortress had to be abandoned. Dienbienphu twitched nervously at the end of a slender air link to Hanoi and Saigon. With good reason. Trenches gradually filling up with human waves, ready to put out those campfires in the perimeter outposts, nearly encircled the fortress. De Castries had named those outposts, so word had it inside the main command center, for his mistresses: Claudine, Marcelle, Huguette, Françoise, Anne-Marie, Gabrielle, Dominique, Beatrice, Eliane, and Isabelle.[65]

4.

> The enemy is worried and speaks of negotiations. . . . We are here to win.
>
> GENERAL RENÉ COTY,
> New Year's Day message
> to French forces, 1954[66]

Navarre was increasingly aware, despite all such boasts, of how easy it could be to snip off the lifeline to Dienbienphu. The thirty-seven-millimeter ack-ack anti-aircraft guns being supplied by China, the general admitted to Ambassador Donald Heath, could seriously impair all operations. He needed more aircraft, more pilots, more aircrew members. Would it be possible in addition for Americans to fly logistic missions to nonbattle areas so that the French pilots could be spared to fly missions against the Vietminh artillery?[67]

This request set off the first full-fledged debate in the National Security Council, on January 8, 1954, over how far the United States would actually go to prevent a Vietminh victory at Dienbienphu. It was now that the first complaints were heard that the French had chosen such a place, and such means, to stage the "showdown" battle that risked losing an entire country to the enemy. General

Robert Cutler, Eisenhower's special adviser on national security affairs, expressed concern at the qualitative change under consideration. "Was not this the camel getting his head through the door?" Cutler's doubts prompted Treasury Secretary George Humphrey to express similar fears.

Throughout the discussion, however, the case was made by the chairman of the Joint Chiefs, Admiral Radford. "We already had a lot of men in Indochina now, though none of them in combat operations. Nevertheless, he insisted, we are really in this war today in a big way."[68] Radford thought very little of French ability, on the other hand, to knock out the Vietminh artillery emplacements. "If we could put one squadron of U.S. planes over Dien Bien Phu for as little as one afternoon, it might save the situation. Weren't the stakes worth it? We were already in this thing in such a big way that it seemed foolish not to make the one small extra move which might be essential to success." Eisenhower began musing on Radford's suggestion. "The President thought . . . [of] a little group of fine and adventurous pilots . . . we should give these pilots U.S. planes without insignia and let them go." This would be "the right way" to use planes from a nearby aircraft carrier—"without involving us directly in the war, which he admitted would be a very dangerous thing." Radford believed it could be worked out.

It is hard to say from the context of these remarks exactly why the president thought it would be "a very dangerous thing" to get directly involved—because of concern about expanding the war so close to China's borders, or scruples about the constitutional oath he had taken at inauguration. In any event the NSC decided to study "all feasible steps, short of the *overt* use of U.S. forces in combat" to aid in achieving success of the Navarre Plan.[69]

Eisenhower's only definitive pronouncement at this meeting—and at subsequent discussions—was a prohibition against sending American ground forces into operation in Indochina. Several times during the course of the discussion he had referred to alternative means of involvement, thereby giving Radford and Dulles a great deal of leeway in using their ingenuity to come up with a plan. And in fact he supplemented his remarks by appointing a special committee headed by his old friend Under Secretary of State Walter Bedell Smith to come up with a plan "in specific terms, covering who does what with which and to whom." As matters stood, the problem of providing what was needed appeared to fall somewhere between the Central Intelligence Agency and the Department of Defense.[70]

Henry II's anguished outcry to his knights regarding Thomas à Becket—"Have I not about me one man of enough spirit to rid me of a single insolent prelate?"—might not have suited Eisenhower's style. But current historical evaluations find Ike far more sophisticated than thought previously, and, on the other hand, they also suggest that clandestine CIA activities in the 1950s did not just "happen," any more than the president's carefully contrived obfuscations at press conferences are explained by Ike's notoriously poor command of syntax.

His reluctance to send ground forces into Indochina indicated no moral reservation holding him back from action against Ho Chi Minh. It is only necessary to recall the unflinching determination with which he accomplished the removal of leftist president Jacobo Arbenz from Guatemala later in 1954 to correct such an impression.[71] The president was clearly upset, nevertheless, by the growing speculations about American ground forces in Indochina. These had been fueled in the first week of 1954 by a Joseph Alsop column in the *Washington Post.* According to Alsop, French foreign minister Georges Bidault had used him to send a message to Washington saying that if the United States was unwilling to come to France's rescue with ground troops—"in a matter of weeks"—then France would withdraw. Almost immediately denials were forthcoming from the Foreign Ministry. And the true story did seem to be that Alsop, perhaps having a glimmer of the debate over Navarre's request, had decided that he would do what he could to force the administration's hand. It was, said Foreign Ministry officials, Alsop's proposal, not Bidault's. Bidault had only responded to a question as to whether he would welcome a U.S. troop contingent.[72]

As the days counted down to the opening of the Berlin Foreign Ministers Conference on January 25, 1954, at which the intractable German "problem" was to be discussed yet again (and out of which the United States did not expect, or even desire, Russian agreement, but hoped instead to secure French consent to the European Defense Community), a flurry of speculations about Vietnam's fate crisscrossed news reports of French intentions in Europe. Perhaps the most intriguing of these was the "trial balloon" launched by Emperor Bao Dai himself. On January 9, 1954, Radio Vietnam in Saigon broadcast a message to the Soviet Union, calling upon the Russians to guarantee "the existence of Viet Nam on a basis other than Communist." The explanation for this apparently bizarre performance was the broadcast's claim that France was about to switch alliances, or at least to accept Moscow's good offices in arranging negotiations with Ho Chi Minh.[73]

Bidault did not deny that it was possible Moscow "will try to sell us Ho Chi Minh in exchange for the European Defense Community," but insisted Paris was not buying.[74] Yet when the Berlin Conference began, Bidault recalled in his memoirs, he responded to Dulles' pep talks rallying the Western "team" around the old Achesonian formula—diplomacy from strength—with some pointed comments about America's performance in Korea. You were not winning, he said, when you negotiated that armistice. France had been fighting in Indochina for twice as long, and now, because of the armistice, China will be able to send additional aid to the enemy. If the Americans had their own reasons for the Korean armistice, fine and good, but the French nation "could not allow its soldiers to fight on alone without the help of the United Nations and without any end to the war in sight," regardless of how much financial aid it received.[75]

Dulles had tried to bolster the French with promises of retaliation against the Chinese, first at a press conference on December 29, 1953, and more dramatically in his "Massive Retaliation" speech on January 12, 1954, when he announced that the basic decision on national security policy had been made: the United States henceforth would "depend primarily upon a great capacity to retaliate, instantly, by means and at places of our choosing."[76]

Repeating his threat that Chinese intervention would lead to "grave consequences which might not be confined to Indochina," the secretary also had a veiled warning for the French: "If we rely on freedom, then it follows that we must abstain from diplomatic moves which would seem to endorse captivity. That would, in effect, be a conspiracy against freedom. I can assure you that we shall never seek illusory security for ourselves by such a 'deal.' "[77]

When the Berlin Conference began, the Soviet Union sought to have China included to discuss all issues, and was turned down. On this point, the Western line held firm. But nothing Dulles said could dissuade Bidault from entertaining proposals for a Five Power conference to deal with Indochina. The secretary objected that it could not be a Five Power conference if the French wanted the United States to attend. The Associated States of Indochina would have to be there. Bidault had a reply for that one, however. If the Associated States attended, the Communists would insist upon having Ho Chi Minh there, too. Did the United States want that?[78]

No, it certainly did not. Later Secretary Dulles changed his mind on that one, but while he sought new arguments to use with Bidault in Berlin, the first "big" stories about the still-pending French requests for bombers and aircrews appeared in the United States. At his press conference on February 3, Eisenhower was asked to comment on a story that the United States had sent 125 technicians to Indochina. Avoiding a direct answer by referring to American military missions throughout the world, the president went on to say in answer to a follow-up question that the Indochinese situation had been critical for some time. But he gave the definition of "critical" a special twist, confusing those present, and requiring the first clarification the White House had had to issue about one of his answers. If the Vietnamese believed that the war would make them free, he had said, then they probably would win against the Communists. "If it goes the other way, you will probably not have the success. So it is critical in the sense that we have had some evidence that there is a lack of enthusiasm we would like to have there."[79]

Later that day the White House said that the president had been referring to those people in Vietnam who had not yet committed themselves to the fight against Communism, and was not commenting on the armies involved, or the leadership of the government. That helped very little. If it had been intended to blunt Bidault's overtures in Berlin by revealing the French requests, Eisenhower's language was unfortunate, and doubly so the clarification, which suggested the inability of the French to arouse Vietnamese loyalties. So it wound up being a criticism of the entire war effort.[80]

But the press conference became incidental to "insider" stories detailing the NSC debates over Indochina, in some versions even featuring accounts of Radford's proposals, and the revelation that the president had established a special committee to advise him on a plan.[81] Congressional leaders were now asking questions about the "drift" in American policy, about possible troop shifts from Korea, and even the use of atomic weapons.[82] At the NSC meeting on February 4, 1954, Eisenhower complained angrily about the leak. Who could have told the press? Silence. Then Walter Bedell Smith, who headed the special committee—and probably had a good idea—cleared the air: "All one could say was that this secret had been kept quite a bit longer than most others."[83]

Eisenhower reverted to the problem he had discussed at the

press conference, but in an operational way. Why, he asked, couldn't we capitalize on the religious issue? Was it possible to find "a good Buddhist leader to whip up some real fervor?" Someone who could inspire the Vietnamese to resistance, the way Europe had responded to the Arab incursions. "It was pointed out to the President that, unhappily, Buddha was a pacifist rather than a fighter (laughter)."[84]

Undismayed, Ike switched religions: "He still believed that there was something in the idea of a religious motivation, and pointed out how Joan of Arc had managed to defeat a large enemy force and place a timid king upon his throne in France. The President said that his religious leader would not attempt to oust Bao Dai, but to support him."[85]

While Eisenhower was thinking about ways of "energizing Bao Dai," Dulles considered threatening Bidault with a withdrawal of American aid, but thought better of it.[86] "I shall do everything possible [to] minimize risks," the secretary assured Eisenhower about the dangers of a Five Power conference on Indochina, but he could not push Bidault beyond a certain point without endangering both the EDC and Indochina.[87]

On February 8, Eisenhower met with legislative leaders, including Senator Leverett Saltonstall, chairman of the Armed Services Committee, who had been publicly critical of the plan to send two hundred technicians to Indochina. He understood their concern about ground troops, the president began, but there were risks involved in all of America's military programs abroad. Saltonstall quickly explained that his objection was to military troops. If civilians could be found, he would go along with expanding the advisory mission.

Eisenhower then replied that he believed that indigenous Asian forces would have to do the fighting, "with the United States providing a mobile reserve for the overall security of the free world." Yet exceptions had to be made until those indigenous forces could be built up. (The persistent problem, of course, from Washington's point of view was French unwillingness to permit the Americans to train Vietnamese forces, and thus set things in motion.) He would like to use Chiang's troops in Indochina, but that risked unacceptable "Chinese Red moves." "But we can't get anywhere in Asia by just sitting here in Washington and doing nothing—My God, we must not lose Asia—we've got to look the thing right in the face."[88]

Walter Bedell Smith, who had been assigned by Eisenhower to

stare the "thing" down, worried that he might not even get the chance to confront the issue. The scheduled visits of René Pleven and General Paul Ely, Admiral Radford's counterpart, on a fact-finding mission to Indochina, he told the president on the telephone, would likely push things a little more toward negotiation. Maybe it would be good to get them to stop off in Washington on their way back to Paris, he suggested. The French opposition would sneer that they had "rushed back here for orders," but that could be overcome. Smith hoped "DDE could stiffen them up a little bit."[89]

For the long term Smith had in mind a regional defense organization. Despite all the talk about such a pact since the time of the Japanese peace treaty, the under secretary confessed he still did not know if it was feasible, as he told British ambassador Roger Makins. The French were impossible. They lacked will and drive, refused to allow the Americans an opportunity to properly train the Vietnamese, and wanted only to negotiate. Eisenhower would never put troops into Indochina, even if he had the power. At this point, in fact, Smith saw a regional defense organization as little more than a lure to Paris to forestall a French bid for a negotiated settlement.[90]

Makins took note of the rising public interest in Indochina, and reported that he was being questioned "constantly" about London's likely reactions to a deepening American involvement. Foreign Secretary Anthony Eden had these messages at hand during the Berlin Conference. He had already made up his mind not to reject out of hand any Molotov proposal for a Five Power conference. He had also decided that the best way to deal with Indochina—and to preserve British interests in neighboring Malaya—was through some sort of partition arrangement that could be guaranteed by the Western powers—joined, he hoped, by India and other Eastern nations.

As things stood, the Chinese had no reason to intervene; the Vietminh were doing well enough (in fact better than that) to win.[91] From the outset, then, American and British conceptions of Southeast Asian "security" treaties reflected very different assessments, not simply of the area to be guaranteed, but what it was that warranted protection. The British thought in terms of specific interests, whereas the Americans thought also of "reputation" and the long-term struggle with Communism in the third world. "We must abstain from diplomatic moves which would seem to endorse captivity," the secretary of state had vowed. "That would, in effect, be a conspiracy against freedom."

But despite all that Dulles could do, the Berlin Conference ended with an agreement that there should be a Five Power meeting at Geneva beginning on April 26, 1954, to discuss Korea and Indochina. The secretary did manage to prevent China being named one of the conveners, and he did succeed in getting the Associated States invited, at the cost of having to send an invitation to Ho Chi Minh as well.[92]

5.

> Now, regrettably but necessarily in our form of government that fact has to be made known, and when we make it known, we also make it known to the Communists—I wish we did not have to tell them, for example, that we have no intention of putting ground soldiers into Indochina; I wish to God that we could leave that suspicion or that fear in their minds. I wish we could leave in their minds the suspicion and fear that we might do a lot of things that we have no intention of doing.
>
> WALTER BEDELL SMITH,
> testimony in Executive Session,
> February 16, 1954[93]

The constraints put on American policy by "our form of government" did not mean that the administration intended to allow things to keep on sliding until an avalanche buried all hopes at Geneva. Americans regarded gathering momentum for a negotiated settlement that would partition Vietnam as a "conspiracy against freedom." India had publicly called for a standstill armistice pending the convening of the Geneva Conference, while in private British and Russian diplomats were beginning to canvas the possibilities of partition.[94] The Indian proposal offended even those congressional doubters concerned about American involvement. Senator William F. Knowland, decidedly not a doubter, warned of an impending Far Eastern "Munich."[95]

One way or another the French had to get out (or be gotten out) of Dienbienphu without surrendering the country, no matter what happened in that battle. An obvious political strategy was to minimize the importance of the fortress in the overall picture, which Smith did, joining Admiral Radford in assurances to Congress that the military situation was not at all critical.[96] Communist forces had won only zigzag "real estate victories," they contended, adding in confidence that the only truly crucial battle taking place was in Paris: would the French have the guts to stick it out there; would they have the nerve to let the Americans take over running the war if the only other choice were defeat?[97]

Yet there was no blinking the fact that Congress was now fully aroused, and the administration fully aware of the legislators' adamant opposition to a land war on the continent of Asia, however much they abhorred the thought of a Chinese-sponsored Vietminh victory. Conservative Democrat John C. Stennis was as blunt as it was possible to be on that score. "I don't want to see any more of our military personnel go into Indo-China," the Mississippi senator said regarding the plan to send two hundred technicians, speaking for many of his colleagues as well. "I want those now in there to be pulled out."[98]

Sometimes domestic political forces canceled one another out. The China lobby, anathema to liberals, played some role, exactly how much cannot be determined despite its fame, in the Eisenhower administration's attitude on the broad swath of Asian policy issues. Yet on the issue of ground forces in Indochina, China lobby people were no more interested than their opposites in sending in American soldiers. The bomb further divided ranks.

The questions at Eisenhower's press conferences became more persistent, the answers more qualified. Would the president comment on Senator Stennis' contention that sending the technicians would lead to a hot war? Yes, he would. "No one could be more bitterly opposed to ever getting the United States involved in a hot war in that region than I am; consequently, every move that I authorize is calculated, as far as humans can do it, to make certain that that does not happen." Did that mean he was determined that the United States should not get involved, no matter how far that war might go? He would not try to predict the course of world events, but there could be no "greater tragedy . . . than to get heavily involved now in an all-out war in any of those regions, particularly with large units."[99]

Meanwhile General Ely and Defense Minister René Pleven had arrived at Dienbienphu. Everyone inside the perimeter was optimistic, including Eisenhower's new military representative to Indochina, General John W. O'Daniel; everyone, that is, except the air chief of staff, General Fay. He did not have enough aircrews to fly the required missions, missions which, in any event, served no useful purpose. Before Ely and Pleven, the air force officer said, "I shall advise General Navarre to take advantage of the respite available to him and the fact he can still use his two airfields, to evacuate all the men he can, for he is done for. That is all."[100]

Pleven and Ely boarded their plane back to Hanoi, the defense minister apparently as untroubled by Fay's dissent as General Navarre and his lieutenants. Ely's austere face gave no indication of what he felt. In Hanoi a correspondent asked if the announcement of the Geneva Conference would not affect morale. "Mademoiselle," Pleven quipped, "if I were in Giap's place, I would be extremely worried precisely on account of the announcement of the Geneva Conference."[101]

Pleven was a better prophet than he imagined. Giap's worries were of a different order, but Pleven was right in thinking that he wanted the battle over before Geneva. The French defense minister then voiced his real concerns to British high commissioner Malcolm MacDonald. The French public, he confided, was weary of the war, it wanted "above all to be able to see the light at the end of the tunnel." Perhaps the only way for France to continue would be to remove all metropolitan troops, before the French people got too tired to carry on.[102]

According to Jules Roy, Pleven had stayed on in Saigon briefly in order to give secret diplomacy a chance to operate. Whether or not a serious attempt was made at this time to initiate bilateral negotiations with the Vietminh, his statement about Geneva may well have been intended in double entendre fashion to suggest to the Vietminh leadership that they stood a better chance in dealing with the French alone than if the Americans got more deeply involved.[103]

If so, it marked a real change, because the French had previously made it a point of honor that should there be negotiations, they would have to be with Russia or China. Secretary Dulles had just made a great show of explaining to the American public, on the other hand, that the Chinese had not been admitted into membership in the great-power game, and that meeting with them at Geneva did not constitute diplomatic recognition. They were not even being invited, but rather called "to account before the bar of world opinion."[104]

Dulles' aversion to "Red China" was certainly strong enough, it ought to be noted, for him to desire to spoil Beijing's debut in international diplomacy—regardless of any other consideration. But he had plenty of other reasons for wanting to preempt the upcoming effort to reach a peaceful settlement of the Indochina conflict.

Among these was the still-pressing desire to "liberate" American diplomacy from Old World influences. Simply agreeing to Geneva he accounted a setback.

Nevertheless, the United States had to be prepared for anything, as Eisenhower told the secretary after his return from Berlin. There may be disappointments in store for the United States, he said, noting that he agreed with Vice-President Nixon that someone with an impeccably anti-Communist record ought to be named to head the delegation so that whatever happened there could be no charges of the administration being soft on Communism. Radio Beijing was already boasting, however, that as a result of Berlin the entire American position in the Far East had been undermined, its effort to deny China its proper role "obviously doomed."[105]

Too close to the truth, Dulles fretted. The best thing from Washington's viewpoint, of course, would be if by the time of the Geneva Conference there was nothing to negotiate. So he discouraged serious preparations for serious negotiations.[106] And Washington dispatched a fifteen-man team from the United States Information Agency to spread the word that the Vietminh were nothing but "puppets of Red China."[107] But everything Washington heard from Paris, from Prime Minister Laniel's statements to the National Assembly to Pleven's private comments to a *Newsweek* editor, argued, as Ambassador Douglas Dillon put it, that the French now believed that for a settlement "it will be up to France's allies to make concessions to Communist China with all that implies for the United States."[108]

Pleven told the editor, Harry Kern, that he believed the Russians and Chinese had their price for ending the war, and France was willing to pay it: free trade with the West, diplomatic recognition, U.N. membership. If the United States persisted in opposition to all negotiations at Geneva, however, the Laniel government would surely fall—leaving France to the neutralist premiership of Pierre Mendès-France. Then there would be no victory in Indochina, no EDC, and an end to Franco-American cooperation in the Atlantic framework.

That was why General Ely was being sent to Washington, for the express purpose of making Admiral Radford understand the situation. The French negotiating position in regard to Indochina itself, Pleven suggested (though he stressed it was his personal view he was talking about), should be to encourage a federation of states, some controlled by the Vietminh, but the majority non-Communist.

If elections were delayed for at least two years there was a good chance that the non-Communist states would remain so. Two years would be enough for the nationalists to offer a genuinely nationalist alternative to Communism. It was a long shot, but "tout est difficile, là-bas."[109]

Pleven's revelations to Kern about General Ely's mission to Washington were somewhat at odds with other accounts, which have Ely charged with finding out precisely what it was the United States was prepared to do if MIG-15's appeared in Indochinese skies, or if China increased its aid to the Vietminh. Would Eisenhower approve U.S. Air Force strikes?[110] If Ely posed the issue in those stark terms, of course, he might elicit—in backhanded fashion—a confession that the United States really had no military alternative to negotiations.

In Washington, meanwhile, Under secretary Smith's special Indochina advisory committee had finished its report on a plan for victory. Much of it was hardly new: increased aid, increased pressure on France to allow American advisers to train indigenous forces, and so forth. Under one heading, however, the committee recommended recruitment of additional forces from Germany, Italy, and Asian countries to serve in Vietnam. Provision should also be made, the committee said, to allow American volunteers to serve in the French military without losing their citizenship.[111] The committee concluded that if its recommendations were implemented, victory could be achieved without an overt use of American military force. If the situation should deteriorate drastically, however, or if French intransigence made it impossible to go forward, "the U.S. may wish to consider direct military action in Southeast Asia to ensure the maintenance of our vital interests in the area."[112]

Before Smith's report could be discussed the Vietminh launched a massive attack on Dienbienphu. It began on March 13, 1954. Within two days perimeter outposts Gabrielle and Anne-Marie had been overwhelmed with a thousand or more dead on each side; and by the end of another day the Vietminh artillery, averaging ten rounds per minute, had rendered the airstrips unusable, making airdrops the only way to resupply the beleaguered men fighting now only for their lives.[113]

General Ely arrived in Washington on March 20, 1954. He was met by Admiral Radford. "If the Communists continue to suffer the losses they have been taking," he told reporters, "I don't know how they can stay in the battle."[114] More and more, however, American political and military leaders concerned themselves with the likelihood that the French would not stay in the battle. A week before Ely's arrival, Admiral Radford had signed a memorandum to Defense Secretary Wilson on behalf of the Joint Chiefs warning that the United States should decline to associate itself with any negotiated settlement, thereby preserving its freedom of action to pursue the struggle without the French.[115]

The admiral preferred, of course, to convince Ely that the French could make it. "The French are going to win," he told reporters. "It is a fight that is going to be finished with our help." Back at the White House, Eisenhower stood at General Ely's side so the photographers could record the scene. Ike whispered to Ely, a reporter overheard, that things had looked bad in World War II at one time. "But we won in the end and we will win again."[116]

What thoughts went through Ely's mind? His mission, as we have seen, was not a clear mandate for such a choice. French planners in Indochina had prepared a contingency plan in the event of a Chinese intervention on the Korean scale. It involved falling back to beachhead positions and invoking American air power. Its code name was Damocles.[117] Whether severed by the Vietminh or by the Americans, French control in Indochina would not survive the loss of Dienbienphu.

CHAPTER SIX

Beyond Dienbienphu

Under the conditions of today, the imposition on Southeast Asia of the political system of Communist Russia and its Chinese Communist ally, by whatever means, would be a grave threat to the whole free community. The United States feels that that possibility should not be passively accepted, but should be met by united action. This might involve serious risks. But these risks are far less than those that will face us a few years from now, if we dare not be resolute today.

JOHN FOSTER DULLES, "Uniting for Action" speech,
March 29, 1954[1]

At the height of the battle of Dienbienphu hardly more than 13,000 men defended the besieged French garrison. In the surrounding hills enemy forces totaled less than 50,000, backed by another 50,000 support troops. Yet it has been called "one of the truly decisive battles of the twentieth century," ranking with the First Battle of the Marne, Stalingrad, and Midway.[2]

Though he wished it otherwise, John Foster Dulles never doubted the comparison. From a purely military point of view it was perhaps not so accurate. But Dienbienphu was etched starkly against a darkening horizon. For a long time Dulles had hoped that when the French finally understood the peril for themselves, they would, somewhat after the fashion of the British in Greece, call upon the New World to deliver Indochina from Communism. He had it in mind, the secretary told President Eisenhower, to paraphrase the Monroe Doctrine in his March 29 speech in New York, extending the boundaries set by that president with a warning that

America could not look upon the loss of Southeast Asia to Communism "with indifference."[3]

The relationship Dulles saw between President Monroe's ancient declaration that the American continents were no longer open to European colonizing and France's war in Indochina was an interesting example of the way the secretary's mind wove together military and political security requirements. America had long ago exceeded Monroe's protected boundaries territorially, but Dulles wished to emphasize the same differences in "systems" that the earlier statesman had emphasized. Extending the Monroe Doctrine to Asia was the way for liberation to work.

Defense Secretary Charles E. Wilson, picking up on the Greek theme, told reporters that Washington wanted to send a military mission to Indochina "similar" to that which had built up the Greek army after World War II, and which had defeated Communist-sponsored insurgency. Wilson admitted, however, that his discussions with General Paul Ely had revealed no change of heart: the French still did not want Americans training "native troops."[4]

"We can, I think, take a lesson from Dien Bien Phu," Dulles admonished a New York audience at the conclusion of the Ely visit, hoping that he could also be heard in London and Paris. "For some days there has seemed to be a lull. But in fact the danger has steadily mounted." Which danger did he mean? Concern about Dienbienphu or, what was to him, the truly frightful threat lurking within the alliance? "Today the free world also feels a sense of lull." Unless they joined ranks, united for action, a day of reckoning was at hand.[5]

American policymakers, only recently hailing French vigor, now seethed at the spectacle they saw of an aging roué, heedless to any warning, squandering away the material and spiritual resources of the West. And always asking for more. Washington had already paid out over a billion dollars to back French wagers, absorbing by 1954 80 percent of the costs of the war. The Eisenhower administration had backed the latest gamble, had, in fact, urged Paris to send an offensive-minded general to Indochina, had even willed itself to believe in the Navarre Plan. All the greater its fears—and frustration.

Before it was too late, America had to demand control over the outcome. As the crisis in Indochina focused on one small place, it drew into itself questions that reached out beyond Dienbienphu's defense perimeter, beyond Southeast Asia as well. Yet to resolve these, or actually even to begin to resolve them, meant going back to the vortex—the besieged fortress where Colonel de Castries rallied his men for the climactic battle.

Admiral Radford, for example, the most confirmed advocate of military action to save Dienbienphu, foresaw a complete collapse *inside France* resulting from a major catastrophe in Indochina. Dulles replied to the admiral during one of their discussions that he believed "we must do some thinking on the premise that France is creating a vacuum in the world wherever she is. How can we fill that vacuum?"[6]

Saving Vietnam, saving France from its folly, filling the vacuum, these all had to be attacked. But there was more to it still. Washington was now under considerable pressure to demonstrate its capacity to conduct U.S. national security affairs and economic foreign policy as befitted the acknowledged leader of the Western alliance. Indochina would thus measure the tensile strength of that alliance at each of several points as well as its overall vitality. If American leaders deplored the "cultural lag" of European colonialism and the anachronistic nationalisms that appeared to hold back European unity, statesmen on the other side of the Atlantic and in Japan had doubts of their own about a foreign policy that increasingly relied upon the theory of massive retaliation, and which had yet to produce a hypothesis about the reintegration of Germany and Japan into the world economy.[7]

The spring of 1954 was a difficult time in which to be doing anything constructive. The Korean War backlash, only part of which could be attributed to the mauling antics of the five o'clock shadow man, Senator Joseph McCarthy, had reached its height. At the same time, a mild economic recession sent an unduly strong tremor of fear racing around Eisenhower's cabinet table. Could the Republicans themselves unite for action to tackle sensitive issues such as trade and tariff policy and beat back an upsurge of economic isolationism?

The administration's New Look military policies, with their emphasis upon atomic weapons delivery systems, encouraged isolationism, both political and economic, an unfortunate side effect of Eisenhower's attempt to fashion a coherent foreign policy that would not overstrain the economy. In the long run he was right about the dangers of that happening, but in the immediate circumstances his advocacy of a New Look at military strategy strengthened advocates of an Old Look in economic foreign policy.

The best thing Americans could do, George F. Kennan told a

Princeton audience, would be to calm themselves. While disavowing the role of Indochina critic—"The time has past when any backseat driving can do any good"—Kennan told his listeners that the general problem in Asia stemmed largely from "profound and wholly legitimate indigenous conditions." The main Communist threat was not of armies crossing borders, but exploitation of existing conditions. The near-hysteria Americans suffered from aided the Communists. In response, we should strive to recover "our inner equilibrium." It was not subversion, but McCarthyite attempts to "protect us all from the impact of ideas" that inspired "false hopes and arrogance" among Soviet rulers. If we wanted to win respect in Asia, the way to do it was to demonstrate seriousness of purpose and belief in ourselves.[8]

Like Kennan, the administration sought an alternative to containment in Asia, but his new voice could not be heard over the din of battle, an uproar that mixed so many sounds from so many different places that the siege of Dienbienphu seemed to be everywhere. For example, it resounded over both the H-bomb and East-West trade. Here were specifics of the New Look and old dilemmas. No account of what happened at Dienbienphu or in Washington or, most important of all, in Western European capitals can be considered anything near complete without reference to those issues. They provide an essential framework for understanding what occurred—and what did not occur.

1.

> It is quite clear that this time something must have happened that we have never experienced before, and must have surprised and astonished the scientists.
>
> DWIGHT D. EISENHOWER,
> commenting on BRAVO,
> March 24, 1954[9]

H-bomb test BRAVO on March 1, 1954, at Bikini in the Marshall Islands, sent shock waves around the world, but whether the scientists were as astonished and surprised as the world's political leaders is an open question. The furor reached its height during Ely's visit to Washington, causing secondary shock waves and anxious speculation about every policy pronouncement relating to Indochina. The largest thermonuclear device ever detonated,

BRAVO was part of the Castle series, for which the United States had unilaterally marked off an area of fifty thousand square miles as its private test site in the Pacific, warning all shipping to stay out.

BRAVO's notoriety arose, in the first instance, because the wind blew in the wrong direction. Shifting in boomerang fashion shortly after detonation, the winds carried deadly radioactive ash back down on American servicemen and inhabitants of the Marshall Islands. That story had broken on March 11, 1954. Three days later a Japanese fishing vessel, *The Lucky Dragon*, which had heeded warnings not to enter the prohibited zone, returned to port laden with twenty-three radiation-stricken seamen. One died soon. Fear of a modern plague falling from the sky spread around the world.

On the morning of the blast, while most of the *Lucky Dragon* crew ate breakfast, one sailor, who had gone on deck to check the nets, saw an awesome sight. "The sun rises in the west," he shouted to his shipmates. The crew thought he had seen a "pikadon," the Japanese word for atomic explosion, but they worked on until a light drizzle fell, coating everything with a sandy white ash. At the end of the day, they decided to return home, still unaware of the danger they had encountered.[10]

Back in America, meanwhile, Congressman Chet Holifield described the blast as so great "that you might say it was out of control." The time had come, he went on, when the people of all nations should know the truth. The danger of destroying civilization "has become real."[11] What was out of control, the H-bomb, or the men who set them off?

Concern about radiation fallout was soon superseded by a new sensation, therefore, as Holifield's statement was juxtaposed with one the head of the Atomic Energy Commission (AEC), Lewis Strauss, made to reporters at a press conference on March 31, 1954. Asked to attend by Eisenhower so that he might dispel the fear that the H-bomb was out of control, Strauss gave the reporters another headline. The bombs could be made as big as one wished, big enough for one to destroy the major cities of the world. "H-BOMB CAN WIPE OUT ANY CITY," began the *New York Times*' front page account of Strauss' answers.[12]

Strauss felt that he had acquitted himself well. A fervent anti-Communist, he suspected that the *Lucky Dragon* was not a fishing boat at all, but a "Red spy outfit."[13] Eisenhower did not think the press conference had gone so well, and neither did the secretary of state. With reporters speculating that the H-bomb popped the genie out of the bottle, Eisenhower's efforts to quiet concern about a "uranium curtain of secrecy" made little headway, especially after his statement about the scientists' surprise. Defense Secretary Wilson further undercut the president by declaring BRAVO's results "so unbelievable the realities are hard to accept." Asked if the United States intended to use the bomb in another war, Wilson said the only thing he could, given New Look assumptions. "Don't you think it would be foolish to spend billions unless you are prepared to use them under some circumstances?"[14]

The sophisticated deterrence justifications of future decades, it must be remembered, had not yet come on the scene. Administration calculations saw the era as one of "nuclear plenty" for the United States. Eisenhower had encouraged planning for the integration of tactical atomic weapons into the standard arsenal, and had made no secret of his intentions in Bermuda. As the leading historian of the "Origins of Overkill," David Alan Rosenberg, writes, "Where Harry Truman viewed the atomic bomb as an instrument of terror and a weapon of last resort, Dwight Eisenhower viewed it as an integral part of American defense, and, in effect, a weapon of first resort."[15]

Plans for the bomb were in the works for local defense in Europe, and Eisenhower had issued veiled warnings about Korea, though, as noted, these were more for political than military requirements, and as much against allied wavering as Russian and Chinese menace. Be these things as they may, next to the Wilson quote in the *Washington Post* that day ran a story entitled "Dulles Talk Stirs Policy Speculation." It began, "Secretary of State John Foster Dulles met with five ambassadors yesterday amid mounting speculation about what he meant by his call for 'united action' to keep Southeast Asia from Communist control."[16]

Two days earlier, on March 29, the AEC chairman and Dulles had a lengthy telephone conversation, during which the secretary expressed concern that Allied fright about the H-bomb was making it difficult to rally support. Admiral Strauss might have countered that it was Dulles who had delivered the "Massive Retaliation" speech, but he chose a different response. The minute of their conversation dictated in the secretary's office records that from the first moment Dulles "mentioned the explosion," Strauss was ready to take on the world. Those who wished "we" did not have such a weapon—and didn't care if Russia had it—had deliberately exaggerated the thing. "Nothing was out of control. Nothing devastated."

Dulles had to disagree. That was not correct, he said. Japan and England were both upset. Strauss reminded him in reply that the Japanese were inside the warning zone. How their tuna got contaminated he did not know, many things were suspicious. That was not the point, Dulles insisted. There was a question of international law. "Can we have an operation that destroys all living things in an 800-mile radius?" No one was killed, Strauss persisted—no fish contaminated, none killed except under the blast.

Obviously Strauss was both bullish and bull-headed about nuclear weapons. The general impression around the world, the secretary replied, was that the United States was appropriating a vast area of the ocean for its personal use, depriving other people, contaminating the fish. But worse than that, people were beginning to feel, especially the British, that their country could be wiped out. Better for them to come to the best terms possible with the Soviets. And so on: "It is driving our Allies away from us. They think we are getting ready for a war of this kind. We could survive but some of them would be obliterated in a few minutes. It could lead to a policy of neutrality or appeasement. They might go into the Soviet-proposed agreement that we will each agree not to use it."[17]

Here was a nice problem for Dulles. That evening he would go to New York intending to stiffen British and French backbones for resisting Communist aggression in Indochina, yet Strauss had gotten backbones stiffened already—with fright. Like Eisenhower, he hoped that Strauss could say something that would "bring this back to the realm of reason."[18] Yet how could he do that? Only two months earlier Dulles had declared that America's strategic policy was massive retaliation at times and places of our choosing. When Strauss told the world that America did indeed have that capability, he demonstrated that while Einstein now ruled physics, old Newtonian principles sometimes dominated politics. For every action, there was an equal and opposite reaction; in this case, as Dulles now feared, a panicked rush toward appeasement.

Indochina was to be the first testing ground for the Eisenhower administration's grand strategy. Postulated as a general theory combining military capability and political courage, the idea was to use atomic superiority not only to hold the Red Army at bay, as in the discarded containment version, but also to impose sanctions on the

Soviet Union's otherwise irresponsible revolutionary behavior, preventing both large-scale aggression as well as new Koreas, i.e., civil wars that engaged outside forces.

After BRAVO it was difficult, and perhaps self-defeating, to get America's allies thinking about atomic weapons in local situations. The H-bomb, it now appeared, deterred America instead. Dulles went on talking about the "brink of war" to reporters, but the general theory had collapsed in a heap at his feet. Who could reconstruct it? Who could think seriously now about winning "limited wars" with "tactical" nuclear weapons, while deterring Communist ground strength (Russian-Chinese-Vietminh), without imagining an escalation to catastrophe? It made America's allies all the more cautious about starting anything that could burgeon upward to a full nuclear exchange.[19]

The French, already paralyzed internally by the disputes over the EDC, had little to say to Americans about the H-bomb, but the British had a great deal to say. Ever since the Bermuda meetings the previous December, Prime Minister Churchill had fretted over Eisenhower's comments regarding the A-bomb. Then, on February 9, 1954, in a long letter signed "Ike E.," the president called upon Churchill to join with him in forming "an association of nations" to include even the "very weak" with clear objectives, an alliance "so firmly confident of its own security that it will have no reason to worry about the possibility that the stupid and savage individuals in the Kremlin will move against us in any vital way."

While Eisenhower would include all "free nations," an inner circle of the most powerful would call the shots. "In some areas and on some subjects, we will have to use cajolery; in others, firmness." It was difficult to fathom Eisenhower's meaning here. Did he intend to say that this new association would substitute for the United Nations, complete with a security council that could mandate its will, when appropriate and necessary? Churchill had long desired an Anglo-Saxon "understanding," had proposed it, in fact, in his 1946 "Iron Curtain" speech. He had always met with a rebuff before, and there was a second question. How would Ike's new inner circle fit into NATO affairs?

In current circumstances, moreover, what stand was the inner circle to take on Indochina? By joining did Great Britain agree to join Washington in putting pressure on France to allow the Indochinese states complete freedom of action as to whether or not they wished to remain in the French Union? Of more concern to the

British at the moment, what would the select few say about Egyptian demands for a British withdrawal? If anything, Eisenhower's letter would push London and Paris closer together to resist American "firmness" or "cajolery."

It was significant, in this regard, that the president listed only third world areas, including Indochina, as points where the Kremlin's ambitions presented serious dangers. What he really seemed to be getting at, once again, was the need for America's allies to follow its lead. Filled with militant images and Manichaean references to history and God, the letter asked the prime minister to link arms in this inner circle to "throw back the Russian threat and allow civilization, as we have known it, to continue its progress." All petty disputes must be put aside. That was the clue, then, to understanding the penultimate peroration and final appeal to destiny that closed the message: "It is only when one allows his mind to contemplate . . . an atheistic materialism in complete domination of all human life, that he fully appreciates how necessary it is to seek renewed faith and strength from his God, and sharpen up his sword for the struggle that cannot possibly be escaped."[20]

Churchill's response, addressed to "My dear Friend," passed quickly from reassurances about their agreement "upon the major issues which overhang the world" to contemplation of the grave changes wrought by the H-bomb. "I understand of course that in speaking of the faith that must inspire us in the struggle against atheistic materialism, you are referring to the spiritual struggle, and that like me, you still believe that War is not inevitable. I am glad to think that in your spirit, as in mine, resolve to find a way out of this agony of peril transcends all else."

To grapple with Eisenhower's religious certitudes, and even more to transubstantiate them back into worldly expressions of a common goal, as Churchill here attempted, required a delicate maneuver by the older man. "Of course," he continued, "I recur to my earlier proposal of a personal meeting between the Three." Then this: "Men have to settle with men, no matter how vast, and in part beyond their comprehension, the business in hand may be. I can even imagine that a few simple words, spoken in the awe which may at once oppress and inspire the speakers might lift this nuclear monster from our world."[21]

Confronted with Churchill's recommendation of a very different "inner circle" to discuss world problems, Eisenhower's answer shifted the subject to the practical difficulties of a meeting of the

Three, citing the issue of French participation and the Russian desire to include China in "oral conversations."[22]

Despite making no progress with the president on the nuclear issue and the value of a summit meeting, Churchill remained loyal to Eisenhower when the Labour party, newly aroused by the BRAVO furor, tried to force both issues in the House of Commons.[23] American possession of the H-bomb weapon, he said in a debate on March 30, 1954, was the greatest possible deterrent there could be to an outbreak of World War III. But the debate did not go well. After he finished his opening statement, former Prime Minister Clement Attlee and Aneurin Bevan, leader of the left wing, pressed him for more facts about the Pacific test series.

His voice thick with emotion, tears in his eyes, the prime minister said almost brokenly, "I haven't got them."[24] It was an awful position for the prime minister to be in. He could say, as he did, that his views were well known on the subject of a summit meeting, as Labour continued to press his most sensitive nerve, Anglo-American relations. But he could not appear to be yielding to Labour, especially to the Bevanites. That would shut off any avenue to Washington, as well as alienating the Tory right.

A full-scale debate was scheduled for April 5, 1954. After a question period in which Churchill was asked if he would invite his French counterpart to London to discuss ways of bringing the fighting to an end in Indochina, and after the foreign secretary was asked if the United States had approached Her Majesty's government about a coordinated defense system for Southeast Asia, Clement Attlee rose to his feet at just after half past three in the afternoon to speak on a motion asking the government to initiate a summit conference, "recognizing that the hydrogen bomb with its immense range and power as disclosed by recent experiments constitutes a grave threat to civilization and that any recourse to war may lead to its use."

It is contended, he said, by "some statesmen in the United States of America" that the "threat of instant retaliation by the use of this weapon can be employed to prevent a resort to armed action anywhere." Avoiding direct reference to the Indochinese crisis, Attlee went on, "Suppose an act of aggression took place now in some part of the world, say on the Burmese border by China." Could one imagine the immediate use of the hydrogen bomb against a capital city of another country? Obviously not. But the danger of a bluff was that it might be called. And even if the bomb were not used—perhaps, indeed, because it could not be used—instead of preventing war, it made it more likely.[25]

Backed into a corner, Churchill lashed out at Attlee for allowing the American Congress to pass legislation in 1946 (the MacMahon Act) effectively nullifying his wartime agreement with Roosevelt to share atomic information.[26] Attlee had done nothing to prevent this, charged the prime minister, when he should have called attention to the agreement. However understandable, especially in the light of his own efforts to move Eisenhower to the summit, Churchill's seeming attempt to turn the debate to partisan advantage caused an outburst in the House.

Amid Labour shouts demanding his resignation, Churchill half-slumped back to his seat. The noise level grew so that the speaker had to call repeatedly for order to hear the prime minister. All at once the debate turned into a review of British dependence on America since World War II. The case was put most effectively by the well-known Labour intellectual John Strachey, who spoke, however, almost as if he had been reading Churchill's private correspondence with Eisenhower or had been privy to the old lion's conversations with his intimates.

The United States had developed a habit of acting first and consulting later, the Labour veteran asserted. It did this in regard to the New Look, and now again in regard to Indochina with Dulles' March 29 speech. "They have actually coined a phrase for this: they call it 'unilateral concerted action'—a very strange phrase indeed." Strachey castigated the American New Look strategic policy, citing American critics for support, as either a bluff or a prescription for nuclear disaster arising from the grotesque notion that atomic weapons could be used in local situations like the current crisis in Indochina. Beware, he warned, of the prophecy in Micah, lest "Zion be ploughed as a field, and Jersualem become heaps."[27]

A younger Labour luminary, Dennis Healey on the party's right, joined with Strachey in calling for a British initiative in the matter of a summit conference, but he believed that the American administration had already realized the uselessness of atom bombs for the Indochina crisis. Yet he was not quite sure. The New Look, he suggested, was "designed for defence against taxation, not against Communism, although one is sometimes inclined to wonder whether some Republicans recognize that there is any difference between the two."[28] Foreign Secretary Anthony Eden closed for the government in conciliatory tones, pledging support for the resolution before the House welcoming an "immediate initiative" for a summit to consider anew reduction and control of armaments and "the strengthening of collective peace through the United Nations Organization." The resolution was agreed to at 10:00 P.M., after more than six and a half hours of floor debate.[29]

American ambassador Winthrop Aldrich observed of the debate that Churchill's decision to assault Labour's supposed supine reaction to the MacMahon Act was, however ill-conceived and poorly executed, an endeavor to demonstrate that the Conservatives could best stand up to the Americans. In the course of the debate, moreover, something else occurred that might bode ill for Anglo-American cooperation. The hitherto fragmented Labour party came together on this issue, as suggested by the agreement between Strachey and Healey.[30]

The previous day, April 4, 1954, Eisenhower had signed a letter to the prime minister renewing his earlier general plea in now very specific terms to join a coalition. Referring to the events of the 1930s, with slightly veiled references to British appeasement, the president averred, "The important thing is that the coalition must be strong and it must be willing to join the fight if necessary. I do not envisage the need of any appreciable ground forces on your or our part." Churchill was not likely to take much reassurance from that statement, nor from the ambiguous warning that followed a few sentences later. "I have faith that by another act of fellowship in the face of peril we shall find a spiritual vigor which will prevent our slipping into the quagmire of distrust."[31]

Seen from London, British choices appeared anything but enviable: the quagmire or the cloud. But Eisenhower's view was also troubled. Referring to the fright caused by the hydrogen bomb tests in the Castle series, he told legislators that he meant to take up with the American people, one by one, the things that were worrying them. "But the important thing, he believed, was to hold 'our coalition' together." It might be well, he mused, to form several new coalitions, "one for every geographical area, especially in view of the slowness of the French in coming around to the right relationship with the natives as regards Indo-China." Exactly how that would address the issues he raised in his various letters to Churchill, or the need to bolster French morale with a willingness to fight, remained unclear, as did the question of how Eisenhower's letter eased Churchill's difficulties in maintaining a loyal posture in regard to the Anglo-American alliance.

The president did realize how much havoc was being wrought by the Castle tests, nevertheless, and thought that once the series was complete, the United States should call for a moratorium on all atomic and hydrogen tests. The crucial point was that the tests continued until May 14, 1954, right through the weeks when Secretary Dulles was pressing hardest for united action in Indochina.[32]

2.

> It is this area of commerce that presents the dilemma to the United States. . . . Since the unmasking of the Soviet designs against western civilization, in conjunction with other free nations we have sought to restrict that trade. This weakened the economies of friendly countries and increased their need for our aid.
>
> Commission on Foreign Economic Policy, January 23, 1954[33]

Churchill sent another long letter on March 24, 1954, expanding the dialogue to include both the H-bomb and East-West trade. He held the view, he said, that easing trade restrictions would aid Russia to develop the kind of consumer-oriented society and political democracy enjoyed in the West. "I hope this process will lead to some relaxation of the grim discipline of the peoples of this vast land ocean of Russia and its satellites." Strategic goods should not be traded, of course, and he admitted that all raw materials and equipment made available to the Soviets went first into Russia's nuclear program, but he asked that Eisenhower consider that the same would be true even under conditions of a total ban on East-West trade.

Having even less to put to alternative uses, the Russians would have correspondingly less reason to modify their hostility to the West.[34] The H-bomb issue dwarfed trade matters, the prime minister believed, but they were related, as efforts to slow Russia's development of the bomb by banning trade could only worsen relations, making war more likely. Churchill's letter was ghostwritten, as it were, by David Lloyd George, who had argued the same case three decades earlier.

As the prime minister sealed his envelope, Harold Stassen, the Eisenhower administration's official in charge of foreign aid programs and East-West trade issues, appeared in London. British efforts to come up with a brand new "short list" of proscribed items led to a "first-class row" with Stassen, and produced the usual American warnings about congressional reactions. Churchill was "hopping mad" at what his efforts had come to, but Anthony Eden, fearing losses of several million pounds in American trade to gain a few million in Russian, sought a compromise. That was not the sort of balance sheet the prime minister thought should be used, but there it was, and little could be done.[35]

The trade issue was not to remain buried in the Eisenhower/Churchill letters, or in second-page stories about Stassen's visit to London. Increasingly, it made cohesion in the West problematical during the Indochina crisis, and was seen in tandem with the hydrogen bomb as American "unilateral concerted action." "If the United States will not let us pay for her goods by rendering reciprocal services and make a reasonable proportion of things your people want or might be attracted by, as is our deep desire, the present deadlock must continue." So wrote Churchill of the general problem during the March exchanges with Eisenhower. And then there was the problem of Germany and Japan. "The arrival of Germany and Japan in the world market make it necessary that we should open out our trade in every possible direction for we have to keep 50 million people alive in this small island as well as maintaining the greatest armaments next to your own in the free world."[36]

Along with Churchill's appeal, Eisenhower had received a 138-page report from the British, outlining what "administration sources" said was a "rather radical revision of the lists of strategic goods."[37] The president's short reply to Churchill merely reiterated the standard American position that "your proposals in this field seem to go a bit further than seems wise or necessary," and expressed the hope that disagreements could be worked out when American negotiators reached London.[38]

"To put the brakes on moves toward relaxing East-West trade restrictions," read newspaper accounts, Eisenhower had sent Harold Stassen to meet with British and French leaders.[39] But the president knew full well that the heart of the matter was the traditional American reluctance to play the role of creditor nation, and its political inability to sacrifice its much greater agricultural interests to achieve free trade, as Great Britain had done after the Napoleonic Wars.

To reeducate the public toward liberalized trade policies, Eisenhower had appointed a prestigious commission headed by steel man Clarence Randall to make the argument so plain that Congress could not ignore its logic. It was a vexing problem indeed. In his *Memoirs*, Ike cited Joseph Stalin's "last public political pronouncement" in October 1952 on the developing crisis in world capitalism. So much of the world had become alienated from the West, Stalin had said, that Britain, France, and the United States could not make room for German and Japanese goods. Inevitably, concluded the Russian leader, Britain and France (on whom the burden fell) would have to "break from the embrace of the United States" and try to "smash United States domination." Then the Soviet Union's "moment for the decisive blow" would arrive.[40]

However far-fetched Stalin's supposed expectations or Eisenhower's fears, the pressure was on. Japan realized that the Korean War bonanza was over, it was reported at the beginning of the year, and that its trade prospects in Europe and the United States would not take up the slack. With the likelihood of a trade deficit in 1954, the Japanese were paying attention to American advisers who were encouraging them to make peace with all their former enemies. "Under these circumstances the lush fields to the south are beginning to look more attractive."[41]

Some German industrialists, noted High Commissioner James B. Conant in testimony to the Senate Foreign Relations Committee, were looking eastward for new markets. But the real threat was to the British in world markets. "They are going to make a strong competition for heavy goods passing to the world." His office thought it was a pity that the Germans were not concentrating more on developing the home market. They were trying to do too much in the export market. "They are not in the long run going to make a stable situation of it, for themselves or the world."

SENATOR [H. ALEXANDER] Smith. You feel there is a real problem there?

DR. CONANT. I do.

SENATOR SMITH. We have the same thing, you see, with Japan. They are increasing their production and cannot do anything about it.

DR. CONANT. That's right. It is the wrong kind of production.

SENATOR SMITH. The British are in trouble, too.

DR. CONANT. You see, this is the old pattern the Germans have.[42]

At the same time it was tabling motions on the hydrogen bomb and a summit conference, the British Labour party was also urging more action on East-West trade. Rumors were widespread that the Soviet Union was prepared to place orders for over $1 billion during the next three years, and the Conservative minister for trade, Peter Thorneycraft, assured the House that the government desired the "maximum degree of trade" with the Soviet Union.[43]

On March 29, 1954, the day that Dulles delivered the "Uniting for Action" speech in New York, the same day, also, that Harold Stassen and Thorneycraft argued over short lists in London, Eisenhower presented Clarence Randall to a legislative leaders meeting for a preliminary discussion of the message on foreign trade he would deliver the next day. When the discussion turned to East-West trade, Randall assured the congressional figures that the president's policy would not strengthen the Soviet Union. But Eisenhower interrupted. The "unpleasant truth we have to face up to," he said, "is that we are going to have to fight Russia either in a trade war or in a hot war—[we have] got to win a lot of people to our side." The allies were saying, "All right, you want to limit trade with us; won't let us trade with Russia—what do you want us to do—starve?"[44] When one legislator, Dan Reed, complained that he had in his office a Japanese doll with a price of three cents on it, Eisenhower again interrupted, this time more vehemently. "Never mind the dolls—let's put our minds to the Pacific testing grounds—Russia can carry three bombs and deliver them—the world is rapidly approaching the cross roads—we have got to help by understanding the problems of our allies and the free world."[45]

At a cabinet meeting on March 26, 1954, Eisenhower had listened to the head of his Council of Economic Advisers, Arthur Burns, describe the need to stop worrying so much about inflation (the traditional Republican concern) and do some thinking about how to prevent the current recession from sliding into depression. "Don't let's get tagged like Mr. Hoover did unjustly of not doing something, we must be out in front," said the president. "We must get going now." Everyone around the table also heard Dulles describe the international ramifications of the tremors disturbing the American economy. The next few months were critical. As critical as any America had faced. EDC, Reds in Italy, Latin American fears: "If on top of all that we do not intend to buy abroad—to give some kind of economic aid—then we cannot hope to prevent an increasing opening of trade with Russia and China."[46]

Eisenhower had come upon a copy of William McKinley's last speech, he later wrote a close friend, delivered the day before he was shot. Fifty years ago that Republican leader had put the case for reciprocal trade agreements and an end to economic isolation. Yet an "astonishing number" of people still did not understand the situation. They failed to see that unless we "pursue a policy that permits them to make a living, we are doomed to eventual isolation and to the disappearance of our form of government."[47]

The Randall Commission proposed two logical remedies: more imports and a higher level of nonstrategic East-West trade. But the commission had not recommended lowering barriers on *any* trade items to North Korea or China. And this was the rub. On March 30, 1954, at the very height of the Indochina crisis, Eisenhower sent the report to Congress asking for authority to reduce American tariff barriers. "Beyond our economic interest, the solidarity of the free world and the capacity of the free world to deal with those who would destroy it are threatened by continued unbalanced trade relationships," the president concluded.[48]

The administration feared, on the other hand, that if Japan was allowed to resume trade relations with China, it might be lost to the Communists. In the long term, Eisenhower's biographer Stephen Ambrose observes, "he wanted to get the Japanese to sell their goods on the Asian mainland, which was one reason he put such stress on holding on in Indochina." As he told the cabinet, "If China finds that it can buy cheap straw hats, cheap cotton shirts, sneakers, bicycles, and all the rest of that sort of stuff from Japan, it would seem to me that would set up the need within China for dependence upon Japan." Japan would have to be watched closely.[49]

The United States was not the only one doing the watching. Both Great Britain and France were also on the alert. In their view, of course, it had always been a mistake to attempt to keep Japan from the mainland. But they meant the Chinese mainland. Holding on to Indochina for the Japanese, possibly risking nuclear war on that account—how could anything be less conducive to allied support for escalating the Indochina crisis into a showdown? French soldiers were to die for that? Since the time of the Japanese peace treaty negotiations, American emphasis on finding Japan outlets in Southeast Asia had also been an irritant in Anglo-American relations. And, as we have seen, the French had imagined that they could do a deal with China that would at one and the same time protect their economic interests in Indochina while opening up contacts with the new regime in Beijing.

These tendencies in both British and French policy reflected "national" interests, and it did not matter that specifics varied, as they naturally would, from Attlee to Churchill, or from Laniel to Mendès-France. The other side of this story, however, reveals both the French and the British gradually turning away from a once-ardent desire to "stand and fight" in Indochina, and especially not so that the United States could find alternative markets for Japan in preference to allowing trade with Communist China, or to keep three-cent Japanese dolls out of America.

It is in this context, as well as the traditional view, that one should consider President Eisenhower's words at his famous press conference on April 7, 1954, ever afterward known as the birth of the "domino thesis." The tale of falling dominoes began when Eisenhower was asked to explain Indochina's "strategic importance." His answer is worth quoting in full:

> THE PRESIDENT. You have, of course, both the specific and the general when you talk about such things.
>
> First of all, you have the specific value of a locality in its production of materials that the world needs.
>
> Then you have the possibility that many human beings pass under a dictatorship that is inimical to the free world.
>
> Finally, you have broader considerations that might follow what you would call the "falling domino" principle. You have a row of dominoes set up, you knock over the first one, and what will happen to the last one is the certainty that it will go over very quickly. So you could have a beginning of a disintegration that would have the most profound influences.
>
> Now, with respect to the first one, two of the items from this particular area that the world uses are tin and tungsten. They are very important. There are others, of course, the rubber plantations and so on.
>
> Then with respect to more people passing under this domination, Asia, after all, has already lost some 450 million of its peoples to the Communist dictatorship, and we simply can't afford greater losses.
>
> But when we come to the possible sequence of events, the loss of Indochina, of Burma, of Thailand, of the Peninsula, and Indonesia following, now you begin to talk about areas that not

only multiply the disadvantages that you would suffer through loss of materials, sources of materials, but now you are talking really about millions and millions and millions of people.

Finally, the geographical position achieved thereby does many things. It turns the so-called island defensive chain of Japan, Formosa, of the Philippines and to the southward; it moves in to threaten Australia and New Zealand.

It takes away, in its economic aspects, that region that Japan must have as a trading area or Japan, in turn, will have only one place in the world to go—that is, toward the Communist areas in order to live.

So, the possible consequences of the loss are just incalculable to the free world.[50]

3.

I feared that unless there was a clear US-UK position, the French would in fact sell out in Indochina, and that the entire area of Southeast Asia would be greatly endangered, with serious consequences to both our countries and to Australia and New Zealand.

JOHN FOSTER DULLES,
conversation with
Sir Roger Makins,
March 30, 1954[51]

During General Ely's Washington visit another State Department official, Douglas MacArthur II, had told Makins that the-French were paralyzing American Far Eastern policy. The general had come without a policy in mind—only a shopping list. The situation, said MacArthur, could not be remedied simply by American pressure. It would take London's support, but not only that, it would also require commonwealth backing. They would all have to put their shoulders to the wheel. American policy was at a crossroads, added MacArthur. If the Indochina and EDC issues were not resolved within a few weeks, he could envision an Asia-first or neo-isolationist move away from Europe.[52]

Always eager to help Anglo-American relations around any awkward corners, Makins put his mind to work. But he encountered a contradiction. If it took British and commonwealth support to move France in directions the United States wanted it to go, how effective could a threat of an Asia-first policy really be? Dealing with American frustrations, however, and reconciling such contradictions, was no new assignment. It went back to World War II days when Britons admonished themselves to be like the Greeks: instructors to the Roman imperium.[53]

Meanwhile, in London, Soviet diplomats stressed the need to end the fighting in Indochina. The Russians insisted that American talk about Chinese aid was exaggerated out of reason. And there was no Russian aid to speak of. Caught out, the Americans would just have to take their medicine, and make the necessary concessions to Ho's forces. In Whitehall no one doubted Moscow's self-interested reasons for striking a disinterested pose—or its desire to reap all the benefits therefrom on every side—but equally apparent was Russian concern about America going off the deep end. What, asked the Soviet charge in London, did the British make of a recent meeting between President Eisenhower and General MacArthur?[54]

For Americans, however, the crucial meetings were with Ely. It is time now to talk about them in detail. Dulles had tried to set the mood by telling the press that the United States could see no reason to abandon the Navarre Plan, nor any possibility of negotiating with the Chinese Communists—until they gave up aiding the Vietminh "and thereby demonstrate that they are not still aggressors in spirit."[55]

When Ely walked into Dulles' office, he believed that Dienbienphu had no better than a fifty-fifty chance and asked straight out what the Americans were prepared to do if Chinese MIG fighters appeared over Indochina. Dulles parried this with a comment about the serious consequences of showing the American flag. "We could not afford thus to engage the prestige of the United States and suffer a defeat which would have worldwide repercussions." There would have to be a full "partnership" not only with the French, but also with the Vietnamese. Asked for specifics, the secretary reminded Ely and his aides that the United States had had considerable experience in Greece and Korea with this sort of problem.[56]

Ely later recalled that the secretary of state impressed him as overly preoccupied with political conditions, evasive on specifics, yet adamant about resisting what Dulles regarded as clear-cut Chinese aggression. He also recalled that Admiral Radford suggested Eisenhower would be less fussy about the political conditions. Much controversy would arise out of the Radford-Ely exchanges, both formal and informal. Suffice it to say here that Ike was playing his cards very close to the vest at this time, allowing both Dulles and Radford to take heart that the president was going along for more than the ride.[57]

Thus when Eisenhower talked with the secretary the following day, the president refused to rule out "the possibility of a single strike, if it were almost certain this would produce decisive results."[58] If he gave Dulles this guidance, or even if he was simply mulling things over, most certainly Admiral Radford would not have been slow to pick up on the theme. Radford had been trying to convince Ely that Indochina was like Korea, meanwhile, steering the talk away from the general's tendency to talk about prospects for a negotiated settlement. Radford even brought up the possibility of an offensive all the way up to the Chinese border. He had some success. As would be the case in general with military men, it was painful for Ely to consider negotiations under present conditions as anything but defeat in disguise.[59]

Ely did not, however, accept the American admiral's insistence that the solution to Indochina's problem was to treat it militarily like Korea. He might have said, but did not, that the American campaign to the Yalu was hardly a good precedent for the French in Indochina. After some further discussion, Radford suggested that Ely stay an extra day, as the National Security Council was meeting on the morning of March 25, 1954. Radford and Dulles held an informal planning session for that meeting over the telephone. The admiral believed that it was time to face facts: (1) the French continue to resist training missions; (2) left alone they might walk out in two to three weeks; (3) "We have to do something to avoid the accusation we would not help them in their hour of need."

Dulles was still reluctant to give the OK to a plan to engage the flag directly, as he had put it, but thought it might be possible to step up activities along the coast of China and from Formosa. But he agreed with the admiral that "we must have a policy of our own even if France falls down." Radford said that he would brief the president and Defense Secretary Wilson before the National Security Council met the next day.[60]

The NSC discussions roamed over political questions, with very little attention devoted to actual military steps that might be taken. Eisenhower brought up congressional and constitutional restraints, canvased a possible approach to the United Nations, discarded that when Dulles talked about how difficult it would be to get a two-thirds vote, and settled for the moment on expanding

ANZUS into a regional defense organization to take up the burden. Of course, said Dulles, the real problem remained France. "Either it would be necessary for the United States to beat the French into line, or else to accept a split with France." Neither alternative looked truly promising.[61]

The discussion had been surprisingly vague and rambling, given Radford's conviction, albeit not entirely shared by Dulles, that immediate action was imperative. Perhaps Radford felt he had gotten all he needed from his private conference with the president before the meeting. In any event, that afternoon he unveiled an intervention plan later dubbed by the French Operation Vulture. If France made a formal request, said Radford with a "certain insistence," the United States would consider using "strategic air power" to save Dienbienphu. B-29s from the Philippines, the admiral added, supported by fighters from American aircraft carriers, could lift the siege. And there was practically no risk of a war with China. According to Ely, moreover, Radford assured him he had the president's approval to say that any request would be considered quickly. What Radford meant to convey and what General Ely understood him to mean became a matter of dispute. In any event, Ely thought he heard a promise.[62]

Radford later claimed that he had intended no such thing. In truth, neither Dulles nor Radford, let alone Ely, could be sure where Eisenhower's arrow would finally point. It spun around the circle of options by the hour, momentarily indicating one thing to a first adviser, another to a second, and still something else to himself. This was common enough in presidential decision-making. Throughout his presidency, however, Eisenhower often used the NSC and his close advisers in a special way. He would lead them along, hinting at something or other, until he could get them to express ideas that he was testing out privately or, alternatively, that he wanted to smoke out so as to clear the boards. Sometimes he wanted to hear what his ideas sounded like bounced back to him like an echo; other times he wanted to haul in an elusive darter much the same way as he scooped fish out of streams in the Colorado Rockies.

One thing is sure. Ely rightly detected the differences in Radford's presentations from what he had heard in Dulles' office. The secretary envisioned a prior French commitment to a two-stage process. Military action to save Dienbienphu was only a holding action until a permanent Southeast Asian regional defense organization could take over the fight. From Admiral Radford, however, Ely gleaned, perhaps mistakenly, that Eisenhower was not so insistent on the second stage, at least not the way the secretary of state insisted it must be.[63]

To Ely's way of thinking, ironically, Radford's proposed air strike would actually be *less provocative* to the Chinese than the political schemes of John Foster Dulles, and certainly less provocative to French sensibilities. Once a defense system was set in place, he pointed out in his memoirs, how could the Chinese not see that as a fundamental challenge? And respond to it as such? "This is why France was not favorable to the conclusion before Geneva of a spectacular military alliance for the defense of this part of the world."[64]

Admiral Radford was frequently heard to say, on the other hand, that if war with China was necessary better to have it sooner rather than later. He made no secret of his views on that score, but neither did he think China would accept the challenge. Ely apparently believed him, if for different reasons than the admiral advanced. Seeking a deal with China, Paris did not want to find out if Beijing could let pass a "spectacular military alliance," one which would seek permanent military bases in Indochina. After all, the situation really was not analogous to the European postwar position, where Russia had established a row of buffer states in Eastern Europe.

A second controversy arose over the question of whether atomic bombs were ever considered in discussions of Operation Vulture, or at a later time during the Geneva Conference itself. On this point General Ely and Georges Bidault present very different accounts of their dealings with their American interlocutors. Bidault's assertion that John Foster Dulles offered to "loan" the French use of atomic bombs at the end of the Dienbienphu crisis is better discussed later.[65] General Ely commented in his memoirs, on the other hand, that the idea that anyone was discussing atomic bombs as part of Vulture was "very fanciful."[66]

Yet not unimaginable. On the day Radford outlined Vulture to his French visitor, a Pentagon study concluded that atomic weapons could be used to lift the siege at Dienbienphu. But army and air force analysts who studied the plan agreed that the loss of Dienbienphu would be less costly than the political consequences of dropping one or more atomic bombs in its vicinity.[67] Even so, and despite further air force studies that disputed the original claim that the Dienbienphu area offered a suitable target, the air force chief of staff, General

Nathan Twining, held to the view that "three small tactical A-bombs" could have saved the day. "It's a fairly isolated area," he later contended, "Dien Bien Phu—no great towns around there, only Communists and their supplies."[68]

He and Radford agreed, added Twining, but they were the only ones. "We didn't want to bomb the mainland of China—the whole area." But Dienbienphu was a good target. And it would do more than lift the siege: "You could take all day to drop a bomb, make sure you put it in the right place. No opposition. And clean those Commies out of there and the band could play the Marseillaise and the French would come marching out of Dien Bien Phu in fine shape. And those Commies would say, 'Well, those guys may do this again to us. We'd better be careful.' "[69]

But instead of atomic bombs, Ike had apparently decided to take a chance on the rainy season. It might not save Dienbienphu, but if the French could only sit down man-to-man and talk it out, they would realize that the situation was not so desperate. "You know," he told the cabinet, "in rainy weather, a pack train will eat up all its food in 60 days. There's no useful food after that time." If only the French would listen.[70]

Maybe they would listen to the British. But who would the British listen to?

4.

> To bring UK to greater recognition its own responsibilities, we are talking very frankly to Australians and New Zealanders here regarding problem (which involves their vital security) in hope they will press British stand firmly with us.
>
> DULLES to American Embassy, London, April 1, 1954[71]

The effort at friendly persuasion began in earnest with the "Uniting for Action" speech on March 29, 1954. The administration, read James Reston's lead article in the *New York Times* the next morning, had taken a "fundamental policy decision to block the Communist conquest of Southeast Asia. . . . It can be stated on the highest authority that this is the meaning of the key paragraph in the speech of John Foster Dulles."[72]

And Dulles so informed Sir Roger Makins, in case he had not had a chance to read Reston's story. "I said that the central paragraph of my address of last night was based on a unanimous position paper of our JCS, who took a very serious view of the situation." Unless the U.K.-U.S. position was made absolutely clear, the French were ready to "sell out," endangering all of Southeast Asia and Australia and New Zealand. The ambassador assured the secretary he had been seeking guidance from London, and asked for a little more time.[73]

Eisenhower did his bit as well. At lunch with newspaper chieftains Roy Howard and Walker Stone, the president said he might have to make a decision to send in squadrons from two aircraft carriers to bomb the Reds at Dienbienphu—"Of course, if we did, we'd have to deny it forever."[74] It was strange to include newsmen, of all people, in such a confidence—if Eisenhower really wanted it to be a confidence. Likewise, what was one to make of Dulles' confidence to English journalist Henry Brandon? Asked in private by Brandon if his speech was meant to herald American entry into the war, the secretary leaned forward, then tipped his chair back: "I can tell you that American aircraft carriers are at this moment steaming into the Gulf of Tonkin ready to strike." Had it all been decided, then? "Not yet."[75]

Not yet was the right answer for any of the variables in this equation. Dulles was in the position of a social-climbing party giver. He needed someone to accept his invitation so that he could persuade all the others to come. So badly did he need that someone that he told a little white lie. The Joint Chiefs were not at all unanimous on the question of American intervention, as he had informed Sir Roger Makins. In fact the service chiefs were unanimously opposed when the question was put to them directly. It was only Admiral Radford, the chairman, who stood out in favor.[76]

Makins had warned London about the "Uniting for Action" speech two days before it was delivered, adding that "it would not be in harmony with your views." So now the Foreign Office had to begin wrestling with the likelihood that America would seek to replace a French holding action with a World War II "V is for Victory" plan. The question for consideration in Whitehall was how to prevent a disaster like Korea from happening again—this time with an atomic ending.[77]

Sir Roger's account of his March 30 telephone conversation with Dulles repeated the secretary's assertion of JCS approval, though in somewhat modified language, and added the note that Dulles had promised the United States would not do anything "silly," such as putting ground troops into Indochina. As Makins explained it, the major emphasis was to be on finding a way to force Paris' hand on the issue of training Vietnamese soldiers up to the standard and size of army needed to defeat the Communists. When Ely had posed the question of Chinese air intervention, the answer he had been given was essentially, nothing, unless you come around.[78]

Even when rephrased in this fashion, the invitation had little appeal. Foreign Secretary Anthony Eden replied on April 1, 1954, welcoming Makins' recent reports that the administration had—"rightly in our view"—rejected intervention by American forces as a solution. After this feigned—"second the motion" and "hear, hear"—ploy, Eden turned to the continuing illusion that Franco-Vietnamese forces with American aid, and possibly under American leadership, could win the war. In the first place, instead of being forced toward that position, the reports he had from Paris indicated that such a policy was in fact becoming "increasingly unacceptable."[79] And while Her Majesty's government fully shared American desire to prevent a Communist takeover, earnest study had convinced them that it would be unrealistic not to face the possibility that conditions permitting a favorable outcome no longer existed. To ignore this possibility, he ended, was likely to increase the difficulty of tripartite agreement "should we be forced at Geneva to accept a policy of compromise with the Communists in Indo-China."[80]

A third guest Dulles needed to have present if the party was to succeed at all was Congress. Before he could even think about a way to get around Eden's polite decline, he had to make sure of Congress. Eisenhower had told him there would be no intervention without a favorable nod from Capitol Hill. An expert in international law, Dulles saw this reticent behavior as more a question of scruple than legal limits on the presidency. The secretary had been working on Eisenhower for some time on this score, although he was also anxious for a regional defense treaty so as to give the president the ability to bypass Congress when an emergency demanded.[81]

The draft congressional resolution Dulles carried in his briefcase to a White House meeting on April 2, 1954, with Admiral Radford and the president attempted to cover both contingencies. It stipulated that since the "Chinese Communist regime and its agents in Indochina" had initiated an armed attack against Vietnam, threatening peace and security throughout the entire Pacific area, including all those nations "with whom the United States has treaties of mutual security and defense," Congress hereby resolves to grant the president authority to employ naval and air forces to assist the forces resisting aggression, and to prevent its extension elsewhere.[82]

Eisenhower liked the draft. But he cautioned Dulles to allow congressional leaders to find their own way to reach a conclusion, and thereby to make it appear that the resolution was their own idea and not one "drafted by ourselves." Dulles said he understood, and would seek to accomplish that end the next day when he and Radford met with them. The secretary casually mentioned there might be "some difference in approach" between himself and Admiral Radford that ought to be clarified before the meeting. What he meant, Dulles explained, was that he would not approve of a military action without having a French commitment to the regional defense system.[83]

Before Eisenhower could react, Radford, who had been urging intervention as almost a question of hours, blurted out that the situation at Dienbienphu did not require American participation. He did not exclude, however, the possibility that at some later stage in the war, American intervention might be useful and necessary.[84] Dulles' position is usually interpreted as the prudent one, as opposed to Radford's volatile "brinkmanship."[85] And the secretary did remind Eisenhower that congressional and public opinion needed the framework of a defensive alliance. But most of all, Dulles hated the thought of giving away the "reward" of a military strike—which might actually get the French off his hook if it worked—before he had a commitment to American political demands. Radford's sudden reconsideration suggests, in this view, not a change of heart so much as his dawning understanding of the secretary's wisdom about the best way to proceed with getting the French out successfully—which might, worse come to worst, involve letting Dienbienphu fall.[86]

More and more, Americans were reaching the conclusion that the French military effort in Indochina had to be separated from American policy. This was a hard thing to consider, of course, since so much had been expended in trying to preserve that effort, but a clean cut was preferable in many ways to events dragging on to a ragged ending. Getting the French out successfully meant preparing the way for a new policy, and that could well mean, therefore, not bombing at Dienbienphu, not further military aid, but cutting losses as soon as possible. The best choice, of course, would be for France to turn over the direction of the war in time for the Americans to save Dienbienphu, or to give it a good try.

When Dulles and his aides met with Sir Roger Makins to initiate discussions of a Southeast Asian defense system, the ambassador only cursorily hinted at Eden's doubts about such a scheme, saying that London was more pessimistic about the outcome than Washington and considered partition the least undesirable of all the solutions. Makins' account of the talk included several points, on the other hand, skipped over in the American record. According to Sir Roger, Dulles implied that if Great Britain would not support the United States, the administration would have to take action with others, i.e., Chiang Kai-shek and Syngman Rhee, rather than see the warning in the "Uniting for Action" speech mocked as an empty bluff.[87]

Balancing his worst case analysis with happier thoughts, Dulles proposed that the British consider that if the Western position were made absolutely clear to China, then surely the Russians would put pressure on Beijing to cease and desist. And surely, also, the greater the number in the alliance, the less chance there would be of war.[88]

All Dulles could tell congressional leaders in response to their sharp questions on April 3 was that he had initiated discussions with America's allies. Radford's position was more ambiguous. He had to admit that none of the service chiefs supported his position in favor of military action. The "consultation" did not really go well at all, in large part because of the confusion Dulles had feared between his position and that, previously and now again, argued by Admiral Radford. Ironically, the main consolation for Dulles was that the single-strike plan was now shelved permanently, as the legislators insisted that before Congress acted the allies would have to be signed up.

The other side of that, of course, was that Dulles would have preferred to have the congressional RSVP in hand before he went ahead with efforts to convince the Europeans to come.[89] When Dulles reported to Eisenhower, who had carefully kept in the background, that "on the whole it went pretty well, although it raised some serious problems," it was the president who suggested that the secretary first go to work in an effort to build his system on the solid base of ANZUS.[90] The American military pact with Australia and New Zealand, ANZUS, had come into being originally as an inducement to Canberra and Auckland to agree to liberal terms in the peace treaty with Japan. Though London had concurred at the time that ANZUS was a good idea, it had become increasingly uneasy with an arrangement that cut across commonwealth lines, and which was a daily reminder of Britain's postwar decline into the second rank of world powers.

On Sunday, April 4, 1954, at 4:00 P.M., Sir Percy Spender of Australia and New Zealand's Sir Leslie Munro were received by Dulles at home.[91] Waiting in the library were Admiral Radford, Walter Bedell Smith, and two other aides. When everyone was comfortable, Dulles began. The administration could see nothing in any of the solutions that might emerge from Geneva except a disguised surrender: either by the French or by the Communists. That being so, and the likelihood of it being a French surrender as matters stood, the situation was fraught with danger for all the Pacific area. He stressed the position Japan would find itself in with the loss of Southeast Asia. Japan would be tempted to seek an accommodation with China, "whereby in exchange for raw materials they would find a market for their industry." What was needed was a new force.

The fact was, continued Dulles (now seconded by Radford), that if things could be held in place until Geneva and the rainy season, the French had no reason to fear defeat. Next to France, Great Britain had the most to lose in Southeast Asia itself. But the United States could not fight alone to preserve the British position in Malaya. With the cooperation of London, however, all things were possible, especially since Congress would then pass a resolution granting extra powers to the president.

In these circumstances Dulles believed that the Russians would rein in their Chinese allies, and simply write off Ho. The impression he had received from Molotov at the Berlin Conference was that the Russians feared a third world war, and would deter the Chinese from extending the war in Asia. When he had discussed the situation with Ambassador Makins, however, Dulles complained gently to the ANZUS diplomats, he had discovered that British thoughts seemed to be directed toward finding the "least bad" exit from Indochina, a partition perhaps along the line of the sixteenth parallel.

At this point, Dulles rose "rather ponderously" and selected the first volume of Winston Churchill's history of World War II from a shelf in back of him. Opening it to a certain page, he referred them to Churchill's account of the 1932 episode when his predecessor,

Henry L. Stimson, had sought in vain to enlist British foreign secretary Sir John Simon in a common effort to block Japanese expansionism. Churchill had excused Simon's behavior on the grounds that the British had no hopes of a securing a corresponding American involvement in Europe, where its primary problems lay, and also could be placing at risk considerable material interests in the Far East just to support this American lead.[92]

But America was involved today, said Dulles, closing the book, and "had definitely proved that she was vitally concerned with Europe." From Australia and New Zealand the United States wanted a commitment of naval forces, probably a carrier from each. But more than that, it wanted political support in Whitehall. Should London not see fit under these circumstances to take a stand, the secretary feared Congress would pull back to the Western Hemisphere, there to build a military version of Winthrop's "City on a Hill." Would America be involved tomorrow, he implied, was the question of questions about Indochina.

5.

> The United States is less and less disposed to risk sending her own men into the melee. . . . Well satisfied that the French are carrying the weight of the battle in Indo-China, she is ready to contribute matériel and money, but wants to decide how that battle is carried on and appears to be ready to throw in contingents of yellow and white peoples supplied by her allies in Asia and Australasia and even to employ her own long range weapons. But she has no thought of contributing battalions.
>
> CHARLES DE GAULLE, press conference, April 7, 1954[93]

Though out of power, de Gaulle was never out of touch. As he spoke to reporters in Paris, Washington had already turned down flat a French request for an air strike at Dienbienphu. Ely had gone home thinking that Admiral Radford's assurances were tantamount to an Eisenhower commitment. His task, then, was to convince the nervous politicians in Paris, and to do that he sent a representative to secure General Navarre's approval.[94]

Dislike of American interference mixed in Navarre's mind with fears that an American air strike would lead to war with China. Ely's messenger spoke of atomic bombs, adding still more controversy over the years to a political landscape already strewn with misgivings. Yet he was tempted. News that another outpost at the besieged fortress Huguette had fallen on April 1 had to be weighed on the other side.

Navarre finally said no. But when Colonel Raymond Brohon returned to Paris with that message, his discussion with Ely was interrupted. A top secret cable had been received from Hanoi: "The intervention of which Colonel Brohon has informed me can have a decisive effect, above all if it is made before the Viet Minh [general] assault."[95]

Ely went at once to Defense Minister René Pleven. An evening meeting was scheduled with Premier Laniel. Around the table sat Pleven and Laniel, Foreign Minister Georges Bidault, and the Committee of National Defense. They were besieged no less than the enlisted men at Dienbienphu. On the right Charles de Gaulle sniped at the government for its sniveling subservience to the United States over the EDC. But the greater threat at the moment was Mendès-France, whose assault from the left was more on the order of a panzer attack.

Colonel Brohon briefed the committee on the situation at Dienbienphu. Questions were asked. The replies fell like the guillotine's blade. Illusions at last severed from reality, the committee considered its choices. To accept the American "offer" meant risking war with China, and perhaps forsaking any chance of détente with the new Soviet leaders. Not to accept risked their careers, and, as it would always seem to men in power, the fate of their country.

In this instance they had some reason to believe that actually might be the case. That very afternoon, five thousand veterans had pummeled Pleven and Laniel at a ceremony near the Arc de Triomphe honoring the dead of the Indochina War. Laniel was chased to his limousine, where demonstrators tried to overturn the vehicle. Shaking their fists, the crowd cried at the premier, "Resign you swine." Another group surrounded Pleven and tore off his glasses. The defense minister was manhandled for ten minutes before police could regain control of the situation. The veterans finally retreated, shouting, "Pleven to Dienbienphu."[96]

More than Dienbienphu might be rescued by the American airplanes. At 11:00 P.M. a call was placed to the American Embassy. To a surprised Ambassador Douglas Dillon, Premier Laniel recited Radford's "personal assurance" that he would do his best to obtain aircraft support at Dienbienphu. Bidault ended the conversation with a melodramatic flourish: "For good or evil the fate of Southeast Asia now rested on Dien Bien Phu."[97]

At about half past eight o'clock the next morning, April 5, Dulles called the president and read parts of the Dillon cable to him. They agreed the answer must be no. The conditions for intervention had been laid down at the meeting with the congressional leaders, conditions, of course, that Dulles had wanted all along. Eisenhower suggested that Radford must have believed he was talking to Ely in confidence, though what difference that would have made was hard to see. For his part, Dulles responded that he was sure Radford had made no commitment. But was he? For then he went on to add that he had spoken already that morning with the admiral, and Radford was "reconciled" to the impossibility of wading in this way. "We can't lose our prestige by going in and being defeated," Dulles said, continuing his old line of argument. We would have to say, the president concluded, this would be unconstitutional and indefensible. But while he ruled out engaging "in war," the president told Dulles to see what alternatives Radford might have for them to consider.[98]

The secretary knew what alternatives there were without asking, at least what ones suited him. Speaking with New Zealand's Leslie Munro the next day, Dulles mentioned the cable as a "rather hysterical request" for action. "The general impression he received from the United States Embassy in Paris was that the French Government is 'running around like a chicken with its head off.' " This country, he went on, was "not to be dragged into the struggle piecemeal or to go in except on a basis that would convince the American public of the justification for the intervention."[99]

At the NSC meeting on April 6, Dulles once again explained why the only course the United States could follow was the one he had devised: no military intervention without a French commitment to "internationalize" the war. Interestingly, Dulles' arguments triggered a response from three NSC members, Vice-President Nixon, Defense Secretary Wilson, and Treasury Secretary George Humphrey, all of whom were concerned about the implications of a deeper American involvement in Vietnamese internal politics—an issue that would come to the fore after Geneva. Humphrey, a thoroughgoing conservative, asked outright if this policy was not getting awfully close to "policing all the governments of the world."

Both Eisenhower and Dulles jumped at him. "We can no longer accept further Communist take-overs," said the latter, "whether accomplished by external or internal measures. We could no longer afford to put too fine a point on the methods." "George," the president intervened, "you exaggerate the case. Nevertheless in certain areas at least we cannot afford to let Moscow gain another bit of territory. Dien Bien Phu may be just such a critical point."

That was the hard thing to decide. He was not prepared to go in alone, but the coalition program would have to go ahead "as a matter of the greatest urgency." "If we can secure this regional grouping . . . the battle is two-thirds won. This grouping would give us the needed popular support of domestic opinion and of allied governments, and we might thereafter not be required to contemplate a unilateral American intervention in Indochina."[100]

Now Dulles would have a clear field, in the sense that the Radford "option" had been argued out, and doubters about the wisdom of getting involved at all in Indochina had the president's word that it would be done through a collective security arrangement. Dulles was ready to make the running.

CHAPTER SEVEN

Mr. Dulles on the Grand Tour

> I have just been talking with President Eisenhower about the quick trip to Europe which I am making. I am getting off tonight for London and for Paris, and I expect to be back by the end of the week. I am going, in order to consult with the British and French governments about some of the very real problems that are involved in creating the obviously desirable united front to resist communist aggression in Southeast Asia.
>
> JOHN FOSTER DULLES, April 10, 1954[1]

A FAMOUS story from the Eisenhower years has a frustrated president exclaim as he watches Dulles rush off yet again, "Don't do something, Foster, just stand there!" Another depicts his arrival in an unnamed foreign country. "We are glad to see you, Mr. Secretary," declares his host. "You shouldn't be," Dulles frowns. "I only go where there is trouble."

Truth be told, John Foster Dulles loved this role. Riding out from Washington, he could pull Paul Revere's cloak around him, and ponder at twenty thousand feet how best to thwart the new redcoats plotting to destroy American independence. On this particular occasion, especially, the problem was not hard to spot. The British were unwilling to consider a Southeast Asian defense organization before the Geneva Conference opened at the end of April 1954. In that case, American policymakers feared, there might not be much left to defend. Certainly the momentum would pass to the Communists, and probably not only in Indochina.

While Dulles' most recent appeal to the ANZUS ambassadors (Australia and New Zealand) had sparked London's interest in such a pact, if only to rectify a situation whereby the United States enjoyed something of a "special relationship" with those commonwealth nations, the maneuver had not succeeded in pressuring the British to move quickly enough to head off otherwise certain defeat at Dienbienphu, or, more fatefully, to rescue the struggle from the defeatist attitude sure to follow a Vietminh victory over de Castries.

Paris, on the other hand, still wavered between invoking United States aid to save Dienbienphu and waiting for a miracle. But neither allied capital, other obstacles aside, was very happy about the way Dulles wanted to proceed. For whatever reasons, the Eisenhower administration seemed bent upon pumping up the issue into a full-scale East-West confrontation. All too casually, it seemed to the allies, Secretary Dulles had baited the Chinese tiger. Now he was riding on its back. Worse still, he seemed to think he could bronco-bust this striped cat by waving atomic bombs under its nose. More likely, if things continued to go the way they were going, either he would succeed in blowing them all to kingdom come, or the tiger would feed on chunks of the British and French empires.

True, Dulles had promised the tiger would slink away if they stood together, but was that likely? On April 4, 1954, after the problematic Dulles/Radford meeting with the congressional leaders, Eisenhower appealed to Churchill to remember where appeasement had led before, and to join with him to erect a wall of nations to block Communist expansion. It was not a new idea or, as we have seen, a fresh appeal. But with Geneva only four weeks away, the president saw the situation as now or never.

Choosing themes from Churchill's war memoirs, again not a new tactic, Eisenhower argued that "today we face the hard situation of contemplating a disaster brought on by French weakness and the necessity of dealing with it before it develops. This means frank talk with the French."[2] Then came that curious warning noted earlier. "I have faith that by another act of fellowship in the face of peril we shall find a spiritual vigor which will prevent our slipping into the quagmire of distrust." Failing to act in time, he said in closing this message, had marked the beginning of "many years of stark tragedy and desperate peril" when Hitler and Mussolini rampaged across Europe. "May it not be that our nations have learned something from that lesson?"

The letter did not go down well in London. Although many in the Foreign Office were also searching for some means to cage the tiger, Eden's private secretary, Evelyn Shuckburgh, called it a "very excitable" message. The prime minister, meanwhile, was aglow with the "splendid news" that *Izvestia* had called for a cease-fire in Indochina. Eden hardly knew what to say or do with Washington talking war with China and his prime minister agog (and gaga) over what he regarded as a clever piece of Kremlin trap-laying. "Don't you see it is a trap," he told the prime minister, "and they would overrun the whole place."[3] Churchill was crestfallen. But Eden approved his brief response to Eisenhower, which promised only a full study of the proposal. "It is, however, a topic which raises many problems for us. . . . We shall be very glad to see Foster here and talk the matter over with him."[4]

1.

> I hope that those critics who thought that we were going to issue some fulminating declaration before the Geneva Conference took place will realize that we are as anxious as they are—and perhaps more so—to see the Geneva Conference succeed.
>
> ANTHONY EDEN, in the House of Commons, April 13, 1954[5]

John Foster Dulles consciously cultivated his image as the most-traveled statesman of his era. It conveyed the proper notion of boundless energy and determination that he wanted to inculcate, a symbolic indication that America was not content to be merely a status quo power, but was always in motion. "USA: Permanent Revolution," the editors of Henry Luce's *Fortune* had once claimed. The world, Dulles constantly reminded listeners, was divided into static and dynamic powers. He had been writing about America's "spiritual leadership" of the latter since before World War II, and deprecating its subservience to the colonial powers for just about as long.[6]

Almost all issues came back, one way or another, in Dulles' mind, to this central proposition. Take British diplomatic recognition of Communist China, for example. Dulles saw that as appeasement dictated by the desire to protect Hong Kong, with its trade and investment opportunities. Such narrow angling for short-run advantage stood in the way of America's future. He was well aware, however, as he left for London on a Saturday in early April 1954 of the difficulties in the way of "saving" Indochina. Hong Kong was only one consideration and, at the moment, less important than other factors. British concern about the H-bomb, perhaps more than any other consideration at the moment, made the Churchill government wary of pursuing a vigorous policy to halt Chinese expansionism, or of allowing the United States to take the lead.

Churchill had barely escaped with the keys to No. 10 from the recent H-bomb debate in Parliament. He was a marked man—in both parties. And the shouted demands for his retirement still rang in Tory ears. Their opponents showed no signs of letting up, especially not if there was any chance of British involvement in Indochina. Aneurin Bevan, leader of Labour's left wing, seized the moment to announce his resignation from the shadow cabinet to protest Clement Attlee's tepid performance as opposition leader, and what others, as well as Bevan, regarded as Churchill's fawning servility to the Americans. In this instance, Bevan overplayed his hand, but that did not become evident immediately. Meanwhile, the H-bomb debate got mixed up with Indochina.

Little wonder that the prime minister's heir apparent, Anthony Eden, was anxious to deprive the opposition of a rallying point on foreign policy. There was trouble enough in holding the Conservatives together, as many chafed, including Eden himself who swore he would not go along, at the prime minister's insistence on fulfilling his destiny by a mission to Moscow.[7] The foreign secretary resented Churchill's using his absence when he was ill in May 1953 as an occasion for delivering a major address on the need for a meeting with the Russians not "overhung by a ponderous or rigid agenda," and feared being at odds with the Americans over something he himself knew would not work.[8]

At every inopportune moment, or so it seemed to Eden, Churchill came out for summitry, and in truth the prime minister made it appear to be the only foreign policy platform the Conservatives had. To Eden it was like walking the plank. Behind him, giving him a shove, was Churchill. Below were sharks, all of whom seemed to be wearing Dulles' rimless glasses. "Bevan's line was full of danger," Churchill averred to his friend and physician, Lord Moran, but not just for Tory prospects, at least not the way Eden perceived them. If America was forced to go it alone, opined Churchill, "she might declare war on Russia and blow her to pieces." That was what American isolationism meant. Bevan and his followers were tempting nuclear fate.

In his imaginings, now daydreams perhaps, the British prime minister envisioned himself the intermediary who would eventually bring the Russians and Americans together. Dulles' current obsession would burn itself out, he was convinced, leaving the field open for him. Of course one had to wait for this Geneva business to be over, bothersome as it was. But he could hold out for that long; and besides, either way it came out, Eisenhower would have to see that Dulles was a poor show.

"If the conference fails, I shall pick up the bits. If it triumphs, I shall go to meet [Soviet Premier Georgi] Malenkov to exploit the victory."[9] How could it end otherwise? In his mind's eye, it could not. "I would pop over to America first, to make it all right with them. I know them so well, they would not think I was up to dirty work." Eden, on the other hand, cared very much whether Geneva succeeded, for he could not imagine decent relations with China—or Russia—if it failed, let alone a summit.[10]

In Washington the political scene was also fragmented, though Eisenhower did not have to worry in quite the same way Eden did. He did not have to feel around on the floor for pieces of the jigsaw puzzle that kept falling off the table. His authority within the Republican party was unchallenged. The China lobby people could hardly be satisfied with anything less than Mao's scalp, but they were a sideshow; distracting at times, but hardly a determining force. Eisenhower had moved to restore the Shah in Iran, would engineer a coup d'état in Guatemala, and, in the end, would decide for himself about Indochina. In the first two instances, as Stephen Ambrose relates, "where he thought it prudent and possible, he was ready to fight the Communists with every weapon at his disposal—just as he had fought the Nazis. There was no squeamishness, no doubts."[11]

Indochina had always seemed more complicated.

Domestic politics on Indochina were especially confused and complex. Anger at Red China was nearly universal in Congress, but sympathy for the French hardly so. And no one wanted to intervene, either in the administration or on Capitol Hill, to save colonialism in Southeast Asia. Thus the odd, and sometimes contradictory, pronouncements from congressional figures. A good example, of course, was the April 3, 1954, meeting at which congressional leaders told Dulles to find out if Britain and France were really interested in "united action" before proceeding any further toward American intervention.

If, as Senator William Knowland, the Republican leader in the Senate, often insisted, European appeasement was the real problem, why should American action depend upon those allied nations? As his critics noted, on the other hand, when it suited him, Dulles had played push and shove with unilateralist sentiments in the United States, serving up booming verbal salvos, "massive retaliation," "agonizing reappraisal," and the like. Was it really surprising that Republican leaders in Congress should expect the administration to follow its own lead? In announcing his forthcoming trip to London to French ambassador Henri Bonnet, on the other hand, Dulles actually tried to bully the Frenchman with the threat of isolationism. "If others would not go along with us, we would know where we stood." The danger was farthest from American shores, he said, and it was "crazy" for anyone to think the United States would get involved just to save one outpost. "If it became necessary for the US to base its defenses on the shores of this country—all right."

But if the French just stopped quaking, and listened to Washington, the dangers could be overcome. NATO did not extend to Indochina. The remedy for this was in French hands. Bonnet said he understood.[12] But did Paris? In France, meanwhile, the Laniel government was being crushed between the never-ending war in Vietnam and the never-ending debate over the EDC. What influence London had in Paris was being used, moreover, to discourage any tendency that might result from panic over the likely—indeed, now inevitable—defeat at Dienbienphu to encourage American bellicosity. A French cry for help might be answered, the British feared, if worse came to worst, by American nuclear weapons.

From the banks of the Potomac, it was easy to imagine London and Paris trying to sneak out the back door as Dulles knocked, scurrying off to bargain for Russian and Chinese goodwill.[13] Who could watch this unfolding tragedy without a profound sense of America's obligation to save the allies from themselves? Already, Republican Senate leader William F. Knowland, whose porcupine nature and Asia-first obsessions made the secretary of state's concerns seem but passing fancies, had threatened to cut off aid to America's allies. "If they want to 'take a reading' based on Geneva, maybe Congress may determine it wants to 'take a reading' based on Geneva and the response to the Dulles inquiries."[14]

Push and shove again, or maybe dare and double-dare, for Knowland's warning disturbed even those, like Admiral Radford, who often spoke ill of the allies. But the view that Washington had to lay it on the line was surprisingly widespread.[15] The *New York Times*, for example, drew a parallel with Truman's dramatic action to save Greece. President Truman had come in for much criticism then for acting unilaterally, read an editorial. "But because of its greater strength the United States is obliged to take the lead. We have to sound the alarm when danger threatens."[16] Even the usually cautious Walter Lippmann observed that American diplomacy had one primary task in the Indochina crisis: to establish the point beyond doubt that the Communists would not be allowed to take over the port cities, "and without them they will never 'have' Indo-China in any effective sense of the word."[17]

Under Secretary of State Walter Bedell Smith capped these statements during a television interview. The French stand at Dienbienphu, he averred, was nothing less than a "modern Thermopylae," a few heroes of civilization against Communist hordes. At stake was the freedom of "masses of people" throughout Asia, as well as the natural resources of the entire Southeast Asian area. "Once the battle is joined," he said on CBS, "nothing should be withheld as long as success is possible."[18]

While awaiting Dulles' much-heralded arrival, Eden spoke with the French ambassador, and was relieved to hear that Paris also believed no plans for a regional defense pact should go forward until agreement "with China" proved impossible at Geneva. The British foreign secretary seconded that position, of course, and remarked that his colleagues could not yet see how these American proposals, which had arisen "in this somewhat haphazard form could best be adopted to serve the interests of our countries in South East Asia." What did the French think? The ambassador reiterated that it was his country's policy to seek an understanding with China, offering valuable transit and port facilities at Haiphong in exchange, apparently, for Beijing's help managing Ho. And, in this regard, he also thought it useful to mention that Russian diplomats had been calling at the Quai d'Orsay "to emphasize that the Soviet Government were sincerely anxious that a settlement should be arrived at in respect of Indo-China."[19]

Dulles had, unfortunately for the success of his visit, confused matters not a little by leaving the impression that he wanted to announce the formation of a regional pact as part of a broadside admonition to the Chinese: cease and desist or pay a terrible penalty.[20] Satisfied that the French were not going to do anything foolish, Eden asked his Far East experts to meet with the military Chiefs of Staff so that he might have their joint conclusions.

Out of that session came a gloomy assessment: even if Chinese aid to the Vietminh ceased, a French victory was not likely. "A mere threat of Allied naval and air intervention," moreover, "is unlikely in itself to have any effect on the Chinese and once made would have to be followed up. . . . No half measures are possible and if the American proposals were accepted the Chiefs of Staff would feel bound to advise Her Majesty's Government that they might lead to all-out war with China."[21]

Eden did not need to hear more. W. Denis Allen, a Foreign Office Far Eastern specialist, received the assignment of preparing the foreign secretary's "brief" for the great debate with Dulles. No threat, Allen wrote, was potent enough to make China accept so humiliating a defeat. "We do not, incidentally, accept the American thesis that China concluded the armistice in Korea because she feared the United Nations would otherwise bomb Manchuria." If the A-bomb had been a bluff at that time, only the Americans were foolish enough to believe it had worked, or would work again.

Given the controversy that would arise (even within British officialdom) over what was agreed to in London, Allen's delineation of how far the foreign secretary could go to meet Dulles' wishes, while not entirely unambiguous itself, is of some interest. "If the United States Government so demand, we could even agree to the issue, before the Geneva Conference, of a joint statement by the *members of the coalition* expressing their common concern with the fall of Indo-China, provided this statement had no minatory character and did not imply any form of military action."[22]

What was meant by "members of the coalition"? An alliance in being? It was complicated even more, because Allen's paper recommended partition as the best of almost equally unappealing choices in Indochina. If unappealing to the British, partition was anathema to Americans. Dulles would not have undertaken to bring about a coalition to defend a line Washington regarded as indefensible morally, and undefendable with arms. Eden, however, could not be coaxed to go across the line.

On Sunday evening, April 11, 1954, Dulles entertained Eden and Allen at dinner in the American Embassy. Once the dishes were cleared and cigars smoked, Dulles made his opening move. The French could not stick it, he asserted, and it was no use thinking that the onset of the monsoon season would save Dienbienphu or Indochina. Given those ineluctable circumstances, he went on, the U.S.

Chiefs of Staff had suggested some three weeks ago that the United States government should intervene "with naval and air support in the fighting in Indochina."[23]

That statement was misleading. In fact, it was not true. Only Admiral Radford held that position. The other service chiefs had demurred, with army chief General Matthew B. Ridgway (and his principal lieutenants) adamantly opposed.[24] Yet ample evidence of American military operations to support the French was not hard to come by. The disagreement over direct intervention within the American military was therefore masked to a degree that allowed the secretary of state to get away with such a statement. Task Force 70's maneuvers off the Vietnamese coast may not have been known to London as yet, but American ferrying of French troops most certainly was, as one of the landing points en route was at a British base in Ceylon (now Sri Lanka). India, moreover, had forbidden the use of its airspace for this operation, necessitating the stopover.

Inside Vietnam, finally, there were the operations of the CIA-owned Civil Air Transport (CAT) line in direct relief of Dienbienphu. On an average day in early April, CAT pilots flying C-119s delivered 137 tons of supplies to the fortress area. April 15 set a record of 250 tons, a figure close to the maximum reached by the German air force during the battle of Stalingrad. Reconnaissance flights were being made not only over Vietnam but over airfields in southern China.[25]

As Dulles continued his story, therefore, a picture of the Americans edging to the "brink of war" took shape. Naval carriers had been moved from Manila down toward the Indochina coast, he confirmed. "On reflection," read the British minutes of the conversation, "Mr. Dulles had considered that the United States should not act alone in this matter. . . . Mr. Dulles had consulted Congressional leaders and had found they shared his views." Accordingly, he had launched the idea of united action.

Insofar as the secretary of state had indeed opposed a plan for military strikes to save Dienbienphu without French agreement to a political program for full independence for the Associated States, this statement was true. In other respects, his own account of his views and the recommendations of the Joint Chiefs was, again to put it generously, a little misleading.[26] All in all, his presentation, with its solecisms, hurt his case more than it helped.

The American record of this initial conversation is remarkable for its brevity, and for not including any of Secretary Dulles' comments on the situation in America. As a result, Eden's later actions seem almost craven attempts to avoid facing the issue. Both records do have Eden responding by making a distinction between holding Indochina, which he thought unlikely, and drawing a line elsewhere. In both records, also, Eden and Dulles spar over who was to be invited to join this still-hypothetical coalition.[27] Dulles feared that British insistence on promoting India and Burma as original members meant there would be a hassle, serious enough perhaps to frustrate efforts to bring the alliance into being. If Burma and India were asked, the United States would have to offer membership to Formosa and South Korea, if indeed not Japan. Then what? The places to be saved would be swallowed up while their would-be rescuers argued over who should carry the rifles and who should just applaud.

Throughout, however, Eden had left no doubt about his determination to scrutinize whatever proposals the Communists made at Geneva before undertaking any action. Using what the French ambassador had told him, the foreign secretary emphasized that the Russians had indicated to the French their belief in Chinese desire for a settlement.[28] The only communiqué Eden said he could agree to, according to the British minutes, was one, according to American views, that might actually encourage the Chinese to intervene as they so pleased: "He (Eden) wondered whether such an announcement should not be confined to the existing military situation in Indo-China with a warning that we should not allow the prospects of the Geneva Conference to be prejudiced by military action. He was more doubtful about making any immediate mention of a decision to begin discussions about the possibility of concluding a South East Asia security arrangement if that were agreed upon."[29]

Dulles closed his comments at this initial session with some provocative musings about France's decline, and "by process of historical evolution [its] inevitably ceasing to be a Great Power." If this were so, he rambled on, it behooved the two of them to give this problem "careful thought." Eden refused to be drawn, saying instead, with some asperity, that British experiences in Malaya made it easier for him to understand what the French faced.

Agreement was reached, therefore, only on the need to consider the possibility of a joint statement on the program to be followed in pursuing the question of a Southeast Asia security pact. Dulles made little effort to disguise his feeling that Eden himself was a major obstacle. While the foreign secretary spoke his piece, Dulles doodled, "looking up occasionally out of the corner of his eye to give Eden a rather quizzical or skeptical look."[30]

The next afternoon, April 12, Eden and Dulles tried again. Not surprisingly, their seconds had reached a complete impasse in the morning. The Americans had tabled a "Declaration of Common Purpose," a wordy document that, British experts decided, went much too far in pledging the proposed signatories to "restore" the territorial integrity of Indochina. That was a telling comment. The British now formally announced that they were for partition. Denis Allen also objected that such an open-ended commitment "might result in an all-out war with China, possibly involving the use of atomic weapons." This was the first specific mention of what really bothered British policymakers.

On their side, Dulles' aides found the British suggestions for a joint declaration far too mild, with its emphasis on seeing Geneva through no matter what happened militarily.[31] Eden repeated that he could agree to no more than preliminary discussions on the "possibility of forming a mutual security system for the area," and he also reiterated that it would be "difficult" before Geneva to give an undertaking about "action to be taken subsequently." Dulles suggested that the language of the American draft might be modified, but that "a situation might nevertheless develop" requiring intervention. "The United States Government were convinced," he went on, "that Indo-China was the place for such intervention," provided its conditions, independence and united action, had been met.[32]

Having threatened the French ambassador with American "isolationism," Dulles put the matter similarly to the British as an "either . . . or" proposition, exaggerating as he did so both Eisenhower's commitment to intervention, and the president's willingness to pressure Congress:

> The last thing the United States desired was involvement in Indo-China. However it would be a greater evil not to make a stand in Indo-China now and to allow the whole area to crumble rapidly. Moreover the present United States willingness to assume additional commitments in South-East Asia would diminish if agreement could not be reached now to make this stand. Mr. Dulles was confident that Congress would authorize the President to use United States air and naval forces, *and possibly even land forces.*[33]

And what was the alternative? To fail to stand up to China as the West had failed to stop Japan in Manchuria in 1931, or to stand by again as had happened when Hitler marched into the Rhineland five years later? Eden denied the situations were analogous, and raised a question about what intervention really meant. Dulles had spoken of air and sea forces, but the British Chiefs of Staff did not believe intervention could be so limited.

Of course, replied the American secretary of state, there could be no "certainty" that intervention could be so limited, but he thought that air and sea power could "restore the position, at least until the rains, provided the Vietnamese armies could be fired with the spark of independence." That he was contradicting at least part of what he had said at dinner about the monsoons offering no respite did not appear to trouble Dulles, but now Sir Ivone Kirkpatrick, permanent under secretary at the Foreign Office, and veteran of diplomatic "hot spots" from before the war, interrupted to say that Korea had not demonstrated the effectiveness of air interdiction, even where there had been clearly defined front lines.

Dulles did not respond to this, but turned to the shortage of French air mechanics in Vietnam. If the British could send some personnel, he said, "this would help the U.S. Government to secure Congressional approval to retain and possibly increase the American personnel already serving in Indo-China."[34] This was a curious argument. Indeed, it came close to an appeal for the British to get him off the hook with congressional leaders. The original response to the administration's plan for intervention, it will be remembered, had been that Dulles should go find out what the allies were ready to do. Besides that, such an argument did little to round out the picture of a firm Ike ready to ask for authority to intervene as Dulles had implied throughout the talks—and it certainly hinted that the sine qua non of congressional support was a genuine British commitment.

In the interstices of the formal conversations, Eden's private secretary, Evelyn Shuckburgh, had a memorable encounter with Walter Robertson, assistant secretary of state for Far Eastern Affairs. Neither he nor Dulles, said Robertson, had any intention of taking a whiskey with the Chinese at Geneva. "You do not take a drink, when the court rises, with the criminal at the bar." But this was not a court, protested Shuckburgh, you are meeting them at an international conference. "No, we are not, we are bringing them before the bar of world opinion." Shuckburgh could not let that go. "I beg your pardon, but you are not bringing them; they are coming." And in his diary, he recorded the remainder of the "debate": "I asked this Robertson whether Dulles had entirely given up any idea of trying to play the Chinese off against the Russians at Geneva. He scorned such a thought, said it was no use, never would be, what good had it done you (British) to recognize China, they just spurn you. A wholly inelastic and opinionated man."[35]

Less polite at lower levels, the differences widened as the hours passed. At dinner that evening with the prime minister, Dulles sought to ease concern about the H-bomb complication by telling Churchill that he and Eden had discussed a possible moratorium on "large experiments." Churchill was glad to hear this, of course, and took the opportunity to plead his case for a truly special relationship between the English-speaking powers. Only they really counted, he asserted, "together they could rule the world." He had definite ideas about how they should rule the world. Among these was Churchill's now frequent references to the need to give the Russians "a vested interest in peace." At least, Dulles noted with relief, he did not this time speak of a Big Three summit.[36]

As always, Dulles thought of summits in terms of Munich and Yalta. What the British wanted, he felt, was for the Russians to collaborate in preserving the remnants of empire, and they would pay whatever price necessary to get this "protection," of little more use than the tributes timid shopkeepers once paid in Chicago to keep Al Capone happy. At a final meeting on the morning of the thirteenth, the communiqué was agreed upon. Where the original American draft had called upon signatories to take action to prevent the fall of "the lands of any of them" (a curious phrase for Dulles to use, given his desire that Indochina be recognized as independent) to "international Communism," the communiqué read that the signatories were ready to take part "in an examination of the possibility of establishing a collective defense."[37]

At the session where the communiqué was agreed upon, Dulles had proposed that after his trip was over, he would "get in touch" to see how best they might proceed "in organizing united will to resist aggression in SEA." One possibility was to establish an "informal working group." Eden said Ambassador Makins "would be available." And that was it. Dulles sent an upbeat message to Eisenhower, proclaiming the talks satisfactory, assuring the president that the British position had been moved toward the American, and closing with a quip that the *London Daily Worker* had called him the most unwelcome guest since 1066.[38]

Yet whatever gloss the secretary of state wished to put on the communiqué, it was evident that he had not gotten what he wanted. Communiqués are designed to disguise disagreement, and permit interpretations that will put the party explaining it to a home audience in a good light. Labour backbenchers assailed Eden that afternoon in the Commons for even saying he had arrived at an agreement with Dulles. But Shuckburgh's account of the outcome of the conference and the Commons debate was more accurate than either Dulles' report or Labour's complaints. "The actual agreement is so favorable to us, and so far from what Dulles's speeches before he came here led everyone to suppose he would demand, that the extremists were quite discomfited, and the opposition cloven in half. A. E. enjoyed this very much."[39]

Needless to say, Dulles did not. He also smelled a rat. Eden's willingness to consider a treaty organization—after Geneva—made sense only if the British were trying to use the Indochina crisis to promote Churchill's vision of a global partnership. Indeed, that is what Dulles wrote Eisenhower: "This would give Churchill the enlarged ANZUS which he has always sought."[40]

Dulles wanted to avoid summitry; given his problems in reconciling Anglo-American agendas, perhaps he was wise to do so.

2.

> Q: In the past, the French have been hesitant about "internationalizing" (whatever that means) the Indochina war. Do you have any reason to believe that they are less adamant on this position?
> A: No, I would not say that I had any present information on that point that is conclusive at all. Of course, it is entirely within the province of the other governments who have vital interests in the country to declare that this threat is a threat to them and that they take appropriate steps to meet it.
>
> JOHN FOSTER DULLES, press conference, April 13, 1954[41]

Dulles' visit to Paris produced more controversy. Argue as he might, the secretary could not get the French to promise more than independence "within the French Union" for the three Associated States of Indochina. "His neck is in a noose still," observed an American reporter after talking with the secretary, "but he has got some soap on the rope."[42]

The secretary had made a triumphal entry into Paris, exuding confidence, as if he had already slipped the noose and was there only to clear up details. The London talks had produced full agreement, he boasted to Ambassador Douglas Dillon, who met him at the airport, and he had British approval to go ahead with really helping the French.[43] Dulles then hinted to French officials that there were also secret British "assurances" that went beyond the communiqué. When Ambassador René Massigli told Eden about these, the foreign secretary pressed for details. It turned out that the U.S. ambassador in London, Winthrop Aldrich, was saying that Churchill himself had promised military collaboration to save Indochina.[44]

Nothing of the sort, an alarmed Eden warned Massigli. The French must not assume a British commitment. "I had made plain that H.M.G. could not undertake any commitment to send military forces to Indo-China. It was as a result of that attitude that our joint statement had taken the form it did."[45] Eden had also made it plain in Parliament that no commitments existed. It would be "completely inaccurate," Eden replied to Aneurin Bevan, to say that the communiqué represented a commitment "to take certain action in certain circumstances."[46]

The American press even noted that it was difficult to reconcile American interpretations of the London communiqué with Eden's statement, but Dulles continued to assure the French that the British had moved "in considerable measure towards the position of France and the US." Indeed, he went on, he had the text of Eden's statement in Parliament, and understood that it had not been too well received by the opposition. Whatever he thought of all this, Premier Joseph Laniel contented himself with a brief comment that "this must have been difficult indeed."[47]

Where Dulles had talked, sometimes misleadingly, in London about the American view of what had to be done to stop Communism in Southeast Asia, in Paris he affected the attitude that the formation of a coalition was now a given, and concentrated here on extracting promises for independence of the Associated States. Paul Reynaud, the minister in charge, recited, in response, all the steps that had been taken, and expressed the hope that France would never again be regarded as colonialists.

Reynaud also complained, however, about a statement that General O'Daniel had made to the effect that France could and would win the war in Indochina. The Vietnamese army, said Reynaud, had been a great disappointment. Well, said Dulles, the Vietnamese were no different from the Koreans. With proper training and inspiration, they would fight as well as the Vietminh. Reynaud and Laniel replied in unison that what was needed was a Syngman Rhee, "even with the disadvantages that entailed." The meeting came to a close on that uncertain note.[48]

Over whiskeys with C. L. Sulzberger that evening, Dulles implied that the trip to Paris had been in the nature of a "stop-over." He could not just visit London on such a mission without going on to the French capital. And the main purpose of his mission, he went on, was to relieve British concern that the United States was about to issue an ultimatum to China: cease and desist by a certain date or risk atomic bombing.[49]

Yet, concluded the secretary, the Chinese had to be made to understand that they were up against "something strong enough" to make them abandon their plans. What he advocated was no more provocative than NATO had been. It was essential to avoid miscalculations if one were to avoid war.[50] Much of the secretary's conversation with Laniel and his aides actually had to do with the EDC debate. Warning that if the EDC did not go forward, the "ancient bonds" that united France to other Western nations would be rent apart, the secretary declared that in such a case he would not envy any man who aspired to the position of premier or minister of foreign affairs, for his task would be "virtually impossible."

Ending his visit with this "fatherly advice," Dulles flew home, landing in Syracuse, New York. On arrival he read a statement that made it appear he had achieved total agreement on a portentous message to Beijing, before rushing off to his upstate New York retreat for a brief respite. Losing mainland China, the statement began, was a great disaster. If in addition "the vast economic resources and the strategic position represented by Southeast Asia and the Pacific Islands" should also fall to the Communists, the West would face calamity. But that grim eventuality need not be. A ten-nation alliance was in the making, was in fact "taking definite form." "Out of this unity . . . will come free-world strength which I believe will lead the Communists to renounce their extravagant ambitions to dominate yet another major portion of the globe."[51]

It was hard to say which part of this statement caused more

trouble in London. In every one of these minatory pronouncements China was the target. While Dulles may have felt it necessary to concentrate on the Yellow-Red peril to gain support from Americans (including Eisenhower?) who had doubts about going in, at least temporarily, in support of the French, he gave every indication of meaning what he said. Probably one would be safe in asserting, however, that the secretary's mention of a ten-nation alliance already taking definite form was enough by itself to give Eden fits. If there was one thing above all the rest that they had not agreed upon in London, it was membership. Perhaps British insistence on having India and Burma consulted was only a way of stalling the whole issue, as Dulles feared, but it was certainly the case that the foreign secretary wanted the option to talk things over with those new commonwealth members.

This was especially true with the Colombo Conference of Asian powers scheduled to meet within days. Britain could not afford to alienate its commonwealth partners before that meeting by appearing to choose the unpopular side in what most of those who would be at Colombo felt was an unabashedly colonial war. Already the *Times* of India had called Eden's "acquiescence" in the Washington program "dangerously near a spineless appeasement of an importunate ally." And Nehru had informed Eden privately that Asian leaders were at one in feeling that the issue was French colonialism. Outside efforts, added the British high commissioner in New Delhi, were seen as nothing more than colonialism disguised as anti-Communist intervention.[52]

Back in Washington, nevertheless, Dulles immediately issued a call for a meeting of the prospective members of the new security organization. Eden was flabbergasted. It would arouse the wildest speculation about moves before Geneva, he cabled Ambassador Makins on April 17, 1954, and the countries Dulles intended to invite would become the original members. No agreement had been reached in London on this point, nor could he now agree. "I cannot possibly accept this." And if a meeting were to be held, Eden added the next day, Washington was the worst possible location. "If this enterprise is to have [a] fair chance of success, it must appear as a spontaneous effort by those countries and not as a response to American crack of [the] whip."[53]

When Makins discussed Eden's reactions with the American secretary of state, he was shown the American records of the London conference, which, the ambassador reported, were unequivocal on the point that agreement had been reached on Washington consultations before Geneva. Dulles' attitude throughout, Makins added, was one of sadness rather than anger, although copies of the American record were also being made available to the Australians and New Zealanders.

Other observers saw the secretary in a very different mood. After he received the initial phone call from Sir Roger telling him that Eden refused to join in the efforts of the working group, for example, he railed at Eden's dastardly behavior.[54] But Makins remained impressed at Dulles' seeming restraint, so much so that Eden took Makins' requests for copies of the British texts amiss. Unable to reach his Foreign Office advisers over the Easter weekend, and perhaps not really wanting to anyway, the foreign secretary drafted a sharp reprimand in the margins of Makins' request.[55] "I am not aware that Dulles has any cause for complaint," Eden snapped:

> Americans may think the time has past when they need consider the feelings or difficulties of their Allies. It is the conviction that this tendency becomes more pronounced every week that is creating mounting difficulties for anyone in this country who wants to maintain close Anglo-American relations. We at least have constantly to bear in mind all our Commonwealth partners, even if the United States does not like some of them; and I must ask you to keep close watch on this aspect of our affairs and not hesitate to press it upon the United States.[56]

Dulles suspected, on the other hand, that while India's increasing role in commonwealth affairs was inevitable, Eden was promoting it so that London could reap the benefits of New Delhi's prestige in postcolonial Asia. As it happened, Eden thought Nehru "blind beyond the end of his nose," a fiddler who foolishly complained about the Americans all the time, while real dangers abounded elsewhere. Nevertheless, a "Far Eastern NATO" proposal had to be handled carefully so as not to alienate the Indians.[57]

It was symptomatic of Anglo-American relations at this time that such mutual suspicions flourished. It was not only that Dulles wanted to run things that irritated the British, but that he was in such a hurry. During the London conversations, American diplomats had given their British counterparts a brief account of their working days, eight in the morning till seven at night, with only the odd Sunday free.[58] Their listeners felt concerned about the shortness of their own workday and British decline, and wondered how the two were related; but the fact was that Dulles' clock ran on different time. For him time was growing short, not simply for Vietnam, but for a strong display of American leadership. Whatever Eden intended about India, the prospect of "neutralism" gaining the edge because of British delays was more than a fantasy spawned by American impatience. So he was determined not to get caught up in any scheme that the British might have in mind for riding India's magic carpet back to Asian leadership.

In this context, Dulles was not entirely displeased at the sudden furor over Vice-President Richard Nixon's statement that if France stopped fighting, the United States would have to send in troops to fight the Communists. At first, Nixon had not allowed reporters at the meeting of the American Society of Newspaper Editors to identify him as the source of the comment. The "mystery" only increased speculation, of course. Accounts of his actual words differed, but in one he was quoted as saying that if the effort to achieve united action failed, the administration must be prepared to take risks. If it was afraid to do what had to be done because of allied views or an uninformed public opinion, the United States might "go right down the road to disaster."[59]

Talking with presidential press secretary James Hagerty, Dulles said that the idea was to keep the Communists guessing. "At present Communists do not know whether we will attack if they move into Indochina and we want to keep it that way." But at Eisenhower's direction, the State Department issued a clarification that sending in troops was not on the immediate agenda. It was, as Dulles liked to say, a delicately balanced matter. He did not want to overly alarm the already skittish European allies, but neither did he want to give the impression that the United States could not act without the approval of London or Paris.[60]

Nixon always insisted that his remarks were not a trial balloon, as contemporary observers and historians labeled them, but instead part of an effort to educate the American people. Yet a minor controversy swirls around even that issue. In his memoirs, Nixon said it was not a trial balloon because he was not trying to reverse administration policy; earlier, in an interview for the Dulles Oral History Project, he remarked that Dulles had not put him up to it to force the issue; and in a contemporary interview with James Reston, the vice-president shaded the meaning slightly differently to suggest that he was not trying to "put over" a policy the administration was not prepared to announce to the public, but rather he was trying to influence the public toward the administration's policy, stated on March 29 by Dulles, that a Communist victory would be a direct threat to American security.[61]

Whether Nixon took some remark by the secretary of state as a clue or acted alone, he certainly did not coordinate his statement with anyone in the White House. What has to be remembered is that an intra-administration debate was raging all this time, if mostly hidden from view. When Dulles and the vice-president talked about the incident on the telephone, nevertheless, the secretary appeared to be in a bantering mood, kidding him about getting his name in the paper. Eisenhower was not disturbed, Dulles assured the vice-president, and the net result might be positive. Within the hour, however, the secretary was on the phone with Senator H. Alexander Smith of New Jersey. Dulles said he was opposed to getting soldiers "bogged down" in Southeast Asia. "Other things we can do are better." He also told Smith that the whole thing was "unfortunate" but would soon blow over.[62]

Nixon himself appeared to retreat from his comment in subsequent speeches in Ohio and Iowa, declaring that the purpose of the administration's policy was to "avoid sending our boys to Indochina or anywhere else to fight."[63] Mixed reactions to Nixon's comments also characterized opinion outside the White House circle. Colonel Robert R. McCormick, owner and publisher of the *Chicago Tribune*, for years—but no longer, it seemed—the authentic voice of American isolationism, had been in the audience when Nixon spoke of sending troops to Indochina. It was ridiculous for the vice-president to tell the audience his remarks were off the record when there were five to seven hundred people present, declared a suspicious McCormick. "He talks like a gibbering idiot," McCormick growled, "we should stay out of Indochina, no matter what happens."[64]

The *New York Times*, on the other hand, usually a harsh Nixon critic, and usually dedicated to preserving an aura of skepticism about Cold War simplicities, ran an editorial that put the vice-president's remarks into a context that reached back to Lenin's legacy. "More than a generation ago Lenin set down the dictum that the conquest of the world for communism lay, first, in the conquest of Asia. We have seen the battle plans that emerged from that dictum." Reciting every adverse development in Asia since World War II, the *Times* writer proposed that the stakes at Dienbienphu were nothing less than "a question of survival in a free world, for us as well as for the Indochinese. This is the reason that the Vice-President and our Administration take the case seriously and the reason why we must do likewise."[65]

3.

> [It was] agreed that there would be little possibility of the strong stand . . . at Dien Bien Phu . . . acting as a spur to morale along the lines "Remember Pearl Harbor"—"Remember the Alamo."
>
> Staff meeting, Department of State, April 23, 1954[66]

Asked about the apparent confusion over Indochina in administration ranks, President Eisenhower replied, "I am not aware of any antagonism between the statements he [Secretary Dulles] has made and I have made." Dulles had never issued an important statement, he said, without sitting down with him and "studying practically word by word what he is to say."[67]

They had hardly had time to talk, let alone sit down and discuss the Nixon episode, however, before Dulles was off again to Paris, on April 20, first to attend a NATO council meeting, and then on to Switzerland for the long-awaited opening of the Geneva Conference. The secretary had many things to say in both meetings. But what he did not say, what was between the lines, was the important thing this time. The secretary still hoped that Indochina "negotiations" could be avoided.

There were a number of matters to be settled, he told reporters in a departure statement, before the Geneva Conference got around to Indochina. At the Berlin Conference back in January, the Big Four had agreed to try to reach a more permanent settlement of the Korean situation. Indochina had been added to the agenda at French insistence. It had not even been decided what nations were to attend that part of the conference, observed Dulles. What he did not tell reporters was what had been decided at a National Security Council meeting on April 13, 1954.

At that session, Dulles' aide, Under Secretary Walter Bedell Smith, explained the State Department position in regard to discussing Indochina at Geneva. "We very much hoped that the Communists would manifest such complete intransigence with regard to a settlement in Korea, that some of the pressure on us to agree to a negotiated settlement in Indochina would be relieved."[68] And to representatives of eighteen nations, hastily assembled when the British vetoed the Syracuse "plan" for a ten-nation "consultation" on military strategy, Dulles said the proper approach at Geneva would be to insist upon the original U.N. program of all-Korean elections.

The Chinese would refuse, he imagined, but it seemed "logical" to him that the purpose of Geneva was to remind everyone that it was "incumbent upon Communist China to purge itself of wrongdoing." As for Indochina, it was at a different stage. He and the president had talked over in Augusta, Georgia, how past Communist aggressions had brought into play Western reactions, how the 1948 Czechoslovakian crisis had brought NATO into being. The purpose of Geneva, it appeared, was not to negotiate seriously about anything, but to demonstrate that "peace for free men meant strength, unity, cohesion and the pooling of our strength to protect the freedom of each of us."

To make sure that everyone was on board, the secretary of state suggested that they agree upon a press statement, and that they bar individual comments on "any questions of strategy or tactics because this would defeat our own purposes at the conference." If he could not report to the world that a preliminary collective defense conference had taken place, Dulles certainly did not want doubts spread about of differences over the prospects for a negotiated settlement at Geneva.[69]

In his departure statement, therefore, Dulles tried very hard to downgrade the likelihood of Geneva coming to anything. He listed a series of "nots." Geneva was *not* a Big Five conference; its purpose was *not* to discuss international problems generally; it did *not* imply diplomatic recognition of Communist China. There was some evidence, he warned, that the Soviet Union might attempt to make it into those things. But the "Communist forces" that had stepped up the scope of their aggression in Indochina, that had "expended their manpower in reckless assaults" in a futile hope to improve their bargaining position, would not succeed. "This is not a good prelude to Geneva. Nevertheless, we shall not be discouraged nor shall we grow weary in our search for peace."[70]

In a private message to Eden issued through Sir Roger Makins, Dulles tried to get the collective defense talks back on track. Congress was ready now, Dulles reported through Makins, and it would be a good thing to strike while the iron was hot. Congress might lose interest if things went sour at Geneva, if, in other words, the French surrendered all or part of Vietnam.[71]

The notion of Congress straining at the leash to intervene in Indochina was still as misleading as Dulles' statement to British policymakers in London that he "had consulted Congressional leaders and had found they shared his views." But no matter. In Paris both Dulles and Eden felt they had to boost French morale, if for somewhat different reasons. They were both shocked, as well, by the ramblings of a nearly exhausted Georges Bidault. The situation at Dienbienphu "obsessed" French leadership, and Bidault was openly despairing that the "flower" of the army in Indochina was in grave peril. Dulles was determined not to allow the moment to pass. How far he went to pressure the French into "internationalizing" the war in these last days before Geneva remains a matter of dispute, far more so than the argument over what had been agreed upon between Dulles and Eden in London a week earlier. Indeed, that episode was now rendered inconsequential, except for its ambiguous legacy.

At a morning session on April 22, 1954, Dulles urged Bidault to subscribe to the Southeast Asian Pact, and to undertake negotiations immediately to that end. The Frenchman retorted that the pact could be of no immediate significance to the outcome of the battle, upon which everything depended. If Dienbienphu was lost, moreover, the French would probably not be interested in joining such an alliance. Calling for emergency negotiations between General Navarre and U.S. military commanders on the spot, Bidault said finally that while he had been opposed to internationalizing the war, "he would favor it now with US if it would save Dien Bien Phu."[72]

Much as he might have wanted to say yes to this "offer," Dulles could not. It is not necessary to repeat all the reasons why it was impossible for him to do so, but the core issue remained the absence of a collective defense system. Congressional demands that the United States not act unilaterally were but a part of this, for Dulles also insisted that France allow the Associated States of Indochina to play an "independent" role in such a system, which meant that they would be able to negotiate for themselves to obtain American military aid.[73] Otherwise, Washington would be compromised. British officials worried that Bidault's tremors would cause Dulles to recommend military action anyway. Everyone present at these talks wondered how long Bidault could go on. His imminent collapse seem to parallel France's plight. "The situation here is tragic," Dulles cabled Eisenhower. "France is almost visibly collapsing under our eyes." Dienbienphu had become a symbol all out of proportion to its military importance. And it was likely that if the fortress fell, "the government will be taken over by defeatists."[74]

The latest in from Dienbienphu was that an effort to retake the outpost Huguette-1, in order to gain a drop-zone area from which to resupply the besieged fortress, had failed. The attempt had claimed his last reserves, General Navarre warned Paris, reducing options to their starkest yet: either the United States must intervene with massive B-29 raids, or the French command must request a cease-fire. Dulles reported that he told Bidault that "B-29 intervention as proposed seemed to me out of question under existing circumstances, but that I would report all this urgently to the President."[75]

Bidault also recalled these sessions, but with some dramatic differences. In his account, the foreign minister referred to the American fleet in the Gulf of Tonkin and to the secretary's public statements that America would not tolerate the expansion of Communism. If he wished, Dulles could now reconcile theory and practice by helping us out at Dienbienphu. "He merely looked glum and did not even promise to back my request at Washington." What he did do, still according to Bidault, was to offer "to give us two atomic bombs." Bidault said that he shunned the idea out of concern that bombing near Dienbienphu would cause the French to suffer as much as the enemy, and dropping A-bombs on supply lines would risk war with China.[76]

Dulles stoutly denied that he ever made any such offer. It may be that Bidault took the secretary's various musings too seriously at one point, but Dulles had no recollection of any conversation with Bidault about the A-bomb.[77] There was discussion of the general issue of atomic weapons as part of "conventional" armor during the NATO council meeting on April 23, 1954, and this took place in a highly charged atmosphere with Dienbienphu's fate on everybody's mind.

The secretary had planned to discuss atomic weapons at the NATO council meeting, not because of the situation in Vietnam, but as a result of the furor over H-bomb tests at the beginning of April and the ensuing debate in Europe. He may also have hoped, however, that reporters would interpret whatever rumors or leaks from the meeting they picked up as indicators that the West was considering atomic weapons for Indochina. That would serve the purpose of keeping the Russians and Chinese guessing.

At 6:00 P.M. Dulles began addressing the NATO council on the issue of atomic weapons. After explaining that Soviet manpower advantages made it impossible militarily, politically, or economically to match Russia in that area, and, as a consequence, that nuclear weapons must be considered part of the West's "conventional" arsenal, Dulles went on to argue that it had to be "our agreed policy," in case of either general *or local* war, to use atomic weapons "whenever or wherever it would be of advantage to do so, taking account of all relevant factors."[78]

He promised that there would be full consultations with the allies on this subject, but there were "certain contingencies" when time would not permit consultation "without itself endangering the very security we seek to protect." Before dinner, Dulles took Eden aside to tell him about Navarre's appeal for American intervention. Unless it came within seventy-two hours, Dienbienphu would be lost. The American secretary of state also read him paragraphs from an Eisenhower message that more than implied British responsibility for any failure to respond to French pleas. "The British must not be able merely to shut their eyes and later plead blindness as an alibi for failing to propose a positive program."[79]

Were these the sorts of "consultations" Dulles had in mind when he addressed the NATO council? Eden responded that he found it hard to believe strikes from American aircraft carriers could save the situation. It was not true, furthermore, that the best French troops were all locked up at Dienbienphu. French officials had told him there were a hundred thousand troops throughout the Tonkin Delta. Dulles said that while all that may be true, Dienbienphu was of such symbolic importance that the West faced a major crisis. If he, Eden, felt able "to stand with him, he was prepared to recommend to the President to ask for 'war powers.' "[80]

One suspects Dulles was imitating Admiral Radford at this moment, not in order to bomb the Vietminh at Dienbienphu, but to achieve his oft-stated political objectives, using shock methods; but it is impossible to be sure. To Eden's repeated request for serious consultations, the secretary gave his standard assurance. But the British foreign secretary went to bed "a troubled man." The next day the "real" Admiral Radford arrived to join Dulles for the climactic effort before Geneva.

4.

The acceptance of risks is necessary in order to avoid being nibbled to death.

ADMIRAL ARTHUR W. RADFORD,
April 24, 1954[81]

Eden and his aides arrived at Ambassador Dillon's residence on the afternoon of April 24 expecting to discuss "a number of assorted and harmless questions." In the garden they found the secretary surrounded by Admiral Radford and a covey of army and navy officers. Dulles took Eden into the study, where he opened the discussion with an ambiguous assurance that the United States had no intention of becoming involved in the battle for Dienbienphu. The president had no power to act with such speed. The French had said, however, that this would be "their last battle" unless the Americans joined in to save the fortress. As Dulles saw it, there was some hope, on the other hand, that if the French received pledges that the British and Americans would come in to defend Indochina—even if Dienbienphu fell—they would continue the fight.[82]

Radford took it from there. "The only thing to do . . . is for US/UK more or less to take over conduct of the war, push the French into the background and hope that the locals will be so inspired by this spectacle that they will rally against the Communists." Vague about what the British would have to put up, Radford only mentioned an RAF squadron and a carrier. Clearly, the British contribution would be mostly political.[83]

So once again Dulles waited for the British to choose. Would it be united action or appeasement? This time, at least, Dulles did not pretend that Congress was straining at the leash, but made it clear that London's participation was an essential prerequisite to Eisenhower's willingness to press Congress for emergency authority. Once again all the arguments for intervention were recited. Admiral Radford played down the likelihood of Chinese action, and when Eden drily commented on the Sino-Soviet alliance, the chairman of the Joint Chiefs dismissed it as but a slight risk, arguing that the Russians could not be provoked into war.*

*On this point at least, Radford had the support, in a fashion, of the Foreign Office. It had been the Foreign Office position for some time that the Russians were really quite sensible about Indochina, and were almost as anxious as the Western powers to restrain the Chinese. The British had taken this as a reason for believing that negotiations would work, whereas, of course, Dulles and Radford saw in Russian

Radford and Dulles then tried to turn this British argument—the risk of war—around by suggesting that if Indochina was lost there was no place else in Southeast Asia where local deterrent measures could be successful. That meant a future war with China. Eden had argued for drawing the line at Thailand. But Radford countered that if the Communists were successful with their present methods in Indochina, the "civil war" tactic would be repeated in Thailand—and then in Malaya. And so on. No military front was possible outside of Indochina, so that an attack on the source of the trouble became inevitable.

In Eden's account of the conversation in Dillon's study, Radford proceeded to deliver a scathing criticism of French military and political ineptitude. Intervention had become necessary to restore French morale, he said, but it also involved "forcing many unpleasant decisions upon the French, including certainly the removal of General Navarre and insistence upon a voice in the planning of the high command, the training of Viet Nam troops, etc."

What this was coming down to, of course, was that the Americans were now asking the British to help them force the French into "internationalization" of the war. For more than a year, Washington had attempted without success to bring the French to yield on this point. Dulles had done battle not only with the French government on this point, but also with Admiral Radford, among others, insisting all the while that military intervention could not take place without prior French agreement. It appeared to Eden, on the other hand, that the crisis was not so dire as the American secretary made it out to be, and that the French were less pessimistic about a post-Dienbienphu collapse than they indicated to the Americans.[84]

Eden was also doubtful about whether air intervention could do very much, either to save the situation at the besieged outpost, or to encourage French morale. He promised only to take the American requests back to London to try to get a speedy answer.

"moderation" reason for assuming that the Chinese would back down from whatever they intended. It was a matter of emphasis. The most recent manifestation of Russian restraint was a conversation Anthony Nutting had had on April 21 with Ambassador Jacob Malik. The latter stressed the danger of the "wild Americans" wanting to return Chiang Kai-shek to the mainland, while Nutting talked about the "wild men" in China. Malik let this pass, and Nutting wrote, "I merely record this because it may be another straw in the wind to show that the Russians are really quite nervous about Chinese ventures in the Far East." FO 371/112054, DF 1071/271.

Admiral Radford said he would like to go to London himself to talk with the British Chiefs of Staff, feeling perhaps that talking soldier-to-soldier would stiffen British resolve at this critical juncture.[85]

The maneuvering continued when Eden and Dulles met later that same day with Georges Bidault. Once again British and American accounts of the meeting vary in important respects. In the former, the American secretary of state demanded to know if the French were prepared to hold on regardless of what happened at Dienbienphu. If so, he said, the United States would try to organize "as urgently as possible" a defense of the entire region "as agreed in the London and Paris communiqués." Eden's objection that the London communiqué did not commit the British to fight in Indochina thus appeared as a proper response to Dulles' apparent effort to portray a united Anglo-American "front."[86]

In the American account, Eden's caveat, on the other hand, appears as a gratuitous interjection before Dulles had had an opportunity to propose his plan for collective defense.[87] Bidault was in an especially awkward position. He wanted American aid at Dienbienphu, but he still did not want to commit France to internationalization. Hence he portrayed the situation in somber terms, but "hastened to agree" with Eden's position (as expressed in the British account) that there was "no commitment whatever" in the London and Paris communiqués.

Dulles then produced a letter which he proposed to send to Bidault explaining why it was impossible for the United States to intervene at Dienbienphu, but offering once again the prospect of a regional collective defense organization. Bidault hesitated for a few moments, then agreed that it should be sent. "Perhaps it would be useful at some stage," he concluded. Dulles was right not to be impressed with Bidault's grudging concurrence. He was under no illusions about French willingness to go on, he reported to Washington, but at least he believed he had staved off "some disastrous course of action" by Paris as the Geneva Conference opened.[88]

After this meeting adjourned, Dulles had a further talk with Premier Joseph Laniel and Maurice Schumann. Laniel renewed the request for immediate intervention at Dienbienphu; and Dulles repeated why it was impossible under the American Constitution for the president to respond. Eisenhower would seek congressional approval for action in Indochina on two conditions only, British willingness to join the fight and a French commitment to complete independence of the Associated States. If the French really wanted

American aid, moreover, they would try to persuade the British to commit themselves to military action.

Having tried to use an Anglo-American front on Paris, Dulles was now seeking to put into operation a Franco-American front against London.[89] He would like to make "one rather delicate comment," concluded Dulles. There were many people who believed that France had never recovered from World War I, and that she had shown by "her tragic experience in the second world war that she could no longer be counted among the great powers." The way in which France now responded to the fall of Dienbienphu would reveal whether or not that conclusion was justified.[90]

Eden had watched Dulles operate with Bidault with mounting concern. The letter promising an American effort to organize regional defense had been passed around during the tripartite discussion, but not having a copy, the foreign secretary could not be sure if anything had been said about British participation as a sine qua non. Before he could obtain a copy, he had to leave for London. As he prepared to do so, however, a telephone call came from Maurice Schumann advising him that both Laniel and Bidault hoped he would urge his colleagues to proceed "on the lines desired by Mr. Dulles."[91]

Dulles had achieved one of his objectives. There was now a Franco-American front: but was it the front he wanted? That remained a question.

5.

> The French go up and down every day—they are very voluble. They think they are a great power one day and they feel sorry for themselves the next day.
>
> DWIGHT D. EISENHOWER,
> private comment, April 26, 1954[92]

Cy Sulzberger had been listening hard in Paris. He had heard what French military and political officials thought, and he had heard what Dulles and Walter Robertson and Admiral Radford had been saying. When Dulles finally told the *Times* reporter that the French had requested intervention, the purpose of the leak was to increase pressure on Paris to internationalize the war. But the front page story in the April 25 *New York Times* headlined the French request for military intervention by U.S. aircraft manned by American crews.[93]

As it turned out, the story did not advance Dulles' objectives. But that became a moot point, because when Bidault sent his reply, it ignored all American stipulations. Not only that, it directly refuted both British and American arguments that rescue bombing missions at Dienbienphu would not be effective. The tone of the letter, finally, strongly suggested that if the Americans failed at this point to strike what might be a "decisive blow," the outcome of the war would be on their shoulders.[94]

Little wonder that the hectic deliberations in this last weekend before the Geneva Conference confused even the closest observers. Eden hurried home to consult with the prime minister and the cabinet. Where the Americans had put the choice as between united action and appeasement, the foreign secretary's advisers saw it as a dilemma: "If we refuse to co-operate with the US plan, we strain the Alliance. If we do as Dulles asks, we certainly provoke the bitterest hostility of India and probably all other Asiatic states and destroy the Commonwealth. Also, a war for Indo-China would be about as difficult thing to put across the British public as you could imagine."[95]

Arriving late at night, Eden's party found the prime minister ruminating about "our wonderful Indian Empire, we have cast it away"; the thought being, recorded Evelyn Shuckburgh, "why should we fight for the broken-down French colonial effort after that?"[96] In London, Anthony Eden met with the cabinet. It took little urging from him for them to reject the American request.

Prime Minister Churchill observed that Dulles had all along been trying to get the British committed first in order to bring the others to the table. "What we were being asked to do," he agreed with Eden, "was to assist in misleading Congress into approving a military operation, which would in itself be ineffective, and might well bring the world to the verge of a major war."[97]

Eden had had prepared a talking paper to use in the cabinet meeting. In it his advisers in the Foreign Office had argued that there simply was no way to hold on to large sections of Vietnam. Partition was the only way to save anything. The objective should be to convince the French that the United Kingdom would stand behind such a partition "border." Immediate military intervention, it went on, would be less effective in reaching those goals than the threat of such intervention. The Chinese, and even less the Russians, could not wish for the struggle to develop into a major conflict with the "uncertainty that non-conventional weapons will be banned."[98]

There were several very big assumptions here, not least the contention that a threat of intervention was more potent than the reality, but the cabinet was in no mood to dispute advice not to get involved in Indochina. After the cabinet met on Sunday morning, April 25, 1954, and rejected the American appeal, the French ambassador, René Massigli, brought an urgent message to Eden. The Americans were now proposing that an immediate declaration be made on behalf of the United States, the United Kingdom, France, the Philippines, and the Associated States, proclaiming their common will to check Communist expansion in Southeast Asia, and to use "eventual military means" to achieve this purpose. This was a new grouping, but one no more acceptable to the British government.

Massigli readily admitted that Under Secretary of State Walter Bedell Smith in Washington had been urging the French to do all they could to get the British to agree "at once." If the British did agree, American forces could go into action as early as Wednesday, April 28. At this point Eden interrupted to point out that even Dulles had said there was no chance of saving Dienbienphu, or of Congress being ready to act so soon. But Massigli insisted Eisenhower was now prepared to seek the authority.[99]

To Eden's continued refusal, Massigli returned a dire warning that the British must now consider the effect on French opinion of their position. Massigli's performance suggests (it is harder to be more definite in these circumstances) that the French hoped to turn the tables on Dulles. Instead of yielding to pressure to internationalize the war, Paris apparently wanted to bring pressure on the Americans to act without such a concession by enlisting the British. If so, it would have been no more successful than any of Dulles' ploys.

Churchill was pretty close to the mark: "The French want us to look after France in Europe while America watches over her Empire. It just won't do."[100] Meanwhile, Admiral Radford had been doing his best to win over the prime minister and the British military. Churchill thought that his arguments "just won't do" as well. When he talked with the British Chiefs of Staff, Radford admitted that to save Indochina would eventually require large numbers of land troops. But these would not come from America or any other white power, he contended, but instead from the Vietnamese themselves—as in Korea. If action were not taken now, before Geneva, the military situation would deteriorate until it would require a "much more serious military commitment." Radford perhaps meant that action had to be taken before the Geneva Conference turned its attention from Korea to Indochina, but the ambiguity of the timing of the intervention was, like nearly everything else, a major stumbling block.

Did the Americans think it vital to save Dienbienphu or not? Radford repeated Dulles' view that it was too late to save the fortress. But immediate action was needed in order to prevent a total collapse, and with it a wholesale mutiny of Vietnamese forces, followed by "large scale riots and massacres of French citizens." Developing his own transcontinental domino theory, the American admiral described the ultimate result of failure as the toppling of the French government, French neutralism, and the final frustration of any prospect for the European Defense Community.

Chinese intervention was highly unlikely, he ended. Photographic intelligence showed no buildup or construction of airfields in southern China. The Russians would not come to their assistance even if asked. And besides, the Chinese and Russians were only going to get stronger. Now was the best time to take a risk.

To all this, the British military men replied that the Vietnamese were not made of the same tough stuff as the Koreans, and in addition, they lacked a leader of any significance. Then they introduced a new consideration. The British were in a position at the Suez Canal that made it difficult for them to spare the forces to build up a "strategic reserve" able to fight Communism anywhere. With American aid, said the British chiefs, it ought to be possible to obtain an agreement with Egypt that would insure the maintenance of the allied position. Radford was totally unfamiliar with this "failure of the Americans to give us their full support" in the Middle East, and could only say he sympathized. Then they adjourned.[101]

Radford was determined to try again with the prime minister. He dined with Churchill at Chequers the night that the Geneva Conference opened, having decided that he would buttress his arguments with at least one other weapon of persuasion: the adverse public reaction in the United States that could be expected if Great Britain finally refused to stand up and be counted in Southeast Asia. Before he reached that point, however, he spoke in Mahan-esque terms of all the dreadful geopolitical consequences of not standing firm in Indochina.

The rest of Asia would be threatened by Communism, he

began, even Australia and New Zealand. "Japanese thoughts would turn towards Asiatic Communism with which they would believe the future to lie." The nationalists in Morocco would rise against the French, spreading the danger throughout Africa and into the Middle East. And this time he was prepared for the Egyptian question, assuring Churchill that if the British cooperated in Southeast Asia "there would be no difficulty in revoking the present policy of aloofness with regard to our difficulties in Egypt."

The prime minister did not deny that the fall of Dienbienphu might be a critical moment in history. It reminded him of 1919 when the Red Army was sweeping toward Warsaw, to be halted by the patriot Pilsudski—with the help of the British and the French. The tide had been checked then, and had rolled backward. "This was another such point in history, but how to roll back the tide in this instance was a very different problem." The British people were not easily influenced by what happened in the distant jungles of Southeast Asia, but they were aware—keenly aware—of American military bases that would become targets for hydrogen bombs in the event of world war.

In one account, Churchill declared that it was impossible to win the war in Indochina without using "that horrible thing," the atomic bomb.[102] It was impossible to commit oneself to a policy that might lead by slow stages to catastrophe: "The Prime Minister went on to impress on Admiral Radford the danger of war on the fringes, where the Russians were strong and could mobilize the enthusiasm of nationalist and oppressed peoples. His policy was quite different: it was conversations at the center." He did not mean by "conversations" appeasement, but it was clear to him and the British people that even if they were not fruitful, conversations were better than fighting in Southeast Asia. It might be true, as Admiral Radford contended, that the Russians would stay clear of a major war, but they were in a position on the fringes to gain a great deal for very little risk.

Sounding once again very much like his old mentor David Lloyd George throughout this "lecture," Churchill laid out the case against chasing will-o'-the-wisps in the name of fighting Communism. Nothing could be done to save Dienbienphu, concluded the prime minister, and it was up to the French to devise a sensible policy for holding what areas they could with the forces at their disposal. He had suffered many reverses himself: Singapore, Hong Kong, Tobruk. He had had those, the French will have Dienbienphu.[103] After Geneva, the British cabinet would be ready to give its answer as to what could be done in those changed circumstances. With a few comments about "greater misfortunes" to come, Radford took his leave, promising to report all this to President Eisenhower.[104]

In his report the admiral stressed several other points not included in the British record of this conference. As Radford remembered it, Churchill was much more in agreement with his geopolitical analysis, yet firmly committed only to the defense of Malaya, and totally unimpressed by the argument that the loss of Indochina would cause the loss of Southeast Asia with immediate consequences in Japan. Radford also emphasized the prime minister's repeated references to the "loss" of India, and the curiously petulant tone he took in saying that if the British people were willing to let India go they certainly would not fight for French Indochina.[105]

The atmosphere in Washington, however, was most influenced not by the British "veto" (if one can say that of the Radford/Churchill exchange), but by Bidault's response to the Dulles offer. It was, as we have seen, a complete turndown of the conditions for American intervention. Having tried and failed to get French acquiescence, even when other officials pushed the cause of immediate intervention, Dulles had finally become convinced that saving Dienbienphu was, if not impossible militarily, a mistake politically. His cable of April 25, 1954, to Under Secretary of State Walter Bedell Smith, sent from Geneva before the final British "veto," discloses what Dulles thought of Bidault's response: it was a trap. "There would be no time to arrange proper political understanding with France with reference to independence of Associated States and training of indigenous forces, and once our prestige was committed in battle, our negotiating position in these matters would be almost negligible."[106]

The Bedell Smith "incident" as it was called in London further exacerbated Anglo-American differences, as "an attempt to bounce us, and to shift the blame for the fall of Dien Bien Phu on to us."[107] So at the end of a hectic two weeks, during which Secretary Dulles had traveled back and forth between London and Paris and Washington, he was finally convinced nothing could be done to budge the French on the key issue. It would be better now for Dienbienphu to fall, under these circumstances, without American aid. Perhaps it would take that shock to bring the French to their senses. Perhaps, finally, that was the only way to start afresh. There had been some ambiguity in recent days about whether Dulles wanted to intervene to save Dienbienphu, and whether his assurances to Eden that he was not interested in such rushed action were not merely ruses to bring the British into play. Probably Dulles was unsure himself. If so, he was also aware, in this context, of what Ambassador Dillon feared: that the fall of the fortress might make it even more difficult for a French government, Laniel's or a successor's, to "accept" American aid. Yes, that was a risk, but, he concluded, "for the reasons stated above, I believe we should accept this risk rather than intervene under present circumstances."[108]

Back in Washington, as presidential press secretary James Hagerty noted in his diary, American military power was poised to intervene on April 24. "French would like us to send in these planes [from offshore carriers] for a quick strike." But the next day Eisenhower had "additional reports" on Indochina to study. These revealed that the British were "getting weak-kneed on cooperative effort" and the French "really wilting." The French had put all their "eggs in Dien Bien Phu." And on April 26, the president told legislative leaders that the French were weary, "weary as hell." But if "we were to put one combat soldier in Indo China, then our entire prestige would be at stake, not only in that area but throughout the world."

The discussion roamed far afield, then came back to Indochina. Eisenhower's troubled state of mind was evident in the groping he did to try to explain himself. He was not "advocating any additional troops for Indo China," he said, "not as a single partner of the French—must keep up pressure for collective security." But there were serious risks involved in turning down the French appeal for massive intervention at Dienbienphu. "Where in the hell can you let the Communists chip away any more. We just can't stand it."

Then, in a remarkable analogy, Eisenhower suggested that the entire American position was in jeopardy. Its Cold War policy could not operate *without* allies, but there seemed no way to operate *with* allies in situations like that which had come down to this dramatic confrontation at Dienbienphu. Gasping for breath, writhing in its death throes, the colonial order yet held the genuine spirit of freedom captive in places like Dienbienphu. An explosion was inevitable. Or, as Eisenhower put it:

> Listen . . . if we ever come back to fortress America, then the word "fortress" will be entirely wrong in this day and age. Dien

Bien Phu is a perfect example of a fortress. The Reds are surrounding it and crowding back the French into a position where they have to surrender or die. If we ever came back to the fortress idea for America, we would have, as I said before, one simple, dreadful alternative—we would have to explode an attack with everything we have. What a terrible decision that would be to make.[109]

The next day, April 27, 1954, Eisenhower continued this ruminating "dialogue" on Indochina in a letter to his old friend, Swede Hazlett. Dienbienphu was the tragic result of a "frantic desire" of the French to remain a world power. For three years he had been urging the French to find some way of internationalizing the war, to prove to the world that it was not colonialism, but only the defeat of Communism they were after. "The French have used weasel words in promising independence and through this one reason as much as anything else, have suffered reverses that have really been inexcusable." The British had a "morbid obsession" with World War III, but Eisenhower still believed a "concert of nations" could save Western interests in "this critical section of the globe."[110]

On the eve of the Geneva Conference, then, the American position had undergone a subtle change—not publicly, of course, and perhaps not entirely consciously—but what Dulles and Eisenhower wanted more than anything else was an end to French obstructionism. They did not want France humiliated at Dienbienphu, that would be a real setback. But more and more such a defeat, with its attendant risks, appeared to be a lesser evil than risking American prestige in support of a lost fortress of colonialism.

CHAPTER EIGHT

The "Setup" in Geneva

> Even . . . if we could by some sudden stroke assure the saving of the Dien Bien Phu garrison, I think that under the conditions proposed by the French the free world would lose more than it would gain. Neither the British nor the French would now agree with the coalition idea—though for widely differing reasons.
>
> DWIGHT D. EISENHOWER to General Alfred Guenther, April 26, 1954[1]

ASKED by American correspondents at a background press conference if he planned to meet with the Chinese delegation before he returned home from Geneva, John Foster Dulles said the expected thing: "Not unless our automobiles collide."[2] Outwardly, Washington's attitude toward Geneva remained as it had always been from the time when, at French insistence during the Berlin Conference months earlier, Dulles had reluctantly agreed to put Indochina on the agenda.

Adding Indochina to a conference called to discuss the possibilities of a more permanent settlement of the Korean War not only ruined American hopes for limiting Communist China's role to that of "defendant" at the bar of world opinion, but, by confusing the nature of the conference, also allowed other nations, specifically "neutralist" India (rapidly becoming Dulles' chief bugbear), to attempt to play a role as a behind-the-scenes mediator, even though New Delhi was not an official participant in the proceedings.

American policymakers, indeed, found themselves constantly fending off suggestions from Berlin onward that Geneva represented China's entrance into the charmed circle, the great power consortium that ruled the world. Seating China at that table—especially under conditions resulting from the Korean and Indochinese wars—involved much more than changing the name of the consortium from the Big Four to the Big Five. It was more important, in some ways, than acknowledging Beijing's right to China's place in the United Nations. Certainly it would undermine American efforts to define the qualifications for participation in the U.N., even if Washington still had the votes to exclude Mao's government.

At the next level, seating China at Geneva meant an end to Euro-American dominance in matters of war and peace. And Russia and China together also meant that the isolation of the Soviet Union was over. From the outset of the Cold War, Russia's isolation in the United Nations had provided the United States and its allies with two great advantages in world politics. First, whenever Moscow resorted to the veto power to protect its interests, the Soviets gave the West another chance to condemn its obstructive behavior. For a time, indeed, U.N. Security Council sessions looked more like a Punch and Judy show, with the Soviet delegate constantly being rapped on the head by all the rest for his dirty tricks. Russian vetoes also justified the Western powers in operating outside the United Nations as reluctant guardians of world peace. Geneva, in sum, threatened to disorient world opinion and produce a topsy-turvy scramble to hold together Cold War certitudes and positions.

And all because of Indochina. Hardly surprising, then, that Dulles feared being mugged in some Geneva alley. He could not stay away, however, if only because of the EDC. To satisfy the French that America was ready to negotiate Cold War issues, he had to put in an appearance. But if the negotiations actually succeeded, that might weaken the case for German rearmament. All he could do was hold tight to his briefcase and stay away from dark corners. Then clear out as soon as possible.

From the beginning, American policymakers had feared that Geneva was a "setup." The conference was to be cochaired by Anthony Eden and Russia's V. M. Molotov. These two also assigned themselves the task, without admitting it, of keeping order amid "all the little yellow fellows who teemed on every side—Burmese, North Koreans, South Koreans, Siamese, Philippinos, Chinese."[3] They also had something of an understanding between them that each shared an interest in moderating his more outspoken ally; i.e., Russia must look after China, and Great Britain do the same with the United States.

What business did he really have here, Dulles kept asking himself? The only object of America's allies, he firmly believed, was to hold on to their colonial empires by any means available. At one point, for example, when Eisenhower felt he was being misquoted in favor of partition as a solution, he wrote Dulles that certain Asian countries were more realistic about the situation "and possibly more courageous than those who are apparently willing to accept any arrangement that allows them by sufferance and for such time as may be permitted by the Chinese Reds to save a bit of face and possibly a couple of miserable trading posts in the Far East."[4]

Specifically, the French may have been planning all along either to force an American entrance into the war on their terms, or to link a negotiated settlement in Korea with a similar solution in Indochina. Whatever Americans suspected of the French, it was true the latter had eyed Geneva originally as a possible opportunity to go around Ho Chi Minh and the Vietminh in an effort to cut a deal with China. As for the British, it had always been clear to their American critics that they, too, yearned for Old World diplomacy—at which they considered themselves masters—even in dealing with Communists, especially if the other choice was "Admiral Radford's War."[5]

Now, however, everyone had to come to terms with Dienbienphu. The fortress had become the funeral pyre of the Laniel government. That changed things considerably. Facing immolation, Bidault and Laniel still refused to agree to American conditions, but they had, as a result, forfeited in addition the chance to be the principal negotiator at Geneva. And the American refusal to come swooping in at the last moment with air and sea power to snatch the fortress defenders from their fate, and thereby preserve Laniel's government from the flames back in Paris, became, partly by circumstance and partly by design, the starting point for a different setup.[6] Maybe some day Dulles might even thank the British from saving him from a foolish misstep. But probably not.

1.

Everything seemed suited to a peace conference—the careless flight of the gulls, the light mist over the lake, even the ghosts

> of Jean-Jacques Rousseau and Madame de Warens. Who could remain unaffected by this pervasive climate of tolerance, by the calm that seemed to soften the very air?
>
> PHILLIP DEVILLERS AND JEAN LACOUTURE, *End of a War*[7]

Geneva was also the city of John Calvin. Heretics had been burned here in his time. And Presbyterian John Foster Dulles gave a pretty good impression of Calvin on his arrival. "We hope to find the aggressors come here in a mood to purge themselves of their aggression."[8] How different was the arrival of Zhou Enlai! Zhou actually "outranked" Dulles, as he combined the posts of prime minister and foreign minister in Mao's government. He started things off at the Geneva airport, with a public relations gambit every bit the equal of any Western diplomatic gesture.

He did it with a smile for an American photographer. "It was a great, meaningful, ironic smile, showing dazzling teeth. It was a smile that would animate the pages of American magazines and be worth months of negotiations for the United States' recognition of the Chinese People's Republic." Greetings over, Zhou sped away in a limousine to the rented villa (one of several used by delegations) built by wealthy Swiss patricians on the lakeshore, where the Chinese government had already put on display a generous sampling of traditional Chinese art and culture.[9]

Bejing sent a delegation of two hundred to Geneva for this its debut in great-power diplomacy. Snub the Chinese all he liked, Dulles knew very well they would play a critical role at Geneva. "For the first time," Zhou told the opening session of the conference, "the Chinese people are the real masters of their fate. No force can or will prevent China from becoming strong and prosperous."[10]

Dulles lay in wait for the British, ready to scourge them once again, not least for getting him into this mess by their stubborn refusal to agree to united action. No sooner had Anthony Eden arrived in Geneva than Dulles appeared at his door, pressing once more all the old arguments for a joint declaration of policy. He was, however, perfectly willing to agree that an immediate air strike would do no good; and, almost for the first time in Anglo-American conversations, the word "partition" escaped his tightly drawn lips. It might—but only as a last resort—offer the least disastrous alternative.

Dulles did not try to hide his irritation that France had hoped to entice the Americans into the war on an indefensible political basis. Maybe he and Eden did have something in common, after all. Even so, the American secretary of state feared a flat turndown might lead Paris to "throw in the sponge." Eden had brought a map of Indochina with him, on which the British Chiefs of Staff had outlined the military position. Dulles spent some time with this map, noting especially "a broken black line at about the seventeenth or eighteenth parallel."

Maybe he was indeed giving partition serious thought, or maybe he was just trying to draw Eden out, trying to find a line that the British would defend. As before, Eden refused to be drawn. The United Kingdom, he repeated once more, could not commit itself to guaranteeing any portion of Indochina until the conference had met and done what it could to find a settlement. If none was achieved, it would "consider urgently what should be done."[11]

Eden and his aides had often talked about Thailand as the place where a defense might be organized. To Americans this was all redolent of Munich. Chamberlain conceded half of Czechoslovakia, then waited until Hitler took the rest before offering a pledge to Poland. By then it was almost too late, and by then, perhaps worse, the West had compromised itself morally. Dulles felt aggrieved that he had moved considerably from his position of early April in an attempt to forge united action, only to be caught between the French, who could use a refusal to intervene on their terms as an excuse for negotiating with the Communists, and the British, who refused to give him anything to use as a counteroffer to the French appeal.

Soon the Geneva negotiators learned that Pandit Nehru had issued his own six-point program for peace in Indochina. In a speech to the Indian Parliament, Nehru had called the Indochina war a colonial struggle. Outside support for the opposing forces had complicated matters, Nehru asserted, but had not altered its basic nature. He condemned talk of massive retaliation, and deplored invitations to form a military alliance as undermining the new hope that negotiations at Geneva might bring peace. He then proposed an immediate cease-fire, requesting that the great powers agree not to intervene. The French should make immediate promises of independence and proceed to negotiate directly with the Vietminh.[12]

Of course the Americans would be unhappy about this, Eden's aides acknowledged, but, "we do not want to give Nehru further encouragement to pose as the sole champion of peace in Indochina and the only one with constructive proposals to make."[13] Neither did the Conservatives want Labour to claim such credits. Already the Labour party executive had endorsed a variation of the Nehru proposals for its own.[14] Aneurin Bevan was at it again as well, telling a "receptive audience" in Leeds, "It was quite natural for revolutionary China, being close to Indochina, to give help because Indochina was trying to get rid of imperialism."[15]

Bevan had no chance to become prime minister, but the British mainstream opinion on Indochina flowed in the same direction. In response, on April 27, the prime minister assaulted Communist Chinese intervention, but repeated for the Commons' benefit that Her Majesty's government would not intervene to prevent the fall of Dienbienphu. What he now called the "episode of the siege of the French fortress" had created, he said, a "violent tension in the minds when calm judgment was most needed." It was all the more important, therefore, not to allow the fate of the fortress to take down with it the chance for a settlement at Geneva.[16]

That same day, Churchill met with French ambassador René Massigli. Still smarting from the Bedell Smith incident, the artifice noted in the last chapter, Churchill was brutally frank about the plight of Colonel de Castries' "lost battalion"—and where he stood. Massigli caught the prime minister at a very bad moment. It did not help that he had brought along a general to vouch for the military efficacy of an American air strike to relieve Dienbienphu. Churchill promised to consider the matter once again, but averred he would not change his mind: "I expressed my deep sympathy with the French in their agony, but I said I thought it a great mistake to have left this large and important force in so isolated a position."[17]

Thus Churchill wrote *finis* to the Dienbienphu "episode." There was a degree of unity inside Britain on Vietnam, unlike most other issues that divided the major parties and splintered them internally. American politics were more complicated. Spring 1954 was an ugly season in American politics. The debate over the censure of Senator Joseph McCarthy was coming to a climax. A special presidential commission was ruling that J. Robert Oppenheimer should be barred from access to classified materials. While some liberals were supporting Senator Hubert Humphrey's bill to outlaw the Communist party, President Eisenhower himself was taking the lead in pushing for legislation to strip persons who advocated the violent overthrow of the government of citizenship rights.[18]

Rightist critics anathematized Geneva, but while they might applaud Dulles' refusal to shake hands with Zhou, and score the British for faintheartedness, demands for American military intervention were not much in evidence.[19] "There is a general sense of bewilderment," reported Sir Roger Makins, and a feeling that if the British and French were not willing to go all out, why should the United States?[20]

Part of the cooling off Makins observed on sending forces to Indochina was the result of sober second thinking about another Korea. Senator William Knowland, the Republican leader in the Senate, would soon be quoted as saying there might have to be sea and air intervention, but no land troops, which would be like "trying to cover an elephant with a handkerchief; you just can't do it."[21] Reporters caught up with former President Truman in a Washington hotel room. Was Indochina like Korea, they asked, when American forces went to the aid of Syngman Rhee? Truman begged off, saying that he did not want to embarrass anyone at a such a time, but as he walked away down the corridor, he could not resist calling over his shoulder: "I'll tell you one thing. I don't intend to announce that I'm going to Indochina."[22]

Everyone remembered that Ike had pledged to go to Korea, and that he had won the presidency because the American people believed he would end the war. Eisenhower's press conference on April 29, 1954, gave him an opportunity to tell the people what he now intended to do about Indochina. The president had been asked to explain a recent reference of his to a possible *modus vivendi* in Indochina. Eisenhower's response left reporters thumbing through their notebooks, a common occurrence at these sessions, in search of his real meaning. A *modus vivendi,* the president began simply, was a middle course between the unattainable and the unacceptable.

Then things got muddled. In Indochina it wouldn't be acceptable to see the "whole anticommunist defense of that area crumble and disappear," but in the present state of world affairs you could not expect to attain "a completely satisfactory answer with the Communists." Whether something could be worked out, he didn't know, but "when you come down to it, that is what we have been doing in Europe—the whole situation from Berlin all the way through Germany is really on a practical basis of getting along one with the other, no more."[23]

The press conference made headlines in Europe, where the French claimed to be aggrieved at Eisenhower's "betrayal."

Georges Bidault, for example, complained that the president's remarks, coupled with recent Churchill statements in Parliament, made it clear that France stood alone. As far as negotiations were concerned, "he had hardly a card in his hand, perhaps just a two of clubs and a three of diamonds."

When Bidault finished, trailing indignation behind, Dulles appealed to Eden to be more forthcoming about military aid to France, or at least to run a bluff in that direction. He received the usual answer.[24] Why did Dulles persist in this fashion—especially since all indications were that he had given up on saving Dienbienphu, too? He did not, of course, want the diplomatic record to show that the United States had abandoned France *in extremis,* and he may actually have had some faint hopes of reviving united action before the momentum of Geneva swept away the last opportunity to salvage the ruin caused, Americans believed, by earlier French obstinacy.

Dulles was stung as well, however, by Zhou Enlai's "violent self-confidence" at the opening sessions of the conference, and, noted one observer, was reduced to "ashen anger" at the spectacle presented by Molotov and Zhou, congratulating one another, smiling and shaking hands all around. There was a powerful feeling on the other side of the table that, despite his moral denunciations, Dulles sensed he was on the defensive.[25]

Yet all the while his mind was at work devising new options. Had he and the president talked over partition? And under what circumstances? What did Eisenhower, in fact, mean by his answer? The British Foreign Office took Eisenhower's comment to mean he, at least, considered partition as a possible solution in Indochina. Certainly the use of the Berlin/Germany analogy would indicate such was the case.[26]

When informed of the furor his comment had caused, the president promptly denied that he had been thinking about partition. Another question, he cabled Dulles, had enabled him to state that partition "was not included in what I considered acceptable."[27] Yet the transcript of the news conference has Eisenhower hedging his bets in obtuse fashion. "I didn't mean . . . to endorse, even by indirection, any specific means of getting along," he told reporters. "I have no particular method that I am thinking about at the moment."[28]

One explanation is that Ike jumped the gun and felt embarrassed about it. Hence the clarification. Another is that he simply happened onto the same wavelength as Dulles. Or he may have been, as he claimed, mystified by press comments that he had cleverly interjected partition into the debate. But if Eisenhower was drifting back in Washington, Dulles was crystallizing his thoughts in Geneva.

2.

> I am beginning to think Americans are quite ready to supplant French and see themselves in the role of liberators of Vietnamese patriotism and expulsers or redeemers of Communist insurgency in Indo-China. If so they are in for a painful awakening.
>
> ANTHONY EDEN TO FOREIGN OFFICE, April 26, 1954[29]

Eden and the Foreign Office had welcomed all hints that the United States was willing to consider partition as the interim, if not the ultimate, solution in Indochina. As the quote above suggests, however, the British foreign secretary also discerned the possibility that the Americans had something else in their minds when they talked about partition: a base for military operations to recapture the whole of Indochina. Dulles' confident talk about the ability of the Vietnamese to fight—given proper direction—and reports in Swiss newspapers about his support for Emperor Bao Dai's refusal to sign any agreement with the French that did not give the Vietnamese government the right to invite foreign troops into Indochina at once, put Eden on guard.[30]

Dulles denied being involved with Bao Dai to that end, but the reports continued to mount up. The secretary, meanwhile, took a flier in an entirely different direction. Seeking out Russian foreign minister V. M. Molotov, Dulles threw out the idea that "all the Indochinese authorities" should be included in the conference. If Ho Chi Minh's Vietminh was represented, he said, it would be impossible to deny the "legal" governments of Vietnam, Laos, and Cambodia seats at the conference table. It was not the best way to do it, perhaps—using a Russian lever to remove a French obstacle—but their presence would confirm their independence, and prevent further stalling.

Vaguer still, Dulles intimated to Molotov that the various Indochinese delegations should take their cues from the American and

Russian delegations. As he put it, "I hinted that Indochinese perhaps lack sufficient experience in international affairs to be able alone to find proper solution." Dulles closed by inviting, indeed encouraging, the Russian to open his mind to him regarding what the Kremlin saw as an acceptable solution. Despite his well-earned reputation for moralistic preaching and ill-chosen phrases, Dulles could conduct out-of-court negotiations, with all their subtleties and deliberate opacities, with the best of them. He had suspected that the Soviets were not a little afraid of China, and not a little resentful, themselves, at having to share the limelight with this young partner. If so, and since he had so singularly failed to get the British and French lined up, what was wrong with probing to see if the two old enemies had a common interest in the Indochina situation?[31]

Whatever it was Dulles was after, he did not get much satisfaction. Excusing himself with a few inconclusive remarks, Molotov took his leave—"having failed to rise to any of the flies I had cast."[32] A tantalizing affair, this maneuver. When one reexamines Dulles' behavior in these opening moves at Geneva, this effort at a tête-à-tête with the Russian foreign minister raises the speculation that the American secretary of state was now flirting with a complicated stratagem involving much more than the establishment of certain ground rules. If he could get things straight with his main adversary, he could go about dealing with America's allies from a position of strength.

From the time of the Berlin Conference, American policymakers thought they detected some unease in Russian diplomatic circles about their Chinese comrades. It was outlandish, perhaps, for Dulles to test the waters in this fashion, but not unknown—even for someone professing guardianship of the nation's morals as well as its national interests.

Summing up what he had found in the opening days of the Geneva Conference, Dulles cabled home that French decline and British weakness had created a situation where, if Americans were clear about what had to be done, they should "take the leadership" in setting the course. The allies would follow, if not immediately then ultimately. About Indochina specifically, he was prepared to favor a plan that would endeavor to collect the anti-Communist forces after the fall of Dienbienphu in "defensible enclaves," where they could have U.S. sea and air protection, while retaining enough territory and enough prestige to develop a "really effective indigenous army."

Defined this way, partition could be transformed from defeat on the installment plan to an effective means of staving off a Communist triumph: "This might, I suppose, take two years and would require in large part taking over training responsibility by US. Also full independence and increased economic aid would probably be required to help maintain friendly governments in areas chosen for recruitment."[33]

This was all very different from what Dulles had in mind when he first proposed united action, but it might turn out for the best after all. The Dulles summary triggered the sharpest debate yet over Indochina in the National Security Council, with practically every one of the president's closest advisers advocating some form of intervention along lines Dulles suggested, even if that meant sending in several divisions of American ground troops.

Stimulated by the first workable plan they had seen, the NSC members seemed raring to go. Only Eisenhower held back. He did not see how anything had changed. How could the United States intervene alone? "This seemed quite beyond his comprehension." Admiral Radford took a turn trying to persuade him by picturing the allies as unable to decide anything for themselves, the French desperate about Dienbienphu and Churchill only a shadow of his former self. Mutual Security Aid director Harold Stassen took up the charge. The United States "had thrust upon us leadership responsibility for the free world," he said, "and we should determine to meet this responsibility." Congress would follow the president's lead, the Vietnamese would welcome American aid, untainted as it was by any colonialist ambitions, and the Chinese would respect American assurances that the United States did not intend to "roll back" Communist advances beyond the Indochinese frontiers.

The president heard all this with raised eyebrow. What Stassen suggested implied that it would be possible to "police the world" alone without risking general war with Russia and China or, equally devastating, losing the support of the free world. The concept of leadership implied associates. "Without allies and associates the leader is just an adventurer like Genghis Khan."[34]

Dulles, of course, was not present. He was still in Geneva and still trading affronts with Anthony Eden, proving, in a way, Eisenhower's point that a basis for allied policy in Indochina had yet to be found. When he got back, however, Dulles would try to fabricate a procedure to get around what he once called the "tyranny of the weak." At another stormy session with Eden, meanwhile, he was practically beside himself with anger at the British foreign secretary's silence in the face of Russian and Chinese attacks on American policy in Korea. It was particularly galling to listen to unanswered assaults on American "imperialism," said Dulles, when everyone knew what sacrifices the United States had been making in terms of its traditional positions on the colonial issue in order to cooperate with Britain and France. If he returned to Washington under these conditions, and had to present explanations to congressional committees, the consequences could be disastrous for the close U.S.-U.K. relations he wanted to maintain.[35]

Eden retorted that he had remained silent to cover the fissure in the Western position on free elections in Korea. At Berlin the West had offered free elections throughout Germany; here, the United States expected its partners to support a South Korean proposal for free elections only in North Korea. Dulles dismissed the point as a "technical" matter and returned to his accusation.[36]

The point was not a technical matter, of course, either in regard to Korea or, later in the conference, to Vietnam. The logic was inescapable. Dulles supported the South Koreans in a proposal he knew would be turned down quite simply because he feared the outcome of all-Vietnamese elections. He suspected the British also knew what the precedent meant, and were playing the game accordingly. The plans that were taking shape in his mind required, as he said, at least two years to mature. If Geneva mandated early elections throughout Indochina, all would be lost.

Eden's muddying the waters interfered, therefore, also with the game of "wink and nod" he was trying to get started with Molotov. Free elections throughout Korea, he guessed, would be just as unacceptable to the Soviet Union, which needed a reliable ally on China's borders, as they would be to the United States. Good fences make good neighbors. Not quite that, of course, but why was Eden being so obtuse? That is what Dulles meant when he said that the differences between them were a "technical" matter, technical in the sense that the West was not there to secure all-Korean elections or all-Vietnamese elections, but to improve stability, to eliminate any remaining "no-man's-lands" in the Cold War.

Dulles did not believe in permanent partition in Indochina, did not think that a line could be drawn to equal even the unsatisfactory one the administration had accepted in Korea. But more than partition, he feared elections, with their unpredictable impact, not only in the locations where they were held, but throughout Southeast Asia. It was much safer, all things considered, to advance positions that brought predictable responses, little winks across the table, if you will, and that could be reported home as reflecting the other side's intransigence. So Dulles continued, much to Eden's annoyance, in arguing the South Korean position in public and at great length, when all the others wanted to end this and "get down to business." "This kind of discussion," Eden insisted, "could do us no good at all."[37]

But Dulles could not bring himself to believe that the British would continue to ignore the purposes of public diplomacy in the Cold War. For years the Russians had been practicing it with great effect in the U.N. and other places. The point was not to get down to business. Hence, despite the sharp words that passed between himself and Eden, Dulles broached his plan for defensive enclaves. "If we could do this, it might be possible to build up from these defensive positions a stronger position in Indo-China. After all, in Korea we had been reduced to a bridge-head."

That might be true, replied Eden, shifting to Oxford Union debating style, "but that military position had been redeemed by massive United States military intervention."[38] At dinner on May 2, 1954, the night before he left for Washington, Dulles brought along Walter Bedell Smith, who had just arrived, for one more try. Smith joined in repeating the Korean bridgehead analogy.[39] Both Americans stressed that Washington was no longer asking for material assistance, not one plane, not one soldier, not one pound, only moral support "in any action that they might take."

"I said that was quite a new approach," Eden reported to London. But what was it Smith and Dulles actually proposed to do? As the conversation wore on there was talk of finding a leader to match Ho Chi Minh's popularity and General Giap's military skills. Eden kept on protesting. "I said that we must really see where we were going." If the Americans went in, and China responded accordingly, "that was in all probability the beginning of the third world war."

No, no, insisted Dulles, there was no thought of large-scale American intervention, rather an effort to train Vietnamese forces to defend their own country. Bedell Smith added that there was already an excellent man on the spot to do that job. The whole process, said Dulles, might take two years. Then came this revealing exchange: "Lord Reading then asked what Mr. Dulles thought would happen in the interval, to which Mr. Dulles replied that they would have to hold some sort of bridgehead, as had been done in Korea, until the Inchon landing could be carried out. Lord Reading commented that that meant that things would remain on the boil for several years to come, and Mr. Dulles replied that that would be a very good thing."[40]

Eden envisioned having to get up in the House of Commons one day after the Americans had gone in to answer the question "Did you know and approve this move?" Most of all, the foreign secretary now just wanted Dulles to go home. He suspected that Bedell Smith, despite his support for Dulles, might have brought new instructions from Eisenhower.[41]

Smith would, in fact, play an intriguing—even somewhat mysterious—role over the next few weeks. Perhaps he warned Dulles about Eisenhower's references to the Genghis Khan peril, for the secretary reported of this very detailed and specific conversation, especially on the American side, only that he and General Smith had given Eden a "far clearer detailed picture of our intent and purposes than he had before."[42] Nevertheless, Dulles concluded, "I feel that Eden was definitely impressed." And so he was. "It was a highly disturbing conversation," the foreign secretary advised London. The Americans, baffled and frustrated, "were searching about for some expedient which would serve to restore or at least to hold the situation."[43]

But Dulles was deadly serious about Inchon. As he boarded his airplane for the flight to Washington, the secretary of state told a member of the French delegation, Jean Chauvel, that "*above all, the Red River and Mekong deltas must be held, in order to prepare for the coming counterattack in two years' time.*"[44] Eden was also at the airport to say good-bye, not at all unhappy about it. "I went to see Foster off. It was meant as a gesture but I don't think it did much good. Americans are sore, mainly I suspect because they know they have made mess of this Conference."[45]

Dulles hardly thought that. But he knew he had to turn his attention to focusing Eisenhower's thoughts on his "counterattack." When Dulles returned home, the American status at Geneva was officially reduced to a "watchdog" role. But there turned out to be much for Bedell Smith to do.

3.

> We have got to give the Vietnamese the feeling that they are not fighting in a vacuum. The fate of Indo-China depends largely on getting the native peoples of Vietnam, Laos and Cambodia, themselves, actively engaged on our side.
>
> Unnamed American official,
> May 1, 1954[46]

In the last days of the battle for Dienbienphu, American officials often seemed to display impatience that the thing dragged on so indecorously—like a mortally ill rich man. Praise for the valiant defenders of the fortress continued, but now all the talk was about filling the military and political "vacuum." Quite naturally, the French bitterly resented this. And their reaction was much the same as a loyal servant might feel about the long-absent relatives who gathered waiting for the will to be read. A few days after Dienbienphu surrendered, George Bidault would remember, Dulles told a press conference in cold-blooded tones that defeat in Indochina need not mean the loss of Southeast Asia.[47]

At least Anthony Eden had the good taste to apologize for this unseemly behavior. "I don't like the job I have to do," Bidault recalled him saying.[48] That was a very open-ended comment. It was unlikely, for example, that the British foreign secretary had much fondness for presiding (along with Molotov) at a conference that oversaw the further collapse of a strong European position in Asia. But it was equally unlikely that he enjoyed listening to John Foster Dulles expound on the wages of sin that had brought the West to this sorry pass, and to his plans for militant redemption.

Nor was he very happy, on the other hand, always to have to take into account the views of the Colombo Conference of former European colonies, whose prime ministers resolved on May 2, 1954, that Communist China be admitted to the United Nations, and that France enter into direct negotiations with the Vietminh. Pandit Nehru had offered an even stronger resolution, not adopted, specifically calling upon the United States to stay out of the struggle.[49]

But there it was. A British foreign secretary's job, increasingly, was to find safe exits, and in this case to try to persuade Dulles that most of Asia regarded the Indochina war as a dirty colonial struggle, and would continue to do so no matter how far Washington managed to distance itself from the defeat at Dienbienphu, or from French policy in general.

Back in Washington, however, administration officials read the outcome of the Colombo Conference differently. Vice-President Nixon told congressional leaders that India's leadership had been firmly rejected, and that the Asian countries meeting there had not ruled out the idea of collective defense. America's "friend," Pakistan, had led the fight against Nehru's one-sided proposals and had won.[50]

Eisenhower reacted to the news from Geneva and Asia as he had from the outset of the crisis, stressing that France was overplaying the consequences of a defeat at Dienbienphu. That was only one battle. But he did not commit himself to anything. As for Geneva itself, the United States had gone along only because so many of the nation's allies had wanted it. "When the conference is over, we will have to have some plain talking with our allies."[51]

What sort of thing did Eisenhower intend Smith to say to the allies in Geneva? The under secretary had served as Eisenhower's chief of staff in World War II, playing more of a diplomatic role than a military one. Smith carried out various negotiations, including the final German surrender, but he was also a fishing companion, which meant he was a special confidant.[52] He had also been ambassador to the Soviet Union in the early days of the Cold War. Although Smith had usually taken a strong interventionist position on Indochina in 1954 NSC debates, Eisenhower may possibly have assigned him a special role at Geneva. At any rate, his appearance produced an immediate calming effect on Anthony Eden. And later Pierre Mendès-France gave him a very large share of the credit for the success of the truce negotiations.[53]

It was not that Smith backed off Dulles' positions—at least not at the outset—but the way he said things lessened European concern that American policy was determined by stringent ideological impulses. Eden may have gotten a "distorted picture of American intentions from Admiral Radford," Smith told him, assuring him also that American troops would be sent in only "over my dead body." Nevertheless, he continued, it seemed to Americans that it was possible now, more so than in future, to take some risks in dealing with the Russians.

The problem, as Smith defined it, was to gain some breathing space for the Vietnamese to organize a more effective defense, while bringing pressure on the Russians and the Chinese to accept a tolerable settlement. "This double purpose lay at the root of all the recent American impatience to be up and doing." Smith's comments gave Eden the opportunity to put a more positive face on British willingness to "play our full part" in upholding any settlement that was reached. The discussion then moved smoothly on to talk about military planning, with Eden agreeing to the holding of Five Power staff talks aimed at devising a defense for any settlement reached at Geneva. The American under secretary had gotten farther with Eden in one dinner conversation than Dulles had been able to do after weeks of importuning and cajolery.[54]

It was also not, therefore, that Eden had changed his own position, at least formally, but that this direct word from someone close to Eisenhower relieved the worst anxieties London had experienced in recent weeks. "I think we have now got this affair back on a realistic basis," Eden cabled the Foreign Office, "and feel that we should not miss this opportunity of restoring Allied unity, which promises solid advantages to ourselves."[55]

But when Smith asked him to expand this commitment to cover any outcome at Geneva, not just a settlement, Eden's suspicions were rearoused; yet, somewhat nervously, he agreed to that as well.[56] While these two were rediscovering the "special relationship," however, Dulles was in conference with Eisenhower and congressional leaders—pouring vituperation to the full measure on the British lion's head. Eden "had the gall," said Dulles, to come to the airport to bid him farewell, and be photographed with him, "although he never said a word in defense of the US at the conference."[57]

When Dulles reported to the National Security Council, he was in a more reflective mood, ruminating about a point that had long been a puzzle to him. Where they found themselves today, he said, was in a predicament just the opposite of the Greek situation in 1947. At that fateful moment the British government had seen that it was unable to continue the struggle against Communist forces in Greece and had called in the United States. France had failed the free world, he implied, by refusing to recognize its obligation to turn over the burden to stronger shoulders.[58]

4.

HANOI, May 7 (U.P.)—The fortress of Dien Bien Phu fell today.

Human avalanches of screaming Communists swarmed over the outnumbered French Union defenders after 56 days of siege.

> With the enemy at his throat, the commander, Brig. Gen. Christian de Castries radioed, "We will not surrender"—then the radio went dead.
>
> *Washington Post*, May 8, 1954

Contrary to expectations, and whatever was fed to reporters in Hanoi, the French commander did not choose death over dishonor. The official French press agency, which gave out the inspirational account, apparently muddled General René Cogny's orders to de Castries that he should not raise the white flag. When the transmitter went dead, de Castries had acknowledged those orders—but said nothing about fighting to the end.[59]

Had the French not been so desperate for some saving remnant, however small, of glory out of the Indochina war, the premature reports of his death would not have been broadcast around the world. Under the conditions of the last days of Dienbienphu, nothing of a coordinated nature could have taken place—not even an individual act of martyrdom.

Vietminh artillery fire and unceasing rain had turned the entire area into a deadly morass, a churning sea of mud. Shelters and blockhouses caved into the quicksand-like earth. Overhead an eerie light of Vietminh flares turned the night of May 6–7 into a phantasmagoric landscape. There were thick showers of mud and gravel, thrown up by Vietminh mines exploding underneath the outer fortifications; and then a tidal wave of General Giap's army, pouring forward, falling back, leaving a debris of corpses, French and their own, in the trenches.

The end came the next day. After de Castries and Cogny talked together for the last time, Dienbienphu's commander changed his uniform and waited for the Vietminh. As usual he was wearing his medal ribbons. When the Viets pushed aside the door curtain to his command post with their submachine guns, he was standing, unarmed, his sleeves rolled up. One account has him reacting to the sight by pleading for his life. "Don't shoot me." That was hearsay. But now he was a prisoner. And that was the ultimate truth.[60]

On the western flank of the fortress, in the last outpost to be occupied, Major Jean Nicolas saw a small white flag or handkerchief on top of a rifle not fifty feet away. "You're not going to shoot anymore?" said the Vietminh soldier. "No, I am not going to shoot anymore," replied Nicolas. "C'est fini?" said the soldier. "Oui, c'est fini." "And all around them, as on some gruesome Judgment Day, mudcovered soldiers, French and enemy alike, began to crawl out of their trenches and stand erect as firing ceased everywhere."[61]

Word arrived of Dienbienphu's fate as flags and bunting fluttered in Paris to celebrate the defeat of Nazi Germany nine years earlier. Town after town sent word that it was canceling V-E Day celebrations. In one city where the parade had not been called off, an honor guard marched under black crepe banners instead of its regimental colors.[62]

On this unhappy anniversary of the German surrender, distraught and puffy looking, Georges Bidault began speaking in emotional tones at Geneva about the gallant soldiers at Dienbienphu. Around him, he could see the lowered eyes of France's allies at the negotiating table; only the Vietminh delegates looked straight at him. After paying tribute to Dienbienphu's defenders, Bidault issued a call for a general armistice; but he made it clear he was talking only about military terms, not the beginning of political negotiations, not even recognition of the Vietminh. The Vietminh gave no answer. Two days later, however, they demanded immediate recognition of the independence of the Associated States, and free elections in each to determine their future. "Pending the setting up of single governments in each country, and after agreement had been reached concerning the ending of hostilities, each side would administer the areas under its control."[63]

It would take more than two months, but this sentence summed up the final declaration of the Geneva Conference. Getting to that point would strain the negotiations to the breaking point, not once but many times. Although Bidault had already toyed with temporary partition as offering an opportunity to regroup for a showdown with Ho Chi Minh, he had always seen that move as a way of forestalling elections. His worst fears had been realized. The French, by holding out, had made the loss of Dienbienphu far more devastating than it need have been. Bidault's call for an immediate armistice, made in the wake of defeat, had given the Vietminh this opportunity for a world platform to advance their political program.

All the worse, because now also there were accusations in Paris that the soldiers at Dienbienphu had been willfully sacrificed. When Premier Joseph Laniel told a tense Chamber of Deputies of Dienbienphu's fall, he implied that France's allies bore a large share of the responsibility. The implication also was that the disaster was the sad culmination of misguided criticism of French policy. "France now must tell her allies that during seven years she has been left alone to defend the common interests in Indochina."[64]

Could matters stand in a more sorry state? Laniel's assertions bode ill for future cooperation. Dulles' first reaction to all this was to try to figure out a way to do without Indochina. Could not the United States, he asked Admiral Radford, negotiate a "chip on the shoulder" mutual defense treaty with Thailand? That way some American troops could be stationed in Southeast Asia, not enough, of course, to defend Thailand against invasion, but sufficient to invoke the "plate glass window" theory.

Radford was cool to the idea. Thailand was a poor place to stand, he grumbled. Without Indochina, the only military solution was to go to the source of Communist power in the Far East, China, "and destroy that power." But, Dulles continued, there was something to be said after all for the British point of view that if you draw a line in advance, then you serve notice on the enemy. You also give him a chance to retreat with honor, unlike intervening in an ongoing war. Moreover, you would probably have a better chance of rallying to your side the maximum number of allies.

The admiral remained unimpressed by all this palaver. Stick to the main point, he insisted; time was growing short. In a few years Russia would have enough nuclear weapons to initiate a general war "on favorable terms."[65] While these gloomy discussions continued in various offices and at various levels in the administration, a surprising message arrived from Paris. Premier Laniel had asked Ambassador Dillon to reconnoiter the prospects of American aid for a French regroupment, and to see, specifically, if Washington would send a general officer to confer in secret with Ely about the best way of accomplishing this goal. The American officer should arrive by the end of the week if a serious effort was to be made. Dillon commented that the premier appeared to be "in a strong and courageous mood," in contrast to his outlook in recent weeks and reminiscent of his attitude at the time the Navarre Plan was formulated.[66]

Was this the sign Dulles had been waiting for all these months, the confession that France was ready to internationalize the war, to turn it over to the United States as Britain had done in the Greek crisis? For the first time, he told Radford on the telephone, they want to sit down and discuss the military situation. "It is encouraging that they seem willing to do business with us so we can move and get Congressional support."[67]

Radford read the cable and phoned back with his dour comment: too bad they hadn't decided to face up to this two months ago. Yes, agreed Dulles, but the big hurdle now was to get Paris to go along without the British. Radford thought they might. But would Eisenhower? That was a bigger hurdle. He would be lunching with the president the next day, suggested the secretary, and could pose all this for his determination. Not soon enough, said the admiral, things should move faster. So Dulles asked for an appointment at the White House for later in the afternoon.[68]

When Dulles walked into the Oval Office, he carried with him a list of familiar conditions for American intervention. But there were some striking differences. Dulles still wanted France to accede to the condition that the Associated States be granted complete independence—but only after a specified number of years. This amendment was directly attributable, one must conclude, to his reaction to the Vietminh proposal at Geneva calling for early elections in each of the countries involved. As Dulles put it, to turn the Associated States "loose" too soon "would be like putting a baby in a cage of hungry lions. The baby would rapidly be devoured."[69]

Also dramatically different was the much shorter roster of nations he produced as constituting a "quorum" to activate united action. Great Britain was absent from the list.[70] Eisenhower had read Dillon's cable, and he also took it seriously. More so than in recent weeks, the president appeared anxious to remove obstacles to intervention, if not yet to affirm his willingness to do so. Eisenhower had also noticed the blank space the United Kingdom normally filled in Dulles' plans, and reminded everyone that he would act only on the basis of collective action—and only if there was evidence that the United Kingdom would participate eventually.

If the conditions were all met, however, the president would go before a joint session of Congress and request authority to use American armed forces to support the free governments the United States had recognized in the area. Of course, said Dulles, adding a cautionary note, Laniel's request was not an official statement of the French government's position. For that reason, in fact, another condition would have to be a prior favorable vote in the National Assembly requesting American aid. Such a commitment, presumably, would prevent "misunderstandings" of the sort that had plagued recent American efforts, and also bind a successor government.[71]

However eager the White House conferees had been at the

outset to "do something quick" to demonstrate that Dienbienphu had not been the last battle for Indochina, nor Geneva proposals the last words, there were still immense obstacles to overcome. The draft cable Dulles had prepared for Paris reflected these dilemmas. "If it became necessary to proceed without active U.K. participation," he confessed in this preliminary attempt, "the implications would be extremely serious and far-reaching." By the last paragraphs, indeed, Dulles was cautioning Ambassador Dillon not to leave anything in writing with Laniel, and, in the event the premier did wish to begin formal talks, to remind him that there would—in fact—have to be consultations with London.[72]

Whether or not Eisenhower had given him permission to explore united action without London as a charter member, Dulles continued to chafe at the "UK veto" on American action in the Pacific. At lunch on May 11, 1954, the secretary kept trying to nail the president down. There were serious disadvantages to going ahead without the British, but greater ones inhered in a situation "where we were obviously subject to UK veto, which in turn was largely subject to Indian veto, which in turn was largely subject to Chinese Communist veto. Thereby a chain was forged which tended to make us impotent, and to encourage Chinese Communist aggression to a point where the whole position in the Pacific would be endangered and the risk of general war increased."[73]

At a press conference that same day, Dulles tried to touch all bases, or perhaps, as some saw it, prepare for the worst. As cautiously as he could, the secretary offered an amendment to the domino theory. When nations came together, he said, as in NATO, that theory ceased to apply. Therefore, if the loss of Vietnam was immediately followed by the creation of a regional defense organization, the resulting situation would be far from hopeless. This was tricky business. Though he repeated he was not giving up in any of the Associated States, in Paris Dulles was immediately accused of delivering a stab in the back.[74]

French reactions were intensified, no doubt, by Ambassador Dillon's decision to delay forwarding Washington's "offer" of military consultations until after the debate on Vietnam in the National Assembly. As it happened, Laniel avoided political oblivion one more time, but only by two votes. The ambassador had been given leeway to do this, but the extra effort at caution backfired. It was not surprising that Laniel and his advisers, lacking any formal response to the plea, took Dulles' words to mean the United States was writing off Indochina, or at least considered it expendable.[75]

Actually, what Dulles was reacting to was the danger that the Geneva Conference might accept the Vietminh plan for early elections. It was a nice question as to whether he would prefer to lose the Associated States militarily, which he could blame on the French, or by elections, which he might have to blame on Woodrow Wilson's championing of self-determination at the Paris Peace Conference. In any event, it was a very unpleasant position to be in, as illustrated in the following exchange when the secretary was asked about the Vietminh proposal.

He would favor "genuinely free elections," affirmed Dulles, but conditions in Vietnam made that impossible in the near future. "At the present time in a country which is politically immature, which has been the scene of civil war and disruption, we would doubt whether the immediate conditions would be conducive to a result which would really reflect the will of the people." Well, came the next question, what if Ho Chi Minh won the election anyway? Dulles evaded a direct answer. "I said that I thought the United States should not stand passively by and see the extension of communism by any means into Southeast Asia. We are not standing passively by." The reporters persisted. Would the United States recognize an elected government led by Ho? "I have just said that I don't think the present conditions are conducive to a free election there and I don't care now to answer the hypothetical situation of what might result if they did have elections." If that were so, suggested another questioner, did the secretary believe the Vietnamese were not mature enough for independence?

No, he had not said any such thing. He meant only that conditions were not conducive for an outcome that would represent the people's will. For that matter, he went on, reaching somewhat safer ground, when the Berlin Conference talked about the so-called Eden Plan for all German elections, it was recognized in the West that these could only be held in East Germany after a period of preparation. "It was felt that the people were so terrorized, so misinformed, that quick elections held there under existing conditions could not be expected accurately to reflect the real views of the people and their intelligent judgment."[76]

The whole issue of free elections in the Cold War was in danger of unraveling here. First there was the question of how, especially in liberal democratic theory, it would be possible to grant independence to a nation without allowing elections. Taken literally, moreover, Dulles' definition of the Western position would make it impossible for there to be an end to the Cold War on any terms except an enforced occupation of former "Communist" territories. How else would the political re-education necessary to qualify the peoples of those areas for elections be carried out? What or who would constitute the government while that process went on?

5.

> In this case we are so mixed up with this colonialism, I can easily understand how the people in Indochina and elsewhere in Asia are not sure we are fighting for the French or Bao Dai or who we are fighting for and what would be the result of our success. That is not a fault on our part. I think we are in a devil of a difficult situation.
>
> SENATOR J. WILLIAM FULBRIGHT
> to John Foster Dulles, May 12, 1954[77]

"We face a very, very fundamental problem," Dulles admitted in response to Fulbright. While the secretary was testifying on Capitol Hill about the difficulties of getting the French to behave like the British had about Greece, he read members of the Senate Foreign Relations Committee a message that was going out to Walter Bedell Smith, clarifying his instructions.[78]

Under no circumstances was Smith to involve himself in the negotiation of any settlement that might have the effect "of subverting the existing lawful governments of the . . . [Associated States] or of permanently impairing their territorial integrity."[79] Early elections equaled subversion in Dulles' calculations, as noted above. The real meaning of the secretary's instructions, it might be argued, was: we prefer temporary partition to all-Vietnamese elections. The catchword here was "permanently." Dulles had already explored temporary partition, so as to get the south ready to launch a counterattack, and Under Secretary Smith was even now testing the waters with Molotov in Geneva.

It would be difficult, however, to square what he suggested to the Russian foreign minister with Washington's instructions ruling out a permanent solution by partition. Speaking with Canada's Lester Pearson on May 12, 1954, Smith said he had told Molotov that he did not fear a resumed war in Korea. But he was worried about Indochina. Molotov readily agreed that the situation was explosive and could lead to "more shooting." What did Smith have to suggest? He had been thinking about the matter a great deal, he told the Russian, and had no specific solution in mind, except that "he felt that if people could not live together in the same area without fighting it would seem reasonable that they should be put in separate areas." And then this: "[Smith] did not like lines of division, but if this was necessary to stop the fighting, he was prepared to accept some solution which would separate the fighting factions. He then suggested that a buffer state could be set up in the northern part of Vietnam. He did not specify the limits of this state but had vaguely suggested the area contiguous to China."

Pearson gathered from all this, not unreasonably, that the United States now accepted partition in "principle." But there was more. Smith had gone on to express his regret that Admiral Radford had so frightened the British "by his rash proposals respecting Dien Bien Phu." Though he concluded this remarkable interview with some remarks about the need to take advantage of Chinese fears of American military power, and the need for a regional security organization, the gist of what Eisenhower's former chief of staff had said could hardly be mistaken.[80]

The question then arises, did Bedell Smith have his signals mixed? Certainly what he told Lester Pearson of his conversation with the Russian delegate went well beyond any utterance from the lips of John Foster Dulles. In fact, it marked a radical departure. And from what Eden was about to learn from commonwealth and French sources, either Bedell Smith had a secret assignment from Eisenhower, or he was part of an American scheme to mislead London while Franco-American negotiations settled on the conditions for American intervention.

It was not beyond the realm of possibility, of course, that both were true. From the time that Dulles opposed a Korean truce in 1953, at least under the terms that Eisenhower would accept, there are little mysteries about Ike's Far Eastern policy. Dulles, as noted, on several occasions did not report everything back to Washington, especially in the pre-Geneva negotiations on united action. Other key players, like Bedell Smith, may have sought to work between Eisenhower and Dulles so as to achieve their own version of what policy should be.

Bedell Smith had encouraged Anthony Eden to agree to Five

Power staff talks (United States, United Kingdom, France, New Zealand, and Australia), but even before the Laniel overture of recent days, Dulles had met with Australian and New Zealand diplomats, expressing to them his doubts about British desires to have the staff talks consider military support for whatever settlement emerged at Geneva. For one thing, said the American secretary, there was nothing in the British proposal about talking with the Associated States to demonstrate we were not "abandoning them."[81]

Dulles called this a "slight difference," but there was every indication that he still hoped somehow to use the commonwealth to bring pressure on Her Majesty's government. More startling to Eden, however, were Swiss press reports of bilateral Franco-American negotiations. Someone, obviously, had gotten wind of the Laniel overture. Was there anything to these, he asked Bedell Smith? Smith knew nothing, he said, about any negotiations; but when Eden asked the French, an evasive first answer was followed by an admission that a "document" stipulating American conditions had indeed been received.[82]

Eden was also informed that the Americans preferred an early date for intervention, rather than waiting until Geneva failed. French coyness infuriated Eden. Returning to Bedell Smith, he received more bad news. The head of the American delegation "exploded with indignation," but the reason for this outburst was "Washington's inability to keep any discussions secret." Shocked at Smith's reaction, Eden pointed out that from the British point of view the seriousness of the situation did not have to do with premature disclosure, but the absence of prior consultation. Smith now agreed it was intolerable that a close ally should receive the news in the press.

The United Kingdom was to have been informed, he said, suddenly more conversant with what was going on in Washington, once French acceptance of the conditions was known. Besides, it was not so serious as the newspapers made out. All that was contemplated was American assistance in training Vietnamese native forces.[83]

From commonwealth representatives Eden was able to fill in the details. It soon emerged that Dulles had let it be known to Australia and New Zealand that his new plan for united action did not make British participation a prerequisite. That may not have been an accurate picture of Eisenhower's view, as the White House conversation on May 11 left things a bit up in the air, but it certainly was Dulles', and the secretary no doubt yearned to be able to go to the president having lined up the ANZUS nations beforehand. Not only would that demonstrate that London's opposition was not shared by the commonwealth nations of the Pacific area, but it would encourage the president to accept Dulles' contention that the British could not stand out for long.[84]

The ANZUS/American "bloc" did not materialize. Whatever inducements Dulles offered the Australians and New Zealanders proved insufficient to overcome traditional loyalties, but that did not ease Eden's mind. Not at all. This constant talk of intervention, coming back again and again, he cabled Churchill, weakened whatever chances had existed for agreement. All along the Chinese and Russians had been saying that America was attending the conference only to cause it to fail, or to promote a cover story. These reports hardly disproved their claim.[85]

Other members of the British delegation, however much they sympathized with the foreign secretary's travails at the hands of Dulles and Bedell Smith, felt that Eden's personal reactions were getting mixed up now with an unhealthy desire to play mediator. The Americans were hardly the only disingenuous ones sitting at Geneva, argued his private secretary, Evelyn Shuckburgh, and they were still Britain's closest ally. Pressed to say why he thought the Russians wanted peace in Indochina, Eden told an associate that it was because it may lead to war. "I am inside right," the foreign secretary joked to a skeptical Shuckburgh, "the Americans outside right. Molotov is inside left, Chou outside left." To Shuckburgh's dismay, Eden even shared the joke with Molotov, who, said the latter, enjoyed it very much. "I'll bet he did," Shuckburgh wrote in his diary, adding, "but he did not criticize *his* outside wing, or show any divergence from them."[86]

"Bedell Smith is clearly unhappy," Eden persisted. "It looks as though the Radford policy has won through in Washington. Perhaps Dulles has been supporting it all the time." The scheme would fail, like all the others. "We shall be left weaker and in greater disarray as on the occasion of every other United States initiative of recent months. But we must do our best to limit the damage."[87]

French diplomats, meanwhile, stoutly denied negotiating with the Americans for immediate intervention; they wanted only something to strengthen their hands in dealing with the Communists. Their country, Ivone Kirkpatrick, permanent secretary at the Foreign Office, was told, remained "determined to seek a peaceful solution at Geneva." Kirkpatrick replied "rather tartly" that considerable damage had been done. If a press leak had not occurred, "we might still be in blissful ignorance." The foreign secretary had been engaged in tricky negotiations with the Chinese and the Russians. "He must have felt last week like a lawyer to whom his clients did not divulge full information."[88]

Bidault was certainly not divulging full information to someone. Neither were the others involved in this chase around Robin Hood's barn. As the *New York Times* reported on May 17, 1954, the British had threatened to withdraw from Five Power talks unless it was made clear that there was no question of American intervention until the conference was over. Bidault hastened to reassure Eden in person that the only reason for the Franco-American talks was to give him a card to play to hasten an end to the hostilities. If that were so, of course, it was unlikely that the threat would be of any real use, given the demonstrated inability of any of the delegations to keep anything secret.[89]

Eden's threat to disassociate the British government from Five Power staff talks also brought an appeal from Bedell Smith that the prime minister instead reassure the House of Commons that Anglo-American relations at Geneva were back on a basis of "full and frank" discussion.[90] It was becoming more and more difficult to reconcile the various declarations made by American policymakers—both in public and in private—with any sort of coherent program for restoring peace or salvaging a position in Southeast Asia. The *New York Times* also reported, for example, that Smith had given personal assurances to Bao Dai that there would be no partition. The head of the American delegation was also supposed to have told Vietnam's nominal ruler that the United States opposed any political settlement.[91]

When French diplomats continued their "confession" to British counterparts about the American negotiations, on the other hand, they insisted that the American conditions were unacceptable as they stood, and that in no case could there have been even a reply for at least two weeks. But they also said that during the course of the negotiations, the Americans had referred to "their possible intervention in terms of two to three marine divisions."[92]

As it happened, the suggestion of American ground forces—a minimum of twenty thousand—had been made by Laniel's advisers as a proviso of their own in response to the American list of conditions for intervention. Maurice Schumann told Ambassador Dillon on May 17, 1954, the same day other French officials spoke of the supposed American proposal for sending marine divisions, that "from the French political point of view, and also from the point of view of the effect in Vietnam it would be absolutely essential to have a limited commitment of American ground troops." Since France had not used conscripts in Indochina, conceded Schumann, Paris could not expect America to send army draftees. "However, they felt that a force of 20,000 marines would be the minimum required to satisfy public opinion here and in Vietnam that US was not simply trying [to] force the French to continue to carry the full burden of the ground fighting."[93]

Yet another game was being played here, for French officials asserted that the National Assembly's willingness to ratify the EDC depended on its ability to withdraw men from Indochina for service in Europe. Laniel's overture, instead of an appeal for help, now took on aspects of blackmail.[94] While Schumann did not foresee that the marines would be required immediately, and repeated the formula that these forces were to constitute bargaining strength, he talked about them as necessary for a "successful conclusion of the war in Indochina." Paris was eager to see an American general to talk over these matters. Of course, Schumann promised, for its part the French government would no longer equivocate on the independence issue, but the right of outright withdrawal from the French Union remained unacceptable.[95]

Such interviews left heads spinning. It was like being in the middle of a Henry James dialogue. All anyone seemed to be getting out of it was a bad case of vertigo. To the chief American diplomat in Saigon, the situation resembled something even worse. "Once as a little boy," he cabled Washington, "I had seen a water snake in a creek which had swallowed a catfish. The spines of the fish had pierced the snake's throat and he could get the fish neither down nor up. We do not want to get ourselves in a similar position here."[96]

6.

> The sooner you get into this war, the better we will like it.
>
> GENERAL PAUL ELY to his American visitors, May 19, 1954[97]

The impasses reached at Geneva, and in Paris and Washington, were perfectly mirrored in Vietnam. Whether one wanted to move peace negotiations forward or to find an entry point for American forces, the situation was the same. Lieutenant General John W. O'Daniel received assurances from Ely that American assistance in the training of Vietnamese forces was welcome, but there was to be no division of authority, no change in the organization of that army to upgrade its status, and no U.S. participation in operational planning.[98]

Faced with reports from Bedell Smith, meanwhile, that Molotov was taking advantage of the deadlock in Western capitals to play upon allied fears and to exploit the "atmosphere of defeat" to Communist advantage, Dulles did not know whom to blame the most. Smith also warned that unless "deeds rather than words" emanated from Washington, Russian overconfidence might lead to war. Again, Dulles did not know exactly whom or what to blame.[99]

The best candidate was, as before, Great Britain. The French persisted in error, but British leadership had lost its scruple or nerve, or both. The problem was to convince the president. How inconvenient, then, that the prime minister should choose this moment to issue yet another of his solemn pledges to the Commons that Her Majesty's government had made absolutely no commitments, had not even "embarked on any negotiations involving commitments," to collective defense in Southeast Asia, and would wait until the outcome at Geneva was known before contemplating such a step.

Dulles told Smith he was full of "a certain righteous—I hope—indignation."[100] Did the British expect the United States to remain silent, he asked rhetorically, while they repudiated, and not only repudiated, but misrepresented, their April 13 pledge to examine collective defense for the area? Meeting with the president, Dulles continued pushing the idea that the U.K. did not have to be an active participant in the newest scheme for regional association. The president agreed. But, he insisted, the United States must not be in the position of "going in alone." Australia and New Zealand would have to participate, as well as the Philippines and Thailand.[101]

Eisenhower also said that he would not rule out in principle the use of marines, as the French had requested, if they were part of a collective effort. Later that day, May 19, 1954, Eisenhower actually told reporters that he thought it was possible to go ahead without Great Britain. "I should say that with the proper Asiatic nations, which of course I lay down as a *sine qua non,* and Australia and New Zealand, we might possibly work out something that would be maybe not as satisfactory or as broad as you would like it, but could be workable."[102]

But try as he might, Dulles could still make no real progress with ANZUS representatives.[103] Questioned about the hugger-mugger surrounding the Franco-American talks, the secretary of state, his feathers ruffled, tried to explain to ANZUS diplomats that, London's having stated over and over again it would not discuss a pact until the Geneva Conference ended, the British had nothing to reproach Washington about. Frustration etching his every syllable, Dulles cautioned them that regional defense plans were of the utmost importance to Australia and New Zealand, and the United States expected those nations to respond favorably to the invitation to form a pact. The response he received was not encouraging.[104]

The ANZUS nations feared being forced to choose between London and Washington, Dulles explained to the National Security Council.[105] He should have added that when this all started back at the beginning of April, Washington was simply hoping to bring moral pressure on the British government through Auckland and Canberra. Now it was attempting something far more difficult: genuine coercion. When he turned to other aspects of situation, Dulles had more discouraging news to report.

Discussions with the French on the preconditions for intervention had, as might be expected, stalled yet again on the question of ultimate independence for the Associated States. French diplomats adamantly opposed any public declaration that withdrawal from the French Union was permissible. Only the constitution of Soviet Russia, said Georges Bidault with heavy-handed sarcasm, acknowledged the right of an individual republic to withdraw from the USSR. Besides, he argued, such a declaration was sure to cause new troubles in Africa, which, in turn, would "necessitate further acts of repression . . . which would be most undesirable."[106]

Dulles had himself been mulling over the dilemma American policy found itself in because of the independence issue. Ever since the Vietminh proposal at Geneva for immediate independence *and immediate elections,* he had been searching for a new formula. His best attempt was a proposal for complete independence at the end of a stipulated period of time. But he could not retreat on the issue of whether independence, when it was gained, was limited by the question of the right of withdrawal.

To the NSC Dulles confessed that "we might be exaggerating the significance of the independence issue." The Associated States already had achieved a "very high degree of independence," and "if we harped on the independence issue it might well rise to embarrass us when the scene shifted from Indochina to Malaya."[107] Yet because the French had so often in the past promised something that on examination turned out to be much less than real independence, it was essential this time not to allow the impression that a "Vietnamese decision to remain in French Union was extorted as price for independence."[108]

Added to these difficulties was another obstacle. When the latest talk about intervention and preconditions for intervention began, the Joint Chiefs of Staff had been consulted for their views. Dulles hoped to present a concrete plan to the five-nation staff talks, but he was alarmed when he saw what the JCS had in mind. In a memorandum signed by Admiral Radford, the JCS declared, "Atomic weapons will be used whenever it is to our military advantage."[109]

Worse, in conversations with the secretary, Radford had given it as his opinion that there was little use in talking about any defense of Southeast Asia or of a substantial commitment of U.S. forces in the area. Instead, American power should be directed at the source of the peril, in the first instance China, "and that in this connection atomic weapons should be used."[110] This was far more strongly put than it had been in the JCS paper on intervention, and it alarmed Dulles.

While he did not question the admiral's military judgment, the secretary told President Eisenhower, such talk did not serve American political objectives with the Five Power discussions pending. "It would lead to U.S. isolation, and indeed it had already done so to some extent in connection with Admiral Radford's last trip to Paris and London." This was as close as Dulles could ever come to admitting that the British had expressed reservations about collective defense schemes, of whatever nature, and that there might be a reason for their behavior beyond a craven desire to protect narrow "imperial" interests.

Eisenhower fully agreed that the JCS should not assume the inevitability of war with China, and should not put its views before other nations in ways that might interfere with the political purposes of the government. And he promised to make sure that did not happen.[111] The JCS paper made Dulles do some more thinking, however, about what it was that he was really after in a collective defense organization. As Samuel Johnson said, the prospect of the gallows concentrates the mind powerfully. Of course if there were overt military action the United States could not rely on a static type of defense, but even that did not seem to warrant consideration of all-out war against China. Not the least thing wrong with that kind of thinking was that it offered absolutely nothing to the "peoples whom we would defend." This was especially true because Dulles did not anticipate overt Chinese aggression, but rather subversion and indirect aggression.

To counter that threat required attention to local defense, as was the case in NATO, backed ultimately by outside power. Militarily, "token participation" of coalition nations would be enough, but the key to success would be "economic and social measures which may cost us some money, but infinitely less than would be required to build a major military defense in the area which I agree seems quite unwise to attempt."[112]

Dulles also believed that this concept would work whether or not all or part of Indochina was lost to the Communists. But these new definitions simply reinforced the view that the United States must disassociate itself from French policy, and that it was time to stop playing around with schemes of intervention such as those under consideration since the early days after the fall of Dienbienphu.

The new instrument of American policy, Ngo Dinh Diem, was actually waiting in the wings in Paris. "We are prepared to accept the seemingly ridiculous prospect that this Yogi-like mystic could assume the charge he is apparently about to undertake," marveled Ambassador Douglas Dillon, "only because the standard set by his predecessors is so low."[113] The setup at Geneva could be changed to suit Washington better, but only if it included a place for Diem. Perhaps it took a "Yogi-like mystic" to rescue American policy. But Diem hovering offstage was only one of several new players to make a difference at Geneva.

CHAPTER NINE

Making Peace on a Bed of Nails

We fought desperately against partition. . . . Absolutely impossible to surmount the hostility of our enemies and the perfidy of false friends. Unusual procedures paralyzed the action of our delegation. All arrangements were signed in privacy. We express deepest sorrow in this total failure of our mission.

TRAN VAN DO TO NGO DINH DIEM
at the conclusion of the
Geneva Conference[1]

It is an anguished peace.

GENERAL PAUL ELY[2]

We got more than I expected—if we can get a coalition going.

WALTER BEDELL SMITH,
on the telephone to
President Eisenhower,
July 23, 1954[3]

JEFFERSON Davis once assured a skeptic that partition would avoid civil war. "War between North and South?" he responded to a challenge put by Benjamin Franklin's great-granddaughter. "My dear Madam, inconceivable! Two friendly nations, rather, living side by side."[4] No one at the 1954 Geneva Conference thought North and South Vietnam would live like "two friendly nations," but there were those who believed Jefferson Davis had, if not the right idea, the only solution to stop the fighting. Beyond that it would be a case of wait and see. Maybe the great powers could come up with a better solution.

Everyone agreed that partition had little to recommend itself otherwise. Everyone—except the two Vietnamese delegations—

also thought that self-determination was fraught with danger, too risky, frankly, for the rest of the world to allow the Vietnamese to determine their own fate. Even a temporary respite was welcome to men who had been fighting for eight years, and all the more so to governments that desperately wanted to avoid a larger war. The new French premier, Pierre Mendès-France, who took office on June 18, promised the National Assembly to bring peace in four weeks or resign. "If the conflict in Indochina is not settled—and settled very soon—it is the risk of war, of an international and perhaps atomic war, that we must face."[5]

Actually the danger of atomic war had receded by mid-June, and was much less an immediate peril than two months earlier, when Operation Vulture had been under active consideration. Mendès-France was quite right, however, to sound the alarm about a possible breakdown in the Geneva talks, however, for that remained a real possibility up until the very last day of the conference.

For Anthony Eden, more than any other statesman present, Geneva came close to being the model Cold War solution. He had a big stake in its success, and, to sum it all up, he thought that it would not take much work to make a virtue out of necessity. Whether he was as afraid of a larger war as he let on to reporters covering the conference, or was simply enjoying upstaging Dulles and company, as his private secretary feared, Eden was convinced that partition was a positive solution for all concerned, and he worked especially hard to convince Zhou Enlai to see its virtues.[6]

Zhou listened carefully and indeed shared many of Eden's views, albeit from a very different perspective. The two were instrumental in forging compromises that permitted the conference to succeed. But the Chinese had no more enthusiasm than Dulles and Eisenhower for Eden's grand design. Tempting a number of fates, the British foreign secretary would liken the design he had in mind to the 1920s European Treaty of Locarno. He could not have chosen a less attractive rubric. Rightly or wrongly, Locarno stood for appeasement and the failure of diplomacy in the interwar years. Little wonder that those who heard him expound on the theme, glowingly at times, recoiled in shock, not least at Eden's seeming naïveté.

Not that the Russians and the Chinese were unwilling to put pressure on the Vietminh delegates to act in a "reasonable" manner, which meant, as Vietminh leaders ruefully discovered, sacrificing territory won on the battlefield. The Vietnamese, North and South alike, soon learned at Geneva that they were expected to volunteer to sacrifice themselves in order to serve the world as "buffer states" between East and West.

Not even those who understood that Eden was not urging a new Munich approved another Locarno, so inappropriately dredged up out of Europe's sad experiences in the interwar years. That wisely forgotten treaty of the 1920s had assumed France and Germany were "satisfied" with the status quo, sought no territorial adjustments to the Versailles Treaty, and were willing to be supervised, as it were, by a consortium of powers. It depended, therefore, upon the willingness of other participants in the pact to guarantee that status quo.

Neither assumption had held water at the time, and neither applied to the current situation in Southeast Asia. But Eden was guilty not so much of an ill-advised nostalgia for appeasement as of confusing and misapplying lessons from the colonial era to the postwar world of revolutionary nationalism. Specifically, when he talked about Locarno, what he really meant was something on the order of a buffer zone between empires, as in the case of India's old northwest frontier.

Nothing was the same. Communist China was not tsarist Russia, however much it wanted to participate in the great-power consortium, and it would not countenance the notion that Eden put forward, that the Russo-Chinese security treaty and a Southeast Asian NATO would balance the diplomatic scales, and provide a sturdy guarantee for the arrangements arrived at by the Geneva Conference. Except for Great Britain, the conferees accepted partition only as the lesser evil—and for a minimum period of time.

Besides the two Vietnamese delegations, only the United States had protested even a temporary partition. Washington eventually came round, as we have seen, to the view that temporary separation of the combatants was the only way to get rid of the French, followed by the initiation of a reunification policy with a genuine nationalist appeal, thereby, it dared to hope, eventually stripping Ho Chi Minh of his false legitimacy as the nationalist prophet of Indochina. Still later, Americans would see South Vietnam as a viable state on its own—even if it required constant transfusions of American aid—as the only alternative to a unified Communist state.[7]

But in 1954, Eden's resurrecting the Locarno, Old World model of diplomacy actually gave Dulles a chance to reinvigorate his own favored model liberation, under the banner of a Potomac Charter, purposely named to revive memories of the Atlantic Charter and FDR's supposed strong stand for universal self-determination. During negotiations for the Potomac Charter in late June 1954, American leaders sometimes even called it Atlantic Charter #2.

If Eden had trouble with the appeasement connection attached to Locarno, however, Dulles had problems with the riddle of self-determination *without* elections in the Potomac Charter. FDR had not lived to face that one. The final declaration of the Geneva Conference on July 20, 1954, called for all-Vietnamese elections at the end of two years. All-Vietnamese elections held about as much attraction for American policymakers as encountering the grim reaper instead of the familiar bartender in a favorite watering place. The Potomac Charter was silent on the possibility.

The Geneva settlement could work, either as Locarno or as the Potomac Charter, paradoxically, only if it was left unfinished. Was it conceivable that the great powers would allow Vietnamese elections to determine the issue of war or peace? Better to leave such questions unasked—you might get a truthful answer.

The Eisenhower administration, finally, was still tormented by the Korean precedent. It taunted policymakers, this Janus-faced statue marking the truce signed at Panmunjon, with the contradiction between liberation and the reality of partition, and it troubled the sleep of anyone who thought about using troops to rectify the disparity by force of arms. On one side the Korean precedent appeared as a graveyard statue, arm raised to warn the quick against intervention with land forces; look again from the other side, and it admonished the viewer that the outcome of that war left the Eisenhower administration in a compromised position.

What future was there for liberation if all it promised was half a country?

1.

The United States cannot lend itself to this game.

JOHN FOSTER DULLES to Ambassador Henri Bonnet, ca. June 8, 1954[8]

In the final days of May 1954, General Paul Ely reported to Paris on his post-Dienbienphu survey of battle conditions and what prospects remained for reorganizing a semblance of defense. The most controversial of his recommendations, promptly leaked to the press, was to use conscripts. British ambassador Sir Gladwyn Jebb wrote Anthony Eden privately that the Ely report would never be accepted, unless—and here was a cruel dilemma—the United States agreed to come in with both feet. If that happened, of course, "a new situation will arise."

This oblique reference to the stillborn Franco-American negotiations and the twenty thousand marines Paris had asked for—perhaps not even expecting a favorable reply, and certainly not prepared for the consequences of one—well indicated the confused, and confusing, state of affairs at the end of one month's labors at the negotiating table. All one could say was that time was growing short on the battlefield. The diplomats had better stop going round in circles.

Jebb was not optimistic about the outcome either in Indochina, or for passage of the EDC, or for what disasters might ensue as a result. "All these gloomy reflections only show how important it is to reach some agreed solution at Geneva *soon.* For that purpose the *threat* of American intervention may well be effective; but Heaven knows what might happen if the threat were carried out. The operation could well be successful and the patient die. Alternatively no solution and no intervention could mean further French disasters which would have unpredictable, but certainly bad, effects in Paris, possibly involving the future of N.A.T.O."[9]

No one could tell, not Jebb, certainly, and not Eden either, what might trigger American intervention. If the French lost Hanoi while the conferees appeared to diddle, Washington might jump the traces altogether, leaping headlong into the war—or, alternatively, the Americans might reduce their conditions so as to make Paris an offer it could not refuse. Their only condition might be that the Geneva talks be called off. Indeed, that was what Jean Chauvel and Paul Boncour confided to the British foreign minister during an "indiscreet" luncheon on June 1, 1954. Chauvel thought Bedell Smith was sensible, but "Dulles was like a man who had been bitten by a mosquito. He seemed determined upon action of some kind."[10]

Jebb's comment that the threat of American intervention might be useful in bringing about success at the negotiating table, therefore, posed the question as to how one could be sure that a mosquito-troubled man, if he was careless, might not carry out his threat to swat the creatures with a two-by-four. Eden noted in his memoirs that Geneva was the first international meeting "at which I was sharply conscious of the deterrent power of the hydrogen bomb.

. . . I was grateful for it," he added, more problematically for the historian. At any rate, what he hoped to achieve with deterrence was not what Washington wished to see. The H-bomb, Eden thought, worked best to spur Russia and Great Britain to press on the others a settlement, however flawed, since the threat of thermonuclear destruction was most vivid to those two vulnerable nations. And by a process of elimination, the H-bomb, having deprived the French of any hope of enlisting British support for joint intervention, left partition the only logical alternative.[11]

That was definitely not the way massive retaliation was supposed to work. Eden further thought the Americans were oblivious to this boomerang effect of the H-bomb because of their military superiority and distance from the Soviet Union. Actually that might not have been the case. Eisenhower sometimes used the H-bomb threat as self-deterrence when he ran down the list of options to accepting half a country or less out of Geneva. When the secretary of state argued that Chinese intervention in Indochina amounted to a "declaration of war against the United States," the president took him up. The United States still would not go into Indochina alone he said, but "if the U.S. took action against Communist China . . . there should be no halfway measures or frittering around. The Navy and Air Force should go in with full power, using new weapons, and strike at air bases and ports in mainland China."[12]

Sobering thoughts, these. And Dulles, who, as noted, worried that Admiral Radford's preparations for allied staff talks much overdid reliance on nuclear weapons, admitted as much in his press conference on June 8, 1954, replying to a question about the administration's plans for approaching Congress with a request for an Indochina resolution by saying there were no plans. "There has so far not been a sufficiently general acceptance of the program to make it, as a matter of practical politics, a question of going to Congress." The prospects for united action had declined, and the objective now would be different. "The objective would be to retain in friendly hands as much as possible of the South East Asian peninsular and island area. Now the practicability varies from time to time. What was practical a year ago is less practical today. The situation has, I am afraid, been deteriorating."[13]

He might have added that the United States was beginning to be in the position of the little boy who cried wolf. The more one talked about using nuclear weapons, the less likely did anyone believe that there was adequate reason to do so—or believe the threat.

In his memoirs, Eisenhower reflected on this phenomenon, suggesting he was troubled by the thought that there was an impression abroad that the United States was carrying primary responsibility for the defense of Indochina. His major concern, he wrote, now became to disabuse *everyone* of that notion.[14]

So the logic of deterrence had failed in this situation, leaving a logic of partition to be put together out of its fragments. If squabbles over an international control commission could be resolved, reasoned Eden, along with the separation of the fate of the three states, it might be done. Where Eden reached, Dulles pulled back. The secretary was aware of the deteriorating situation on the battlefield, and had realistically appraised the failure to move the ANZUS states, and had, indeed, reasoned out the logic. But still he resisted the final step: acceptance.

What Walter Bedell Smith now reported from Geneva, by depriving him of any last hopes, at least made that step easier. In recent conversations with American diplomats, Smith cabled, the new minister for the Associated States, Frederic-Dupont, had talked about partition. What he had in mind, Bedell Smith cabled, was "likely to be the best we will be able to get." As Vietminh military victories piled up, Ho's representatives were behaving with even greater truculence about political matters at Geneva:

> I believe also that the Chinese Communists have considered and are willing to risk the chance of what we might do in Indochina. They probably would welcome the introduction of some US ground forces there because of the opportunity this would give them directly to intervene for the ostensible purpose of repelling US aggression and because of the initially adverse effect our participation would have on Asiatic public opinion for many reasons well-known to you. *I believe it already has involved in the minds of Australia and New Zealand some of the thoughts of "supporting colonialism" judging by the apprehensive reaction of their representatives here to our military talks in Paris.*[15]

Eisenhower's first reaction to this predicament was to consider reducing the status of the American delegation at Geneva. The continuing stalemate over separating Laos and Cambodia from Vietnam gave him a perfect argument for doing so. That position Dulles shared. By "disengaging," as he put it in a telegram to Bedell Smith, the United States would absolve itself of any arrangement that gave a stamp of approval to the captivity of previously free peoples.

Dulles always had Yalta on his mind, and what the 1952 Republican platform statements he had drafted said that agreement had done in regard to Eastern Europe. But it was more than consistency he worried about. Signing any agreement that now seemed possible out of Geneva would, he feared, preclude later action. It would be used, a signature, to commit Washington to uphold a settlement deliberately designed "to preclude any efforts on the part of the U.S. at liberation of the peoples who were subject to captivity."[16]

Of course, that was indeed why there was a Geneva Conference in the first place. Every time, then, he was defeated on the issue of intervention—and even after he accepted the logic of partition—Dulles acted to preserve his future options. How aware Eisenhower was of these hedges, and whether he approved, remains a moot question.* In carefully phrased speeches on the West Coast at Seattle, San Francisco, and Los Angeles, the secretary appeared to be reiterating old positions, but he was engaged in fact in dragging bushes across his trail, pioneer fashion, to cover his tracks. Warning the Communists with one swipe not to test the administration in the western Pacific by attempting to drive the United States "back to California," he insisted with another that the Eisenhower administration harbored no desire for war with China, and then, with a series of rapid strokes, discussed allied relations:

> Diversity often seems a troublesome fact. But the richness of life is, above all, due to differences. No two human beings are exactly alike. . . . There is no problem more difficult than that of trying to build unity on a foundation of diversity. . . . On the other hand,

*This pattern, still relatively new in 1954, would become more and more standard in Cold War Washington, as the bureaucracy grew, and the decision-making circle included more and more points on the compass. At the height of the foreign policy crisis of the Reagan administration, Secretary of State George Shultz testified, about the sale of arms to Iran, "Nothing ever gets settled in this town. It's not like running a company, or even a university. It's—it's a seething debating society in which the debate never stops, in which people never give up, including me. And so that's the atmosphere in which you administer. And what I try to do is stay as close to the President as I can, and I feel very close to him." See *New York Times*, December 9, 1986, p. A13. What Shultz implied about staying close, perhaps unconsciously a double-entendre (and perhaps not), could have been said by Dulles in 1954 about Vietnam.

we must not be blind to the fact that differences can mount to a point where they become a real danger . . . and there come times when differences must be voluntarily submerged.[17]

Given their recent conversations, it is interesting to speculate that Dulles was also ruminating about his differences with Eisenhower. That he was in the doldrums when he delivered this obituary for united action can hardly be doubted. Yet Dulles' season of discontent was about over. It began, not surprisingly, with the fall of the Laniel government. The surprise was his successor, Pierre Mendès-France. Who could have predicted that the radical socialist premier would provide the Eisenhower administration as well as Paris with new options in dealing with the Indochina crisis?

For months Washington had feared that Mendès-France spelled nothing but disaster for Indochina, for the EDC, for the decline of the West. What a good omen instead Mendès-France turned out to be. Indeed, he helped Dulles launch the Potomac Charter. Without him—*mirabile dictu*—it might not have been accomplished.

2.

> The two parties should take a few steps toward each other—which doesn't mean that each has to take the same number of steps.
>
> ZHOU ENLAI to Mendès-France[18]

Washington was much too alarmed at first about the new premier's socialist principles to see Mendès-France as a blessing in disguise, but that he was. For one thing, whatever he did about resolving the French predicament, Mendès-France could not emulate Laniel in shifting the blame to the United States for not coming to the rescue at Dienbienphu or afterward. A new French government, dedicated to correcting past errors in dealing with Vietnamese nationalism, could hardly criticize the United States for following its lead and dealing directly with an "independent" South Vietnam. There was now nothing to prevent the United States from exerting its influence with Bao Dai, or whomever, to name new anti-Communist nationalists to power. And with that accomplished, to achieve what Washington had always wanted: a fresh start in Southeast Asia.

Second, Mendès-France could deal with Ho and the Chinese to get the best deal he could; and while the Americans had always feared that situation, in a new context, it gave Dulles even more room to maneuver an American replacement of French colonialism. It began to develop, therefore, that the United States had a stake in Mendès-France's success—and, most unexpectedly, in the success of the Geneva Conference itself. Since the end of March, and his "Uniting for Action" speech, Dulles had sought to save Southeast Asia from the outcome of Geneva. Now, he was beginning to see that the way ran through Geneva, for that was the only way Vietnam could become truly independent; and for that purpose, Mendès-France turned out to be a vital contributor to American policy.

The crucial issue at Geneva, it had soon appeared, was the issue of whether the war in Vietnam could be treated separately from the situation in Laos and Cambodia, and the related question of a political settlement. When Eden and Zhou first met for serious discussions on May 20, 1954, the British foreign secretary insisted that Laos and Cambodia were easy matters to settle. All that had to happen was for the Vietminh to withdraw their invading troops. As expected, Zhou insisted that Indochina was a "single colonial war," started by the French, for which the only solution was a simultaneous and indivisible cease-fire.[19]

Eden pointed out that this inflexible approach courted the dangers of a wider war. It strengthened the conviction in the West that the Vietminh were out to "grab the whole of Indo-China," using the fiction of resistance movements in Laos and Cambodia. Zhou responded in kind that the French were in danger of emulating the American attitude at the outset of the Korean negotiations, which only prolonged that war. And so the deadlock.[20]

The differences—argued in foggy terms about whether the rebel forces in Laos and Cambodia were genuine or fabricated out of Vietminh resources—were really about where to draw the line. Eden wanted not to surrender most of Indochina; Zhou feared Western military bases close to China's borders. Dulles could take some credit, surely, for this Chinese wariness, with his repeated harangues about Beijing's evil intentions, as if that nation's new leaders were glowering demoniac figures come to life from ancient Chinese prints.[21]

The Eden-Zhou conversations took place in an environment colored by many other factors. The most dramatic change was Mendès-France's accession to power. Georges Bidault had often let it be known that he was considering cutting a deal with the Chinese Communists, but he lacked whatever it took, skills, imagination, or maybe realism, to succeed. Perhaps he was merely bluffing.

But Mendès-France had pulled off a daring gamble and wrenched himself free to negotiate with anybody he pleased to end the war. He had refused to accept the Communist votes cast in favor of his premiership in the Assembly. Though Communist leader Jacques Duclos denounced the action as "unconstitutional," Mendès-France had adroitly slipped out of the ideological grasp of the left and sped past the gendarmes of the right into the premiership with votes to spare.[22] Instead of then following standard procedures, Mendès-France named a highly personalized cabinet, including several conservatives, and then went about his scheme in relative safety, using his self-defined mandate to end the war in four weeks as a talisman against domestic and foreign criticism. By the time he was finished, moreover, he had won over such disparate authorities on Cold War *savior faire* as Molotov and Dulles.

It did not look that way at the beginning. Upon assuming the premiership, Mendès-France first had to cope with what seemed to be an early collapse of the peace negotiations. Frustrated by his inability to move the Chinese or the Russians, Anthony Eden had informed his colleague Walter Bedell Smith that he was ready to see the conference go into recess. This was treated as good news by the American delegation, not fully aware as yet of the favorable implications of Mendès-France's accession to power, and not a little pleased with an opportunity to say "I told you so" to the "mastermind" of the conference.[23]

As Eisenhower recalled the situation, he had decided that if the French continued the negotiations despite their obvious futility, "our best move would be to reduce our delegation in stature rather than completely withdraw it."[24] Smith then explained to Eden that the president felt the "Communists were only spinning things out to suit their military purposes and the time had now come to decide where the West intended to draw the line in South-East Asia. He was convinced that the Communists would carry on until such a line had been drawn and the Communists warned 'thus far and no further.' "[25]

Eden and Zhou had met several times in an effort to resolve the basic impasse over whether Laos and Cambodia were the same as Vietnam. Perhaps because he had been warned by Eden that collapse was imminent, Zhou hosted a friendly lunch for Mendès-France.[26] Toward the end, the Chinese diplomat even hinted he would accept a pro-French tilt: "The two parties should take a few steps toward each other—which doesn't mean that each has to take the same number of steps."

Mendès-France was placed in a position to accomplish what his predecessors had only talked about: a bargain with China over the head of Ho Chi Minh. No single factor explains why he was so advantageously placed, but Mendès-France knew how to make the best of it. A bargain of sorts was also discussed by Smith and the new premier. Informing the American of his decision to meet with Zhou, Mendès-France promised not to accept a peace that was a surrender to the Vietminh, and asked that Washington in turn use its influence with the newly appointed Vietnamese premier, Ngo Dinh Diem, and with Bao Dai to prevent needless obstruction of "any honorable truce which the French might reach with the Vietminh."[27]

Mendès-France's request that Washington intervene with Vietnamese leaders amounted to a tacit recognition that the United States now had a key political role to play in Vietnam, not in immediate military intervention, but in the survival of a "partitioned" Vietnam. As such, it was also a step—if a small one—toward acceptance of long-standing American terms for such a presence.

Smith's report of this conversation noted that Mendès-France had repeatedly stressed the difficulty of selling any agreement with the Vietminh to the new Vietnamese government. Diem was a fanatic like South Korea's Syngman Rhee, he added, but he would undoubtedly place great weight on any advice that came from Washington. All this was perhaps only realistic on the French leader's part, but it was certainly different in both tone and purport from the fruitless negotiations over conditions for military intervention when Laniel and Bidault had wriggled free of a final commitment. Smith reserved his attitude on this "one important request," but even that argued well for an understanding.[28]

Mystery still surrounds the appointment of Diem as Bao Dai's prime minister. Aloof, a devout Catholic in a country with a Buddhist majority, and endowed with few of the charismatic qualities associated with political leadership, Ngo Dinh Diem had served in the French colonial administration in the 1920s, and then briefly as secretary of the interior in Bao Dai's almost powerless government in the early 1930s. He left in protest at French interference in Vietnamese internal affairs and stayed out of government thereafter, being tempted to return only once, in 1945, when the Japanese invited him to become premier in their client government.

His nationalist credentials were further weakened, then, by his exile in Europe and the United States during the last years of the struggle against the French, even though he kept up a steady stream of criticism of Bao Dai for not pursuing the cause of Vietnamese independence with more vigor. The Vietnamese community in Paris, a powerful factor at this time, at first refused to vet him for the post, and relented only reluctantly when its first choices were ruled out. What overcame all these adverse factors? Speculation has always centered on Washington's influence.[29]

Recent works have added little to what has long been known about Diem's activities, and those on his behalf by American supporters. He had powerful friends in the United States, a range of acquaintances remarkable in this era because it stretched across the political spectrum. The account offered by a sometime participant in various negotiations with the Vietnamese, Chester L. Cooper, is intriguing, however, both for pointing out some obvious truths and adding some new twists to the story. Cooper dismisses the notion that Diem's appointment was the result of a successful American cloak-and-dagger operation, or some conspiracy by private interests that hoped to gain something out of Vietnam economically.[30]

Diem definitely was *not* the candidate, on the other hand, observes Cooper, of French capitalist interests. Those groups had been putting considerable pressure on Laniel (whose tottering government could not resist such a powerful lobby) to see that Bao Dai appointed "a pliable man who could be induced to preserve French economic and, perhaps, even some political influence in Vietnam." Here, revealed incidentally, is another powerful reason why Laniel had so stoutly resisted American conditions for intervention, conditions that would have introduced Vietnam into the world market, with the inevitable decline in French advantages.

Because it is so important to understand the ramifications of American management of the free world "system," it is worth elaborating on Cooper's point. The former CIA official recounts that in the midst of this French turmoil over who could be considered a "safe" prime minister for Vietnam, Dulles met with Bao Dai in the spring of 1954 to urge on him a compact with Diem to defend the south. The last emperor wanted nothing to do with a partitioned Vietnam. Fine, said Dulles, who was himself changing his mind, if not yet his heart, let them agree that Bao Dai should remain in France "and return to Vietnam after Diem had won over the country."[31]

That nicely ambiguous phrase covered a number of possibilities. Bao Dai might not be a suitable "Founding Father" for Vietnam, but if Diem was to be anything of a match for Ho Chi Minh, this was probably the best way to proceed. As two French observers concluded:

> From that day on, Dulles felt reassured and "resigned himself" to partition. He no longer saw any need for the United States to intervene on behalf of a moribund colonialism or to fight for the "unity" of that distant country. The opening move had been made, the principal pawn had been advanced; and given patience and wise maneuvering, it should lead to the establishment in Southeast Asia of a political and strategic system that was wholly under American direction.[32]

Dulles had recently reiterated, moreover, the American belief that Japan could not survive as a member of the free world without access to Southeast Asia. "Today," he said in Los Angeles,

> the vast Pacific is a friendly ocean only because the West Pacific islands and two peninsular positions are in friendly hands. . . . We are giving supplies to the French Union forces in Indochina. But close behind this island and peninsular screen lies a mainland with many hundreds of millions of people under a despotic rule that is fanatically hostile to us and demonstrably aggressive and treacherous. . . . Japan's population, now grown to 87,000,000, depends for its livelihood upon foreign trade. Trade is offered by the Communists—at a price. The price is that Japan—the only industrial power in Asia—should cease to cooperate with the United Nations and with the United States.[33]

Lest it be supposed this was simply Dulles' way of building a case, cramming in every possible argument, there is Eisenhower's address to the National Editorial Association a few days later.

> Japan cannot live, and Japan cannot remain in the free world unless something is done to allow her to make a living.
>
> Now, if we will not give her any money, if we will not trade with her, if we will not allow her to trade with the Reds, if we will not try to defend in any way the southeast Asian area where she has a partial trade opportunity, what is to happen to Japan?
>
> It is going to the Communists.[34]

Or, again, his private lecture to Republican legislative leaders:

> If we don't assist Japan, gentlemen, Japan is going Communist. Then instead of the Pacific being an American lake, believe me it is going to be a Communist lake. If we do not let them trade with Red China, with Southeast Asia, then we are going to be in for trouble. Of course, we do not want to ruin our own industries to keep Japan on our side, but we must give them assistance. It is a delicate, difficult course we have to follow, but I am sure we can do it in the long run.[35]

Although the president admitted that no one of these enumerated alternatives to help Japan would be enough, "and any one of them pursued to an extreme would ruin us," this vision disturbed the French for obvious reasons, not least the image projected therein of a revived Japan dominating Asia economically, for the United States had no other way to meet the problem except to lower its own tariff barriers and emulate British policy in the nineteenth century—a most unlikely occurrence, however confident Ike might be about successfully completing the difficult course over the long run.[36]

Awaiting Diem's arrival in Saigon, meanwhile, was an expert in "nation building," Colonel Edward Geary Lansdale, recently arrived from the Philippines where he had been helping President Ramon Magsaysay secure his country against a Communist-led rebellion. As Dulles hoped he would, Lansdale soon became Diem's chief political adviser.[37]

Actually, Lansdale had been picked for this mission long before Washington had accepted Diem's credentials as the leading anti-Communist nationalist for Vietnam. Back in January 1954, at a meeting in the Pentagon, Dulles asserted his belief in the inevitability of Vietnamese independence; and when this happened, he assured those present, including Lansdale, the United States could start channeling aid directly, instead of via the French. "Dulles turned to me and said that it had been decided that I was to go to Vietnam to help the Vietnamese much as I had helped the Filipinos."[38]

After a month in Vietnam, Lansdale concluded that whatever was going on in Geneva, the French in Vietnam had not heard of independence—and they responded emotionally whenever an American went near one of "their" Vietnamese. A Swiss journalist gave Lansdale a fitting analogy: "The French are like a man giving up his mistress. He knows the affair is over, but he hates it when he sees his mistress ride by in the big car of a rich man she has just met."[39]

Lansdale wrote with feigned innocence, "I gathered that we Americans were the rich newcomers."[40] His own personal mission to Asia began at the end of World War II, when, as a young officer assigned to civil duties in the Philippines, he first saw great "appeal . . . in the U.S. military's part in the creation of democratic institutions in postwar Germany and Japan. There were examples all about me in the Philippines of what a previous generation of American military men had done there."[41]

No rich newcomer, Lansdale pictured himself standing in Walter Reed's shoes, dedicating himself to stamping out "Red fever," and preventing future outbreaks by inoculations of political vaccine. It had not been John Foster Dulles who recommended he be sent to Vietnam, but Allen Dulles, the director of the Central Intelligence Agency. At the January meeting in the Pentagon it had been the CIA director who "inquired if an unconventional warfare officer, specifically Colonel Lansdale," could be added to the American military mission. That was agreeable to Admiral Radford, who then appointed Lansdale also to the working group charged with drafting position papers on Vietnam.[42]

When Lansdale arrived in Vietnam on June 1, he wondered, according to his memoirs, "Was I going to be able to help them?" A paper he may have helped to draft framed the issue this way: "To set forth a program of action without resort to overt combat operations by U.S. forces, designed to: (a) secure the military defeat of Communist forces in Indo-China, and (b) establish a western oriented complex in Southeast Asia incorporating Indo-China, Thailand, Burma, Malaya, Indonesia, and the Philippines."[43] Working with Diem's brother, Ngo Dinh Nhu, Colonel Lansdale was instrumental in creating the Front for National Safety, and was soon assisting in a public relations campaign geared toward demonstrating that only Diem could salvage the situation.[44]

Thus while France struggled to regain control of its political fortunes, by the time Mendès-France came to power Franco-American rivalry in Vietnam was much altered, tilted away from Paris. The Americans had come in too late to save Dienbienphu, and not with soldiers. But they were there. Denied entrance via high-level negotiations for so many crucial months, the Americans gained access to Vietnam in a variety of ways. Lansdale came attached to the military advisory group and attached himself to Diem. Diem, in turn, had been promoted by Dulles and others. And so on. By early July 1954, a tacit understanding existed between Mendès-France and the Eisenhower administration based on their mutual interest in seeing Geneva succeed. Mendès-France would get an end to the war, and the United States, recognition of the independence of the Associated States of Indochina. What happened after that—well—it would happen.

That the French premier dealt successfully with this change, saving what he could for France, balancing off allies and enemies, was much to his credit as a diplomat. He had few trumps, but he played them with skill. He realized that any future hope for French interests in Indochina now rested on the goodwill of the Americans, but that first he would have to assist Anthony Eden, and V. M. Molotov (and whomever else), in mediating between the Americans and the Chinese.

Mendès-France, Eden, and Molotov all acted as go-betweens at one time or another, offering their services for mutual reassurance that neither China nor America desired military outposts in Laos or Cambodia. Walter Bedell Smith before he left Geneva, for example, advised Molotov that the United States had no desire for military bases in those two countries, so long as they were "adequately equipped to defend themselves and their security guaranteed." Zhouenlai likewise communicated back through Eden and Mendès-France that if the Americans kept their guns out of Indochina, China would recognize the independence of Laos, Cambodia, and Vietnam, and even said that he favored their continued membership in the French Union.[45]

At one of their meetings, Zhou left Mendès-France with a word to the wise: he should see the chief Vietminh delegate, Pham Van Dong, as soon as possible. Too much was being decided, he hinted, without proper attention to diplomatic good manners.

Mendès-France and his aides had agreed upon a three-part strategy, now that the crucial face-to-face sessions with Zhou had turned out favorably. The *objective* was division, at least provisionally, at the eighteenth parallel, for political as well as military reasons; the *procedure* was dialogue with the Vietminh; the *pressure tactic*, the possible sending of draftees.[46]

Openly resentful of the cozy little tête-à-têtes Mendès-France was having with the Chinese, the Vietminh delegation suddenly became balky, contrasting the Sino-French "understanding" with the lack of attention they had received at the ministerial level. The Vietminh also resented growing Soviet and Chinese pressure upon them to compromise, especially given their continuing military prowess. To put this discontent in concrete terms, Ho's representatives demanded the provisional partition line be set at the thirteenth parallel, a difference of six hundred kilometers and four million inhabitants from the French proposal.[47]

Partially obscured by the fuss over a demarcation line, a far more intractable question loomed: that of an ultimate political solution and, obviously closely related, the timing of the proposed all-Vietnamese elections. Dulles had given his answer, it will be remembered, to the original Vietminh call for immediate independence and elections during an exchange with reporters in mid-May. "At the present time in a country which is politically immature, which has been the scene of civil war and disruption, we would doubt whether the immediate conditions would be conducive to a result which would really reflect the will of the people."

So spoke their enemy. But the Vietminh could hardly have been happy about the low priority, or even indifference, their Russian and Chinese allies were evidencing on what was the crucial point.[48] Rather than rely on such inconstant friends, the Vietminh decided to do their own talking. If there was to be not simply territorial but also political partition, they would have a say in setting the boundaries. Before Mendès-France came to power, a Vietminh delegate had spread out a map of Indochina before French negotiators and, placing his hand on the Red River Delta, declared imperiously, "We must have this. We need a state, we need a capital for our state, and we need a port for our capital."[49]

His listeners were astounded. Did this mean Ho accepted permanent partition? The Vietminh spokesman, Ta Quang Buu, did not respond directly, but he insisted that the bilateral nature of the discussion was better than supervision by the great powers. Obviously, the diplomacy on the Communist side was fully as complicated as the relations between Paris and London and Washington. Even the bickering over the timing of elections took on great importance in this context. What the Vietminh might offer the French on any issue varied, not only for sound strategic or political reasons, but because of issues of independence connected with strained relations between Ho and his two "big brothers."

The Franco-Vietminh interview of June 25, 1954, thus reflected, besides other considerations, a truculent response to being treated as a ward of the great powers. As such, however, it threatened Mendès-France's favored procedure for arriving at peace terms and nudged him toward Washington.

3.

> I am proud to have been in on the talks, which produced this document, which was of course essentially your inspiration and drafting. It made a welcome departure from the conventional "communiqué."
>
> JOHN FOSTER DULLES
> to Dwight D. Eisenhower,
> July 6, 1954[50]

The document referred to here by Dulles was dubbed the Potomac Charter by administration spokesmen, in conscious imitation of the 1941 Atlantic Charter signed by Roosevelt and Churchill. This time it would come to something, vowed American policymakers, and not be set aside when FDR brushed off the Atlantic Charter as a few words scribbled down somewhere on a piece of paper he could not find.[51]

For some time Churchill had been seeking a meeting with Eisenhower to clear the air. The Dulles/Eden feud, which had been at the boiling point since mid-April, provided him with enough of a reason to request that they sit down to talk about "family matters," but he had a wide-ranging agenda to discuss. Eisenhower, however, was considerably less enthusiastic about playing host. "I've decided to let the old man come over for this visit," shrugged the president to his press secretary, James Hagerty.[52]

The prime minister's recent letters had an irritating sameness about them, and always ended in a call for a Big Three summit. In a message Eisenhower received on June 21, for example, Churchill again warned against becoming involved militarily in the local affairs of Vietnam. Constantly harping on French incompetence in Indochina, the prime minister recalled the mournful story of how the Labour government had cut and run in India. More and more he sounded like a ruminating old character out of Dickens, fixated on some grievance no one could repair—and which had become, by repetition if nothing else, a treasured private sorrow. Yet he did say, on the other hand, that he would seriously consider a Southeast Asian counterpart to NATO.

In return, Eisenhower would have to listen to his complaint that Great Britain, by hosting American air bases, had become the "bull's eye" for Russian nuclear weapons, and hear him out when he proposed carrying a message to Moscow that "there is a thoroughly friendly and easy way out for her in which all her hard-driven peoples may gain a broader, fuller and happier life."[53]

Churchill's traveling companion and heir apparent, Anthony Eden, moreover, had recently singed the air with a speech criticizing American policy in East Asia, and, to make matters still worse, had advanced his Locarno proposal for consideration. And what, in heaven's name, was Eden doing on June 23, 1954, on the eve of departure for Washington, introducing his plan to the House of Commons with an arch reference to the dispute of mid-April over what had been decided on during Dulles' failed mission to London and Paris? He spoke as if it were up to him to pick up the mess made by the bull in the china closet—and as if he were the only one who could do it:

> I hope it will be possible to agree on some system of South Asian defense, and to guard against aggression. In other words, we-could have a reciprocal arrangement in which both sides took part, such as a Locarno. We could also have a defensive alliance, such as NATO is in Europe, and such as the existing Soviet-Chinese treaty provides for the Far East. These two systems would, I admit, be quite different, but need be in no way inconsistent.
>
> My belief is that by refraining from any precipitate move toward the formation of a NATO system in Southeast Asia, we have helped to create the necessary conditions under which both systems can possibly be brought into being.[54]

A more unpromising family get-together, as Churchill called these meetings, could hardly be imagined. Dismay and indignation spread through the administration and Congress, said the press, and a move was under way on Capitol Hill to deny American funds to any treaty scheme that had even a smell of Locarno about it.[55] That the Chinese evidenced no interest in Eden's Locarno model, and vehemently denied any relationship at all between the Sino-Soviet Treaty and what the West was after in Asia, hardly mattered.[56]

As Eden and Dulles drove in from the Washington national airport on June 25, the atmosphere was uncomfortably heavy, presaging a thunderstorm on the way. Distant rumbles could be heard inside the limousine as the two fell to arguing about yet another family matter, American pressure on Britain to support Washington in the United Nations on the Guatemalan dispute. The administration was endeavoring at this moment to chase a leftist government out of power in Guatemala, and had come under fire as violating international law. The British were currently supporting efforts by the Guatemalans to bring the issue (and by implication the U.S. behavior) before the Security Council.[57]

"If the first thing that happens after they arrive," Dulles said on the telephone to Ambassador Henry Cabot Lodge at the United Nations from his office, "is that we split on this, they better pack up and go home. Things are bad enough." Lodge commiserated. If that released us to do what we wanted on the colonial question, he said, "it's not a bad deal." The secretary had no argument with that judgment. "The happiest day in his life," vowed the secretary, "will be when we don't have to modify our policies etc. to keep up a facade of unity."[58]

After the limousine arrived, and Eden talked with the prime minister, a compromise was reached. The British representative on the Security Council, Sir Pierson Dixon, "abstained," explaining that the U.N. could await the outcome of the Organization of American States' deliberations. Eden was very foolish sometimes, the prime minister told an aide. "He would quarrel with the Americans over some petty Central American issue which did not affect Great Britain and could forget about the downtrodden millions in Poland."[59] Eden did not think it quite so petty an issue. The argument had begun, in part, because Dulles had threatened to stop any British ship delivering arms to the Guatemalan regime. It rankled the British that Americans felt unrestrained, nay fully justified and obligated, in condemning European imperialism while at the same time behaving about Central America as if the "Roosevelt Corollary" protectorates were still in full force.[60]

Eisenhower decided the best way to deal with the Locarno idea if the British brought it up, meanwhile, would be to bore them to death. A nonaggression pact, in itself, was not a bad idea, but, as Dulles said, the Eden proposal involved guaranteeing the Geneva settlement. And they both agreed that anything out of Geneva "we would have to gag about." "I'll tell you what we'll do, Foster. Let's you and I listen and refuse to be committed and look bored at some times."[61] Eisenhower felt he could do this because he believed Eden had intended it only to soothe ruffled feathers in Parliament and with an eye cocked toward commonwealth reactions.[62]

The white dominions in Asia, Australia, and New Zealand, while opposed to intervention in Vietnam, preferred a post-Geneva SEATO organization. India's Nehru and Zhouenlai, who were starting their own talks on Asian affairs, declared themselves for Asian coexistence, or *Panchasheel,* and ruled out both SEATO and a Locarno-type treaty. When they adjourned this first Asian summit, the Chinese foreign minister told reporters, "Revolution cannot be exported, and at the same time outside interference with the expressed will of the people should not be permitted."[63]

As the first formal session in Washington was breaking up on the afternoon of June 25, on the other hand, Eden turned to Ambassador Winthrop Aldrich and said, "You know, Mr. Ambassador, as far as I'm concerned I am going to drop this Locarno matter."[64] The next day, June 26, the president announced he would like to try his hand at something he called Atlantic Charter #2. Churchill wanted to talk, instead, about a summit conference, but after an interruption so that the prime minister could witness a real thunderstorm from the White House solarium, he finally consented to read the president's draft and pronounced it "damned good."[65]

Perhaps he had needed time to cool off as Washington was being drenched, so that he could bring himself to say something nice to Ike about his manifesto. But having given the president a pat on the back, Churchill had second thoughts. Memories of 1941 came back to him, for after further consideration the prime minister thought he espied some Dulles "anticolonial sentiments" lurking in the draft, and wanted to spend some time making sure that Atlantic Charter #2 did not apply to the British Empire, just as he had denied that the original had any application to affairs within His Majesty's domains.

Obviously unsettled by all these diversionary matters, Churchill changed his mind again. The first priority had to be obtaining Ike's approval for an East-West summit, with, of course, himself leading the way to Moscow. Such thoughts quickly overcame reservations about Eisenhower's typically American penchant for grand pronouncements.

While the Atlantic Charter #2, or the Potomac Charter as Dulles would baptize it, was still struggling to be born, an urgent message came in from Mendès-France. Describing the next few weeks as decisive for Indochina, the French premier asked for help in achieving a "regrouping which will assure the State of Vietnam a territory as solid as possible." The problem, as he saw it, was to overcome the opposition of the Vietminh on the one hand, and to forestall the "dangerous reactions" of the current Vietnamese government on the other. The Anglo-American conference could provide much help if its final communiqué warned that failure to reach a "reasonable settlement at Geneva" would produce a "serious aggravation of international relations."[66]

Mendès-France's previous hints that he would welcome a firm statement of American policy had suddenly culminated in this appeal of June 26, 1954, addressed to both Dulles and Eden. No longer, it appeared, would the Laniel/Bidault tactics of saying one thing to London and another to Washington dominate French policy.[67] By soliciting Washington's aid in handling the new Vietnamese premier, Mendès-France offered an interesting choice: the United States could remain aloof for principle's sake, risking an even worse outcome if the military situation continued to deteriorate, or it could opt for a "regrouping" (as Mendès-France had so nicely put it) in an effort to assure the "state of Vietnam a territory as solid as possible."[68]

It was an intriguing proposition, whatever Mendès-France's underlying motives. The appeal conceded Washington's interest in the internal politics of Vietnam, an original condition for intervention back in early April; in fact, it called on Washington to *increase* its involvement, to become, as it were, Vietnam's champion—but first a wise trustee and counselor. Thus, Mendès-France had concluded, he offered the Vietnamese nationalists a chance to consolidate themselves in the face of the Vietminh, and to create an authentic state:

> It is for this reason that the French Government strongly hopes it can count on the United States at the proper moment to intervene with the Vietnamese to counsel upon them wisdom and self-control and to dissuade them from refusing an agreement, which, if it is reached, is dictated not by the spirit of abandoning them, but on the contrary by the desire to save in Indochina all that can possibly be saved, and to give the Vietnamese state, under peaceful conditions, opportunities which have not always been possible heretofore because of the war.[69]

One might resent the advice that Dulles would do well to emulate Father Flanigan, but there was something *different* about this appeal. Not only that, Eisenhower was already impressed with Mendès-France. Even though he called the French a "hopeless, helpless mass of protoplasm" at dinner with Churchill and aides from both countries, he later observed in his memoirs that Mendès-France was "moving in high gear." He was especially impressed with the way Mendès-France conducted negotiations with Zhouenlai, and his ability to extract from the Chinese diplomat a "two-state" formula for Vietnam.[70]

Finally, the timing was right. The appeal from Paris completed a syzygy, a rare alignment indeed of Anglo-French-American political resolve—or, it might be argued, entanglement. Either way, Mendès-France had given the Americans at once what they had said they wanted all along, a chance to make a go of it in Southeast Asia, and an opportunity to corner the British, leaving them a Hobson's choice between deeper involvement (leading to a commitment to SEATO) and letting down possibly the last French leader before the deluge.

Having asked for the meeting, the British were ill-placed even to raise very many objections about the language of the Potomac Charter, which now became—not little thanks to Mendès-France—the focal point of the Anglo-American talks.[71] Actually, the conference gave birth to paternal twins. The Potomac Charter was divided into two parts, a public declaration and a formal Anglo-American response to the Mendès-France aide-mémoire of June 26. Both had seven points, but the response to Mendès-France specified requirements France must fulfill at Geneva to make itself eligible to receive Anglo-American blessings for a settlement, which, in any case, would be reserved to a promise not to upset the terms of a Vietnamese "solution."

Whether Dulles could ever have "cornered" Eden without Mendès-France's help is doubtful. Of course, Churchill had helped, too, for he had initiated the meeting. What a turnaround. A dubious beginning now promised a happy ending. The public declaration signed by Eisenhower and Churchill began with a reaffirmation of the Atlantic Charter; promised a good faith effort to achieve a nuclear sanity and a "just and fair peace"; urged the establishment of regional associations of "appropriate nations" to preserve the security and independence of peoples living there; offered assistance to such associations, when desired; and scrambled together the preservation of economic and military strength with a pledge to seek a fuller and freer exchange of goods.

Point three, however, was the crux:

> We uphold the principle of self-government and will earnestly strive by every peaceful means to secure the independence of all countries whose peoples desire and are capable of sustaining an independent existence. We welcome the processes of development, where still needed, that lead toward that goal. As regards formerly sovereign states now in bondage, we will not be a party to any arrangement or treaty which would confirm or prolong their unwilling subordination. In the case of nations now divided against their will, we shall continue to seek to achieve unity through free elections supervised by the United Nations to insure they are conducted fairly.[72]

The response to Paris promised to "respect" an agreement that got the Vietminh out of Laos and Cambodia, preserved the southern half of Vietnam, and did not deny Laos, Cambodia, and "retained" Vietnam the right to maintain adequate security forces. Furthermore, such an agreement must provide the new states the essential subsidiary right to import arms and employ foreign advisers. As for Vietnam specifically, the terms of settlement could not contain political provisions which would risk the loss of the retained area to Communist control, nor, on the other hand, preclude the possibility of ultimate reunification by peaceful means. And, finally, it must allow for the peaceful and humane transfer of people from one zone to another, and for effective international supervision of the agreement.[73]

When the French pointed out that two of the seven points contained a contradiction—the ban on any provision that risked the loss of the retained area by political means as against the possibility of reunification by peaceful means, i.e., an election, under Communist domination—Dulles replied coolly that that was why the United States opposed any date being set for elections. Banking on traditional Communist refusal to allow the United Nations to supervise such elections, the secretary believed that if the democratic elements were given a chance to create a "state" in the "retained" area under American aegis, Ho Chi Minh would back away from the challenge. Moreover, he added to Ambassador Dillon, what was being offered here was a promise to respect the settlement, not to guarantee it.[74]

The Potomac Charter and its seven-point twin response to Paris allowed Washington to accept what it had previously refused to countenance in public, a Vietnamese partition, yet to lay the foundations for a postcolonial order in Southeast Asia. If everything worked out (admittedly still long odds), South Vietnam just might become a model reclamation project, snatched out of the wreckage of French colonialism, just as the Philippines had been saved from the evils of Spanish rule, to find new life as a symbol of the superiority of American methods and the desire of peoples everywhere to associate themselves with the fruits of those methods: capitalism and democracy.

4.

> If you think appropriate please orally say to Mendès-France that while many aspects of the Indochina settlement obviously reflect a sense of compulsion rather than of choice, I feel that it is at least a good augury for France that he has demonstrated a capacity to take decisions and carry them out.
>
> JOHN FOSTER DULLES to
> Ambassador C. Douglas Dillon,
> July 21, 1954[75]

It was not so easy to clue in the press about what had been achieved in the Potomac Charter. Dulles told a background press conference that it meant the British had toughened up, and there now existed a possibility that if negotiations broke down "we will press forward." To legislators, however, he pictured the Potomac Charter as drawing a line in Southeast Asia, although regrettably, because of British and French dilatoriness, the time had passed when military intervention in Vietnam could be considered.[76]

Churchill's public appearances belied the notion of a British "toughening up." If he failed to stir up things inside the White House, he more than compensated for that failure in public pleas for renewed efforts to end the Cold War. He portrayed the outcome of the Washington talks as a green light for pursuing a rapprochement with both Russia and China. Churchill's impassioned remarks to reporters on the perils of the "doom-laden" present and the utter futility of victory on a heap of ruins, and his call for a summit conference, put the Geneva Conference in a somewhat different perspective. Those who cared little about Indochina before, and would not be willing to send troops now, were made a little uneasy about "buying" a summit with someone else's country.[77]

So now the administration had a new problem. It had been delighted with the outcome. After all, the prime minister and Eden had been converted from Locarno to the Potomac Charter, which, with Mendès-France's timely suggestion, had provided the first sound basis for a policy toward Southeast Asia. But it was difficult to say all this, especially so in the wake of Churchill's public expiations. When reporters asked Eisenhower for a definitive statement, the president fell back on a familiar tactic, a gallop through field and forest to syntactical havens known only to him:

> Q. JAMES B. RESTON, *New York Times.* Does your statement on Indochina, sir, mean that you will not cooperate in any way with an armistice in Indochina that partitions Viet-Nam?
>
> THE PRESIDENT. Oh, no, I don't say that I am going to stand here, and in the absence of studies and analyses of any proposal made, I don't say that I won't go along with some of it.
>
> I say I won't be a party to a treaty that makes anybody a slave; but to make such a statement doesn't mean you are not going to study every single region, every single incident that comes up, and decide what to do at the moment.
>
> Q. MR. RESTON. But if Vietnam is partitioned, will not the northern part of the country then be left under Communist control?
>
> THE PRESIDENT. I don't know what kind of a thing it's going to be yet. As a matter of fact, let us assume this: let's assume that

> there is going to be ample opportunity given for the migration within these areas of any people, not merely the Armed Forces, but any peoples, and ample time to do it if they want to transfer. I don't know what kind of a deal there will be there; I am just as puzzled as anybody else on that one.[78]

But there were additional reports that the British were going to support the admission of "Red" China to the United Nations. Eisenhower simply could not cover all the flanks no matter how fast he rode. Senate leader William F. Knowland declared that if the Chinese Communists were admitted to the U.N., he would quit his job and lead the fight to take the United States out of such disreputable company and back up to the City on a Hill. Lumping supposed British arguments for a new policy toward China with Churchill's statements about the danger of atomic destruction, and the weak-kneed French posture at Geneva, Knowland declared he would have none of it.

While the French allowed much of Indochina to slip into Red hands, he declared, the free nations groveled their way to a "new Munich." Then it was the Senate chaplain's turn. His Fourth of July sermon assailed Britain for its readiness to "clasp the bloody hand of the aggressors who have slaughtered thousands of American youth." Rev. Dr. Frederick Brown Harris went on to say that perhaps the time had come for America "to declare again its independence from England if she decides to barter truth for trade. . . . That Liberty Bell of ours, which neither Moscow nor Peiping can stifle, must sound the death knell so far as American participation for [*sic*] any new Munich which expediency may propose."[79]

Such fulminations made Ike yearn for the peace and quiet of World War II, when he could command subordinates, even generals, to stop making inflammatory public statements. He could be forgiven for lamenting the absence of a command structure in politics, but it did not let the president off the hook. On July 8, 1954, Eisenhower replied to a letter from Churchill concerning the progress he had made toward arranging a trip to Moscow. Playing down their differences over that issue, the president urged the prime minister not to attempt to bring the issue of Chinese membership in the U.N. to the fore. At the moment, he warned, the international question that "most engages the attention of our people is the possibility that some kind of armistice in Indo-China will be used as an excuse for raising the issue of Red China's entrance into the United Nations."[80]

Regretting that Knowland had "somewhat taken the bloom off the peach of our visit," Churchill replied with a long message reassuring the president that he fully understood that Indochina had become ensnared in the Red China issue, complicating the processes going on at Geneva, and troubling Anglo-American relations needlessly. The British would not bring up U.N. membership for China in the fall, no matter what happened; and, in return, he hoped that the Geneva negotiations would not be harmed. A settlement would in no way weaken his resolve to go ahead with SEATO, "on the widest lines including the Colombo Powers and bringing Great Britain in for the first time to ANZUS affairs."[81]

When Senator Mike Mansfield, a Democrat, joined the chorus of criticism about American participation in the Geneva Conference, calling it a profoundly humiliating experience, Dulles prepared an answer that was never used, perhaps because it undermined Cold War truisms. The fundamental blunder, he wrote, was made in 1945, when "our Government allowed itself to be persuaded . . . by the French and the British." The French had maintained themselves in Vietnam only by "bloody massacres which started the colonial war." Everyone had been paying for this blunder ever since. It was a grave disservice for Senator Mansfield, or anyone else, to assume that the United States is "Mr. Fixit" throughout the world.[82]

At length Eisenhower decided in favor of sending a high-level representative back to Geneva. It was a tough proposition, given the confusing reports on the Churchill visit, risking the further criticism that the United States was deliberately enmeshing itself in the hypocrisy of Old World diplomacy, breaking a promise that the administration would liberate American policy from all those evils. But otherwise, Eisenhower told James Hagerty, the stories from Geneva would be colored by Red propaganda and, equally displeasing, by French attempts to put the blame on the United States for everything that went wrong.[83]

Mendès-France's fly casting had succeeded in snaring something. Whether it was a rotting log or a fat trout remained to be seen. But Ike admired a skilled fisherman. The cover story for the decision to send a major representative back to Geneva was supplied by Dulles, who traveled to Paris to meet with the French premier and

Eden, supposedly to insure that the allies would live up to the seven-point memorandum, i.e., make it a minimum standard for an agreement.

In Paris Dulles played out his assigned role as the reluctant bystander, hoping his name would not get in the papers. He was quite sincere, however, in explaining to Mendès-France that the Eisenhower administration feared being associated "with a settlement which would be portrayed in the US as a second Yalta." He was equally sincere, on the other hand, in saying that there was absolutely no chance now that the United States would come to France's aid militarily, even if *all* the conditions were met. Things had gone too far, the military situation had deteriorated too much; if there ever had been a moment, it had passed.[84]

Reports that the United States had agreed to send Bedell Smith back to Geneva to speed a truce, despite all of Dulles' precautions, caused some stir, if not the outburst the secretary had feared. Congressman John Vorys of Ohio called Dulles in an effort to get it all straight. He was about to be interviewed on a radio program and he wanted to make sure what the administration position really was on "guaranteeing" any settlement. Moreover, he said, he couldn't understand the purpose of this last trip to Paris, which, to his mind, was not very good. Dulles replied that if he knew the whole story, he would think it was good. As to the issue of guaranteeing the settlement, it was the same as Korea. "We would not go to war, but we are free to work peacefully against it."[85]

If it was the same as Korea, Vorys probably thought, liberation had met its Yalta—perhaps something worse. Whatever the congressman may have thought, the Alsop brothers, Joseph and Stewart, flayed the administration in their *Washington Post* column: " 'Liberation'—'Recaptured Initiative'—'The New Look'—'Massive Retaliation!' It is downright unkind, nowadays, to recall these optimistic catchwords, which have turned out to have no more practical value than an old country-woman's runes to cure warts."[86]

No serious effort had been made, complained the Alsops, to halt the march to a Far Eastern Munich. What consoled Dulles, however, was the thought that he had traded an asset of declining value for a potential big gain. At Paris, Mendès-France had even convinced the secretary that he was holding out for *more* than the seven points and that he could get it if the United States sent its top man back to Geneva. "This guy is terrific!" Dulles marveled at the end of the talks.[87]

A few days later he put this sentiment in written form: "I admire and respect the rectitude with which you approach the vital problems that confront us today. Indecision is the worst of evils, and you have done a great deal to dissipate it." All the many friends of France, said a grateful Dulles, "are supporting you with their prayers."[88]

5.

Suppose we said two years?

V. M. MOLOTOV on the date for all-Vietnamese elections[89]

Mendès-France also dealt skillfully with the Russians in the final stages of the Geneva Conference. Anthony Eden, who participated in these sessions with Molotov, agreed that the Frenchman "had fought his corner brilliantly."[90] At a meeting on July 16, Molotov had pressed for early elections in Vietnam "to set at rest doubts which might be aroused in Vietnam by the military division of the country." Mendès-France raised a series of objections. If difficulties and disappointments were to be avoided, he countered, the date fixed must be a distant one.[91]

There must be time for passions to cool, he went on. After all, elections had not been held in France for fourteen months after the end of the war in Europe. Molotov's faith in elections to settle any dispute, let alone one that could involve the great powers in a "local" matter, put him on the same side—now that he had said his piece—as Mendès-France. Three days later, on July 20, 1954, the Russian foreign minister asserted himself on both the election issue and the truce line.

Pham Van Dong, the Vietminh delegate, had fought bitterly for the thirteenth parallel as the temporary dividing line and for elections within six months. Molotov waited until everyone had talked themselves out on both issues, then said, "Let us agree on the seventeenth parallel," and moments later, "Suppose we said two years." Having watched Mendès-France in operation, even for this short time, Molotov may well have concluded, like Dulles, that for some time to come Moscow would be dealing with this French leader.

The composition of the international commission to supervise the truce agreement having been settled by naming a three-member team (Canada, India, Poland), all that remained was the question that had troubled Zhouenlai from the beginning: militarization of Southeast Asia and specifically, of course, American bases in the Associated States of Indochina. He had hinted more than once that he no objection to Cambodia and Laos and, presumably, even Vietnam (whatever its political complexion, and divided or not) remaining in the French Union.

Speaking to Eden on July 17, Zhou asked if the Dulles visit to Paris meant that SEATO was going ahead. If so, the chances for peace were dim. Eden told the Chinese leader that he thought that if an agreement was reached at Geneva, the states of Indochina would not join a regional security pact. When he repeated this to Walter Bedell Smith, the latter said that the United States accepted the caveat.[93]

Had this been agreed to when Smith left Washington? It is an interesting question. In the past Smith had considerably moderated American positions on the spot, much to the relief of British negotiators at Geneva. He advised Washington only that he planned to say, if asked, that the participation of the Associated States "depends on outcome of conference." Eden, he explained, had already "made the mistake of saying that no consideration had been given to inclusion of Laos and Cambodia. . . . This final gambit," he ended the report, "is going to be extremely difficult to play and I do not now see the moves clearly."[94]

Acting as a middleman between Smith and Zhou, Eden took the message back to Zhou. The Chinese were perfectly satisfied, and gave assurances that whatever the outcome politically, the Associated States would also be debarred from joining a military pact uniting them to China.[95] To the surprise of all the great powers, the Cambodian delegate, Sam Sary, extracted a concession from Molotov at the last minute that almost undid Eden's efforts. Sary refused to sign any agreement that did not give Cambodia the right to receive military aid from nations other than France. "Bases?" said Molotov. "Out of the question, quite out of the question. But certain forms of joint defense might be considered. What if Cambodia could call on support from abroad if there were specific threats, a real danger." Sary said he had another seventeen demands to make, but generously allowed the weary negotiators to go on through the draft terms until, early in the morning, Molotov asked if everyone was content. Mendès-France raised a hand. It was simple justice, he said, to allow Laos the same right of self-defense.

All patience exhausted, Molotov replied with a wry look, "All right—Laos too."[96]

In a sense, Molotov had given Dulles a working premise for SEATO. Eden and Smith had earlier counseled together about the problem of defending Laos and Cambodia, as well as "retained" Vietnam (the first euphemism for what would become the Republic of Vietnam in American usage). They had agreed between them, Eden advised London, that SEATO should cover the Associated States, "although we have naturally said nothing to the Chinese."[97]

Without doubt the most unhappy people in Geneva on July 21, 1954, were the Vietminh representatives and Bao Dai's delegation. The final declaration, unsigned, of July 21, 1954, denied to the Vietnamese the right to join a military alliance or to have any military base on their territory under the control of a foreign state. If this declaration were in fact carried out—even after all-Vietnamese elections—the Vietnamese would still remain in limbo, a neutralized (or neutered) sovereignty in place of colonial status. These were the terms dictated by the great powers. Walter Bedell Smith's unilateral declaration promised not to upset the settlement by threats or use of force. Then it piously cited the Potomac Charter as governing American policy. Nothing in his declaration, said Smith, indicated any departure from this "traditional position."*

At a farewell dinner given by Zhouenlai, the Vietminh delegates were astonished to find that one of the guests was Ngo Dinh Luyen, younger brother of Ngo Dinh Diem and a member of Bao Dai's "puppet" commission to Geneva. Worse was to come. Turning to Luyen, Zhou suggested that Saigon open a diplomatic mission in Beijing: "Of course, Pham Van Dong is closer to us ideologically, but that doesn't rule out representation from the south. After all, aren't you both Vietnamese, and aren't we all Asians?"[98]

Ten years earlier, Vice-President Henry A. Wallace had undertaken an effort, on Franklin D. Roosevelt's behalf, to make peace between the Kuomintang and the Chinese Communists. Speaking to Kuomintang leader Chiang Kai-shek, Wallace told him that the American president felt that, inasmuch as they were all Chinese, they were basically friends, and that "nothing should be final between friends."[99]

Perhaps Communist and capitalist diplomacy was not so different after all. But neither could control all the forces of revolutionary

*For the wording of these documents, see Appendix.

nationalism all the time or, it soon appeared, for very long. The outcome of the Geneva Conference bought peace for a few years, but once again the intervention of a great-power consensus was fated to end the same way as the earlier American attempt to patch up the quarrel between Chinese "factions." Peace had been made. But it could not rest on a bed of nails.

CHAPTER TEN

Nation Building

> Can we make a synthetic strong man of him, and can we associate with him competent people who may compensate for his deficiencies in administrative ability and governing capacity?
>
> WALTER BEDELL SMITH's inquiry to the American Embassy in Vietnam, September 28, 1954[1]

In a few years, if things went right, said the nation builders, doubts about Project Vietnam would disappear. People would be proclaiming Ngo Dinh Diem the George Washington of his country, a selfless patriot, austere and distant like that great man, a symbol to rally around. If anyone could save Southeast Asia, they would say, that man was Premier Diem. The feather in Yankee Doodle's cap—an offshoot of the American Revolution—that was what might be made out of Ngo Dinh Diem. Project Vietnam was the first undertaken by the nation builders. It was to be the most important one as well. Pessimists looked hard for the evidence and saw only dried macaroni, brittle, polished, and hollow inside. But their number was shrinking, a process accelerated by natural selection and self-preservation politically.[2]

At first John Foster Dulles had reserved final judgment. But he was committed and put it as a challenge. "Frankly, Collins," Dulles had confided to General J. Lawton Collins when the latter left on his first mission to Indochina in 1954, "I think our chances of saving the situation there are not more than one in ten."[3] And those were generous odds. Few army professionals thought that much of anything could be done, or that Diem had the right stuff to do it. The Joint Chiefs went along with a training mission, recalled one army general, out of sheer relief that the administration had taken their advice not to commit combat forces. "We were in no mood to quibble," noted James Gavin, because "we had blocked the decision to commit ground troops."[4]

No one could really foresee Vietnam's future very far ahead. Two years was about the limit, and what everyone saw happening then was an embarrassing Communist election victory. Thus Eisenhower would write in a now-famous paragraph in his memoirs, "I have never talked or corresponded with a person knowledgeable in Indochinese affairs who did not agree that had elections been held as of the time of the fighting, possibly 80 per cent of the population would have voted for the Communist Ho Chi Minh as their leader rather than Chief of State Bao Dai."[5]

The Geneva Conference had imposed a two-year deadline on all-Vietnamese elections. Diem had to be strong enough by then either to win those elections or, what was at least possible, to lead a government powerful enough to resist demands that they be held. He would have to overcome powerful factions and sects within the territory of retained Vietnam, substitute a "national" force for the French army, and build a political structure to house the new state.

It was not simply that Ho Chi Minh had at least an eight-year lead in all these areas; it was the pace of political change, the wildfire nationalism sweeping across Asia that tried men's souls in Washington in those post-Geneva days. Whatever doubts members of the Eisenhower administration felt about Diem's qualifications had to be put aside, as necessity made nation builders out of skeptics. Having sought this opening for so long, they could hardly do otherwise.

When Secretary of Defense Charles Wilson, the closest approximation to a devil's advocate in the administration, raised serious questions about the stability of the foundations of Diem's regime, Dulles hardly blinked. "This is, of course, the familiar hen-and-egg argument as to which comes first but I would respectfully submit that the U.S. could profitably undertake two courses of action in Free Viet Nam: one to strengthen the government by means of a political and economic nature and the other, to bolster that government by strengthening the army which supports it."[6]

If the military engineers did their part, Dulles argued, he would take care of the rest. Vietnam's outer walls were his beat; he would pace around the perimeter, tightening a connection, examining a weak spot, smoothing over rough spots. At the end of two years, he surveyed the construction project in its final stages and pronounced it a solid success. Draped over the whole area was a large banner: "These Walls Under Construction to Protect Vietnam, arch., J. Dulles; builders, SEATO Alliance Inc., Washington and Manila."

Alliance was a bit of a misnomer in this instance, as those involved in Vietnam policy planning well understood. Dulles liked the symmetrical rhyme, in Europe NATO, in Asia SEATO. It sounded very impressive at congressional budget time, and in between times for press releases detailing the accomplishments of the administration. But the secretary was under no illusions that SEATO would ever become a mutual aid arrangement.[7] "I never got the impression," Richard Bissell, a policy planner from those years, said about the origins of SEATO, "that he [Dulles] thought that the governments we were committing ourselves to help were particularly strong or stable or that there was any chance, really, of forming a military coalition with any effective strength greater than that that we ourselves invested in it."[8]

Dulles once explained the general approach in sentences about Eastern Europe that he would himself have also applied to the particular situation in Vietnam: "Liberation normally comes from within. But it is more apt to come from within if hope is constantly sustained from without. And that we are doing in many ways."[9]

Foster Dulles had always believed that circumstances had tied American hands, preventing timely military action to save Dienbienphu. What he meant by circumstances, however, was actually the absence of an international position under law that would have permitted military intervention without a congressional declaration of war. SEATO's purpose was to fill that gap.

The truth was, the administration was doing much more, both within and outside Southeast Asia, than it had ever done to roll back Soviet power in Eastern Europe. Once lost, it was argued, it would be far more difficult to reclaim Southeast Asia from Chinese influence than it would be to defeat the Red Army—if it ever came to that. The truth also was, though not talked about, the administration had no intention of disturbing the Soviet sphere of influence in Eastern Europe.

Only one thing continued to disturb the equanimity of the dedicated corps of nation builders: cultural lag in Paris. To Eisenhower's great disappointment, it now appeared that France was backsliding. Great hopes had been held out for Mendès-France. But, alas, despite Mendès-France's socialism, here was an instance of *Plus ça change, plus ç'est la même chose.* As the president put it in a letter to an old friend, "Mendès-France is Churchillian in his attitude toward 'dependent' peoples." He was obsessed with fear that his prestige would be lowered, continued Eisenhower, "if he should lose one iota of the area or function over which he exercises some degree of influence or control."[10]

During the American Revolution, France had come to the colonies' aid, sending the Marquis de Lafayette and money to support the cause. Louis XVI, an absolute monarch, had actually helped to start a republican nation. It was questionable whether Pierre Mendès-France, a socialist, would see any advantages to lending a helping hand to Ngo Dinh Diem. And where was the counterpart to Benjamin Franklin to persuade him to do so?

Franklin had taken the measure of the old diplomacy, according to historical tradition, had spied out the weak spots, played upon French ambitions. John Foster Dulles was cunning, too, but these were different times, and very different men. As the Vietminh bottled up the French in the cities and within the perimeters of their military bases, said a National Intelligence Estimate submitted to the president by the CIA on August 3, 1954, the situation would rapidly deteriorate. When that happened, Mendès-France might—probably would—bargain with the Vietminh to retain French economic and cultural interests. "Such an arrangement might include an agreement to hold early elections, even with the virtual certainty of Viet Minh victory."[11]

There it was again—that recurrent specter that kept Dulles up at night. At an August 1954 National Security Council meeting, Dulles and Eisenhower both undertook to answer the charge that all-Vietnamese elections were an honorable obligation imposed by Geneva. The secretary said he was concerned about the language of a certain paragraph in a draft policy paper dealing with elections. He did not believe that there was "any way to bring about a non-Communist victory in any all-Vietnam elections. He thought our real objective should be to avoid having any such elections." Secretary of Defense Charles E. Wilson then asked "if we were going to undermine the Geneva agreements." Dulles pointed out to his cabinet colleague that the United States had not "become a party to these agreements." Eisenhower agreed, and ordered that the paragraph be rewritten to end with the language "prevent a Communist victory through all-Vietnam elections."[12]

The French saw things somewhat differently. They resented

being shoved aside, especially to yield to Ngo Dinh Diem, who they believed was certainly not the savior of South Vietnam. More likely its nemesis. Close advisers of Mendès-France had hoped that partition would not continue long beyond 1956, but that a progressive regime in the south would attract enough supporters from the north to "make it possible to seek the reestablishment of unity outside communism."[13] But the situation had degenerated too far for that to happen, limiting even the chances for a Syngman Rhee type regime in the south. Whatever Mendès-France might have opted to do, argued French authorities, the main trend in the government's policy was not to seek negotiations with Ho, but to fall in, however reluctantly and after much resistance, behind the Americans and hope for the best.[14]

The events of 1954–1956 in Vietnam left behind a legacy of mutual suspicion that would break into the open one day soon, but it was hard for the Americans to be much concerned what Paris thought. They were too busy finding a formula that substituted macaroni for straw in the bricks for Saigon's presidential palace.

1.

> There is nothing in the agreements which will prevent a line being drawn which would include the free nations of Laos, Cambodia and the southern part of Viet-Nam, the transgression of which by the Communists would be treated as an active aggression calling for the reaction on the part of the parties to a Southeast Asian Pact. In the same way, let us say, the Rio Pact draws a line which includes Canada and Greenland, although neither Canada nor Greenland are parties to it.
>
> JOHN FOSTER DULLES at a press conference, July 23, 1954[15]

Almost at once Dulles started calling South Vietnam a country, linking it with Laos and Cambodia at first and then, as various audiences got used to the idea, speaking of it alone without mentioning the other two. He did so, for example, in the next sentence at this press conference forty-eight hours after the Geneva Conference ended. "The extent to which these three countries can actually participate as members in the Pact is not entirely clear." Besides providing an umbrella for Indochina, it was urgent to create SEATO so as to give added legitimacy to the new government in Saigon. Thus, retained Vietnam became the Republic of Vietnam, a new nation with international standing.

Whether the administration had given up hopes for a reunited country under Diem's (or his successor's) leadership soon became a moot issue. Certainly it had to be put off to the distant future. The creation of SEATO took the place of earlier plans, such as they were, for using the allotted time before the scheduled elections to work out some sort of offensive to "liberate" North Vietnam. Dulles could argue, of course, that American objectives had not been scaled back, only the method of achieving those objectives. He would have something to say on this and related questions after the Manila Conference was held and SEATO came into being.[16]

From the outset of the post-Geneva era, the principal obstacle to American plans was no longer Great Britain, but France. In Washington's view, European colonial powers, and France in particular, had learned nothing from the 1930s experience. They just could not seem to keep themselves from trying to appease the enemy to protect the sorry remnants of power and glory they had once held. Hence the urgent need to bulldoze straight through the mess with aid programs for the states of Indochina, before the French, wittingly or unwittingly, by reactionary policies in the south and diplomatic deals with the north, undercut Vietnam's chances for survival.

A message setting forth American intentions to commence direct support to the Associated States went out from Washington on August 18, 1954, along with a cautionary word to Mendès-France that they needed to "move strongly together" in Vietnam. Dulles confided to Ambassador Dillon that he was worried about "backward-looking elements" in France, and the threat that they would take advantage of the premier's preoccupation with European problems to seek the kind of government in Vietnam that had always failed. As for the American view of Diem, "We do not wish to make it appear Ngo Dinh Diem [is] our protégé or that we are irrevocably committed to him. On other hand, we do believe kind of thing he stands for is necessary ingredient of success and we do not now see it elsewhere."[17]

Dillon transmitted the message and sent back an apt metaphor describing the emerging, or reemerging, French attitude. Diem's early difficulties, said the ambassador, had convinced them that they were right to have held out against premature independence. The French believe, he said,

> that if the Vietnamese are given, without restriction, an erector set with all the parts for a ten story building they will end up with a one story cabin and the remaining parts will either be sold or end up in the pockets of the builders. On the other hand if the parts are handed out with care and supervision, a well-built five story building will emerge after many trials and tribulations. Furthermore, the French believe that their past sacrifices on behalf of Vietnam and their obligation as a member of the French Union dictate that they should be the construction supervisor.[18]

Worrisome also, for vastly different reasons, was the visit Syngman Rhee paid to Washington even as the Geneva shock waves continued to reverberate, and word of a mini–air battle involving the Chinese air force and planes from U.S. carriers reached Washington. Rhee started off strongly at the airport reception in his honor, asserting the war in Korea could have been won on the Yalu, but "some people had a little cold feet." Addressing Congress on July 28, the diminutive seventy-nine-year-old Korean nationalist had to stand on a box behind the speaker's podium to deliver his message, a call for war against China. Perhaps the Russians might come to China's aid, he admitted, but that was all to the good, because it would allow American bombers to destroy the Soviet capacity to make hydrogen bombs.[19]

Rhee had also delivered this message inside the White House, to be told by Eisenhower that any war to reunite Korea or Indochina or any other tragically divided country was out of the question. Rhee was not to be put off quite so easily. Now that the Communists had won in Indochina, he said, Thailand would be next. And then South America. He was not talking for Korea alone, he ended, but the world. "We are holding to that little spot in Korea to create courage among anti-Communist nations to oppose Communism."

Eisenhower told Dulles to tend to the man. Yes, of course, Dulles said, trying to smooth things over, that was what the stand in Vietnam was about, holding a spot to create courage so that the rest could be held. Dulles said he felt sympathy for everything Rhee said, about the meaning of what had happened in Indochina, about

Korea's role as a rallying point, and about Soviet dreams of world conquest. But that was all he felt, sympathy. The test was one of perseverance. Just as Korean nationalists could not have known when their trials under Japanese occupation would come to an end, so it was today. "It is up to us to keep the pressures on. The other side will crack."

What Dulles did not want to see at this moment, or in the foreseeable future, was an impulsive surge in Congress that might get out of control. "Mr. President," he told Rhee, "you as a devoted Christian, must agree with me that there are things that happen for the right that cannot be foreseen at the present time but they will happen without resort to a terrible worldwide global atomic war."[20]

After this session, Rhee pulled in his horns, explaining to the Washington Press Club that he had been "misunderstood."[21] No doubt Dulles had also learned some things about the limitations of power, yet it also seems likely, given other evidence, that he was growing more confident about what *could* be done in South Vietnam to turn things around, despite all the problems still to be faced. Once this vision appeared, as his successors would learn for themselves, it would not go away easily.[22]

Unlike the Korean situation, the opportunity in Vietnam was not bound to any specific territorial limit, and it was an opportunity to start afresh ideologically as well. Not only was there a brand new government in Saigon, there was no blemish of military stalemate on the record to inhibit American initiatives. The Korean War had marked a new phase in the Cold War. The standoff (equal to a defeat in many eyes) could be blamed on unpreparedness—the famous Pearl Harbor syndrome. Now, under new leadership, America was geared up to win. Just as it had recovered from the shock of the Japanese attack and mobilized its resources to defeat the Axis, so now it would overwhelm the Communists.

The first significant aid to reach Vietnam came in the form of a sealift to resettle a purported hundred thousand refugees from the north, who, Washington said, were "unwilling to face the grim uncertainties of life under the Communists." This was the first investment, approximately $2 million, in Vietnam's future.[23]

It was a good send-off for the SEATO Conference. Only later would Diem have to face the dilemma created by all those new citizens crowding out the others, demanding special consideration, irritating the "native born" southerners.[24]

2.

A protocol extends the Treaty benefits to Cambodia and Laos and the free territory of Vietnam. The Indochina armistice created obstacles to these three countries becoming parties to the Treaty at the present time. The Treaty will, however, to the extent practicable, throw a mantle of protection over these young nations.

Speech draft by DULLES,
September 15, 1954[25]

The Philippines had special significance as the site for the SEATO Conference. The island nation had been liberated twice by the Americans, from the Spanish and then from the Japanese, at considerable cost the second time—and then set free to enjoy its place in the sun. It was the perfect place to begin. Yet there were clouds covering the sun when Dulles arrived in Manila. Some had followed him from all the way from Washington.

It had recently occurred to the secretary that, as the situation had developed, he had exposed himself and the administration to certain risks. Dulles had worked so hard for this meeting, had coaxed, entreated, cajoled, and importuned the others to come. Now, he suddenly realized, looking at the chairs around the table—they had the power to render it all a nullity, simply by not raising their hands to support any motion with teeth in it.[26]

He could not come home without a treaty, Dulles had told an aide on the eve of his departure, and given the reluctance of the British to include the word "Communist" in the operative clauses defining who the enemy was, perhaps it would be better if he did not go at all. "They are more concerned with trying not to annoy the Communists," he complained to Livingston Merchant, "rather than stopping them."

Besides that, Eden was even refusing to allow representatives of the Associated States to take part in the conference as observers. Then, at the last minute, the British foreign secretary decided not to come to Manila, sending regrets via a second-level man that the impending "crisis" over the EDC in the French Assembly was more important. In his mind's eye, Dulles saw himself standing alone, watching the rain fall outside his hotel window, while the Europeans settled things among themselves. Henry James had written this scene, too, several times over.

"The French and British are blocking everything we want to

do," lamented the secretary of state, feeling himself unfairly bested once again by practitioners of the black arts of Old World diplomacy. In this instance, the *Washington Post*'s editors agreed: "It almost seems as if Britain has created a posture in foreign affairs with which she can take her duties according to her convenience. Or is it that Premier Nehru, who has frowned on the Manila Conference, has become the high priest of Britain's foreign policy in Asia?"[27]

Dulles could not be happy, either, about reports he read out of Saigon that Premier Diem was threatened with a coup d'état by the leaders of the sects: the crafty General Bay Vien, who ran most of the vice operations in Saigon as head of the Binh Xuyen, and assorted generals from the Cao Dai and Hoa Hao groups. The American ambassador Donald Heath threatened them all with a cutoff of American aid, but even to him it looked very much as if Diem would go down in his first innings, a victim not only of the plotters but of self-inflicted wounds.

"This may sound a bit like lecturing," Heath advised his superiors, "but it is a lecture that needs to be repeated again and again. Substantial part of Diem's difficulties resides in his suspicion and distrust of people not possessed of same ideals and motivation as himself and in his lack of personal warmth."[28]

In what would become something of a pattern in later years, those who brought bad news about Diem were blamed for the "mess." "He [Heath] will be changed," promised the secretary in a conversation with Congressman Walter Judd, the China lobby specialist in Congress on dealing with Foreign Service messengers who brought bad news.[29] Dulles may have thought that Heath had been wrong about Vietnam "up to the present," as he said, but he was not blind.

Whatever chagrin and forebodings he felt underneath, or perhaps because of them, Dulles opened the Manila Conference on September 6, 1954, by invoking a higher power: "We are acting under the authority, and in accordance with the principles, of the United Nations Charter." What they would do there, he continued, was directed against no nation. "We are united by a common danger, the danger that stems from international communism and its insatiable ambition." He went on to define that danger: "We know that wherever it makes gains, as in Indochina, these gains are counted on, not as final solutions, but as bridgeheads for future gains. It is that fact which requires each of us to be concerned with what goes on elsewhere."[30]

A fairly long list of the reasons why Dulles was so intent upon identifying "international communism" as the aggressor and not naming names, not even Russia or China, can be attached to any account of the proceedings at Manila. At this moment, for example, Dulles was very concerned not to offend India, whose boundary disputes with Pakistan, a future member of SEATO, could lead to war. If one nation could be named, so could another in the cause of resisting aggression.

As believers in the agent theory of Communist revolution, American policymakers also wanted to dispel the notion that local Marxists ever acted on their own, undirected from Moscow or Beijing. The task was to describe an enemy powerful enough to warrant an international response, and clever enough to use subversion for conquest. What would save SEATO from being an updated version of the British raj in India, protecting local princes against their enemies, would be Dulles' ability to establish "international communism" as the enemy, and place Ho and other "agents" in subordinate roles in the grand scheme of things.

But try as he might, Dulles could not get the word "Communist" into the treaty itself, necessitating a special addendum or "understanding," whereby it was stipulated that the United States recognized aggression and armed attack to mean only "communist aggression."[31] He put the best face he could on things at a press conference on September 12, 1954: "If that [the SEATO treaty] had been in existence three or four months ago, I don't believe that the free world would have had to take the losses that it did take in Indo-China."[32]

Manila had also strengthened and "solidified" the situation in Asia, Dulles insisted, not because he now had his legal basis for military action, though that was certainly important, but because a "big step forward" had been taken in meeting the Communist charge that the West stood for colonialism and imperialism. "By proving that the east and west can work together, we have made a very considerable step forward. Perhaps that, in history, will be looked upon as the most significant aspect of our conference."[33]

There had, in fact, been considerable discussion about East and West working together at Manila. Reporting to the National Security Council, Dulles said that suggestions had been made for an Asian Marshall Plan. He had responded to these by saying that of course the United States was ready to consider economic problems, but could not commit itself to a specific commitment or organization. He had also pointed out that "the participation of other countries in the Far East would be required for the solution of economic problems of the area." And that meant Japan.[34]

Japan was much on American minds whenever Far Eastern problems came up. As the SEATO Pact was being signed, in fact, the ruling Liberal party in Japan, through Prime Minister Shigeru Yoshida's right-hand man, Hayato Ikeda, was issuing a number of statements about the nation's economic needs, pairing them, unfortunately, with comments that the United States had failed to contain Communism in Asia. Asked to comment, Dulles said that the United States recognized Japan's needs for foreign markets to achieve a viable economy. It was unlikely, however, that many of these would be found in America.[35]

After Manila, the secretary of state had gone to Tokyo to deliver this message in person. "Japan must find markets elsewhere for the goods they export," Dulles told Yoshida. "If Japan can find some export markets in Southeast Asia," the secretary of state then told the National Security Council, there was every reason for optimism about the future.[36] Becoming Japan's new "Co-prosperity Sphere" was not what SEATO delegates, Asian or European, had in mind in terms of economic cooperation.

But as the delegations wrangled over treaty language, a real fight was going on in the Formosan Straits. Despite the Nehru/Zhou accord, the Chinese Communists had vowed to liberate Formosa. These tit-for-tat challenges erupted into artillery attacks in early September, with the Nationalists bombarding the mainland, and the Communists returning the favor against the island fortresses, Quemoy and Matsu, held by Chiang Kai-shek's forces.[37]

Eisenhower pondered what to say to Churchill in the light of reports about the situation in the straits. The foundations of multilateral action had to be the closest possible "understanding and purpose" between Washington and London, he proposed to argue, but

> an awkward situation arises out of the fact that some years ago your government recognized Red China while we clung, and still cling, to the theory that the Communist ruling clique there is a conspiracy and is not a government in the civilized meaning of that word. As a result of this divergence, we might conceivably

> have great difficulty in concerting our policies and actions in the event that there should begin an aggression out of continental China against Formosa.[38]

The situation centered on that one issue: the United States needed it written down somewhere, in some official document, that the enemy was "international communism." Dulles had not gotten it at Manila. Eisenhower added in this draft that he believed America was "morally bound" to take action against the "conspiracy" should it seek to spread its tentacles to Formosa. To do so, moreover, "would be definitely in the interests of the whole free world."

Outlawing "international communism" and spurring others to do the same did not make it any less absurd to go to war over Quemoy and Matsu—however hard Dulles tried to persuade the British of their psychological value—and that was at the core of the problem, not only in the Formosan Straits but throughout Southeast Asia as well.[39]

SEATO looked to be a very leaky umbrella indeed, at this stage at least.

3.

> The heart of the problem in South Vietnam is that we really don't yet know Mendès-France's game.
>
> JOHN FOSTER DULLES at National Security Council meeting, September 24, 1954[40]

At the end of September, administration policymakers were also glum about the internal situation in Vietnam. As they saw it, the French were backing General Nguyen Van Hinh against Diem, and trying to get Bao Dai to do their dirty work by getting rid of the only man who could overcome Ho Chi Minh's challenge.[41] On September 25, Dulles moved to show his displeasure with Paris by cutting back on foreign aid. "We would like to see the reserves of the Bank of France come down," said the secretary. And, at the same time, Washington would go ahead with dollar aid directly to Saigon.[42]

Accordingly, Harold Stassen, Mutual Aid director, informed French officials that there would be "unavoidable delays" in certain categories of foreign aid. Walter Bedell Smith told those same officials that in channeling aid directly to the three new states, instead of continuing the joint Franco-American plan, the only idea was to enhance the prestige of those new nations, not to replace the French.[43]

The communiqué issued at the conclusion of these talks reported agreement that an additional $335 million would be made available to the Associated States by the end of the year. It also reported that the French government "is determined to make every effort to break up and destroy the regular enemy forces in Indochina." Press reports indicated, however, that this was really a face-saving way of saying that the French had surrendered again, this time to the Americans. Washington was putting it about that the French military would be out of Vietnam by the spring of 1956.[44]

Things were starting to move, at last, in the right direction. Under Secretary Smith cabled new instructions to Ambassador Heath in Saigon. He was to go to Paris to tell Bao Dai to stop supporting General Hinh's conspiratorial efforts to take power. Merely passing the word along through the French was no longer enough. Smith's cable also explained what the recent communiqué meant to Americans: "What we want from Bao Dai as well as what we believe we have obtained from French is a reasonable period of time during which, with our support and in absence organized or inspired opposition, Diem can make an effort, and we hope achieve, a strongly nationalist, anti-Communist government."[45]

It was up to Heath to decide the best method of obtaining Bao Dai's blessings for Diem, but he was to make it clear that American policymakers did not consider any of the alternatives worthy of support. Heath's visit would also make it clear, presumably, that the French were no longer in a position to make any decisions about who received support. As if to put the final seal on the Franco-American "treaty" ending the political wars over Vietnam, Mendès-France promised Dulles personally that despite all his doubts, he would "give Diem a good try."[46]

The SEATO umbrella might be leaky, but maybe the political rainy season in Vietnam was over. By the time the 1956 election date came, a surprisingly confident Dulles told his staff, "We would have ample grounds for postponing or declining to hold them in the South. The problem is not one of getting ready for a political election but combating subversion and infiltration in the immediate future."[47]

As he went on describing the scenario for Vietnam's future, it became evident that he envisioned American military aid performing a very different function than that which had preoccupied the French since World War II, or indeed what the Joint Chiefs now had in mind. Pentagon planners had suggested a ten-division army, at a cost of about $500 million a year, and trained for offensive action. Half a billion dollars a year, Dulles responded? That was "silly." He was thinking in terms of a police force, rather than an army. Such a force should not cost more than $100 million a year.

There was no point, he said, in preparing the Vietnamese army to defend against a "full-fledged attack" from the north. Nor was the new-style army he envisioned to be a NATO-type national force, capable of linking up with other national forces in a general Southeast Asian conflict. Its mission was "psychological," to provide the Vietnamese people "assurance of internal security and the government a sense of stability."

How, then, asked an aide, did the Manila Pact apply in case of overt aggression? In that event, replied the secretary, there would be "American" bombing of the north, and probably general war with China. "Our concept envisages a fight with nuclear weapons rather than the commitment of ground forces."[48] Actually, he was increasingly sure of himself at this point precisely because he no longer expected (if he ever did expect) a nuclear war in Southeast Asia. The Chinese had already shown their hand at Geneva. All they wanted was reassurance that the United States did not desire military bases next to their borders.

Show the dragon you were not afraid of him, all the while building South Vietnam's strength. Some day, as in Western Europe, the economic miracle would take place and Ho's grip on the imagination of the Vietnamese would loosen. All it needed was time—and an end to French obstructionism. That was basically what Dulles had in mind when he wrote Eisenhower on October 19, 1954, explaining the need for a shift in emphasis in Far Eastern policy. Before the fighting came to an end in Korea and Indochina, it had been policy to encourage the Chinese Nationalists to harass the mainland from Formosa. Now it was necessary to negotiate a new treaty with Chiang stressing the status quo:

> The treaty should be defensive in nature and this aspect should be accepted by the Chinats. It would not be consistent with our basic policy of non-provocation of war were the United States to

> commit itself to the defense of Formosa, thus making it a "privileged sanctuary", while it was used, directly or indirectly, for offensive operations against the Chicoms.
>
> The policy should be the same as in relation to Germany where Adenauer has renounced the use of force to unite Germany, and in relation to Korea where we oppose the use by Rhee of force to unite Korea.
>
> This does not exclude taking advantage of opportunities by joint agreement, as for example, if there were large scale insurrections against the Chinese Communist leadership or if their regime collapsed.[49]

Inside the United States, meanwhile, Dulles had achieved a major political triumph. Democratic leaders, who had joined the Republican right in condemning Geneva, were now almost as joyous about SEATO as the administration, seeing in it a triumph over the go-it-alone "Old Guard." Adlai Stevenson, for example, gave a rousing election speech in mid-October, calling upon voters to elect Democrats to provide support for John Foster Dulles! "The Southeast Asian defensive alliance Secretary Dulles has negotiated has definite military value, and it could and will, we hope, become far more than what the Asians call the 'white man's protective association.' . . . We can even encourage the Secretary of State to be himself and to sponsor a foreign policy which will represent the country as a whole and not just a reactionary minority." What had stimulated Dulles' unfortunate comments from time to time, Stevenson now told his San Francisco audience, was the influence of the Republican Old Guard, isolationist and divisive. "A Democratic victory in November can lay the basis for national unity."[50]

Objectively speaking, there would seem to have been little reason for this bullish attitude toward SEATO's prospects. The organization still largely existed only on paper, written, much of it, in invisible ink. The reasons for this surge of optimism are not entirely clear. Only weeks before, newspaper columnists and political figures had looked upon the results at Geneva with jaundiced eye. Certainly no one said a thing about the settlement being a cause for celebration. Perhaps Dulles had been right. All it needed, to adapt Stevenson's phrase, was for the Europeans to let Ike "be himself"—with the secretary right behind.

Well, of course, it would take more than that. Harold Stassen would have to make a few bookkeeping entries in his foreign aid ledgers, transferring dollars from French accounts to new ones opened up over Diem's signature. The Pentagon would have to come through with good police training. Ed Lansdale would have to do his bit. But the corner had been turned. Things were moving, momentum was gathering. After months and years of standing on the sidelines, America was in the game. Inside Vietnam prospects did seem to be looking up. After a combined assault by the French commander General Paul Ely and Ambassador Heath, General Hinh did an about-face and agreed to cooperate with Diem.

Even Ho Chi Minh seemed in a mood to cooperate. Calling on the Vietminh leader in Hanoi, Pandit Nehru obtained his promise to apply the Sino-Indian outline for peaceful coexistence to Vietminh relations with Laos and Cambodia. But one step he would not take. He would not allow the United States to maintain a consulate in Hanoi. Whether he, too, feared subversion or merely diplomatic cleverness, a sort of backhanded blessing in exchange for leaving the south alone, is impossible to say.[51]

Ho never retreated either from his post-Geneva pledge to redeem all of Vietnam. But who expected him to? Adenauer had not renounced reunification of Germany, but he was held in check by Washington. From what Americans could see at Geneva, Ho was being kept on a tight rein by his "big brothers." At this juncture, Washington released a letter Eisenhower had sent Diem, saluting him as "President of the Council of Ministers."

Given the later emphasis on Eisenhower's original "pledge" to Diem's government as the basis for Lyndon Johnson's decisions (along with the equally problematic SEATO commitment) to send half a million men to Vietnam, it is worth noting that the letter made continued aid contingent upon Saigon's ability to use the assistance effectively, and to carry out a program of needed reforms. When critics of Johnson's handling of the political aspects of the Vietnam War began lodging their complaints in the aftermath of defeat, they seldom looked back to Eisenhower's stipulations. But both the letter and Dulles' definition of the mission of the South Vietnamese army affirm their understanding that South Vietnam could not exist without establishing a government at least as useful to the population (whether democratic or not was another issue) as Ho's appeal in the north.

Ho might only have captured nationalism for his own purposes, but one couldn't dislodge him with a deception. Thus Eisenhower's message said American aid would help to make it possible for Vietnam to achieve true independence, "so enlightened in purpose and effective in performance, that it will be respected at home and abroad and discourage any who might wish to impose a foreign ideology on your free people."[52]

Dulles was certainly right on one score: Washington had found a way—to its own satisfaction—to do "it" legally. When the French protested the Eisenhower letter as in violation of the Washington talks and provisions of the Geneva agreements banning the introduction of new weapons, Dulles shrugged it off, suggesting that the French had put themselves "on the spot because they had made some sort of secret agreement with the Vietminh."[53]

Only "Doubting Charles" Wilson dissented from what he regarded as overly facile explanations for the situation in Vietnam. He did not know whether the French were involved with the Vietminh, but he thought it was time to get out. Eisenhower shot back that he preferred Admiral Radford's position: it was time to get the French out. Wilson did not back down. "As matters stood . . . he could see nothing but grief in store for us if we remained in this area."[54]

Dulles admitted that the situation in Vietnam, despite recent reports, remained "confused," and proposed sending a high-ranking general, someone who would not have to report back to Washington constantly on detailed matters. Ike liked the idea. What about J. Lawton Collins? They agreed—Collins it would be. Certainly such an appointment would clear up any lingering doubts about American intentions.[55]

4.

> I appreciate your undertaking this difficult and delicate mission which is of such great importance to the United States. This assignment and these instructions are convincing evidence of the firm intention of the Government of the United States to help the Vietnamese people preserve and promote their liberty and welfare.
>
> EISENHOWER to General
> J. Lawton Collins,
> November 3, 1954[56]

Collins' arrival in Saigon was treated with all the ceremony Washington could have desired. He arrived surrounded by the aura of a high commissioner. And was treated as such, for Collins was there not merely to replace Ambassador Heath, but, with personal instructions from the president, to coordinate all American activities. The transfer of power was nearly complete.[57]

Actually, Collins and Ely worked well together. They hit it off from the beginning. Four days after Collins arrived in Saigon, on November 8, 1954, Bao Dai finally ordered General Hinh to report to him in Paris. With Hinh out of the way, Collins had a clear field for his Operation Vietnam, a seven-point program for refugee resettlement, land reform, economic development, and political democracy. Operation Vietnam, though it was never called that, thus fell somewhere between the missions entrusted to the Generals MacArthur, father and son, in the Philippines after the Spanish-American War and in Japan after World War II.

As Dulles had insisted, the military training plan Collins developed after reconnoitering the situation actually scaled down the Vietnamese army from 170,000 to form a smaller but well-equipped 77,000-man force completely under Vietnamese control.[58] Collins also saw to it that the French departure proceeded on schedule. With SEATO in place, Dulles cabled Ambassador Douglas Dillon in Paris, there was no need for a large force or, more important, for the French to pretend that they were there to prevent a renewal of the hostilities. The real reason they were there, he said, was the desire to retain their influence in the internal affairs of Vietnam and a role in Far Eastern affairs in general. Hence the United States would no longer share the costs of maintaining French forces after December 31, 1954.[59]

General Ely had an interesting observation to make, however about the risks these American saviors were courting. Was it true, he asked Collins in mid-November, that many Americans supported Diem because the premier was dead set against all-Vietnamese elections in 1956? Because if that were the case, and should the Vietminh launch an all-out military offensive when elections were not held, there would be insufficient forces to resist. The Vietminh might even provoke a revolution in the south, he went on, if it should appear that the Saigon regime was becoming firmly established. "I assured Ely we are not backing Diem for any such reason," Collins reported. But it was a delicate question, he admitted, suggesting it be referred to higher authorities, perhaps even Mendès-France.[60]

Mendès-France and Dulles did talk about the elections during the premier's first visit to Washington in mid-November 1954. But on this occasion the premier took pains to dispel the notion that

France wished to see the provisions of the Geneva settlement implemented in any way that would give the Vietminh an advantage. Instead, Mendès-France suggested, one way to handle the situation would be to find candidates at the local level who could block an overall Communist victory. The only thing that seemed to worry the premier about American policy, on the other hand, was its overreliance on Diem, and the risk of providing an excuse to the Vietminh to break the truce. Dulles promised only to take no actions "which in our judgment" would violate the Geneva agreements.[61]

Mendès-France was in a particularly difficult position at this time. Not only had Hanoi shown little interest in maintaining economic ties, but French fortunes were once again on the downswing, this time in North Africa. At the beginning of the month the smoldering discontent in Algeria had been transformed by large-scale terrorist attacks into another confrontation with revolutionary nationalism. Conservatives leaped to the attack: the premier and his conciliatory policies were responsible for these outrages. With the shameful defeat in Vietnam as a model, revolutionaries felt they could attack with impunity. But the Eisenhower administration saw the Algerian situation as once again too little, too late. In between, Mendès-France felt trapped.

Dulles reported to the White House that the premier was almost desperate about getting support in Algeria. He wants us in, said the secretary. He says he is fighting for his life and his government will fall without an American commitment. And then there would be chaos. The president replied that Dulles should be philosophical and noncommittal. There were going to be no more Vietnams, with the French asking for more and more aid and unwilling to listen to any suggestions about a political settlement.[62]

5.

> This is a new kind of situation, but it's a test of our guts and resilience.
>
> LIEUTENANT GENERAL JOHN W. ("IRON MIKE") O'DANIEL, December 16, 1954[63]

New generals reporting into Saigon for duty always made such statements. And that was as true of the Americans as it had been of Henri Navarre, and those who came before him. Iron Mike O'Daniel had been given the job of training the Vietnamese army. "I still believe this country can be saved," he asserted. "I have not even begun to think of writing it off." Things are on track now. He might as well have said, "We have just begun to fight."

In Paris, meanwhile, Premier Mendès-France's predicament deepened, with critics now seeking to make the Indochina portion of the budget into a vote of confidence. A former minister for the Indochinese states, Jean Letourneau, asked point-blank: Was France about to abandon Vietnam again? Such a shameful retreat, he asserted in the debate over the budget for the Associated States, would sacrifice all French interests in Southeast Asia, and shake the foundations of the French position in North Africa.[64]

Mendès-France was thus being whipsawed between domestic critics on the right, who pressured him not to yield to the Americans to get out yet who wanted few concessions to Ho, and the Americans, who now held the power of the purse and with it Mendès-France's fate. Reporters had a chance to ask Dulles about "certain things" that had come up in the debate in the National Assembly. Some French deputies were saying that the French were having to pull out because America was cutting off its financial support. It was also said that the situation was deteriorating because Washington had insisted upon imposing Diem on Vietnam, and forcing the French to back him. Was there any justification for these allegations?

Of course not, replied Dulles. There was complete cooperation between France and the United States and their representatives, Generals Ely and Collins. "I would say there is no basis whatever for any idea of our imposing our views on the French."[65] As Dulles spoke to reporters, however, foreign aid director Harold Stassen was meeting with French officials to discuss the $100 million gap between what the United States would allot France essentially as a quit fee over the next year in support of an orderly withdrawal, and what was in the French budget.

Stassen repeated what the secretary of state had been saying about Washington's strategic outlook, that there was no need for Vietnam to have an army of more than a hundred thousand at most. For protection against direct aggression, Vietnam could depend on SEATO. The American cut, said Stassen, had come as a result of a review of "world-wide commitments, resources and priorities."[66]

In Washington the nation builders were in full control, as they would be through the next decade. Out on the construction site, on the other hand, Saigon's heat and confusion had begun taking its toll. There was the case of Lawton Collins, for example. By mid-December the man who headed up the entire Operation Vietnam project had begun wondering aloud in his reports to Washington whether it might not be well to start considering alternatives to Diem—even Bao Dai. Criticisms of Diem, he warned, were cropping up on every front, centered, as usual, on the premier's personality, family nepotism, and poor, indeed absent, record in fulfilling promises to get reforms under way. Collins thus worried lest too many commitments be made in terms of training and promises of future military aid.

And he even hinted that it might be preferable to turn the whole mess back over to the French. "Should it be determined that in view of the unsound situation in Vietnam the US should gradually withdraw support from this country, then it would be necessary, in my opinion, to increase the aid to the French expeditionary corps so that it would remain strong enough during the next year to permit the US to withdraw essential equipment which might otherwise fall into Communist hands."[67]

Collins' objections were treated, in what would become a pattern, as aberrational symptoms of tropical localitis, brought on, said the nation builders, by some dark influence, in this case the French disease carried by Paul Ely. Every doubt, every question even, that arose in regard to Diem over the next several years would be charged off in this fashion. Dumping Diem was just what the French wanted, came the response, they wanted the Americans to back out of Vietnam without even giving it a fair try.

Replying directly to Collins on Christmas Eve, Dulles reviewed what he called the basic factors in the Vietnamese situation. First, he said, there was no reason to admit defeat. The people of South Vietnam were fundamentally anti-Communist. The problem presented by General Hinh's threatened rebellion had been dealt with successfully. The Communists had problems, too. It was important not to forget that. The immediate task was to create a situation "such that they can only take over by internal violence." If that could be done, "we will have faced them with serious dilemma because of unfavorable effect such action [would have] on Asian countries like India."

Having long ago decided to block all-Vietnamese elections in 1956, Dulles felt sure that he had doped out the problem the Vietminh would face. Given the time restraints, moreover, the effort to build up South Vietnam's forces to resist internal violence meant that there was no time to search around the Vietnamese countryside for a more able leader. Diem was it. True, there was the "extremely delicate" problem of influencing Diem to move along the "right lines." It was natural, therefore, that the general should feel some frustration. The Communists had exploited the land reform issue, which had a "powerful propaganda value." "Something should be done on our side, with our help, [to] put this emotional and basic element to work for us."[68]

What that might be, he did not say. It was indeed one of those "extremely delicate" problems that eluded solution not only in Vietnam, but throughout much of what was already becoming known as the third world. At various times, and in various ways, American policymakers tried out some plan to deal with fundamental issues but never succeeded, not in Vietnam in the 1950s and 1960s, nor in Central America in the 1970s and 1980s.

Brought into the administration from the Luce "empire" as an expert in psychological warfare (whose association with Eisenhower went back to World War II days), C. D. Jackson outlined one way the land reform issue might be attacked in a problem-solving memorandum to Dulles on the 1954 situation in Guatemala. Its recommendations demonstrated why Americans would find it rough going in Vietnam as well. "A profound effect might be obtained by initiating discussion of programs for settlement of landless or marginal subsistence farmers on underdeveloped lands. United States tradition holds that farmers should own the land they till. Thus, we might demolish communist claims on land reform without alienating any economic group."[69]

To accomplish land reform without alienating any economic group, especially the group supporting Diem, would take a master illusionist. But with enough American economic aid the day of reckoning could be put off to sometime in the future. As Dulles had argued with Collins, the bottom line was sufficient American investment in Vietnam to "buy time" to build up strength elsewhere in Southeast Asia. But by the end of 1954, the reification process had already proceeded quite far in Vietnam, as American aid became the paste holding together the cards that made up the House of Diem. Indeed the whole of that country had assumed a fateful abstraction in American thinking as the place where the line had been drawn against the spread of "international communism."

In the decade and a half from Roosevelt's prewar declaration of national emergency, the United States had achieved a position of dominance unlike any great colonial empire of the past. Yet it was also exposed to dangers greater than those of any past empire. The domino theory Eisenhower popularized to explain America's interest in Southeast Asia only summarized a few of those perils. Raw materials, markets for Japan, the future of democracy as against Communism, these were all serious considerations for the leader of the postwar system.

But there were other hazards to be concerned about in becoming involved in Vietnam. Dulles began to recognize that if the French pulled out too quickly, America could be held responsible for a likely disaster. Even if the transition went perfectly, America would be in an exposed position for an indefinite period as the liberator of Vietnam. So much was at stake. Trying to insure against failure, Dulles and his successors simply shut their eyes to anything that might undermine their belief in the chosen instrument of policy, Ngo Dinh Diem, and their ears to the ever-louder complaints against the social and economic policies of his regime.

Rightly suspicious of the "colonial powers" already by December 1954, American policy was heavily encumbered with self-justifications that what was wrong could be always be traced back to Grendel's cave, the lair of that greedy beast Old World diplomacy. Not only was he ravenous all the time, he was slow-witted and little able to adapt to the new environment. But he had infinite capacity for destruction. This attitude was perhaps the greatest danger of all, for while it was a common enough human reaction to criticism, it blinded policymakers to what they might do, given the limitations of Cold War ideology, to accommodate the forces of revolutionary nationalism.

The nation builders were convinced that Vietnam could demonstrate what they wanted to be true, that the American Revolution could be exported, materially and spiritually, to benefit the world. It took a great deal of imagination to see Dienbienphu as Yorktown in disguise, but getting rid of the French was the key. After that all things were possible. Diem's neglect of land reform, the postponing of elections, the strength of antidemocratic forces in South Vietnam (working both for and against the Saigon government), all these could be overcome. Vietnam had been liberated.

CHAPTER ELEVEN

The Contradictions of Liberal Empire

We are prepared to spend several hundred million dollars in Vietnam, Laos and Cambodia. I hope it will be appreciated that in so doing, we are not disloyal to our obligations under this Treaty or that we are extending favoritism to others. The United States is guided in these matters by the calculation as to how best to serve the cause of freedom in the West Pacific and Southeast Asia area, a cause which cannot be served unless we approach the problem as a whole.

JOHN FOSTER DULLES,
presentation to the SEATO
Council, February 1955[1]

WATCHED over and nurtured by the Eisenhower administration, Diem's Republic of South Vietnam survived the crises of late 1954 and a military showdown with the sects the following spring. In the latter affair it has been estimated that CIA operatives distributed as much as $12 million in bribes to key military figures in the Cao Dai, Hoa Hao, and Binh Xuyen, to insure their neutrality while Diem's forces attacked the strongholds of their masters. Spending a few million this way got Diem out of a tight spot, not only in Vietnam, but also in Washington, where General Lawton Collins had nearly convinced Eisenhower that it was time for a change.[2]

So Vietnam disappeared from the front pages. No news was good news. But the money Dulles talked about at the SEATO meeting in February of 1955 was still being spent years later, much of it, just to keep Diem out of trouble. The bribes to the sects replaced subventions the French had traditionally paid out to maintain the peace. That was low-cost colonialism compared with what

America would pay. There was now more money to go around, of course, than had ever been distributed in the years of French rule. An initial grant to Diem of $322.4 million in 1955 was expanded so that by the end of the Eisenhower years, Washington had provided nearly $1.5 billion to keep the Saigon regime healthy. In addition to this economic aid, Diem received another half billion in military subsidies.[3]

American munificence enabled the Saigon government not only to cultivate the support of the notoriously unreliable sects in South Vietnam, the French goal, but to launch a new urban bourgeoisie, creating a class that had not existed under the French. Quite naturally, and as hoped, these "people of substance" soon became accustomed to the "good life," and looked to Diem to provide for their expanding needs. Yet Saigon's budget remained in the black, also thanks to American aid, which meant that Diem was relieved of any necessity to tax this class beyond token amounts.

Vietnam might not be so rich as the Arab oil kingdoms, but Diem's "natural resource," the U.S. Treasury, yielded enough revenue to enable him to preside over a welfare state—if he cared to take advantage of the situation.[4] He did—and he didn't. Distribution of American aid he took as a divine right, no questions allowed. The South Vietnamese elections of October 1955, by which Diem engineered the ousting of Bao Dai as chief of state, made it clear that he subscribed to a novel form of political organization, "one-man democracy." Within his inner circle of advisers only his family really counted. The odds were practically nil, then, that on truly substantive issues, such as land reform, Diem would ever yield anything to the National Assembly, a body that he created in 1956 à la Syngman Rhee in South Korea, to substitute for all-Vietnamese elections. Nicholas II of Russia could hardly have treated the Duma with more contempt.

The truth was, the National Assembly as designed by Diem hardly deserved to be treated any differently. In 1956 he reached down to the village level to abolish local councils, and replaced them with officials appointed from Saigon. The partial autonomy that the villages had enjoyed under the French was gone. Wholesale political repression followed, under the provisions of Ordinance No. 6, which gave officials "virtually a free hand to eliminate opposition." With these actions, and with his refusal to carry out a serious agrarian program to win over the peasants, Diem declared his willingness to go it alone.[5]

Little wonder that despite an aid program larger than that for any other country except Korea, the Saigon government compiled an abysmal economic record. The South Vietnamese economy actually went backward. In 1958, to take but one index, South Vietnam imported $232 million in American, French, and Japanese goods, but sold only $57 million abroad. Despite this permanent trade imbalance, Diem somehow managed to keep a reserve of over $200 million on hand. The South Vietnamese economy thus displayed a ruddy complexion to the casual observer, but more astute witnesses saw the condition for what it was: the flushed appearance typical in a fatal case of tuberculosis.[6]

Answering questions about world trouble spots in 1956, however, Dulles treated Vietnam as a patient cured of colonialism and resistant to new strains of Communist infection, a textbook example to go along with the expulsion of leftist regimes in Iran and Guatemala: "We aren't worried any more, as we did so critically about Indo-China." He took special pride in a situation "salvaged from almost, what many people thought was certain disaster, [and] a building up of a bulwark there so that the defeat of the French in Dienbienphu did not open the gates so that the whole flood of Communism poured through into the Pacific."[7]

Yes, it was a bit troubling that Diem sometimes paid so little attention to the wishes of his benefactors. Even a staunch group of nation builders would recall times during the Eisenhower years when Diem's behavior was, to put it gently, puzzling. Former Assistant Secretary of State Walter S. Robertson remembered that during one visit, President Diem (his title after the 1956 "elections") talked and talked—then got up and left. "Wouldn't you think that here in Washington," Dulles mused to Robertson, "he might be interested in what our Secretary of State had to say?"[8]

On the other hand, the secretary usually took pride in these displays of "independence." In Paris, after yet another round of talks on Franco-American differences, Dulles replied to a hostile question about Washington's role that if Diem's were the kind of government that could be controlled, it could not succeed. "The only government that can succeed there is a government which is independent of foreign controls and which is really operating on a national basis."[9]

This comment came, of course, as an answer to French critics, who had continued to insist that Diem was nothing more than America's creature. Maurice Couve de Murville never denied, for example, that French policy both before and after Mendès-France had been to do a deal with China, based on mutual interest in keeping the Associated States neutral. Neither could he deny the accusation that Paris had little enthusiasm for Ngo Dinh Diem, and wished him gone. But from the moment the Geneva agreements were written down in July 1954, he said later, the Americans "took possession of South Vietnam and tried to work it out the other way; that is, taking that place that we had held before while we were at war, trying to create South Vietnam as a Western country and, therefore, establishing a sort of American protectorate under the Diem government."[10]

However little American policymakers recognized themselves in Couve de Murville's mirror, deep down Dulles believed that just as America's intervention had brought Vietnam back from almost certain disaster, it could also shape the future. From that point it was only a small step to the conclusion that if, at some future date, after due deliberation, getting rid of Diem for the welfare of the new state was necessary, then so be it. And it might not be just a question of the welfare of the new state, for, as he always remembered, others had a big stake in Vietnam's survival in the free world; Japan, for example.

Occasionally, Dulles would let something slip publicly that hinted at his inner thoughts on the matter. Picking up on one of Dulles' comments during another press conference in Paris that no one seemed to have an alternative name to Diem's to suggest, a reporter started to ask Dulles what he meant by that, but the secretary interposed his own question and (ambiguous) answer. No, the United States had not "fallen in love" with Diem, he began. "We found him there." If anybody had a miraculous new idea, he would not close his mind to it. "After all, we don't choose the head of the government of Indo-China. Indo-China does not belong to us. We support what is there and as long as it is competent, honest, anti-communist and vigorous—Diem seems to fit the bill—we don't seem to see any particular reason to throw him out."[11]

All this recalls Woodrow Wilson's strenuous efforts to design his foreign policy around the concept of *de jure* recognition principles as opposed to traditional *de facto* practices. Such a departure attempted to establish not only a right but an obligation to pass judgment upon the governments of other nations, especially those that came to power as the result of revolution. It also looks forward to Ronald Reagan's attempts to unseat the Sandinistas in Nicaragua.

So long as Diem "fit the bill" no reason existed "to throw him out."

As events unfolded into the next decade, Saigon and Washington continued to believe that each depended on the other. After all, everyone agreed, there was no alternative. Both were wrong; but on another level both were also right. Fed up with Diem in 1963, American policymakers came to believe that the Communist-led insurgency could not be defeated while he remained in power. What role the Kennedy administration played in the actual coup d'état that ended the brief Diem dynasty remains at dispute, at least in regard to details. Eisenhower's successors might have tried to seek an accommodation with Diem, despite all their frustration, however, if they had not come to fear that his last desperate act was to be an effort to save himself by exercising the sovereign right of an independent nation to negotiate peace with the enemy.

A bustle of alarmed reports appeared on President Kennedy's desk in mid-September 1963, alerting him to the new threat. The CIA's Chester Cooper wrote, for example, that despite the Diem brothers' antipathy to the Hanoi regime, "it would be quite in character for Nhu [the President's brother and closest adviser]—and Diem—to seek some measure of maneuverability vis-à-vis the US to avoid being boxed between two unacceptable alternatives: abject surrender to US demands or a loss of all political power."[12]

Should that be the case, continued Cooper's memorandum, it might be expected that Hanoi's minimum demand would be the removal of U.S. military forces. Some attention was paid in later memos to finding a "pretext" for intervention in such an eventuality, but it was easier simply to let the dissident generals know that Washington would not stand in their way, nor deny them aid afterward, if they felt it was their patriotic duty to overthrow the repressive Diem regime.

Events had come full circle since the CIA had distributed $12 million to the shadowy military figures in the sects opposing Diem. In their stead now appeared a parade of generals who marched up and down the palace steps while the war went on around them—worse than before. The parade ended with Nguyen Van Thieu. Thieu was fated to witness the final, ironic spin as the centrifugal force that had held Saigon and Washington paired in suspension finally failed.

On November 23, 1972, President Richard Nixon wrote Thieu complaining about the negative "press campaign emanating from Saigon." The subject of that campaign was the draft agreement to bring about a truce in the second Vietnam War. Nixon was furious at these "dilatory tactics" employed by Thieu in an effort to "scuttle" the proposed settlement. "If the current course continues and you fail to join us in concluding a satisfactory agreement with Hanoi, you must understand that I will proceed at whatever the cost."[13]

So in 1963 Diem was deposed for seeking negotiations, and in 1972 Nixon was ready to abandon Thieu for refusing to negotiate.

1.

> We granted independence to the Philippines and now after they get their independence they in turn are helping another country, Vietnam, to become independent. There is a certain drama about it which appeals to me, at least, and it is having an excellent effect in Vietnam.
>
> JOHN FOSTER DULLES,
> press conference, Manila,
> March 2, 1955[14]

The first meeting of the SEATO Council in early 1955 found Dulles in a self-congratulatory mood. He was close to several goals. Before leaving for Bangkok, the meeting place, Dulles planned what he would say. It would be a triumphant declaration of victory. Although the battlefront had been Indochina, this was an ideological success that involved more than any geographical area. SEATO's creation had demonstrated that East and West could cooperate, that former colonies, emerging nations, and Old World powers could band together, with America playing a crucial role, to strengthen the social fabric of the free world.

Fond of quoting Soviet leaders on the importance of controlling the nonwhite peoples of the world, the secretary of state thought of reminding his Bangkok audience how the United States had foiled the Russian design:

> The Communists in Asia are preaching a form of racial and geographical segregation. They are trying to divide the free peoples of Asia from association with non-Asians. They do so because, Stalin explained, this will facilitate the "amalgamation" of these peoples into the Soviet orbit. Actually, the power situation in the Eurasian land mass is now such that there is no balance of

> power unless the free nations of Asia and indeed of Europe are supported by power from outside.[15]

In notes he chose not to use in the formal speech, Dulles outlined how he thought history had brought him, as a representative of America, to this place:

> First concern of Americans historically was freedom of peoples of the Americas; American foreign policy as reflected Monroe Doctrine was early devoted to this end; historically next concern of American Republic was development of these principles in the Far East. At the close of the last century United States interest in the freedom and welfare of Asian peoples symbolized by the "Open Door"; in this century this traditional American interest further developed with relinquishment of special privileges in Asian countries and with American cooperation in the development of Philippine independence.[16]

The Philippine example had long been used in this way, as a talisman to ward off charges of American imperialism whether they issued forth from the Kremlin's dark towers or from the threadbare frock coats in West European capitals. Nine months earlier, as Geneva got under way, Anthony Eden had confided to an aide what probably passed through Lord Salisbury's mind on occasion. All the Americans want to do, Eden said, is to replace the French and run Indochina themselves. "They want to replace us in Egypt too. They want to run the world."[17]

The American reply was that formal colonialism, colonial attitudes, and even association with colonial methods or attitudes promised only defeat in the Cold War. Just as the metropolitan powers had appeased Germany and Japan in the prewar era to preserve their narrow advantages and imperial prerogatives over others, so now they would follow a similar short-sighted policy, buying time with Russia or Red China, in a misguided belief that the masters of "international communism" would leave them alone.

The Soviets and their Chinese allies were perfectly ready to accept concessions in Europe or Korea, say, while they merely held in abeyance the forces of "revolutionary nationalism." French rigidity had created (and would continue to provide) a fertile field for the activities of Ho Chi Minh and other party operatives. The need was to halt that process, and if it looked as though all America wanted to do was replace the French, then that was a problem for others, not the secretary of state or the administration he represented.

Dulles would, naturally, have preferred stronger support from the NATO allies, as he told them on a different occasion. "If you like the kind of U.S. you see here [in Paris], you should give it your confidence, as we apply the same policies in Asia, and join us if you will."[18] This was a crucial point in the American worldview of the 1950s, and in the Eisenhower administration's interpretation of the Cold War.

Washington did not refuse to negotiate with Moscow in those years, and, with Walter Bedell Smith in charge at Geneva, it held arms-length talks with the Chinese through third parties, reassuring Zhouenlai that the United States did not seek military bases in Indochina. Where Communism's frontiers were well established, Dulles recognized them. (He even cautioned the Soviets against the dangers of allowing nationalism to make a comeback in Eastern Europe.) The Soviet Union and the United States had a common interest in the rules of war.

America and Russia both represented truly international systems, Dulles and his successors would argue. Both might believe that only one would survive the contest, but neither would survive a nuclear war. Operating from different imperatives, then, each sought control in such areas as Southeast Asia. The colonial powers, on the other hand, represented an inherently unstable anomaly, a congeries, a polyglot, which when powerful had wreaked havoc with the world economy, producing war and revolution, and which now constantly needed propping up. Unless American views prevailed, those holding opinions prevalent in the Victorian age, and working in offices filled with period furniture, would either negotiate away the peoples and resources of Asia and Africa or lose them to "international communism." Dulles regarded it as crucially important to have those words, "international communism," at the center of the SEATO Treaty, and dominant in its discussions.

They would be a constant reminder that the world that had existed when the empires had been founded no longer existed—anywhere. How, then, could any nation negotiate with a subordinate division of the Communist operation, under the delusion that it, too, was acting independently? Whether intended that way or not, the words "international communism" reduced the world to two dimensions.

"One little thing I might mention," Dulles clued reporters at the conclusion of the Bangkok session.

> You'll find the words "international communism" are mentioned in the communiqué—a hurdle which some people found a little hard to take. They were not in the communiqué that came out from the working group. The word Communism never found any mention at all. I called attention to the fact that it seemed rather extraordinary, when we were making all this effort to combat something, that we couldn't even give it a name. And so the words "international communism." I think that from now on it will be respectable in this circle to talk about international communism.[19]

The resistance he had met at the Manila organizing session for SEATO, when the phrase had been excluded, had somehow been overcome. It was a fateful triumph. Based upon a worldview no less out of touch (in some ways actually more so) with reality than that which he criticized among the Europeans, the communiqué put the seal on any significant chance that the United States might find it possible to deal with revolutionary leaders except in a Cold War context and, more important, that it could come to terms with a world soon to be shaken by tremors from Cairo to Cuba.

2.

> The U.S., perhaps more than any other member of the Manila Pact, views this situation from a fairly broad standpoint because we have other security ties with other countries. . . . So, to US, this is part of a total security structure, and I think of it in relation to the whole.
>
> JOHN FOSTER DULLES, press briefing, February 22, 1955[20]

From Bangkok, Dulles traveled directly to Saigon. Here many questions awaited the man who had done so much to bring about this new "state." No secret documents are needed to fill out the story. Simply following Dulles around and listening to his answers at press conferences is enough. What about the 1956 elections? The standard answer now was that "we can all hope that there will in fact be established conditions where there will be free elections."[21]

Cold War policy, on both sides of the line(s) dividing the "free world" from the "Socialist bloc," had long since decided on this euphemism to protect the larger interests of the superpowers against the vagaries of an unpredictable system of choosing rulers.

Indochina, and specifically Vietnam, was probably the only place in the world, however, where Washington believed from the beginning that it had little chance of winning such a contest. In other places, such as Germany, the stakes for both sides were simply too high even to think about trying out the system. Suppose anti-Communists triumphed in East Germany? What then? The Russians could not tolerate such an outcome. To a much lesser degree that was the situation in Vietnam. The idea of Communism triumphing by an electoral process was far worse for the future of American interests in Asia than if the Vietminh took up arms against the creation of the Saigon government and actually succeeded in winning on the battlefield.

Linking Vietnam to other unnaturally divided countries in this fashion, denying that there could be anything like free elections in Communist-held territory, served as a useful method of integrating the country into the Cold War proper. In other divided countries, the superpowers kept things quiet by letting it be known in local circles that the boundaries were not to be crossed except for visitation purposes. When the war resumed in Vietnam, the United States put the blame largely on China, in part to maintain the aggression-response model intact. That helped to justify American intervention, beyond the shaky SEATO commitment and Eisenhower's qualified letter to Diem.

Other questions put to Dulles on this first visit required more involved responses. Did the United States seek to replace the French economically? He had seen news reports in the Saigon press to that effect, but it was not so. Now that dollars were coming into Vietnam directly it was true that by the "law of economics" a more competitive situation would exist as American business became aware of the area. "But there is not the slightest support by the U.S. Government of any efforts by American business people to come in here and supplant French, we are not attempting any economic or commercial exploitation of this area at all."[22]

Saigon press reports carried the story, however, that the secretary had chastised the French for not supporting Diem. In Manila, on March 2, Dulles also denied that accusation. France had helped America establish its liberty, he said, then the United States had saved France's independence in the world wars. "Now we were both standing side by side, arm in arm, working for the independence of Vietnam."[23]

Arm in arm? Dulles admitted in answer to another question that outside competition, especially the anticipated boost of Japanese trade in Vietnam, would not be pleasant for some individual French concerns. But the change would not hurt the overall French economy, which was doing pretty well in his estimate. Washington had long believed that Southeast Asia was a natural outlet for Japan, if it was to survive the transition to liberal capitalist democracy. "I don't blame the French for being concerned about it but I don't think you can go on indefinitely having a protected preferential market for the French if . . . Vietnam is to be an independent country."[24]

To Paris the options might have appeared as more like a choice between seeing Vietnam slip behind the iron curtain or into the dollar net. Of course there was no question which was to be preferred, but the road to Suez, and the greatest crisis in the Western alliance, was signposted starting from Saigon. Traveling on to Paris later that spring, Dulles acknowledged that there had been serious misunderstandings about Vietnam. Important as Vietnam was, he vowed, it could not become a cause of "ill will between the French government and French people and the American government and American people. I wouldn't let that happen."[25]

Now it is necessary to refer once again to private conversations to complete this part of the account. When Dulles vowed not to "let that happen," he had just concluded an exhausting four-day tripartite conference with the French and British. Vietnam was the most difficult subject they discussed. After the Bangkok meeting, which ended for Dulles on such an upbeat note, conditions inside Vietnam had rapidly deteriorated. He went to Paris to demand a final decision to support Diem, or provide an alternative.

It all seemed to be coming apart. Bao Dai was agitating against Diem from the outside, threatening to "take the matter into his own hands and establish a new government himself." This would create real problems, for, as Dulles admitted, he "so to speak represents the only legitimate governmental authority." Americans suspected that the French were egging on the sects again, but General Lawton Collins was on his way back to Washington with the bad news that "Diem's number was up." Meeting with the National Security Council on April 28, 1955, Collins insisted that General Ely had been loyal, and that his original doubts about Diem went back to his very first week in Saigon. Diem simply had no knack for politics, nor any skill in handling men.[26]

Collins advocated not getting out, but finding someone else to carry the banner of Vietnamese self-determination. "I thought we were over the hump," Dulles confessed in a letter to the general, but there were reasons not to act hastily. Could Congress be persuaded to fund a new man, he asked Collins? Probably not, especially since an alliance of such different types as Walter Judd and Mike Mansfield had expressed themselves as opposed to any shift. And could it be taken for granted that Diem would go quietly, or was it not more likely he would raise his own banner against a successor "colonialist" regime? "If he has the idealistic and stubborn qualities which have been attributed to him, I would think that there was a risk about this."[27]

But Collins had gotten to the White House. And for a brief moment at the end of April 1955, Eisenhower almost authorized the final option. Messages had in fact gone out to Saigon to prepare to back off from full support for Diem. These were almost immediately countermanded, however, when reports of fighting in Saigon made it appear that the presidential palace had been assaulted by the Binh Xuyen sect's forces, and that Diem's army was proving itself loyal—and capable. Who started the fighting remained a mystery for a time, but Colonel Lansdale was with Diem throughout his ordeal by fire.[28]

At first it was thought that a civil war might make it easier to withdraw. Allen Dulles turned over that idea. "It takes us off the hook." But his brother believed the situation offered a different kind of relief. "The Sec[retary] does not know if Diem is losing control or possibly emerging a hero."[29] It did not take long for Foster Dulles to decide: Diem was a hero. "In the US and the world at large," he informed Collins, "Diem rightly or wrongly is becoming symbol of Vietnamese nationalism struggling against French colonialism and corrupt backward elements."[30]

The secretary of state thus went to Paris with a mind made up. He would not allow Vietnam to divide France and the French people from America, but neither would he allow Diem to replay Kerensky's hapless role in the Russian Revolution. "We believe," he told the French, "that Diem has the best chance of anyone of staying on top of revolution and keeping it within 'tolerable' limits. Diem is only means US sees to save South Vietnam and counteract revolution. US sees no one else who can. Whatever US view has been in past, today US must support Diem wholeheartedly. US must not permit Diem to become another Kerensky."[31]

The French were brought round. And Diem dodged Kerensky's fate. Midway through the 1954 Geneva Conference Dulles and Eisenhower had briefed Republican congressional leaders on the basic American positions that governed policy. The secretary of state reviewed all of Asia, and concluded that the objective beyond simply salvaging something from the taint of French colonialism was to "keep the Pacific a free ocean." Then Eisenhower gave a final overview:

> The President said that every individual is the center of the universe so far as that individual is concerned; in the same manner, every nation is the center of the universe in working out its own problems. Yet, in a general sense . . . it is correct to say that the United States is the central key, the core of democracy, economically, militarily and spiritually. Consequently in simple terms, we are establishing international outposts where people can develop their strength to defend themselves. Here we are sitting in the center, and with high mobility and destructive forces we can swiftly respond when our vital interests are affected. We are trying . . . with these programs to build up for the United States a position in the world of freedom of action. . . . One of our greatest hopes . . . is to get our troops back home. As we get these other countries strengthened economically, to do their part to provide the ground forces to police and hold their own land, we come closer to the realization of our hopes. . . . we cannot publicly call our Allies outposts . . . [but] we are trying to get that result.[32]

3.

> The issue is can we do what we are trying to do in Vietnam. I do not think we can.
>
> DEAN ACHESON, addressing the gathering of "Wisemen," March 26, 1968[33]

Every president since Lyndon Johnson has suffered from the aftereffects of Vietnam; yet the nation has been cautioned against drawing the wrong lessons. Particular attention has been focused, for example, by one group of critics on the "mistake" of supporting the 1963 coup, which, in getting rid of Diem, it is now argued, actually decapitated the nationalist movement itself.[34] This line of argument often extends into a critique of the liberal fascination with nation building, the presumed desire to plant some version of Lyndon Johnson's Great Society in the valley of the Mekong. Having purged the only man capable of rallying anti-Communist forces because he failed to measure up as a social democrat, how in the world could one hope to win a war?

Among those who argue this way is General Maxwell Taylor, once a favorite of John Kennedy and the New Frontiersmen. Looking back on the Vietnam experience, Taylor wondered whether the emphasis on solving that country's social and economic problems had not gotten in the way of fighting a successful war. "We should have learned from our frontier forebears that there is little use planting corn outside the stockade if there are still Indians around in the woods outside."[35]

As it happened, unlike some other recent critics, General Taylor was consistent in this view. Returning from a special mission to evaluate the situation in 1963, Taylor lost patience with contemporary critics who charged that Diem was unworthy of support. Testifying in closed session to the Senate Foreign Relations Committee, the general said he would like to make a point he thought "we have all had in mind." "We need a strong man running this country, we need a dictator in time of war and we have got one. I seem to rule [*sic*] that in our civil war we also had a dictatorial government. We also suspended the writ of habeas corpus."[36]

Taylor's frontier days analogy, however, is a bit mixed up. Try feeding the stockade without planting corn. It was this point that the Joint Chiefs made back in 1954, when Taylor himself was involved in Pentagon planning. A JCS requirement for a successful training mission was political stability. Now it was true that it hardly followed that South Vietnam had to become more democratic than the democracies in order to qualify under that criterion. Yet it was Defense Secretary Charles Wilson who raised the issue about the worthiness of the Diem regime, and it was Dulles who answered, "This is, of course, the familiar hen-and-egg argument as to which comes first but I would respectfully submit that the U.S. could profitably undertake two courses of action in Free Viet Nam: one to strengthen the government by means of a political and economic nature and the other, to bolster that government by strengthening the army which supports."[37]

Hens and eggs, cornfields and stockades—you can't have one without the other. Eisenhower's famous letter to Diem delivered in late October 1954, often cited in the next decade as the basic commitment to, and justification for, sending five hundred thousand troops to defend South Vietnam's independence, was perfectly explicit in this regard: "The Government of the United States expects that this aid will be met by performance on the part of the Government of Viet-Nam in undertaking needed reforms."[38]

If there is a case to be made either for or against undertaking nation building in Vietnam, then, it must be pushed back to the Eisenhower years, if not earlier, as Truman recognized, into the Roosevelt years when that president attempted to boost China up by its own bootstraps into the rank of the Big Four. Commenting on what Roosevelt had undertaken in Asia, Truman wrote in his memoirs: "The task of creating a new nation was colossal. President Roosevelt had built up the idea that China was a great power because he looked to the future and wanted to encourage the Chinese people."[39]

It was argued above that Saigon and Washington wrongly assumed that each depended on the other, but that, on a different level, there was a certain truth involved in that assessment. After Diem, things were never the same. Secretary of Defense Robert McNamara, testifying at the same session of the Senate Foreign Relations Committee, tried to make Taylor's point in less argumentative fashion: "It isn't is the Diem government an effective government. The proper question is[,] is the Diem government the most effective government we can obtain under the circumstances."[40]

Though the answer finally decided upon by McNamara and other policymakers was no, Diem would have to go, after the coup things were never the same. With the overthrow of Diem, the last anticolonialist rationale disappeared; the self-protective coating that Roosevelt had applied to American policy, and that Dulles had used, and that, despite everything, had substance as well as sheen, was gone. The contradictions of a liberal empire now stood revealed, and the only response was to attack nation building, as if it were the same sort of ideological aberration born in the decade that saw LSD become fashionable on college campuses.

Having accepted a measure of responsibility for changing the Vietnamese government—one may dispute the degree—it was impossible to disengage. Policy decisions rested on a weak analytical base, a distorted syllogism that went this way: Only colonial nations lose wars in Asia; America is not a colonial nation; therefore America cannot lose. Defending those propositions strained American material and spiritual resources to the limit. When, at long last, political leaders decided it couldn't be done, critics blamed a supposed obsession with exporting democracy. Now, said neoconservative critics, the syllogism read: America supports only liberal democracies; Vietnam is not a liberal democracy; therefore America does not support Vietnam. Restated that way, America was bound to lose—and the Communists sure to win.

In either version, such logic lacked real content. Instead, it mocked reality. From the beginning of the Vietnam War, American policymakers were caught in a web of abstractions and contradictions. Thus Dulles believed—deep down—that he could change the government of South Vietnam, to save the country from the Communist menace or its own foolhardiness. His sucessors used that final option, only to find out the truth about their creation.

In December 1964, General Taylor, now ambassador to Saigon, stood before the so-called Young Turks, a group of Vietnamese generals who had locked themselves into a cycle of coups and countercoups that threatened total collapse. He dressed them down in words he might have used as commandant at West Point:

> I told you all clearly at General Westmoreland's dinner we Americans were tired of coups. Apparently I wasted my words. Maybe this is because something is wrong with my French because you evidently didn't understand. I made it clear that all the military plans which I know you would like to carry out are dependent on governmental stability. Now you have made a real mess. We cannot carry you forever if you do things like this.[41]

Dulles did not face a situation like this because he did not have to use the final option. He was also protected from having to come to terms with the contradictions in nation building by the conviction, shared before him by people all the way back to Roosevelt with his plan for a trusteeship, that America had a special talent for liberating colonized peoples. "What we are hoping for now," he told a reporter during a private session, "is the emergence of some Asian leader who could take the initiative in bringing together an alliance of the free Asian nations which we could support, but which would not be dominated by the Western powers."[42]

Eisenhower had spoken about the United States as "the central key, the core of democracy, economically, militarily and spiritually. Consequently in simple terms, we are establishing international outposts where people can develop their strength to defend themselves." What happened, of course, was just the opposite. In a sense core and periphery were transposed. It was not just that instead of bringing troops home the Vietnamese intervention caused Eisenhower's successors to send a great army abroad, but that the fundamental object—"We are trying . . . with these programs to build up for the United States a position in the world of freedom of action"—was contradicted. The United States lost all freedom of action in Vietnam, as the periphery held hostage the nation's political and economic destiny.

After listening to former advisers in the State Department, Truman's secretary of state, Dean Acheson, concluded in 1954, "Our difficulty [about colonialism], I think we see so clearly now in connection with Indo-China. That if this thing goes to pieces, does the whole thing go to pieces? Everything? Maybe it does. One reason why perhaps it does that is there isn't anything to fall back on."[43]

From the time he spoke it would take two more decades to find that out.

Endnotes

INTRODUCTION: AFTER THE FALL

1. "The Princeton Seminar," from the copy in the Harry S. Truman Library, Independence, Missouri. This "seminar" was conducted by Acheson in the first two years after he left the State Department, and was attended by high-level policymakers from that administration. Its purpose was to discuss what had been done, and to fill in details, before memories faded.
2. With the appearance of Raymond Bonner's *Waltzing with a Dictator: The Marcoses and the Making of American Policy* (New York: Times Books, 1987), the American record in the Philippines from World War II to the present has been filled out in much less flattering detail. Particularly noteworthy is the persistence of a "colonial" bias in American policy that permits Washington to rationalize interference in Philippine politics. The fateful election of 1986, for example, was largely run by two American public relations agencies, one for Ferdinand Marcos, and the other for Corazon Aquino. The real "voters" were in Washington, with the Reagan Administration setting itself up as final judge. See pp. 419–40.
3. "Princeton Seminar."
4. Kennan to Harry S. Truman, September 3, 1952, the Harry S. Truman Papers, President's Secretary's File (PSF), Harry S. Truman Library, Independence, Missouri.
5. July 22, 1954, the Dwight D. Eisenhower Papers, Whitman File, International Series, Dwight D. Eisenhower Library, Abilene, Kansas.
6. Churchill to Eisenhower, August 8, 1954, *ibid.*
7. Both common interests and contradictions bind such "allies" together, as Thorne so brilliantly demonstrates. *Allies of a Kind: The United States, Britain, and the War Against Japan, 1941–1945* (New York: Oxford Univ. Press, 1978).
8. *New York Times*, May 21, 1954.
9. Hagerty Diary, the James Hagerty Papers, Eisenhower Library, Abilene Kansas.
10. "Secretary's Exposition of American History at the Kraft Dinner, November 13, 1952," by an unknown note taker, Dean Acheson Papers, Truman Library, Independence, Missouri.
11. See *New York Times*, December 9, 1986, p. A13.
12. Bonner, *Waltzing with a Dictator*, p. 34.

NOTES

CHAPTER ONE: ROOSEVELT'S DREAM

1. Cited as "a story which circulated in Algiers during the war," by Robert Murphy, *Diplomat Among Warriors* (New York: Pyramid, 1964), p. 187.
2. Diary Entry, March 3, 1944, in John Morton Blum, ed., *The Price of Vision: The Diary of Henry A. Wallace, 1942–1946* (Boston: Houghton Mifflin, 1973), pp. 307–8. For an example of concern about the president's pledges to the French, and a brief list of the occasions on which he offered them, see Cordell Hull, *The Memoirs of Cordell Hull*, 2 vols. (New York: Macmillan, 1948), 2:1597.
3. *Time*, October 25, 1971, p. 20.
4. Blum, *The Price of Vision*, pp. 307–8.
5. Minute by Gladwyn Jebb, August 18, 1942, in Public Record Office (PRO), Foreign Office (FO) 371/31526; Minute by L. H. Foulds, March 5, 1945, and J. C. Sterndale-Bennett to M. E. Dening, April 14, 1945, both in FO 371/46304, F 1269/11/G.
6. Quoted from an excerpt in William Appleman Williams, Thomas McCormick, Lloyd Gardner, and Walter LaFeber, eds., *America in Vietnam: A Documentary History* (New York: Doubleday, 1985), pp. 22–27.
7. "Transform Liberal Words into Concrete Action," a speech delivered at the Union for Democratic Action, and *New Republic, Vital Speeches*, 11 (February 1945): 273–75.
8. Hull, *Memoirs*, 2:1597.
9. Minutes of Subcommittee on Political Problems, April 10, 1943, Harley Notter Records, National Archives of the United States, Washington, D.C.
10. For an excellent survey of the ways in which the war in the Pacific changed societies in both Asia and the West, see Christopher Thorne, *The Issue of War: States, Societies, and the Far Eastern Conflict of 1941–45* (New York: Oxford Univ. Press, 1985).
11. On India, see Lloyd C. Gardner, *Economic Aspects of New Deal Diplomacy* (Madison: Univ. of Wisconsin Press, 1964), pp. 181–83; the quotation is from a diary entry, December 30, 1941, in Beatrice Bishop Berle and Travis Jacobs, eds., *Navigating the Rapids: From the Papers of Adolf A. Berle* (New York: Harcourt, Brace Jovanovich, 1973), pp. 391–92.
12. See Robert Sherwood, *Roosevelt and Hopkins: An Intimate History* (New York: Harper and Row, 1950), pp. 449–51.
13. For a general look at the thesis suggested in my discussion of Luce and Wallace and the consensus they represented, see Robert Divine, *Second Chance: The Triumph of Internationalism in America During World War II* (New York: Atheneum, 1967).
14. Quoted in Elliott Roosevelt, *As He Saw It* (New York: Duell, Sloan, and Pearce, 1946), pp. 35–37. The authenticity of Elliott Roosevelt's account of his father's exact words has often been questioned, but not his general sentiments.
15. William D. Leahy, *I Was There* (New York: Whittelsey House, 1950), p. 9.
16. *Ibid.*, p. 44.
17. *Ibid.*, pp. 44–45.
18. Statement by Acting Secretary of State, August 2, 1941, quoted in R. B. Paper to Commanding General, CBI, August 6, 1943, Record Group 332, National Archives, Washington, D.C.

19. On the general issue of Anglo-American appeasement of Japan in Indochina, see Ellen Hammer, *The Struggle for Indochina, 1940–1954* (Stanford, Calif.: Stanford Univ. Press, 1966), pp. 17–20; for specifics on the American refusal to enter trade negotiations, so as to "present the Japanese with a fait accompli and prevent Indo-China from falling under the complete economic domination of Japan," as one member of the Vichy government put it directly to Leahy, see Leahy to State Department, January 27, 1941, National Archives (NA), State Department (SD), 611.51G 31/10, and Memorandum of Conversation, May 5, 1941, where the counselor of the French Embassy, Georges Picot, asserted that outside pressure in support of the "open door" principle would "bolster up Indochina in opposing the southward march of Japanese aggression." NA SD 611.51G 31/12.
20. For a brief discussion of neutralization, see Chester L. Cooper, *The Lost Crusade: America in Vietnam* (New York: Dodd, Mead, 1970), pp. 20–21; Press Release, July 24, 1941, in U.S. Department of State, *Papers Relating to the Foreign Relations of the United States (FR): Japan, 1931–1941* (Washington, 1943), 2:316–17.
21. At the Yalta Conference in 1945, of course, occurred the most famous of all of Roosevelt's "dispensations," the arrangements made with Stalin dealing with China's future. See Akira Iriye, *The Cold War in Asia* (Englewood Cliffs, N.J.: Prentice-Hall, 1974), for a discussion of the "Yalta system" Roosevelt negotiated with the Soviet leader.
22. Churchill to Anthony Eden, August 11, 1941, in Winston S. Churchill, *The Second World War*, vol. 3: *The Grand Alliance* (Boston: Houghton Mifflin, 1951), p. 439.
23. *Ibid.*, p. 442. Churchill admitted, however, that the president had first raised the question of a joint declaration. He also avoided another issue connected with the origins of the Atlantic Charter, Roosevelt's concern about "rumors" that the British had already made special arrangements concerning postwar frontiers. See Roosevelt to Churchill, July 14, 1941, in Warren F. Kimball, ed., *Churchill and Roosevelt: The Complete Correspondence*, (3 vols. Princeton, N.J.: Princeton Univ. Press, 1984), 1:221–22. Though this issue emerged as perhaps the most interesting for later historians of the Cold War, during World War II the Atlantic Charter and the colonial issue were uppermost in everyone's mind.
24. Christopher Thorne, *Allies of a Kind: The United States, Britain, and the War Against Japan, 1941–1945* (New York: Oxford Univ. Press, 1978), p. 61.
25. 992nd Press Conference, in *Public Papers and Addresses of Franklin D. Roosevelt*, Samuel I. Rosenman, ed., 13 vols. (New York: Harper, Macmillan, Random House, 1938–1950), 13:563.
26. Diary Entry, March 17, 1944, in *The Diaries of Edward R. Stettinius, Jr., 1943–1946*, Thomas M. Campbell and George C. Herring, eds. (New York: New Viewpoints, 1975), p. 40. For general surveys on this theme, see Gary R. Hess, "Franklin Roosevelt and Indochina," *Journal of American History*, 59 (1972): 353–68; Walter F. LaFeber, "Roosevelt, Churchill, and Indochina: 1942–45," *American Historical Review*, 80 (1975): 1277–95; Christopher Thorne, "Indochina and Anglo-American Relations, 1942–1945," *Pacific Historical Review*, 45 (1976): 73–96.
27. Campbell to Sir Alexander Cadogan, August 6, 1942, FO 371/3153, U 512/27/70.

28. Campbell to Sir Alexander Cadogan, August 6, 1942, FO 371/3153, U 513/27/70. On the racial aspects of the Pacific war, see John Dower, *War Without Mercy* (New York: Oxford Univ. Press, 1986).
29. Minutes by Ashley Clarke and F. K. Roberts, August 18, 1942, FO 371/31513, U 512/27/70.
30. Memorandum by Law, September 21, 1942, FO 371/31514, U 841/27/70.
31. William Roger Louis, *Imperialism at Bay* (New York: Oxford Univ. Press, 1978), pp. 198–200; Robert Sherwood, *Roosevelt and Hopkins: An Intimate History* (New York: Harper and Row, 1948), pp. 634–36.
32. Clark Kerr to Foreign Office, September 28, 1942, FO 371/31514.
33. *New York Times*, October 7, 1942.
34. Sherwood, *Roosevelt and Hopkins*, pp. 634–36, and *New York Times*, October 28, 1942.
35. LaFeber, "Roosevelt, Churchill, and Indochina," p. 1278.
36. The publicity surrounding the North African campaign did not obscure for a keen observer like Robert Sherwood the importance of the developing interallied tussle over postwar issues. See, for this quotation and development of the theme, *Roosevelt and Hopkins*, p. 656.
37. For a discussion of the general reception of Willkie's views in wartime Britain, see Thorne, *Allies of a Kind*, pp. 210–11.
38. *Ibid.*, pp. 349–50.
39. Johnston sent a copy of this speech to Roosevelt on September 15, 1943. The president then expressed a desire to talk over its subject matter with Johnston. See Johnston to Roosevelt, in President's Personal File, 1483, the Papers of Franklin D. Roosevelt, Franklin D. Roosevelt Library, Hyde Park, New York.
40. Diary Entry, January 26, 1943, in Harold Macmillan, *War Diaries: The Mediterranean, 1943–1945* (New York: St. Martin's Press, 1984), p. 8.
41. Murphy, *Diplomat Among Warriors*, p. 192.
42. *Ibid.*, p. 197.
43. Harold Macmillan, *The Blast of War, 1939–1945* (New York: Macmillan, 1968), pp. 200–1.
44. Thorne, "Indochina and Anglo-American Relations," p. 78; Robert Dallek, *Franklin D. Roosevelt and American Foreign Policy, 1933–1945* (New York: Oxford Univ. Press, 1979), pp. 378–79.
45. Halifax to Foreign Office, March 28, 1943, PRO, FO 371/35366, U 1430/G. During this discussion, Sumner Welles reminded the president once more that he had given promises about returning the French Empire intact at the end of the war. Roosevelt parried the remark by saying he thought that only referred to North Africa, but in any event, "in the ironing out of things after the war this kind of position could be rectified."
46. See, for example, Thorne, *Allies of a Kind*, pp. 548–49.
47. Minute by John Carter Vincent, June 23, 1943, on Clarence Gauss, Ambassador to China, to Secretary of State, December 31, 1942, NA 851G.00/81. See also John Paton Davies to Gauss, March 9, 1943, in the Papers of Joseph Stilwell, Hoover Library, Palo Alto, California; China Information Committee Daily Bulletin, August 10, 1942, FO 371/31514.
48. "Present and Future Status of Indochina," January 5, 1944, with enclosures, NA 851G.00/96.

49. Memo by A. L. Moffatt, August 24, 1944, on Gauss to Secretary of State, July 26, 1944, NA 851G.00/8–2444.
50. LaFeber, "Roosevelt, Churchill, and Indochina," p. 1280; Sherwood, *Roosevelt and Hopkins*, pp. 718–19.
51. Thorne, *Allies of a Kind*, p. 312.
52. "Roosevelt-Chiang Dinner Meeting," November 23, 1943, in *FR: The Conferences at Cairo and Teheran, 1943* (Washington, 1961), pp. 322–25.
53. "Roosevelt-Stalin Meeting," November 28, 1943, *ibid.*, pp. 483–86.
54. "Tripartite Dinner Meeting," November 28, 1943, *ibid.*, pp. 509–12.
55. Macmillan, *War Diaries*, p. 318.
56. Roosevelt, *Public Papers*, 12:68–70.
57. Halifax to Foreign Office, January 18, 1944, F360/66/G, handwritten copy in FO 371/38508; Churchill to Eden, December 21, 1943, PRO PREM 3 178/2.
58. Eden to Churchill, December 20, 1943, FO 371/41723, F 118/66/61.
59. Eden to Churchill, December 24, 1943, PREM 3 178/2; Minute by Ashley Clarke, January 12, 1944, FO 371/41723, F260/66/61; "The Future of Indo-China and Other French Pacific Possessions," W.P. (44) III, February 16, 1944, FO 371/41723, F980/66/61.
60. Mountbatten to Chiefs of Staff, London, November 9, 1943, FO 371/46307. The episode is treated briefly in Philip Ziegler, *Mountbatten: The Official Biography* (New York: Harper and Row, 1985), pp. 244–45.
61. M. E. Dening to Sir A. Cadogan, January 11, 1944, PREM 3 178/2.
62. Halifax to Foreign Office, January 19, 1944, FO 371/41273, F 360/66/61.
63. Churchill to Eden, May 21, 1944, PREM 3 180/7.
64. Ronald Campbell to Foreign Office, July 10, 1944, FO 371/41958, Z 4435/1555/67; Dallek, *Roosevelt and Foreign Policy*, pop. 458–62.
65. Mountbatten to Eden, August 16, 1944, FO 371/41719, F 3948/9/G.
66. Thorne, "Indochina and Anglo-American Relations," p. 83.
67. "Record of a Meeting . . . ," August 24, 1944, FO 371/46305, F 4028/66/G.
68. M. E. Dening to Foreign Office, September 30, 1944, FO 371/41720, F 4495/9/G.
69. See LaFeber, "Roosevelt, Churchill, and Indochina," pp. 1287–88.
70. Sir Horace Seymour, Chungking, to Foreign Office, June 27, 1944, FO 371/41663, F 3310/1776/10.
71. The fullest discussion is in Archimedes L. A. Patti, *Why Viet Nam?* (Berkeley: Univ. of California Press, 1980), pp. 48–53.
72. *Ibid.*, pp. 53–54.
73. Records of the Philippine and Southeast Asia Office, box 9, National Archives, Washington, D.C.
74. Halifax to Foreign Office, August 30, 1944, FO 371/41719, F 3975/9/G.
75. Memorandum of Conversation, September 4, 1944, copy in Stilwell Papers.
76. Quoted in Thorne, *Allies of a Kind*, p. 464.
77. October 16, 1944, SD 851G.00/10–1644.
78. Memorandum by Charles Taussig, March 15, 1945, *FR 1945* (Washington, 1967), 1:121–24.
79. See Churchill to Eden, October 11, 1944, PREM 3 180/7; Churchill to Eden, October 21, 1944, FO 371/41720, F 4930/66/G; J. C. Sterndale-Bennett to M. E. Dening, October 23, 1944, FO 371/41720, F 4930/9/G; Memorandum by Stern-

dale-Bennett, November 4 and 13, 1944, FO 371/41721, F 5305/9/61; Moffat to Stettinius, November 1, 1944, SD 851G.00/11–144; Moffat, "Indochina and Southeast Asia," November 16, 1944, Records of Philippine and South East Asia Office, box 9. A suspicion persisted that the "secret" reason for American delay in responding to British requests concerning the Blaizot mission was Washington's desire not to deny France Indochina, but to make sure the reconquest took place under an American aegis. Eden told Churchill that there were "most secret sources, which cannot be quoted," confirming this view. "There is reason to fear that if our reply . . . is much longer delayed, the French may throw themselves into the arms of the Americans. You will understand Admiral Mountbatten's probable state of mind if . . . he is hamstrung in relation to Indo-China." Minute, October 10, 1944, FO 371/41720.

80. Minutes of Subcommittee on Security Problems, February 26, 1943, Notter Records.

81. M. E. Dening to Foreign Office, December 9, 1944, FO 371/41746, F 5800/993/G, and F 5802/993/G.

82. Dening to Foreign Office, December 9, 1944, FO 371/41746, F 5802/993/61.

83. A. L. Moffat, "The Dependent Territories in Southeast Asia," January 17, 1945, Philippine and Southeast Asian Affairs Records, National Archives.

84. "Memorandum of Conversation with the President," January 2, 1945, Papers of Charles Bohlen, National Archives, Washington, D.C., box 4; Halifax to Foreign Office, January 2, 1945, FO 371/46304, F 85/11/G. "This throws us back to where we were before the Quebec Conference," minuted L. D. Foulds in the Foreign Office. "The President refuses to discuss Indo-China with anyone save the PM and when he meets the PM he does not mention it." January 4, 1945, FO 371/46304, F 85/11/G.

85. Stettinius to James C. Dunn, January 4, 1945, SD 851G.00/1–445. Hopkins himself met with French officials in Paris on January 30, 1945. Minutes of the meeting reported a "very frank discussion on both sides about colonies, especially Indo-China." The French went into their proposed plan for advancing Indochina to "complete equality with Metropolitan France—politically and otherwise." To all this, including, however, a great number of topics lumped together, it was added, "Mr. Hopkins was most sympathetic and made an excellent impression." Jefferson Caffery to Secretary of State, January 30, 1945, the Papers of Harry L. Hopkins, Franklin D. Roosevelt Library, Hyde Park, New York.

86. Halifax to Foreign Office, January 9, 1945, FO 371/46304, F 85/11/G, and Halifax quoted in a Foreign Office Memorandum to Eden, February 12, 1945, FO 371/46304, F986/11/G.

87. "Meeting of the President with his Advisers," February 4, 1945, *FR: The Conferences at Malta and Yalta* (Washington, 1955), p. 566.

88. For Churchill's determination to avoid such a talk, see Churchill to Eden, February 13, 1945, FO 371/46304, F986/11/G.

89. "Roosevelt-Stalin Meeting," February 8, 1945, *FR: Conferences at Malta and Yalta*, p. 770.

90. *Ibid.*

91. Gardner, *Economic Aspects*, pp. 190–92.

92. Thorne, *Allies of a Kind*, pp. 597–99.

93. Leahy, *I Was There,* p. 314. The fate of the trusteeship plan as FDR had originally planned it was also linked to the Yalta discussions on Europe and the Declaration on Liberated Europe, a State Department plan for preventing the solidification of Eastern Europe under Russian rule. When the latter was brought up, Churchill wanted it "clearly understood that the references [in the proposed Declaration on Liberated Europe] to the Atlantic Charter did not apply to the British Empire." He had made a speech in Parliament on that subject, he said, and had given Mr. Wendell Willkie a copy. Roosevelt made a joke of the situation, wondering "if that had been the reason for Mr. Willkie's death." But the memory of that episode in 1942 had several meanings for both men. "Sixth Plenary Meeting," February 9, 1945, Bohlen Notes, *FR: Conferences at Malta and Yalta,* p. 848.
94. Cited in Williams et al., *America in Vietnam,* p. 31.
95. Dening to Foreign Office, February 26, 1945, FO 371/46304, F 1231/11/G.
96. Minutes, March 10 and 13, 1945, FO 371/46305, F 1470/11/G.
97. Eden to Churchill, March 3 and 11, 1945; Churchill to Roosevelt, March 17, 1945; and Roosevelt to Churchill, March 22, 1945, FO 371/46305, F1829/11/G.
98. Minute, March 24, 1945, FO 371/46305, F 1829/11/G; C.O.S. to Mountbatten, March 21, 1945, FO 371/46305, F 1824/11/G; Churchill to Hollis, March 31, 1945, FO 371/46306, F 2140/11/G; Mountbatten to British Chiefs of Staff, April 8, 1945, FO 371/46306, F2230/11/G; Churchill to Roosevelt, April 11, 1945, Kimball, *Churchill and Roosevelt,* 3:626–27.
99. Press Conference #998, April 5, 1945, transcript in President's Personal File (PPF:1-P), Roosevelt Papers.
100. Draft, July 9, 1954, in the Papers of John Foster Dulles, Mudd Library, Princeton University, Princeton, New Jersey.

CHAPTER TWO: A CROWDED BOAT

1. U.S. Department of State, *Foreign Relations of the United States (FR)1947* (Washington, 1972), 6:95–97.
2. "Matthews Minutes," February 9, 1945, *FR: The Conferences at Malta and Yalta* (Washington, 1955), p. 854.
3. "Truman-Stalin Meeting," July 17, 1945, *FR: The Potsdam Conference, 1945* (Washington, 1960), 2:43–46.
4. Harry Truman, *Years of Trial and Hope* (Garden City, N.Y.: Doubleday, 1956), pp. 61–62.
5. Dean Acheson, *Present at the Creation: My Years in the State Department* (New York: Norton, 1969), p. 730.
6. *Ibid.*, p. 734.
7. United States Senate, Foreign Relations Committee, *Hearings Held in Executive Session: Legislative Origins of the Truman Doctrine,* 80th Cong., 1st sess. (Washington, 1973), p. 197.
8. Truman's Speech to Congress, March 12, 1947, "The Truman Doctrine," reprinted in Walter LaFeber, ed., *America in the Cold War* (New York: Wiley, 1969), pp. 49–55.
9. Senate Foreign Relations Committee, *Legislative Origins of Truman Doctrine,* p. 198.

10. *FR 1945* (Washington, 1969), 6:300–1.
11. "Memorandum on Indochina," April 23, 1945, National Archives (NA), State Department (SD), 851G.00/4–2345.
12. *Ibid.*
13. Grew to Caffery, May 9, 1945, *FR 1945*, 6:307.
14. Minute by N. B. Butler, July 10, 1945, Foreign Office (FO) 371/46307, F 4240/11/G.
15. Hurley was still fuming in 1951 when the Senate investigated the events leading to the Korean War and General Douglas MacArthur's removal by Truman. See United States Senate, *Military Situation in the Far East: Hearings Before the Committee on Armed Services and the Committee on Foreign Relations,* 82nd Cong., 1st sess. (Washington, 1951), p. 2893. On skirmishes in SEAC between Wedemeyer and Lord Mountbatten, see papers in FO 371, 46306, and 46307. Halifax to Foreign Office, July 9, 1945, FO 371/50193, U 5559/5559/G.
16. Reprinted in Senate, *Military Situation in the Far East,* pp. 2890–92. For a general picture of OSS (Office of Strategic Services) concern with "rumors" of change, see Archimedes L. A. Patti, *Why vietnam? Prelude to America's Albatross* (Berkeley, Calif.: Univ. of California Press, 1980), pp. 118–23. A detailed survey of the Truman administration's decisions in 1945 is found in George C. Herring, "The Truman Administration and the Restoration of French Sovereignty in Indochina," *Diplomatic History,* 1 (1977): 97–117.
17. Joseph Grew to Hurley, June 7, 1945, in Department of Defense, *United States–Vietnam Relations, 1945–1967,* 12 vols. (Washington, 1971), 8:30–32. Franco-American relations were a delicate subject in the late spring of 1945. British and American objections to de Gaulle's policies in the Levant and in Europe had led to several sharp exchanges and warnings among the allies. All the more reason, it was argued, not to alienate the general in Southeast Asia. On the eve of a Bidault visit to Washington, Truman was advised that a "growing anti-American campaign by the Communists" required answering with specifics of the lend-lease program of "$1,600,000,000 to be used in France in spite of the termination of hostilities in Europe." Memorandum of Conversation with the President, May 17, 1945, the Papers of Joseph Grew, Houghton Library, Harvard University, Cambridge, Massachusetts.
18. Langdon to Ellis O. Briggs, May 18, 1945, Record Group 84, National Archives, Washington, D.C.
19. Harriman's speculation is not conclusive evidence, certainly, for the position that Stalin accepted the San Francisco system and sought to turn it this way, but it tallies well with the various discussions at Potsdam. *FR: Potsdam Conference,* 1945, 2:260; also see pp. 253–60, 43–44, 1582–87.
20. "Memorandum of 3rd Conversation . . . ," May 28, 1945, *FR: Potsdam Conference, 1945* 1:41–52; and see John Paton Davies, Jr., *Dragon by the Tail* (New York: Norton, 1972), pp. 396–98. Davies was in Moscow at the time to take up a new post after several years in the Far East, and learned about the conversations firsthand from Hopkins and Ambassador Harriman. Conversations in Washington also suggested that the Russian threat in the Far East was beginning to surface as discussions of the postwar treatment of Japan took on a new meaning. See, for example, Henry Wallace's critical observation about a comment Mrs. Joseph Grew, wife of the sometime ambassador to Japan and acting secretary of state,

made deploring a Russian attack on Japan in Manchuria. "Well," she had said, "in that case we must now begin to think about strengthening Japan." Wallace was, of course, highly sensitive to such comments, but clearly this was a frequent topic of conversation at several dinner tables. July 24, 1945, *The Price of Vision: The Diary of Henry A. Wallace, 1942–1946* (Boston: Houghton Mifflin, 1973), p. 470.

21. Truman, *Memoirs: Year of Decisions* (Garden City, N.Y.: Doubleday, 1955), p. 455.

22. On the reluctance to be closely associated with European policies in SEAC, and the preference for benign neglect, see Robert J. McMahon, *Colonialism and Cold War: The United States and the Struggle for Indonesian Independence, 1945–49* (Ithaca, N.Y.: Cornell Univ. Press, 1981), especially pp. 82–83.

23. The American Joint Chiefs of Staff had decided that French military aid in Indochina "has relatively little if any value" vis-à-vis Japan, while the Department of State believed it desirable to respond favorably to French requests to participate in the Pacific war, which meant Indochina, "from the point of view of relations with the French Provisional Government." The JCS also felt that American troops should not be used "in Indochina except in American military operations against the Japanese." All this was a complicated way of saying that the United States had no military or political goals in Indochina *as such* that warranted any delay in attacking the Japanese home islands. Put differently, if getting France out of Indochina had once seemed important to Roosevelt and other policymakers in order to construct the postwar system, it now seemed more important to let the British and French take care of that area, while America preempted any unwanted "allied" help in the "real war" against Japan. See *FR 1945*, 7:307–12; and Department of Defense, *U.S.–Vietnam Relations*, 8:26–32.

24. Department of Defense, *U.S.–Vietnam Relations*, 8:34–44.

25. Foreign Office to Chungking, August 14, 1945, FO 371/46252, F 5235/1147/G. And Chungking to Foreign Office, August 17, 1945, FO 371/46252, F 5236/1147/G.

26. Truman, *Memoirs: Year of Decisions*, pp. 494–96.

27. United States Senate, Committee on Foreign Relations, "The United States and Vietnam: 1944–1947," a staff study based on the Pentagon Papers, study no. 2, 92nd Cong., 2nd sess. (Washington, 1972), p. 4.

28. *Ibid.*, p. 1.

29. Patti, *Why Vietnam?* pp. 244, 368–69, 372–73.

30. Nguyen Ai Quac or Quoc was already a pseudonym. Ho Chi Minh was first named Nguyen Sinh Cung and was renamed according to Vietnamese tradition by his father, at the age of ten, Nguyen Tat Thanh, a name he changed at least twice, adopting Nguyen Ai Quoc or Nguyen the Patriot as he began serious political activities. For general surveys covering a spectrum of Western non-Communist opinion, see John T. McAlister, Jr., *Vietnam: The Origins of Revolution* (New York: Knopf, 1971); Dennis J. Duncanson, *Government and Revolution in Vietnam* (London: Oxford Univ. Press, 1968); David G. Marr, *Vietnamese Tradition on Trial, 1920–1945* (Berkeley: Univ. of California Press, 1984); and Paul Mus, *Viet Nam: Sociologie d'une guerre* (Paris: Editions du Seuil, 1952). On Ho, see Jean Lacouture, *Ho Chi Minh: A Political Biography*, trans. by Peter Wiles (New York: Random House, 1968), and the "official" Vietnamese biography, Truong Chinh,

President Ho Chi Minh, Revered Leader of the Vietnamese People (Hanoi: Foreign Languages Publication House, 1966).
31. McAlister, *Origins of Revolution*, pp. 85–86.
32. Lacouture, *Ho Chi Minh*, pp. 69–70.
33. *Ibid.*
34. *Ibid.*, pp. 83–85
35. Ellen J. Hammer, *The Struggle for Indochina, 1940–1955* (Stanford, Calif.: Stanford Univ. Press, 1966), pp. 96–102.
36. Senate, "United States and Vietnam," p. 3.
37. Patti, *Why Vietnam?* p. 250.
38. *Ibid.*, pp. 244–46.
39. Quoted in Stanley Karnow, *Vietnam: A History* (New York: Viking, 1983), p. 138.
40. Hammer, *Struggle for Indochina*, pp. 142–44.
41. See Department of Defense, *United States–Vietnam Relations*, I, C-66–C-104.
42. Quoted in Karnow, *Vietnam: A History*, p. 153.
43. Record Group 331, National Archives of the United States, Washington, D.C.
44. Peter M. Dunn, *The First Vietnam War* (New York: St. Martin's Press, 1985), p. 152.
45. Karnow, *Vietnam: A History*, p. 148.
46. Patti, *Why Vietnam?* pp. 257–59; Duncanson, *Government and Revolution*, pp. 158–59.
47. Duncanson, *Government and Revolution*, pp. 160–61.
48. Cited in Philippe Devillers and Jean Lacouture, *End of a War: Indochina, 1954* (New York: Praeger, 1969), p. 6.
49. Cited in Chester L. Cooper, *The Lost Crusade: America in Vietnam* (New York: Dodd, Mead, 1970), p. 46.
50. "New French Colonial Policy . . . ," September 5, 1945, SD 851G.00/9–545. Hammer, *Struggle for Indochina*, pp. 11–13. For a succinct statement, see R. F. Holland, *European Decolonization, 1918–1981* (New York: St. Martin's Press, 1985), p. 96. "Ultimately the French judgement boiled down to a shrewd gamble that the cliques which surrounded Ho Chi Minh would opt for the not insubstantial rake-offs available to them in the French scheme of things rather than risk smashing their febrile political organization in a confrontation with a sophisticated European opponent whose capability to bring force to bear within the region was growing all the time."
51. "American Interests in Southeast Asia," March 26, 1945, Records of the Philippine and Southeast Asian Affairs Office, National Archives, Washington, D.C.
52. *Ibid.*
53. "New French Colonial Policy . . . ," September 5, 1945, SD 851G.00/9–545.
54. Patti, *Why Vietnam?* p. 210.
55. *Ibid.*, pp. 210–11.
56. Dening to Bevin, October 5, 1945, FO 371/46309, F 7907/11/G. Both Bernard Fall, *The Two Viet-Nams* (New York: Praeger, 1963), pp. 68–69, and Chester L. Cooper, *Lost Crusade*, p. 40, emphasize the psychological scars this episode left on France and French policymakers involved in the events of later years. For

Sainteny's own account, see *Histoire d'une paix manquée* (Paris: Amiot-Dumont, 1953), pp. 135–40.

57. Cooper, *Lost Crusade*, pp. 41–42.

58. Richard W. Klise, Special Agent, to Commanding General, Counter Intelligence Corps, October 4, 1945, Record Group 332, National Archives of the United States, Washington, D.C.

59. *Ibid.*

60. Karnow, *Vietnam: A History*, p. 139. One version of Dewey's behavior and his death is presented here. Patti, *Why Vietnam?* pp. 319–22, puts the slaying into the context of Gracey's passive approval of French violence against the Vietminh in Saigon. A much more critical account of Dewey, favorable to Gracey, is Dunn, *First Vietnam War*, pp. 155–58, 214–16, which also denies he had been ordered to leave. See also Michael Maclear, *The Ten Thousand Day War: Vietnam: A History, 1945–1975* (New York: Avon, 1981), p. 15.

61. Karnow, *Vietnam: A History*, p. 156.

62. Dening to Foreign Office, September 10, 1945, FO 371/46308, F 6636/11/61, and Dening to Foreign Office, September 19, 1945, FO 371/46308, F 7161/11/61. Some weeks later, SEAC commander Lord Mountbatten sent another warning to London, this time, however, about the delay in the arrival of British troops and Gracey's decision to employ Japanese troops to keep order. Mountbatten to Chiefs of Staff, October 2, 1945, FO 371/46309, F 7789/11/G.

63. Bevin to Sir H. Seymour, September 17, 1945, FO 800/461, F 7205/186/10.

64. Cabinet, Far Eastern Planning Unit, "General Conclusions," Gen 77/75, November 25, 1945, FO 371/46504, F 10650.

65. See various minutes in FO 371/46308, F 7161/11/61.

66. Mountbatten to Cabinet Offices, September 24, 1945, FO 371/46308, F 7489/11/61.

67. Killearn to Foreign Office, April 21, 1946, Papers of Ernest Bevin, FE/46/72, Public Record Office, London. A similar, but less optimistic view was expressed by a member of the Philippine and Southeast Asian Affairs Office in the State Department, who wrote an even more detailed memorandum on the precariousness of the American position in Southeast Asia. Pointing out that during the war the European powers had been unable to meet the basic needs of their dependent peoples, Phillip Bagby argued that "this suffering more than anything else served to fan the flames of nationalism. For the same conservative classes who formerly supported their foreign rulers now had to divert the upsurge of the masses into nationalist channels in order to maintain their privileged economic position." Bagby also thought that a Russian success in the old imperial areas would be "a threat to the very existence of the United States and would bring on a third world war." "United States Policy with Respect to the Decline of Western European Imperialism," March 13, 1946, PSEA Papers.

68. Lacouture, *Ho Chi Minh*, p. 126.

69. *Ibid.*, pp. 130–34.

70. Hammer, *Struggle for Indochina*, p. 163.

71. *Ibid.*, pp. 168–70.

72. *Ibid.*, p. 173.

73. Different interpretations of the series of events that led to the outbreak of the war can be found in Hammer, *Struggle for Indochina*, pp. 183–87, and Fall, *Two*

Viet-Nams, pp. 76–77. The broad context, however, is illuminated best by Holland, *European Decolonization,* pp. 96–97.

74. Hammer, *Struggle for Indochina,* pp. 191–92; Devillers and Lacouture, *End of a War,* p. 13.

75. Department of Defense, *United States–Vietnam Relations,* 8:91–92.

76. Bernard B. Fall, "Tribulations of a Party Line," *Foreign Affairs,* 33 (April 1955): 499–510.

77. Reed to Marshall, July 19, 1947, *FR 1947,* 6:119–20.

78. Marshall to Caffery, February 3, 1947, *ibid.,* 6:67–68. See also the analysis in Senate, "United States and Vietnam," pp. 20–22.

79. For the view that the Communist revolution was essentially one phenomenon, even if not so conspiratorial in nature as Americans insisted, see R. B. Smith, *An International History of the Vietnam War* (London: St. Martin's Press, 1983), 1:11. "It is not necessary to invoke the much-derided 'orders from Moscow' in order to recognize the historical unity of the world revolution which has always been inherent in Marxist-Leninist thought." China is the great exception, according to Smith, while Vietnam, a much smaller country, never dared to challenge the Moscow line. Smith does not, however, discuss Yugoslavia in these terms, although he does mention the independence Tito displayed in 1956 during de-Stalinization (p. 86). Neither does he comment, perhaps because his book really starts with Geneva in 1954, on the number of efforts that Ho Chi Minh made to enlist American political support from 1945 to 1947. East European Communists never behaved in this fashion, except for sporadic requests for economic aid. For the conspiratorial view straight in its most recent manifestation, see Hugh Thomas, *Armed Truce* (New York: Atheneum, 1987).

80. Hammer, *Struggle for Indochina,* pp. 207–17.

81. *Ibid.,* pp. 234–36.

82. A superb account of the impact of the Chinese Revolution and the themes discussed in this paragraph is Robert Blum, *Drawing the Line: The Origin of the American Containment Policy in East Asia* (New York: Norton, 1982), especially chap. 12.

83. Minute by Neville Butler, January 13, 1946, Bevin Papers, US/46/13.

84. Bevin to Attlee, January 23, 1947, Bevin Papers, FE/47/3.

85. For general background on the convertibility crisis, see Richard N. Gardner, *Sterling-Dollar Diplomacy,* rev. ed. (New York: McGraw-Hill, 1969); on Bevin's troubles and the context for his comments on relations with the former colonial areas, see Alan Bullock, *Ernest Bevin: Foreign Secretary, 1945–1951* (London: Heinemann, 1983), chap. 11. Quotation is from Bullock, p. 454.

86. Bevin to Attlee, July 7, 1947, and Attlee to Bevin, July 8, 1947, Bevin Papers, US/47/29.

87. "Record of a Conversation Between the Secretary of State and M. Bidault," November 29, 1947, Bevin Papers, Conf/47/9.

88. PPS/23, "Review of Current Trends in U.S. Foreign Policy," February 24, 1948, Records of the Policy Planning Staff, National Archives, Washington, D.C., box 9.

89. Department of Defense, *U.S.–Vietnam Relations,* 8:226–64.

90. *Ibid.*

91. Kennan quoted in Lloyd C. Gardner, *A Covenant with Power: America and World Order from Wilson to Reagan* (New York: Oxford Univ. Press, 1984), p. 112. Thomas quoted in United States Senate, Committee on Foreign Relations, *Hearings Held in Executive Session: Economic Assistance to China and Korea, 1949–50*, 81st. Cong., 1st and 2nd sess. (Washington, 1974), p. 159. For a general survey of this problem, see William S. Borden, *The Pacific Alliance: United States Economic Policy and Japanese Trade Recovery, 1947–1955* (Madison: Univ. of Wisconsin Press, 1984), chap. 3.
92. Memorandum of Conversation at the White House, February 4, 1950, Papers of Dean Acheson, Harry S. Truman Library, Independence, Missouri. It is significant that this conversation occurred the day after the cabinet and the president decided to recognize the Bao Dai government. See untitled minute, February 3, 1950, *ibid.*
93. Department of Defense, *U.S.–Vietnam Relations*, 8:226–64.
94. Ritchie Ovendale, *The English-Speaking Alliance: Britain, the United States, the Dominions, and the Cold War, 1945–51* (London: Allen and Unwin, 1985), pp. 160–61.
95. *Ibid.*, pp. 165–66.
96. "Record of a Meeting," September 13, 1949, Bevin Papers, FE/49/22.
97. "Record of a Meeting at the State Department," September 13, 1949, Bevin Papers, FE/49/21. See also "Conversation Between the Secretary of State and the United States Ambassador," August 26, 1949, FO 371/75814, F 128843/1023/10.
98. MacDonald to Sir William Strang, August 19, 1949, and Strang to MacDonald, September 2, 1949, FO 371/75814, F 13405/1023/10.
99. See High Commissioner in Australia to the Foreign Office, September 6, 1949, and Minute by P. D. Coates, September 9, 1949, FO 371/75814, F 13343/1023/10.
100. Gladwyn Jebb to Dening, December 8, 1949, and Dening Minute, December 9, 1949, FO 371/75828, F 19217/1023/10.
101. The analysis in these paragraphs is informed by Andrew J. Rotter's article "The Triangular Route to Vietnam: The United States, Great Britain, and Southeast Asia, 1945–1950," *International History Review*, 6 (August 1984): 404–23.
102. Bevin to Attlee, July 7, 1947, Bevin Papers, US/47/29.
103. "Conversation with the President," November 17, 1949, Records of the Policy Planning Staff. For a thoroughgoing study that also stresses Southeast Asia as a key determinant of China policy, see Blum, *Drawing the Line.* With a somewhat different emphasis, Warren I Cohen, "Acheson and China," in Dorothy Borg and Waldo Heinrichs, eds., *Uncertain Years, Chinese-American Relations, 1947–1950* (New York: Columbia Univ. Press, 1980), pp. 13–52, makes the same point. "He was much more interested in British and French opinion, in pacifying major allies, than in the fate of Chiang Kai-shek or Southeast Asia" (p. 50).
104. See, for example, Cohen, "Acheson and China," p. 51.
105. Bevin to British Ambassador in Paris, December 16, 1949, FO 371/75827, F 18978/1023/10, and Franks to Bevin, December 17, 1949, Bevin Papers, FE/49/40.
106. "Memorandum for the President," February 2, 1950, Department of Defense, *United States–Vietnam Relations*, 8:276–77.
107. "Memorandum of Conversation," January 6, 1950, Acheson Papers.

NOTES

CHAPTER THREE: THE KOREAN RESCUE MISSION

1. Papers of Harry S. Truman, Harry S. Truman Library, Independence, Missouri, President's Secretary's File (hereafter, PSF).
2. Speech, June 30, 1950, Harry S. Truman, *Public Papers of the Presidents, 1950*, National Archives (Washington, 1965), p. 515.
3. See, for example, John Lewis Gaddis, "Was the Truman Doctrine a Turning Point?" *Foreign Affairs*, 53, no. 2 (1974): 386–402.
4. See Lloyd C. Gardner, *A Covenant with Power: America and World Order from Wilson to Reagan* (New York: Oxford Univ. Press, 1984), pp. 98–99.
5. See the insightful essay on America's role in the Cold War by Thomas J. McCormick, "Every System Needs a Center Sometimes," in Lloyd Gardner, ed., *Redefining the Past: Essays in Diplomatic History in Honor of William Appleman Williams* (Corvallis: Oregon State Univ. Press, 1986).
6. "Statement by Senator Taft on Formosa," January 11, 1950 (Washington, 1950), p. 3.
7. Secretary of State Acheson attempted to blunt the impact of British recognition of Communist China and to bring home some truths by telling Republican leaders that (a) Formosa (Taiwan) was almost impossible to defend militarily; and (b) it was the wrong moment to suggest, by interfering in the Chinese civil war, that the United States behaved in any fashion like the Soviet Union. His arguments were met with much skepticism by H. Alexander Smith, senator from New Jersey, who warned that abandoning Chiang to his fate "might affect his future attitude of support of a bipartisan foreign policy." Senator William Knowland of California threatened more active opposition in the Senate. The meeting ended in a strained atmosphere. "Courteous but restrained goodbyes were offered by those present." Memorandum of a Conversation, "Formosa Problem," January 5, 1950, Acheson Papers, Truman Library, Independence, Missouri. Early French indications of a desire to buy off Mao came even as the ambassador in Washington was pleading for an initial commitment to military aid for Indochina on February 16, 1950. Memorandum of Conversation, "Indochina," *ibid.*
8. American policymakers believed that the British pursued the two-Chinas policy at bottom out of a desire to divert Japanese economic competition from European colonial markets to mainland China. They were constantly chagrined to find this old appeasement theory, as they saw it, resurfacing at a whole series of points in diplomatic discussions over the Japanese peace treaty, as well as in attitudes toward Southeast Asia. See, for example, a memo by John Foster Dulles, "Japan and China," January 11, 1952, Dulles Papers, Mudd Library, Princeton University, Princeton, New Jersey.
9. On this last point, see especially Acheson's conversation with Carlos P. Romulo of the Philippines on March 10, 1950. "I told him we have to be careful here that the French did not get discouraged by internal difficulties at home and withdraw from Indo China. If their troops were withdrawn there would be a real danger of the first magnitude." Acheson Papers.
10. U.S. Department of State, *Foreign Relations of the United States (FR) 1950* (Washington, 1976), 6:711–15.
11. For a well-reasoned view that Acheson *was* in hopes of splitting the Chinas, see Warren I Cohen, "Acheson, His Advisers, and China, 1949–1950," in Dorothy

Bord and Waldo Heinrichs, eds., *Uncertain Years: Chinese-American Relations, 1947–1950* (New York: Columbia Univ. Press, 1980), pp. 13–52, and commentary, pp. 52–59.

12. "Address by the Secretary of State," January 12, 1950, in Department of State, *American Foreign Policy, 1950–1955: Basic Documents*, 2 vols. (Washington, D.C., 1957), 2:2310–22; Dean Acheson, *Present at the Creation* (New York: Norton, 1969), p. 355.

13. Acheson, *Present at the Creation*, p. 355.

14. "Memorandum for S/S," by L. D. Battle, March 8, 1950, and "Memorandum of Conversation with Ambassador Bonnet," March 13, 1950, Acheson Papers.

15. "Conversation Between the Secretary and Representative Herter," March 21, 1950, Acheson Papers.

16. January 20, 1950, Department of State, *American Foreign Policy, 1950–1955*, 2:2527–28.

17. Acheson, *Present at the Creation*, p. 358.

18. Ronald W. Pruessen, *John Foster Dulles: The Road to Power* (New York: Free Press, 1982), pp. 435–36.

19. "Memorandum of Conversation with President Truman," enclosed in Dulles to Acheson, May 2, 1950, Acheson Papers.

20. May 18, 1950, Dulles Papers.

21. John Chang Myun, Oral History Interview, *ibid.*

22. Pruessen, *Dulles: Road to Power*, pp. 450–51.

23. Joint Chiefs statement cited in Matthew Ridgway, *The Korean War* (New York, 1967), p. 7 (emphasis added). For similar statements and background, see Lloyd C. Gardner, Walter F. LaFeber, and Thomas J. McCormick, *Creation of the American Empire: U.S. Diplomatic History* (Chicago: Rand McNally, 1973), pp. 484–85.

24. Department of State, *American Foreign Policy, 1950–1955*, 2:2539–40.

25. For general surveys of American policy leading to the Korean War, see David Rees, *Korea: The Limited War* (New York: St. Martin's Press, 1964), and William Stueck, *The Road to Confrontation: American Policy Toward China and Korea, 1947–1950* (Chapel Hill: Univ. of North Carolina Press, 1981).

26. "Meeting of the NSC . . . ," June 29, 1950, National Archives (NA), State Department (SD), 795.00/6–2950.

27. "Bukit Serene Conference," Minutes, Papers of John Melby, Harry S. Truman Library, Independence, Missouri.

28. "Memorandum of Conversation: Korean Crisis," June 30, 1950, Acheson Papers.

29. Cited in Ritchie Ovendale, "Britain and the Cold War in Asia," in Ritchie Ovendale, ed., *The Foreign Policy of the British Labour Governments, 1945–1951* (Leicester, Eng.: Leceister Univ. Press, 1984), p. 131.

30. Franks quoted in William Steuck, "The Limits of Influence: British Policy and American Expansion of the War in Korea," *Pacific Historical Review*, 55 (February 1986): 65–95.

31. Quoted in Ritchie Ovendale, "Britain, the United States, and the Recognition of Communist China," *Historical Journal*, 26: (1983): 139–57.

32. Ovendale, "Britain and the Cold War in Asia," pp. 132–33.

33. Ritchie Ovendale, *The English-Speaking Alliance: Britain, the United States, the Dominions, and the Cold War* (London: Allen and Unwin, 1985), pp. 168–69.
34. *Ibid.*
35. "Memorandum by Mr. John Foster Dulles . . . ," August 7, 1950, *FR 1950*, 6:128–30. One of the few dissents voiced to this general proposition was offered by the retiring head of the Policy Planning Staff, George F. Kennan, who expressed doubts about the implications of the Dulles approach to Far Eastern policy in a memorandum to Secretary Acheson, dated August 23, 1950. Said Kennan: it should be "an objective of policy to terminate our involvements on the mainland of Asia as rapidly as possible and on the best terms we can get." And "with respect to Indo-China, we should let . . . [the French know] that the closer view we have had of the problems of this area . . . has convinced us that that position is basically hopeless." Acheson Papers.
36. Vo Nguyen Giap, *People's War, People's Army* (New York: Praeger, 1962), p. 22.
37. See the discussion in Melvin Gurtov, *The First Vietnam Crisis* (New York: Columbia Univ. Press, 1967), pp. 8–14.
38. *Ibid.*
39. Allan W. Cameron, ed., *Viet-Nam Crisis: A Documentary History*, 2 vols. (Ithaca, N.Y.: Cornell Univ. Press, 1971), 1:152–53.
40. *Ibid.*
41. Quoted in R. E. M. Irving, *The First Indochina War* (London: C. Helm, 1975), p. 103.
42. See the long discussion of this problem in Ambassador David Bruce's telegram from Paris, November 3, 1950, *FR 1950*, 6:917–19.
43. Irving, *First Indochina War*, p. 83.
44. "Memorandum of Conversation . . . ," October 16, 1950, *FR 1950*, 6:896–97.
45. As Assistant Secretary Dean Rusk put it in a cable over Acheson's signature, "We have not felt US should take leadership in attempting organize such groupings particularly in view problems which naturally arise, such as possible misunderstanding US motives, varying conceptions and aims of states which might be concerned, and choice of members." India and Nationalist China were at the center of this problem. October 12, 1950, *ibid.*, pp. 148–49.
46. *Ibid.*, pp. 900–1, 935–36.
47. Bruce to Acheson, November 3, 1950, *ibid.*, pp. 917–19.
48. "Final Report of the Joint MDAP Survey Mission . . . ," December 6, 1950, *ibid.*, pp. 164–73.
49. *Ibid.*
50. David Rees, *Korea: The Limited War* (Baltimore: Penguin, 1970), p. 174. The most recent survey is Rosemary Foot, *The Wrong War: American Policy and the Dimensions of the Korean Conflict, 1950–1953* (Ithaca, N.Y.: Cornell Univ. Press, 1985).
51. The standard work remains Allen S. Whiting, *China Crosses the Yalu: The Decision to Enter the Korean War* (New York: Macmillan, 1960).
52. *FR 1950*, 6:941.
53. "Meeting in the Secretary's Office," December 5, 1950, Acheson Papers.
54. Assistant Chief of Staff, G-2, "Intelligence Estimate of World-Wide and Soviet Reaction to the Use of Atomic Bombardment in the Korean Conflict," July 13, 1950, Record Group 319, National Archives, Washington, D.C.

55. "First Meeting of the President and Prime Minister Pleven," January 29, 1951, Truman Papers, PSF.
56. *Ibid.*
57. "Third Meeting of the President and the Prime Minister," January 30, 1951, *ibid.*
58. National Security Council, "Progress Report by the Under Secretary of State . . . ," March 15, 1951, *ibid.*
59. Acheson to Certain Diplomatic Offices, January 19, 1951, *FR 1951* (Washington, 1977), vol. 6, part 1, pp. 349–50.
60. Irving, *First Indochina War,* p. 88.
61. Bruce to Acheson, December 16, 1950, *FR 1950,* 6:944.
62. George C. Herring, *America's Longest War: The United States and Vietnam, 1950–1975,* 2nd ed. (New York: Knopf, 1985), pp. 20–21.
63. Bruce to Acheson, March 14, 1951, *FR 1951,* 6:395–96, and Bruce to Acheson, March 18, 1951, *ibid.,* pp. 404–6.
64. Acheson to the American Legation in Saigon, October 15, 1951, *ibid.,* p. 532.
65. Dulles Papers.
66. United States Senate, Committees on Armed Services and Foreign Relations, *Hearings: The Military Situation in the Far East,* 82nd Cong., 1st sess. (Washington, 1951), p. 172.
67. *Ibid.,* pp. 324–25.
68. Nancy Bernkopf Tucker, *Patterns in the Dust: Chinese-American Relations and the Recognition Controversy, 1949–1950* (New York: Columbia Univ. Press, 1983), p. 36.
69. *Ibid.,* pp. 204–5; and see also the works cited by Borden, *The Pacific Alliance* (Madison: Univ. of Wisconsin Press, 1984), chap. 3, and Rotter, "The Triangular Route to Vietnam," *International History Review,* 6:404–23.
70. William Sebald, Oral History Interview, Dulles Papers, pp. 53–54; on Philippine opinion, see, *FR 1951,* vol. 6, part 1, pp. 1136–37.
71. *FR 1951,* vol. 6, part 1, pp. 1116–18, 1247–48.
72. "Memorandum of Conversation . . . ," April 18, 1951, *ibid.,* pp. 985–89.
73. Notes for a letter to General MacArthur, undated, 1950, Dulles Papers.
74. Minutes, First Meeting of Study Group on Japanese Treaty Problems, Council on Foreign Relations, October 23, 1950, *ibid.*
75. March 18, 1951, *FR 1951,* vol. 6, part 1, p. 932.
76. See *ibid.,* p. 1253.
77. *Ibid.,* pp. 254–55.
78. The story is most easily followed in Pruessen, *Dulles: Road to Power,* pp. 484–98. But Dulles could also talk tough to the Japanese, at least on this single issue of China. Ambassador William Sebald recalled the following exchange on December 12, 1951. "Dulles pointed out that he wished to find out now, whether the foreign policy of Japan will parallel ours or whether it will be such as to be inimical to our national interests. In the former event, solution of our many problems would be relatively easy; in the latter event, we should have to take stock of our position and be guided accordingly." Sebald, Oral History Interview, Dulles Papers, pp. 61–62. On Yoshida's fears of British retaliation, see a paper prepared for Truman's use when he met with Prime Minister Winston Churchill in January, 1952, "Japanese Relations with China," January 2, 1952, Truman Papers, PSF.

79. United States Senate, Committee on Foreign Relations, *Hearings: Japanese Peace Treaty and Other Treaties Relating to Security in the Pacific*, 82nd Cong., 2nd sess. (Washington, 1952), p. 47.
80. *Ibid.*
81. *FR 1952–1954* (Washington, 1982), vol. 13, part 1, pp. 124–29.
82. "Memorandum by the Assistant Secretary of State for Far Eastern Affairs," February 11, 1952, *ibid.*, pp. 28–34.
83. Heath to Department of State, January 30, 1952, *ibid.*, pp. 22–24.
84. Herring, *America's Longest War*, pp. 21–22.
85. Steering Group on Preparations for Talks Between the President and Prime Minister Churchill, "Divergence of U.S. and British Policies Respecting China," January 5, 1952, Truman Papers, PSF.
86. Steering Group on Preparations for Talks Between the President and Prime Minister Churchill, "Prospects for an Acceptable Settlement of Major Issues with the USSR," December 29, 1951, *ibid.*
87. "Memorandum of Dinner Meeting . . . ," January 5, 1952, *ibid.*
88. *Ibid.*
89. "Truman-Churchill Talks," Third Formal Session, January 9, 1952, *ibid.*
90. *Ibid.*
91. "Memorandum of Conversation . . . ," March 21, 1952, *FR 1952–1954*, vol. 13, part 1, pp. 75–77.
92. "General Discussion with Prime Minister Menzies of Australia," May 20, 1952, Acheson Papers.
93. Minutes of Tripartite Foreign Ministers Meeting, May 28, 1952, *FR 1952–1954*, vol. 13, pp. 157–65.
94. *Ibid.*
95. Herring, *America's Longest War*, pp. 24–25; Stephen Jurika, Jr., ed., *From Pearl Harbor to Vietnam: The Memoirs of Admiral Arthur W. Radford* (Stanford, Calif.: Hoover Institute Press, 1980), p. 357.

CHAPTER FOUR: TRUE LIBERATION

1. Dulles Papers, Mudd Library, Princeton University, Princeton, New Jersey.
2. January 20, 1953, National Archives and Records Service, *Public Papers of the Presidents: Dwight D. Eisenhower, 1953* (Washington, 1960), pp. 3–4.
3. "War or Peace" speech, draft of July 16, 1952, Dulles Papers.
4. Interview, Dulles Oral History Project, *ibid.*
5. Robert H. Ferrell, ed., *The Eisenhower Diaries* (New York: Norton, 1981), p. 213.
6. "Private Memo," January 5, 1951, Papers of Arthur Krock, Mudd Library, Princeton University, Princeton, New Jersey.
7. June 30, 1952, Papers of Bernard Baruch, Mudd Library, Princeton University, Princeton, New Jersey.
8. Dulles Papers.
9. He thought so even when he could find no alternative. In the summer of 1953, Eisenhower ordered a series of studies, known collectively as the Solarium Project, on options for future national security policy. Roughly speaking, these broke down

into three alternatives: liberation (up to and possibly including military initiatives, although how far to go was never completely spelled out); traditional containment; and fortress America. At the end, the president summed up the findings this way: "[T]he only thing worse than losing a global war was winning one; that there would be no individual freedom after the next global war. If you demand of a free people over a long period of time more than they want to give, you can obtain what you want only by using more and more controls; and the more you do this, the more you lose the individual liberty which you are trying to save and become a garrison state (American model)." "Memorandum by the Special Assistant to the President . . . ," July 16, 1953, U.S. Department of State, *Foreign Relations of the United States (FR). 1952–1954* (Washington, 1984), 2:397–98.

George Kennan, who presented the containment task force's conclusions, believed that the president's words indicated a continuing commitment to that policy. *Memoirs, 1950–1963* (Boston: Atlantic–Little, Brown, 1972), pp. 180–82. The text of the above memorandum does not indicate such presidential certainty, although it is not a verbatim account.

10. Eisenhower to Dulles, June 20, 1952, Dulles Papers. One should keep this memorandum in mind when reviewing the American policy toward elections in post-Geneva Vietnam.

11. Transcript of the "Princeton Seminar," May 15, 1954, copy in the Acheson Papers, Harry S. Truman Library, Independence, Missouri.

12. *Ibid.*

13. "Memorandum of Meeting at the White House," Acheson Papers.

14. Lodge to Eisenhower, June 26, 1956, copy in Dulles Papers.

15. Quoted in Lloyd C. Gardner, "The Dulles Years, 1953–1959," in William Appleman Williams, ed., *From Colony to Empire: Essays in the History of American Foreign Relations* (New York: Wiley, 1972), p. 386.

16. Interview with Eisenhower, March 29, 1965, Dulles Oral History Project, Dulles Papers.

17. Interview with W. Walton Butterworth, *ibid.*

18. Press Conference, December 7, 1954, transcript *ibid.*

19. Quotation from Interview with Elliot Bell, Dulles Oral History Project, *ibid.* Dulles had a hard time convincing Treasury Secretary George Humphrey that it would be worthwhile to ease conditions on American loans so that the undeveloped world could have access to capital on terms that would not be so onerous as to alienate them forever from the West. Said Dulles, "It might be good banking to put South America through the wringer but it will come out red." "Memorandum Re NAC Meeting, September 30, 1953," October 1, 1953, *ibid.* And to a White House adviser, he wrote on August 24, 1954, "I am personally convinced that it is going to be very difficult to stop Communism in much of the world if we cannot in some way duplicate the intensive Communist effort to raise productive standards. They themselves are increasing their own productivity at the rate of about 6% per annum, which is about twice our rate. In many areas of the world such as Southeast Asia, India, Pakistan and South America, there is little, if any increase. That is one reason why Communism has such great appeal in areas where the slogans of 'liberty', 'freedom', and 'personal dignity' have little appeal." Dulles Papers.

20. The original article appeared in *Foreign Affairs*, 25 (July 1947): 566–82.

21. Interview with Joseph C. Harsch, Dulles Oral History Project, Dulles Papers. See also George F. Kennan, *Memoirs, 1950–1963* (Boston: Atlantic–Little, Brown, 1972), pp. 180–82.
22. Eisenhower revealed in 1965 that he had called Dulles on the telephone at one point in the campaign to remind him that they had agreed that whenever they talked about Eastern Europe and liberation they would say the United States "should use all peaceful means." Dulles had transgressed in a speech on the captive nations in Buffalo, leaving out the qualifier "peaceful." Eisenhower accepted Dulles' explanation that it was "just a complete oversight." Interview with Dwight D. Eisenhower, March 13, 1965, Dulles Oral History Project, Dulles Papers. In the future, however, the secretary took some pains to clear his remarks with the White House. Whether Dulles would have followed a bolder liberation policy in Eastern Europe without Eisenhower's restraining hand resting on his shoulder remains open to question. I have discussed this question in *A Covenant with Power: America and World Order from Wilson to Reagan* (New York: Oxford Univ. Press, 1984) chap. 6.
23. For information on Eisenhower and Korea, see Burton I. Kaufman, *The Korean War: The Challenges in Crisis, Credibility, and Command* (New York: Knopf, 1986), chap. 9.
24. For convenient summaries of recent literature on Eisenhower and his presidency, see Robert Griffith, "Dwight D. Eisenhower and the Corporate Commonwealth," *American Historical Review*, 87 (February 1982): 87–122; Richard Challener, "The National Security Policy from Truman to Eisenhower," in Norman Graebner, ed., *The National Security: Its Theory and Practice, 1945–1960* (New York: Oxford Univ. Press, 1986), pp. 39–75.
25. China's appeal to Asian nationalists was being used by the Russians to advance their own aims, but they were very clever about it, and the battle could be lost. "Many Orientals fear," Dulles noted in an article, "Security in the Pacific," "that Westerners are incapable of cooperating with them on a basis of political, economic and social equality and this fear divides the East and West. It has a long background of growth, and Communist propaganda in Asia concentrates on keeping it alive and whipping it up. The Communists scream that there cannot be a genuine 'Asia for the Asiatics' until every vestige of Western influence has been driven out of Asia—leaving, of course, 'Asia for the Russians.'" *Foreign Affairs*, 30 (January 1952): 184–87.
26. United States Senate, Foreign Relations Committee, *Executive Sessions of the Senate Foreign Relations Committee, 1953*, 83rd Cong., 1st sess. (Washington, 1977), 5:142.
27. "JFD Statement, China," November 21, 1950, Dulles Papers.
28. *Ibid.*
29. Transcript of broadcast, February 10, 1952, *ibid.* These paragraphs draw heavily upon the thesis advanced in David Mayers, "Eisenhower's Containment Policy and the Major Communist Powers, 1953–1956," *International History Review*, 5 (February 1983): 60–83.
30. "Summary of JFD remarks . . . at Kanohe," December 11, 1952, Dulles Papers.
31. Stephen Ambrose, *Eisenhower: The President* (New York: Simon and Schuster, 1984), p. 164.

32. National Archives, *Public Papers of the Presidents, 1953,* p. 17.
33. Eisenhower Interview, Dulles Oral History Project, Dulles Papers.
34. JFD to Charles E. Wilson, December 30, 1952, *ibid.*
35. F. S. Tomlinson, British Embassy Washington, to Foreign Office, February 19, 1953, Foreign Office (FO) 371/105180, F1023/5G. Dulles had thought a great deal about the importance of causing trouble in "communist territory." See, for example, Dulles to David Astor, March 24, 1952. "Surely, there is a vast range of possible policies between the one extreme of total abandonment of the loyal representatives of Free China on Formosa and the other extreme of now escorting them to the military reconquest of the mainland." Dulles Papers. Of course, Dulles was at this time engaged in a "debate" with the president over Korean policy. Eisenhower was determined to bring the war to a speedy end, while the secretary was arguing that it was terribly important not to withdraw under circumstances suggesting appeasement. Hence he would use arguments about Indochina as additional reasons for staying tough in Korea, as well as the need to maintain an extended battle line on China's frontiers. For Eisenhower's views, see Interview with Mark Clark, Dulles Oral History Project, *ibid.*
36. Roderic O'Connor Interview, Dulles Oral History Project, Dulles Papers.
37. General Matthew Ridgway remembered that Dulles came to Paris in the spring of 1953, full of ideas about a military offensive in Korea, the unleashing of Chiang, and amphibious operations in the Indochina region against Hainan Island. Here was another version of the three-pronged assault on China. Ridgway heard nothing more about the plan, however, after he returned to Washington that same summer. Interview, Dulles Oral History Project, *ibid.*
38. For a fuller explication, see John Lewis Gaddis, "American Policy and Perspectives: The Sino-Soviet 'Wedge' Strategy, 1949–1955," paper delivered at Beijing Conference on Sino-American Relations, 1986.
39. February 18, 1953, transcript in Dulles Papers.
40. Quoted in R. H. Scott to Sir Eisler Dening, April 10, 1953, FO 371/105486, FK 1071/130.
41. Minute on Makins to Foreign Office, February 21, 1953, FO 371/105180, F1023/7.
42. *Ibid.*
43. Extract of Conversation, March 6, 1953, FO 371/105180, F1023/8/G.
44. Ferrell, *The Eisenhower Diaries,* p. 223.
45. *Ibid.*
46. Diary Entry, January 6, 1953, in John Colville, *The Fringes of Power: 10 Downing Street Diaries, 1939–1955* (New York: Norton, 1985), p. 660.
47. January 7, 1953, *ibid.,* p. 662.
48. JFD to DDE, November 14, 1952, Dulles Papers.
49. David Carlton, *Anthony Eden* (London: Allen Lane, 1981), p. 325.
50. Judd's Memorandum of the Conversation, March 4, 1952, reprinted in the transcript of his interview, Dulles Oral History Project, Dulles Papers.
51. Henry Cabot Lodge, *As It Was: An Inside View of Politics and Power in the Fifties and Sixties* (New York: Norton, 1976), pp. 26–27.
52. Dulles was made aware of this request by Douglas MacArthur II, who held a policy-making position in the State Department in the Eisenhower administration. MacArthur discouraged the idea because, on the other hand, it seemed to

promise too much of a commitment to Indochina and current French policies. See MacArthur to General Al Greunther, November 16, 1952, Dulles Papers.

53. May 5, 1952, Dulles Papers (emphasis added).

54. *Ibid.*

55. See Norman A. Graebner, *The New Isolationism: A Study of Politics and Foreign Policy Since 1950* (New York: Ronald Press, 1956), and the same author's "Limits of Nuclear Strategy," in Graebner, ed., *The National Security*, pp. 275–304.

56. "Memorandum of Discussion at the 160th Meeting of the National Security Council . . . August 27, 1953," *FR 1952–1954*, 2:443–55.

57. *Ibid.*

58. Graebner, "The Limits of Nuclear Strategy," p. 280.

59. Less appreciated than the "sanctuary" provided by China, or the military aid, was the example of a successful war of national liberation. See Vo Nguyen Giap, *People's War, People's Army* (New York: Praeger, 1962), p. 69.

60. Sherman Adams, *Firsthand Report* (New York: Popular Library, 1962), pp. 127–28.

61. Radford had been the American commander in the Pacific. "Widely known for his Asia-first views, the Pacific commander was an articulate champion of air and sea power and in particular of the giant aircraft carriers. He was reported to be close to Senator Taft and those who believed America should tell the neutrals in Asia that it was join our side 'or else.' " Marquis Childs, *Eisenhower: Captive Hero* (New York: Harcourt, Brace, 1958).

62. Stephen Jurika, Jr., ed., *From Pearl Harbor to Vietnam: The Memoirs of Admiral Arthur W. Radford* (Stanford, Calif.: Hoover Institute Press, 1980), p. 295. See also pp. 357–58.

63. "Memorandum of Conversation . . . ," February 4, 1953, *FR 1952–1954*, vol. 13, part 1, pp. 384–86. Such predictions always had the built-in escape clause, of course, that allowed the military (French or American) to say later that the war had not been fought in the "right way," or with the "right weapons," or with the full support of civilian policymakers. Much of the recent writing in the United States favors such an interpretation of why the war was ultimately lost. See the very popular book by Harry G. Summers, *On Strategy* (San Francisco: Presipio Press, 1982).

64. "Notes Taken at the First Plenary Session of Project Solarium," June 26, 1953, *FR 1952–1954*, 2:390.

65. Ambrose, *Eisenhower*, p. 52. See also "Discussion at the 131st Meeting of the National Security Council," February 11, 1953, Papers of Dwight D. Eisenhower, Ann Whitman File, Dwight D. Eisenhower Library, Abilene, Kansas.

66. Emmett John Hughes, *The Ordeal of Power: A Political Memoir of the Eisenhower Years* (New York: Atheneum, 1963), pp. 103–5.

67. Ambrose, *Eisenhower*, p. 94.

68. Dulles to Embassy in France, March 19, 1953, *FR 1952–1954*, vol. 13, part 1, pp. 416–17.

69. "Memorandum of Breakfast Conversation," March 24, 1953, Dulles Papers.

70. R. E. M. Irving, *The First Indochina War* (London: C. Helm, 1975), p. 104; R. F. Holland, *European Decolonization, 1918–1981* (New York: St. Martin's Press, 1985), p. 102.

71. Holland, *European Decolonization*, p. 102.

72. "Memorandum of Discussion at the 138th Meeting of the National Security Council . . . ," March 25, 1953, *FR 1952–1954*, vol. 13, part 1, pp. 426–28.
73. Dulles to Embassy in France, March 27, 1953, *ibid.*, pp. 432–34.
74. *Ibid.*, pp. 436–37.
75. Dulles, "Notes on Remarks at NSC Meeting," March 31, 1953, Dulles Papers.
76. Douglas Dillon to DDE, April 9, 1953, Dulles-Herter Series, Eisenhower Papers.
77. Senate Foreign Relations Committee, *Executive Sessions, 1953*, 5:300–1.
78. "Discussion at the 139th Meeting of the National Security Council . . . ," April 8, 1953, Whitman File, Eisenhower Papers.
79. *Ibid.*
80. "Memorandum of Conversation . . . ," April 9, 1953, *FR 1952–1954*, vol. 12, part 1, pp. 300–2.
81. Kaufman, *Korean War*, p. 320.
82. JFD to DDE, May 22, 1953, Dulles-Herter File, Eisenhower Papers.
83. Saruepalli Gopal, *Jawaharlal Nehru: A Biography* (Cambridge, Mass.: Harvard Univ. Press, 1976), 2:148. Nehru specifically stated in a memorandum of September 16, 1953, that there was no warning to China conveyed through him at Dulles' behest. For a detailed examination, see Edward C. Keefer, "President Dwight D. Eisenhower and the End of the Korean War," *Diplomatic History*, 10 (Summer 1986): 267–89. Keefer documents the point that the atomic threats, while real, were hardly part of a comprehensive policy.
84. "Outline of Major U.S. Statements and Actions . . . ," Dulles Papers.
85. Kaufman, *Korean War*, pp. 329–30.
86. *Ibid.*, pp. 329, 337. For specifics, see "Memorandum for the President," June 14, 1953, Dulles-Herter File, Eisenhower Papers.
87. DDE to JFD, June 2, 1953, Eisenhower Diaries, Eisenhower Papers.
88. "Memorandum for the Secretary of State," June 18, 1953, *ibid.*
89. JFD to DDE, June 24, 1953, *ibid.*
90. JFD to Dillon, June 5, 1953, *FR 1952–1954*, vol. 13, part 1, pp. 603–4. See also "Statement of Secretary Dulles at April 23 [1953] Session of North Atlantic Council Ministers' Meeting," Dulles Papers.
91. "Statement of Secretary Dulles at April 23 [1953] Session," Dulles Papers.
92. Carlton, *Anthony Eden*, p. 328; Lord Moran, *Churchill: The Struggle for Survival, 1940–65* (Boston: Houghton Mifflin, 1966), p. 405.
93. Kaufman, *Korean War*, p. 339. On American responses to Churchill's call for a summit, see Harold MacMillan, *Tides of Fortune* (new York: Harper and Row, 1969), pp. 522–25.
94. Dillon to JFD, April 30, 1953, *FR 1952–1954*, vol. 13, part 1, pp. 528–29.
95. DDE to Dillon, May 6, 1953, *ibid.*, pp. 550–1.
96. Draft DDE to Mrs. Robert Patterson, June 15, 1953, Whitman File, Eisenhower Papers.

CHAPTER FIVE: THE FRENCH DEFENSE

1. Quotation from "Massive Retaliation" speech, included in "Outline of Major U.S. Statements and Actions Reflecting Recent U.S. Policies Towards Indo-

china," Dulles Papers, Mudd Library, Princeton University, Princeton, New Jersey.

2. Walter Korn, ed., *Modern Chess Openings*, 9th ed. (New York: McKay, 1962), p. 92.

3. Eisenhower, *The White House Years: Mandate for Change, 1953–1956* (New York: Doubleday, 1963), p. 246.

4. DDE to Everett E. "Swede" Hazlett, December 24, 1953, in Robert Griffith, ed., *Ike's Letters to a Friend, 1941–1958* (Lawrence: Univ. of Kansas Press, 1969), pp. 112–18.

5. Jules Roy, *The Battle of Dienbienphu* (New York: Carroll and Graf, 1984), p. 19; C. L. Sulzberger, *A Long Row of Candles: Memoirs and Diaries, 1934–1954* (New York: MacMillan, 1969), pp. 908–9.

6. Eisenhower, *Mandate for Change*, p. 246.

7. Achilles to State Department, July 8, 1953, U.S. Department of State, *Foreign Relations of the United States (FR) 1952–1954* (Washington, 1982), vol. 13, part 1, pp. 643–44.

8. *Ibid.*, pp. 701–19.

9. Roy, *Battle of Dienbienphu*, pp. 18–21. See also Guy de Carmoy, *The Foreign Policies of France, 1944–1968*, trans. by Elaine P. Halperin (Chicago: Univ. of Chicago Press, 1970), pp. 142–43.

10. For background details, see M. Steven Fish, "After Stalin's Death: The Anglo-American Debate over a New Cold War," *Diplomatic History*, 10 (Fall 1986): 333–56. Somewhat surprisingly, Fish does not mention the Asian issues, or Eisenhower's threats to use atomic weapons in China, a major factor in London's reluctance to follow Washington's lead about Indochina.

11. Roy, *Battle of Dienbienphu*, pp. 8–9.

12. *FR 1952–1954*, vol. 13, part 1, pp. 616–18, 624–26, 647–48.

13. "United States Minutes of the First United States–French Meeting . . . ," July 12, 1953, *ibid.*, pp. 656–67.

14. "Outline of Major U.S. Statements and Actions Reflecting Recent U.S. Policies Towards Indochina," pp. 5–6, Dulles Papers.

15. R. E. M. Irving, *The First Indochina War* (London: C. Helm, 1975), p. 106.

16. Dillon to Department of State, August 29, 1953, *FR 1952–1954*, vol. 13, part 1, pp. 740–41. More of what Dillon conveyed to Laniel was noted by C. L. Sulzberger in his diary. "Dillon said the Navarre plan for Indochina is going to be paid for by the United States. . . . Indochina now has top priority. The necessary amount will be earmarked for Indochina, and funds for all other countries will be proportionately cut." If this was not sufficient, a special bill would be presented to Congress at the next session. "The idea would be to have a sort of 'Truman Doctrine' for Southeast Asia emphasizing the great need to dam the Communist tide there." Entry for September 1, 1953, *Long Row of Candles*, pp. 894–95. Little wonder Laniel was enchanted.

17. Ronald Spector, *The United States Army in Vietnam, Advice and Support: The Early Years* (Washington, 1983), p. 179.

18. "Substance of Discussions . . . ," September 4, 1953, *FR 1952–1954*, vol. 13, part 1, pp. 751–57.

19. Stanley Karnow, *Vietnam: A History*, p. 189.

20. Roy, *Battle of Dienbienphu*, pp. 12–17.

21. *Ibid.*, pp. 18–19.
22. Philippe Devillers and Jean Lacouture, *End of a War: Indochina, 1954*, trans. by Alexander Lieven and Adam Roberts (New York: Praeger, 1969), p. 40; Gurtov, *First Vietnam Crisis* (New York: Columbia Univ. Press, 1967), pp. 60–61.
23. Roy, *Battle of Dienbienphu*, p. 23.
24. Devillers and Lacouture, *End of a War*, pp. 44–45; Spector, *Advice and Support*, p. 182.
25. *Washington Post*, September 4, 1954.
26. Bernard B. Fall, *Hell in a Very Small Place: The Siege of Dien Bien Phu* (Philadelphia: Lippincott, 1966), pp. 54–55.
27. *Ibid.*, p. 57.
28. Karnow, *Vietnam: A History*, p. 142.
29. Roy, *Battle of Dienbienphu*, p. 298.
30. *Ibid.*, p. 140; Fall, *Hell in a Very Small Place*, p. 141.
31. Karnow, *Vietnam: A History*, pp. 193–94.
32. Roy, *Battle of Dienbienphu*, p. 85.
33. Irving, *First Indochina War*, p. 117.
34. United States Senate, Committee on Foreign Relations, *Executive Sessions of the Senate Foreign Relations Committee*, 83rd Cong., 2nd sess. (Washington, 1977), 6:16.
35. Fish, "After Stalin's Death," pp. 333–56. As this article makes clear, Bermuda was acrimonious not because it was unimportant, but for the opposite reason.
36. *Ibid.*
37. Undated, "Memorandum for the President," November 1953, Eisenhower Papers, Dulles-Herter Series, Eisenhower Library, Abilene, Kansas.
38. See my review "45/85," *Journal of American History*, 73 (December 1986): 833–34, and my *Safe for Democracy: The Anglo-American Response to Revolution, 1913–1923* (New York: Oxford Univ. Press, 1984), for an account of Lloyd George's attempt to come to terms with the Bolsheviks, an attempt Churchill opposed at the time.
39. DDE to Everett E. "Swede" Hazlett, December 24, 1953, in Griffith, *Ike's Letters*, pp. 112–18.
40. Lord Moran, *Churchill: The Struggle for Survival, 1940–65* (Boston: Houghton Mifflin, 1966), pp. 423, 428.
41. *Ibid.*, p. 508.
42. Diary Entry, December 6, 1953, in Evelyn Shuckburgh, *Descent to Suez: Diaries, 1951–56* (New York: Norton, 1986), p. 115.
43. *Ibid.*, p. 114.
44. *Ibid.*
45. "Memorandum of Conversation," December 4, 1953, Dulles Papers.
46. "First Plenary Tripartite Meeting . . . ," December 4, 1953, 6:00 P.M., *FR 1952–1954* (Washington, 1983), vol. 5, part 2, pp. 1754–61.
47. Compare note 46 with Diary Entry, December 4, 1953, by John Colville, *The Fringes of Power: 10 Downing Street Diaries, 1939–1955* (New York: Norton, 1985), pp. 682–84, and Moran, *Churchill*, p. 505. "Infiltration" use quoted in Shuckburgh, *Descent to Suez*, p. 113.
48. Colville, *Fringes of Power*, p. 683.
49. "Eisenhower-Churchill Dinner Meeting," December 5, 1953, *FR 1952–1954*, vol. 5, part 2, pp. 1786.

50. "Informal Meeting Held after Dinner . . . ," December 5, 1953, Foreign Office (FO) 371/105574, FK 1241/G. See also Colville, *Fringes of Power,* pp. 685–86, and Carlton, *Anthony Eden* (London: Allen Lawe, 1981), pp. 335–36.
51. Colville, *Fringes of Power,* pp. 685–86, has the most complete account of the reaction to Eisenhower's wording.
52. An edited version of the speech is in Walter LaFeber, ed., *The Origins of the Cold War* (New York: Wiley, 1971), pp. 136–39.
53. Colville, *Fringes of Power,* pp. 685–86; and see Churchill to DDE, December 6 and 7, 1953, Eisenhower Papers, Whitman File.
54. Testimony, January 7, 1954, in United States Senate, Committee on Foreign Relations, *Executive Sessions of the Senate Foreign Relations Committee,* 83rd Cong., 2nd sess. (Washington, 1977), 6:16.
55. "Fifth Plenary Tripartite Meeting . . . ," December 7, 1953, *FR 1952–1954,* vol. 5, part 2, pp. 1823–33.
56. *Ibid.*
57. Eisenhower, *Mandate for Change,* p. 243.
58. Michael Maclear, *The Ten Thousand Day War* (New York: Avon, 1981), p. 37.
59. Nixon's comments on Indochina are printed in *FR 1952–1954,* vol. 13, part 1, pp. 929–31; the comments on China are in the record of that meeting in the Eisenhower Papers.
60. Vo Nguyen Giap, *People's War, People's Army* (New York: Praeger, 1962), p. 168.
61. Fall, *Hell in a Very Small Place,* p. 51, barely develops this point, which is worthy of much more attention.
62. See the *New York Times,* January 1, 1954, for the sort of information available to Giap. There were also private responses that Giap may have had no inkling about, or may indeed have been aware of. See J. F. Dulles to Eisenhower, December 22, 1953, enclosing Ambassador Charles Bohlen's account of a conversation with V. M. Molotov on atomic issues, indicating at least "a slight shift" in Soviet positions. Dulles-Herter File, Eisenhower Papers. On the newest variation of the diversion theme, British Labour's insistence that Japanese trade with China be resumed so as to ease pressure on the sterling bloc, see *New York Times,* February 2, 1954.
63. On trade with China, Conservative Chancellor of the Exchequer Rab Butler told the House of Commons in early January 1954 that Britain looked forward to trade with China to benefit the sterling area once the Berlin Foreign Ministers Conference was over. "We had hoped that arising from the armistice in Korea it might be possible to discuss these matters more rationally than hitherto." *New York Times,* January 5, 1954. That might be regarded, in turn, as a warning to Russia to be reasonable, but also to the United States. From yet another perspective, there was always the chance that Russia and China had different agendas, and that one or the other would approach American policymakers. On December 30, 1953, *New York Times* correspondent James Reston had a conversation with Dulles reporting on a luncheon he had with a Soviet Embassy spokesman on the Far East that hinted at a possible "deal," with the United States abandoning Chiang Kai-shek in exchange for vague, and at best implied, suggestions that it would be better for America to have China sitting with the great powers. Dulles Papers.

64. The most recent account of the battle, which supplements Fall, *Hell in a Very Small Place*, is Thomas D. Boettcher, *Vietnam: The Valor and the Sorrow* (Boston: Little, Brown, 1986), pp. 91–103.
65. *Ibid.*, p. 94.
66. *New York Times*, January 1, 1954.
67. Heath to Department of State, January 3, 1954, *FR 1952–1954*, vol. 13, part 1, pp. 937–38.
68. "Memorandum of Discussion . . . ," January 8, 1954, *ibid.*, pp. 947–54.
69. *Ibid.*, emphasis added.
70. "Memorandum by C. D. Jackson," January 18, 1954, *ibid.*, pp. 981–82. The importance of these musings by Eisenhower should not be underestimated, as they set forth precedents that grew into an unofficial warrant that permitted intelligence agencies to speculate on the president's desires, and to act upon answers that suited their particular outlook. See Fletcher Prouty's book *The Secret Team* (Englewood Cliffs, N.J.: Prentice-Hall, 1973), pp. 76–94, for a "parable" about how the CIA could use such a charter to take things into its own hands. Prouty served in the air force during World War II and was a close observer in the Pentagon of CIA clandestine operations throughout the first two decades of the Cold War. The official NSC discussions, as well as the discussions in the Smith committee, provide specifics for Prouty's discussion of the activities of an American "major," who in turn closely resembles Colonel Edward Lansdale. How quickly this charter went into full operation is illustrated by the events of April 1955.
71. Stephen Ambrose, *Eisenhower: The President* (New York: Simon and Schuster, 1984), pp. 193–96; and for the fullest treatment, Richard Immerman, *The CIA in Guatemala: The Foreign Policy of Intervention* (Austin: Univ. of Texas Press, 1982).
72. The story can be followed in *FR 1952–1954*, vol. 13, part 1, pp. 940–41, and *Washington Post*, January 7, 1954.
73. *Washington Post*, January 10, 1954.
74. *New York Times*, January 11 and 21, 1954.
75. Georges Bidault, *Resistance: The Political Autobiography of Georges Bidault*, trans. by Marianne Sinclair (New York: Praeger, 1967), p. 194. General de Gaulle, awaiting a call to return to power, held much the same view. If anything, however, he was less convinced of an American desire to go to war again in Asia. The turning point, he told C. L. Sulzberger, had been the Truman-MacArthur fight, when the United States decided against attacking China. "The English want business with Russia. The French want an arrangement in Indochina. The United States wants export markets. These are the imponderables that make for a *modus vivendi.* This is not an entente; it is armed peace." De Gaulle's prophecy about Bao Dai is still more striking. The French had failed with Bao Dai, he said. "We will regret it greatly, but we must go. In 1863 Napoleon III went to Mexico. He supported Maximilian. But all the United States was against him. He had to get out. It is the same thing in Indochina." *Long Row of Candles*, pp. 949–50.
76. "The Evolution of Foreign Policy," January 12, 1954, Department of State, *American Foreign Policy, 1950–1955: Basic Documents*, 2 vols. (Washington, 1957), 1:80–85.
77. *Ibid.*; and see Anthony Eden, *Full Circle: The Memoirs of Anthony Eden* (Boston: Houghton Mifflin, 1960), p. 96.

78. "Memorandum for the Record . . . ," January 27, 1954, *FR 1952–1954*, vol. 13, part 1, pp. 998–1000.
79. National Archives, *Public Papers of the Presidents of the United States: Dwight D. Eisenhower, 1954* (Washington, 1960), pp. 226–27.
80. James Reston in the *New York Times*, February 4, 1954.
81. *Ibid.*, and Joseph Alsop in the *Washington Post*, February 3, 1954.
82. *New York Times*, February 9, 1954; and "Memorandum by the Assistant Staff Secretary . . . ," undated [February 8, 1954], *FR 1952–1954*, vol. 13, part 1, pp. 1023–25.
83. "Memorandum of Discussion . . . ," February 4, 1954, *FR 1952–1954*, vol. 13, part 1, pp. 1013–17.
84. *Ibid.*
85. *Ibid.*
86. W. B. Smith to Saigon, February 5, 1954, *ibid.*, pp. 1019–20; unsent letter, February 6, 1954, Dulles Papers.
87. JFD to DDE, February 6, 1954, *FR 1952–1954*, vol. 13, part 1, pp. 1020–21.
88. "Memorandum by the Assistant Staff Secretary . . . ," undated [February 8, 1954], *FR 1952–1954*, vol. 13, part 1, pp. 1023–25; Diary Entry, February 8, 1954, James C. Hagerty Papers, Eisenhower Library, Abilene, Kansas.
89. Telephone call to General Bedell Smith, February 9, 1954, Dwight D. Eisenhower Diaries, Eisenhower Papers.
90. Makins to Foreign Office, February 8, 1954, FO 371/112047, DF 1071/19.
91. Makins to Foreign Office, February 17, 1954, FO 371/112047, DF 1071/28; Eden, *Full Circle*, p. 97.
92. Eden, *Full Circle*, pp. 99–101.
93. Senate Foreign Relations Committee, *Executive Sessions, 1954*, p. 111.
94. Eden, *Full Circle*, p. 101; see FO 371/112048, DF 1071/50, for indications of preliminary soundings. Serious Anglo-Russian discussions began in mid-March when a member of the Russian Embassy, M. Zhivotovski, called at the Foreign Office. The Russian indicated that the key question was the borders of China, not Vietminh rule. Memorandum by J. G. Tahoudrin, March 18, 1954 (seen by Eden), FO 371/112048, DF 1071/68.
95. *New York Times*, February 23, 1954.
96. *Washington Post*, February 17, 1954.
97. See also Makins to Foreign Office, February 19, 1954, reporting on conversation with Smith in which the latter said that he would favor a blockade of China not only in case of Chinese intervention, but also if there were a "French collapse and withdrawal." The French military situation, he insisted again, was not so bad. "The trouble lay with defeatism in Paris." FO 371/112047, DF 1071/32.
98. *Washington Post*, February 11, 1954.
99. *FR 1952–1954*, vol. 13, part 1, pp. 1034–35.
100. Roy, *Battle of Dienbienphu*, pp. 140–43.
101. *Ibid.*, p. 144.
102. "Memorandum of Conversation," February 21, 1954, FO 371/112102, DF 1092/21.
103. Roy, *Battle of Dienbienphu*, pp. 144–45.
104. *Washington Post*, February 25, 1954.

105. "Memorandum of Luncheon Conversation . . . ," February 24, 1954, Dulles Papers; *New York Times*, February 23, 1954.
106. "Memorandum . . . ," March 1, 1954, *FR 1952–1954*, vol. 16: *The Geneva Conference* (Washington, 1981), pp. 427–28.
107. *New York Times*, March 8, 1954.
108. *FR 1952–1954*, 16:435–45 (quotation on p. 444); *ibid.*, vol. 13, part 1, pp. 1106–7; Harry F. Kern to J. F. Dulles (with enclosure of luncheon conversation with Pleven, dated March 11, 1954), March 14, 1954, Dulles Papers.
109. Kern to Dulles, March 14, 1954, Dulles Papers.
110. Devillers and Lacouture, *End of a War*, p. 68.
111. "Memorandum by the Chairman . . . to the President," March 11, 1954, *FR 1952–1954*, vol. 13, part 1, pp. 1108–16.
112. *Ibid.*
113. Fall, *Hell in a Very Small Place*, pp. 154–55; Heath to Department of State, March 16, 1954, *FR 1952–1954*, vol. 13, part 1, pp. 1124–25.
114. *New York Times*, March 21, 1954.
115. Wilson to Dulles, March 23, 1954, *FR 1952–1954*, 16:471–79.
116. *New York Times*, March 23, 1954.
117. Fall, *Hell in a Very Small Place*, p. 297.

CHAPTER SIX: BEYOND DIENBIENPHU

1. "Views of the United States on the Eve of the Geneva Conference," U.S. Department of State, *American Foreign Policy, 1950–1955: Basic Documents*, 2 vols. (Washington, 1957), 2:2371–81.
2. Bernard Fall, *Hell in a Very Small Place: The Siege of Dienbienphu* (Philadelphia: Lippincott, 1966), p. vii.
3. "Memorandum of Conversation with the President," March 24, 1954, Dulles Papers, Mudd Library, Princeton University, Princeton, New Jersey.
4. *New York Times*, March 24, 1954.
5. U.S. Department of State, *American Foreign Policy, 1950–1955*, 2:2380.
6. "Telephone Conversation with Admiral Radford," March 24, 1954, Dulles Papers.
7. Differing viewpoints on these issues can be found in Richard Barnet, *The Alliance: America-Europe-Japan, Makers of the Postwar World* (New York: Simon and Schuster, 1983), and David P. Calleo and Benjamin M. Rowland, *America and the World Political Economy: Atlantic Dreams and National Realities* (Bloomington: Univ. of Indiana Press, 1973).
8. *New York Times*, April 1, 1954.
9. Quoted in Stephen Ambrose, *Eisenhower: The President* (New York: Simon and Schuster, 1984), p. 168.
10. A full account of the BRAVO "fallout," political as well, is in Robert Divine, *Blowing on the Wind: The Nuclear Test Ban Debate, 1954–1960* (New York: Oxford Univ. Press, 1978), chap. 1, on which these paragraphs are based.
11. *Washington Post*, March 31, 1954.
12. Divine, *Blowing on the Wind*, p. 13.
13. *Ibid.*, p. 11.

14. *Washington Post,* March 31, 1954.
15. Rosenberg, "The Origins of Overkill," in Norman Graebner, ed., *The National Security: Its Theory and Practice* (New York: Oxford Univ. Press, 1986), pp. 123–95. Quote is from pp. 141–42.
16. *Washington Post,* March 31, 1954.
17. "Telephone Conversation with Adm. Strauss," March 29, 1954, Dulles Papers.
18. *Ibid.*
19. For an excellent introduction and commentary on the dilemmas of "limited war" in the H-bomb era, see Lawrence Freedman, *The Evolution of Nuclear Strategy* (New York: St. Martin's Press, 1983), chap 7.
20. DDE to WSC, February 9, 1954, Eisenhower Papers, DDE Diaries, Eisenhower Library, Abilene, Kansas. British policymakers reacted strongly to this last passage, with its Armageddon-like quality, and believed, with Churchill, that a strong response must be found. See Evelyn Shuckburgh, *Descent to Suez: Diaries, 1951–56* (New York: Norton, 1986), pp. 144, 147.
21. WSC to DDE, undated (received March 12), 1954, Eisenhower Papers, International Series.
22. "Draft of Suggested Reply," March 17, 1954, *ibid.*
23. WSC to DDE, received March 29, 1954, *ibid.* Included in this letter was a rather supplicating appeal for greater sharing of information, a subject that Churchill was particularly vulnerable to vis-à-vis the Labour party and very anxious to turn against it.
24. *New York Times,* March 31, 1954.
25. Hansard, vol. 526, cols. 38–39.
26. For a discussion of Attlee's predicament when the MacMahon bill was being considered, see Margaret Gowing, *Independence and Deterrence: Britain and Atomic Energy, 1945–1952,* 2 vols. (London: Macmillan, 1974), vol. 1, chap. 4.
27. Hansard, vol. 526, cols. 65–66.
28. *Ibid.,* cols. 132–33.
29. *Ibid.,* cols. 152–53.
30. Aldrich to Dulles, April 6, 1954, Eisenhower Papers, International Series.
31. DDE to WSC, April 4, 1954, U.S. Department of State, *Foreign Relations of the United States (FR) 1952–1954* (Washington, 1982), vol. 13, part 2, pp. 1239–41.
32. Ambrose, *Eisenhower,* p. 170.
33. U.S. Department of State, *American Foreign Policy, 1950–1955,* 2:2925–26.
34. WSC to DDE, March 24, 1954, Eisenhower Papers, International Series.
35. Diary Entry, March 29, 1954, in Shuckburgh, *Descent to Suez,* pp. 154–55.
36. WSC to DDE, March 24, 1954, Eisenhower Papers, International Series.
37. *New York Times,* March 28, 1954.
38. DDE to WSC, March 27, 1954, *ibid.*
39. *Ibid.*
40. Eisenhower, *The White House Years: Mandate for Change, 1953–1956* (New York: Doubleday, 1963), p. 208. On the general problem, see Lloyd C. Gardner, "Economics and National Security," in Graebner, ed., *National Security,* chap. 2.
41. *New York Times,* January 3, 1954.

42. United States Senate, Committee on Foreign Relations, *Executive Sessions of the Senate Foreign Relations Committee, 1954 (Historical Series)*, 83rd Cong., 2nd sess. (Washington, 1977), pp. 227–33.
43. *New York Times*, March 26, 1954.
44. Diary Entry, March 29, 1954, Hagerty Diary, Hagerty Papers, Eisenhower Library, Abilene, Kansas.
45. *Ibid.*
46. Hagerty Diary, March 26, 1954, Hagerty Papers.
47. DDE to Everett E. Hazlett, August 3, 1956, in Robert Griffith, ed., *Ike's Letters to a Friend, 1941–1958* (Lawrence: Univ. of Kansas Press, 1984), pp. 164–67.
48. U.S. Department of State, *American Foreign Policy, 1950–1955*, 2:2932.
49. Ambrose, *Eisenhower*, pp. 201–2.
50. National Archives, *Public Papers of the Presidents of the United States: Dwight D. Eisenhower, 1954* (Washington, 1960), pp. 381–90.
51. Dulles Papers.
52. Makins to Foreign Office, March 23, 1954, Foreign Office (FO) 371/112048, DF 1071/79.
53. See chapter 1, note 1.
54. "Memorandum of Conversation with Soviet Charge," March 23, 1954, FO 371/112049, DF 1071/104.
55. Press Release #154, March 23, 1954, Dulles Papers.
56. JFD to DDE, March 23, 1954, and "Memorandum of Conversation," March 23, 1954, both in *FR 1952–1954*, vol. 13, part 1, pp. 1141–4. The best account of the Ely visit and negotiations is George C. Herring and Richard H. Immerman, "Eisenhower, Dulles, and Dienbienphu: 'The Day We Didn't Go to War' Revisited," *Journal of American History*, 71 (September 1984): 343–63.
57. Paul Ely, *Memoires: L'Indochine dans la tourmente* (Paris: Plan, 1964), pp. 65–67. On the controversy, see Herring and Immerman, "Eisenhower, Dulles, and Dienbienphu," pp. 343–63.
58. "Memorandum of Conversation with the President," March 24, 1954, Dulles Papers.
59. Ely, *Memoires*, pp. 70–71. And see John Prados, *The Sky Would Fall* (New York: Dial Press, 1982), pp. 76–77.
60. "Telephone Conversation with Admiral Radford," March 24, 1954, Dulles Papers.
61. "Memorandum of Discussion . . . ," March 25, 1954, *FR 1952–1954*, vol. 13, part 1, pp. 1163–68.
62. Ely, *Memoires*, pp. 76, 85–88.
63. For another account of the nuanced relationships that were at play here, one that also suggests Radford and Eisenhower were not so concerned with the "more remote problem" of a political alliance, see Victor M. Bator, *Vietnam—a Diplomatic Tragedy* (Dobbs Ferry, N.Y.: Oceana Publications, 1965), p. 34. The issue dissolved, of course, because whatever he thought in late March, Eisenhower quickly became committed to the Dulles position, adding still more qualifications about his constitutional responsibilities.
64. Ely, *Memoires*, p. 88.
65. See below, pp. 347–48.
66. Ely, *Memoires*, pp. 88–90.

67. Ronald Spector, *United States Army in Vietnam, Advice and Support: The Early Years, 1941–1960* (Washington, 1983), pp. 200–1.
68. Transcript of Oral History Interview, March 16, 1965, Dulles Oral History Project, Dulles Papers.
69. *Ibid.* When Twining spoke those words it was 1965. And already many had regrets of all sorts about what had happened "back then" to cause the awful mess in Vietnam. "We might not have had this problem we're facing in Vietnam now had we dropped these small 'A' weapons."
70. Hagerty Diary, March 26, 1954, Hagerty Papers. See also Dulles to American Embassy, Taipei, March 26, 1954, *FR 1952–1954,* vol. 13, part 1, p. 1174.
71. *FR 1952–1954,* vol. 13, part 1, pp. 1202–4.
72. *New York Times,* March 30, 1954. Reston was being given very full briefings, as his column for March 31 indicated. In this evaluation of the Dulles plan, the writer called attention to the ambitious effort not merely to line up old allies, but to convince India's Nehru that this was a war that had to be fought. "He has set out to change the political basis of the Indo-China war, and to demonstrate that it is of such consequence to the security and principles of the Western world that all the non-Communist nations must take 'united action' alongside the French." *New York Times,* March 31, 1954.
73. Memorandum, March 30, 1954, Dulles Papers. Dulles had talked earlier with White House aide C. D. Jackson, and had noted that the speech was not well received by his immediate audience, which was 75 to 80 percent Democrats, but TV and radio coverage were good. And anyway, that was not the main audience. "The Sec. said Britain and France are most eager for appeasement, and he felt he had to set it back." "Telephone Conversation with C. D. Jackson," March 30, 1954, *ibid.*
74. Hagerty Diary, April 1, 1954, in *FR 1952–1954,* vol. 13, part 1, p. 1204.
75. Prados, *The Sky Would Fall,* pp. 91–92.
76. Joint Chiefs to Secretary of Defense, March 31, 1954, *FR 1952–1954,* vol. 13, part 1, pp. 1198–99.
77. Makins to Foreign Office, March 27, 1954, FO 371/112049, DF 1071/100, and Minute by J. P. Cloake, March 29, 1954, FO 371/112049, DF 1071/89.
78. Makins to Foreign Office, March 30, 1954, FO 371/112049, DF 1071/107.
79. Anthony Eden, *Full Circle: The Memoirs of Anthony Eden* (Boston: Houghton Mifflin, 1960), p. 102.
80. *Ibid.*
81. On March 17, 1954, during a telephone conversation with Eisenhower, Dulles elaborated on both points in the context of the Indochina crisis: "When Constitution was up for adoption, original language was that Congress shall have power to conduct war. That was changed to read 'power to *declare* war' on ground that circumstances might arise requiring President to repel attack with[out?] intervention of Congress. That was very thoroughly considered. At time of debate on North Atlantic Treaty, I took position that when the treaty declares that certain area is vital to U.S., then President has Constitutional authority in case of emergency to act without Congress. I said, 'I think that is the power of the President. Whether or not he uses it or does not wait for Congressional authority would depend upon facts of the case and degree of the emergency.' " Eisenhower did not respond to all this. Eisenhower Papers, DDE Diaries.

82. "Draft Taken to WH by JFD 4/2/54," Dulles Papers. The proposed resolution made reference to action taken by the U.N. or by other free nations. The question of the U.N. often came up, and so the draft resolution tried to cover that possibility as well.
83. "Memorandum of a Conversation with the President," April 2, 1954, *FR 1952–1954*, vol. 13, part 1, pp. 1210–11.
84. *Ibid.*, and "Telephone Conversation with Admiral Radford," April 1, 1954, Dulles Papers.
85. Herring and Immerman, "Eisenhower, Dulles, and Dienbienphu," pp. 343–63.
86. "Memorandum of Conversation with the President," April 2, 1954, *FR 1952–1954*, vol. 13, part 1, pp. 1210–11. In fact, Dulles went out of his way to demonstrate the different positions to Eisenhower: "Mr. Dulles suggested that perhaps Admiral Radford looked upon this authority as something to be immediately used in some 'strike' and irrespective of any prior development of an adequate measure of allied unity."
87. "Memorandum of Conversation . . . ," April 2, 1954, *ibid.*, pp. 1214–17; Makins to Foreign Office, April 3, 1954, FO 371/112049, DF 1071/121/G. Rhee had in fact made a public offer of troops for Indochina, and although it had been rejected, Dulles' threat must have seemed credible. See Spector, *Advice and Support*, p. 198.
88. Makins to Foreign Office, April 3, 1954, FO 371/112049, DF 1071/121/G.
89. Prados. *The Sky Would Fall*, pp. 94–97; Herring and Immerman, "Eisenhower, Dulles, and Dienbienphu," pp. 343–63.
90. "Telephone Conversation with the President," April 3, 1954, Dulles Papers.
91. The account presented here is based on "Memorandum of Conversation . . . ," April 4, 1954, *FR 1952–1954*, vol. 13, part 1, pp. 1231–35; portions of Leslie Munro's diary, quoted by him in his oral history interview in the Dulles Papers; High Commissioner in Auckland to Colonial Office, April 7, 1954, FO 371/112051, DF 1071/164; and Munro to Auckland, April 6, 1954, #91, FO 371/112052, DF 1071/207/G.
92. Dulles' gloss on Churchill is mostly accurate, but the emphasis in the original was a bit different, as one might expect. The Churchill account is less specific about Stimson and Simon, not surprisingly, since Americans tended to follow Stimson's memoirs in heaping blame on Sir John; but a close reading of the Churchill version also suggests (albeit in the most cautious fashion), in contrast to his usual attacks on appeasement, that he thought Simon's behavior was not only excusable, but justified in terms of Britain's long-term policies in Asia. Winston S. Churchill, *The Gathering Storm* (Boston: Houghton Mifflin, 1948), p. 87. (Incidentally, Sir Leslie Munro's account has Dulles reading from page 68.)

A final word here. The position Churchill would take in 1954 could almost be predicted by reading what he had written about 1932, especially the veiled criticism of the "strongest hostility" Americans felt about Japan's first shot in the outrage committed against China. The reality of Anglo-American disagreements, however, suggested that neither Britain nor the United States had a truly developed and consistent Far Eastern policy to meet Japan's outward thrust. The picture of British shilly-shallying presented by Churchill came mostly from American retrospective accounts, like Stimson's memoirs. On this point, see the invaluable book

by Christopher Thorne, *The Limits of Foreign Policy: The West, the League, and the Far Eastern Crisis of 1931–1933* (London: Oxford Univ. Press, 1972), pp. 247–72.
93. *New York Times*, April 8, 1954.
94. Good accounts are Prados, *The Sky Would Fall*, pp. 98–102; Jules Roy, *The Battle of Dienbienphu* (New York: Carroll and Graf, 1984), pp. 212–23; Ely, *Memoires*, pp. 85–87; and Fall, *Hell in a Very Small Place*, pp. 300–6.
95. Cited in Prados, *The Sky Would Fall*, p. 99.
96. *Washington Post*, April 5, 1954.
97. Dillon to State Department, April 5, 1954, *FR 1952–1954*, vol. 13, part 1, pp. 1237–38.
98. "Telephone Conversation with the President," April 5, 1954, Dulles Papers.
99. Munro to Auckland, April 6, 1954, FO 371/112052, DF 1071/207/G.
100. "Memorandum of Discussion . . . ," April 6, 1954, *FR 1952–1954*, vol. 13, part 1, pp. 1250–65. Richard Nixon concluded, on the other hand, that Eisenhower had backed off a good deal on Indochina, and was not now even especially eager to put pressure on America's allies. Nixon's feeling may account for his behavior in the next opportunity he had to talk to the public; on April 16 he suggested that America might have to bite the bullet and put ground forces into Indochina. See *ibid.*, pp. 1265–66, for an excerpt from Nixon's *Memoirs.*

CHAPTER SEVEN: MR. DULLES ON THE GRAND TOUR

1. White House Press Release, copy in Dulles Papers, Mudd Library, Princeton University, Princeton, New Jersey.
2. Eisenhower to Churchill, April 4, 1954, U.S. Department of State, *Foreign Relations of the United States (FR) 1952–1954* (Washington, D.C., 1982), vol. 13, part 1, pp. 1239–41.
3. Diary Entries, April 6 and 8, 1954, in Evelyn Shuckburgh, *Descent to Suez: Diaries, 1951–56* (New York: Norton, 1986), pp. 160–61.
4. Churchill to Eisenhower, received April 7, 1954, Eisenhower Papers, Whitman Files, DDE Diaries, Eisenhower Library, Abilene, Kansas.
5. Quoted in David Carlton, *Anthony Eden: A Biography* (London: Allen Lane, 1981), p. 342.
6. See Ronald W. Pruessen, *John Foster Dulles: The Road to Power* (New York: Free Press, 1982), especially pp. 440–47.
7. Shuckburgh, *Descent to Suez*, p. 161.
8. See Robert Rhodes James, *Anthony Eden* (London: Weidenfeld and Nicolson 1986), pp. 364–76.
9. Lord Moran, *Churchill: The Struggle for Survival, 1940–65* (Boston: Houghton Mifflin, 1966), p. 541.
10. *Ibid.*, p. 542.
11. Ambrose, *Eisenhower: The President* (New York: Simon and Schuster, 1984), p. 130. And see pp. 192–97.
12. "Memorandum of Conversation . . . ," April 8, 1954, *FR 1952–1954*, vol. 13, part 1, pp. 1290–92.

13. *Ibid.*, p. 540; "Telephone Conversation with Senator Wiley," April 7, 1954, Dulles Papers.
14. *Washington Post,* April 9, 1954.
15. "Telephone Conversation with Admiral Radford," April 9, 1954, Dulles Papers.
16. *New York Times,* April 8, 1954.
17. *Washington Post,* April 8, 1954. Periodical opinion throughout the 1954 crisis remained divided. Catholic journals and some business journals tended to favor American intervention of some sort, fearing the implications of a Vietminh victory, while liberal journals, reflecting also the views of commentators like Richard Rovere and Theodore White, thought the administration was leaning too much in the direction of intervention. The point remains, however, that Dulles enjoyed more support for his plan of action in Southeast Asia than the administration had garnered for its other policy initiatives after Korea. See Carl Krog, "American Journals of Opinion and the Fall of Vietnam," *Asian Affairs,* 6 (1979): 324–32.
18. *Washington Post,* April 12, 1954.
19. "Memorandum," April 9, 1954, Foreign Office (FO) 371/112051, DF 1071/182/G.
20. Shuckburgh, *Descent to Suez,* p. 161.
21. Minutes, April 10, 1954, FO 371/112051, DF 1071/199. For their part, the British chiefs had been advised by Lieutenant General Sir Charles Loewen that the war in Indochina was very definitely a civil war. Loewen to CIGS, April 9, 1954, FO 371/112057, DF 1071/363.
22. Allen, Paper on Points for Discussion with John Foster Dulles, April 9, 1954, FO 371/112052, DF 1071/202 (emphasis added). On Allen's own perplexity about the Anglo-American "misunderstanding," see Carlton, *Anthony Eden,* p. 343.
23. "Record of Conversation . . . ," April 11, 1954, FO 371/112054, DF 1071/267/G. A very complete paraphrase of this record is provided by Eden himself in *Full Circle: The Memoirs of Anthony Eden* (Boston: Houghton Mifflin, 1960), pp. 107–8.
24. Ronald Spector, *United States Army in Vietnam, Advice and Support: The Early Years, 1941–1960* (Washington, 1983), pp. 202–3; Matthew B. Ridgway, *Soldier: The Memoirs of Matthew B. Ridgway* (New York: Harper, 1956), pp. 279–80.
25. John Prados, *The Sky Would Fall* (New York: Dial Press, 1983), pp. 118–22; William M. Leary, "CAT at Dienbienphu," *Aerospace Historian,* 31 (September 1984): 177–84.
26. "Record of Conversation . . . ," April 11, 1954, FO 371/112054, DF 1071/267/G.
27. *Ibid.*, and "Memorandum of Conversation," April 11, 1954, *FR 1952–1954,* vol. 13, part 1, pp. 1307–9.
28. Once again the American minutes are silent. The disparity in the written records of this conversation are such as to make it difficult to believe the participants were present at the same meeting.
29. It is easy to understand why Denis Allen would be confused at this point, for Eden's language seemingly reversed what had been in the prepared brief. See note 22.
30. Walton Butterworth, Oral History Interview, Dulles Papers.
31. *FR 1952–1954,* vol. 13, part 1, pp. 1311–15.

32. "Meeting Between the Secretary of State and Mr. Dulles on Indo-China on April 12, 1954," FO 371/112054, DF 1071/268/G. Once again the American record of this meeting fails to include the key statements by both men. See Dulles to Department of State, April 13, 1954, *FR 1952–1954*, vol. 13, part 1, pp. 1319–20.
33. Dulles to Department of State, April 13, 1954, emphasis added; Eden's memoirs, which paraphrase so accurately the first meeting with Dulles, do not provide equal details of this second talk and the crucial reference to land forces. *Full Circle*, p. 108.
34. "Meeting Between the Secretary of State and Mr. Dulles . . .," April 12, 1954, FO 371/112054, DF1071/268/G. For the American record and drafts of the proposed statements, see *FR 1952–1954*, vol. 13, part 1, pp. 1311–15.
35. Diary Entry, April 12, 1954, Shuckburgh, *Descent to Suez*, p. 164.
36. Dulles, "Memorandum of Dinner with Sir Winston Churchill," April 12, 1954, Dulles Papers.
37. *FR 1952–1954*, vol. 13, part 1, p. 1321.
38. *Ibid.*, pp. 1322–23.
39. Shuckburgh, *Descent to Suez*, p. 164.
40. *FR 1952–1954*, vol. 13, part 1, p. 1323; C. L. Sulzberger, *A Long Row of Candles* (New York: Macmillan, 1969), pp. 996–97. On this point, see also Eden to Makins, April 14, 1954, FO 371/112053, DF 1071/223.
41. Dulles Papers.
42. Sulzberger, *Long Row of Candles*, p. 995.
43. Dillon, Oral History Interview, Dulles Papers. See also Prados, *The Sky Would Fall*, p. 130.
44. Eden to Paris, April 15, 1954, FO 371/112055, DF 1071/302.
45. *Ibid.*
46. *New York Times*, April 14, 1954.
47. *Ibid.*; "Memorandum of Conversation," April 14, 1954, Eisenhower Papers, Whitman File, Dulles-Herter Folders.
48. "Memorandum of Conversation," April 14, 1954, Eisenhower Papers, Whitman Files, Dulles-Herter Folders.
49. Sulzberger, *Long Row of Candles*, p. 996. Interestingly, British information about the Dulles conversations in Paris tallied with the secretary's own rather offhand comments to Sulzberger. There was no effort to enlist an immediate American intervention, and most of the debate centered on the issue of independence. See W. D. Allen, "Tripartite Meeting in Paris on Indo-China," April 16, 1954, FO 371/112055, DF 1071/290.
50. Sulzberger, *Long Row of Candles*, p. 996.
51. *New York Times*, and *Washington Post*, April 16, 1954.
52. *New York Times*, April 16, 1954. High Commissioner to Foreign Office, April 16, 1954, FO 371/112053, DF 1071/242. For Eden's comments on commonwealth restraints, see *Full Circle*, p. 109.
53. Eden to Makins, April 17 and 18, 1954, FO 371/112053, DF 1071/232/G.
54. Makins to Foreign Office, April 18, 1954, FO 371/112053, DF1071/238/G; Prados, *The Sky Would Fall*, p. 142.
55. Shuckburgh, *Descent to Suez*, p. 167.
56. Eden to Makins, April 19, 1954, FO 371/112053, DF 1071/238/G; the quoted extract is also to be found in Eden, *Full Circle*, p. 110. Makins did not believe Eden

could get off the hook quite so easily, however. In reply to the foreign secretary's criticism of his behavior, Sir Roger wrote to Ivone Kirkpatrick, complaining that he had not been kept well-informed and that the American record appeared to indicate very clearly that an agreement had been reached on preliminary consultations. "All I have to date on the Dulles' [*sic*] talks is one flimsy copy of a draft record, which I am bound to say I found very scrappy." Makins felt that what the Americans wanted did not commit London, and was in line with the conclusions of the Dulles/Eden conversations. Indeed, a subsequent telegram to commonwealth capitals he quoted to Kirkpatrick said that very thing: "Further consultation on collective defense in South East Asia will take place in Washington as soon as possible." "I am quite unable to reconcile these passages with the telegrams which I received over the week-end and I hope I may be forgiven in the circumstances for being almost as taken aback by these telegrams as were the Americans." In short, the controversy turned on the word "preliminary," which Eden took to mean additional Anglo-American discussions, and which Dulles (with Makins agreeing) took to mean discussions with a list of invited powers. FO 371/112059, DF 1071/409/G.

57. Shuckburgh, *Descent to Suez*, pp. 164, 166.

58. *Ibid.*, p. 163.

59. *New York Times* and *Washington Post*, April 17, 1954.

60. Hagerty Diary, April 19, 1954, Hagerty Papers, Eisenhower Library, Abilene, Kansas. For a different emphasis, see George C. Herring and Richard H. Immerman, "Eisenhower, Dulles, and Dienbienphu: 'The Day We Didn't Go to War' Revisited," *Journal of American History*, 71 (September 1984): 343–63.

61. Nixon, *RN: The Memoirs of Richard Nixon* (New York: Grosset and Dunlap, 1978), p. 153; Interview, Dulles Oral History, Dulles Papers; *New York Times*, April 20, 1954.

62. "Telephone Conversation with Vice President Nixon," April 19, 1954, 5:15 P.M.; "Telephone Conversation with Senator Smith," April 19, 1954, 6:30 P.M., Dulles Papers.

63. *New York Times*, April 22, 1954.

64. *Ibid.*, April 19, 1954.

65. *Ibid.*

66. *FR 1952–1954*, vol. 13, part 1, pp. 1365–66.

67. National Archives, *Public Papers of the Presidents of the United States: Dwight D. Eisenhower, 1954* (Washington, 1960), p. 387.

68. *FR 1952–1954*, vol. 13, part 1, pp. 1323–26.

69. "Memorandum of Conversation," April 20, 1954, *FR 1952–1954* (Washington, 1981), 16:119–24, 535–38.

70. "Statement Made by the Honorable John Foster Dulles on Departure for Paris," April 20, 1954, Dulles Papers.

71. Makins to Foreign Office, April 20, 1954, FO 371/112054, DF 1071/255 (A).

72. Eden to Foreign Office, April 22, 1954, FO 371/112055, DF 1071/282; Dulles to Department of State, April 22, 1954, *FR 1952–1954*, vol. 13, part 1, pp. 1361–62. Dulles spoke to Eden about this talk with Bidault, remarking that it was now clear that the French would not be interested in a coalition even to save Laos and Cambodia. Since the United States would not send in ground troops, Dulles thought they ought to consider what the maximum concessions were that could

be made to promote a settlement. France was collapsing, ended Dulles, there was no resolution, no government capable of taking action. And the result would be a vacuum not only in the Far East, but also in Africa. Eden to Foreign Office, April 22, 1954, FO 371/112055, DF 1071/280/G. This appears to be one of the few times that Dulles seriously contemplated the likely outcome of Geneva and what had to be done to limit the damage, instead of talking about united action and the resolve of free men making a negotiated surrender unnecessary. It was a passing mood.

73. C. L. Sulzberger, who was in Paris at the time, caught exactly what Dulles had been intent upon doing. "What he is really saying is, 'If you sign up on the Southeast Asia pact, we will give you the airplanes you are asking for.' " As for direct intervention, Dulles told Sulzberger straight out that "the request might be regarded differently if there were actually an operational Southeast Asia alliance with France and the United States as members. Congress would have to approve American participation—probably by a resolution. Then, perhaps in a fashion similar to Korea where the United Nations intervened, the United States might be able to intervene." *Long Row of Candles,* p. 1002.

74. Dulles to Eisenhower, April 23, 1954, *FR 1952–1954,* vol. 13, part 1, pp. 1374–75.

75. Dulles to Department of State, April 23, 1954, *ibid.,* p. 1374.

76. Bidault, *Resistance: The Political Autobiography of Georges Bidault,* trans. by Marianne Sinclair (New York: Praeger, 1967), pp. 196–97.

77. The fullest account is in Prados, *The Sky Would Fall,* pp. 152–56. He concludes that the general question cannot be answered. Obviously, consideration was given to using the bomb in the 1954 crisis. Prados believes that there is circumstantial evidence for the specific offer, but available documentation does not uphold Bidault's version.

78. "Statement by the Secretary of State . . .," April 23, 1954, *FR 1952–1954* (Washington, 1983), 5:509–14.

79. Eden, *Full Circle,* pp. 112–13; Eisenhower to Dulles, April 23, 1954, *FR 1952–1954,* vol. 13, part 1, pp. 1366–67.

80. Eden, *Full Circle,* pp. 113–14; the wording differs somewhat from Eden's cable to London, April 24, 1954, FO 371/112055, DF 1071/305/G.

81. "Memorandum of Conversation . . .," April 26, 1954, *FR 1952–1954,* vol. 13, part 1, pp. 1386–91.

82. *Ibid.,* and Eden's account, in Eden to Foreign Office, April 24, 1954, FO 371/112056, DF 1071/314/G. These accounts differ considerably on certain points, as will be noted in the text.

83. Diary Entry, April 24, 1954, in Shuckburgh, *Descent to Suez,* pp. 171–72.

84. Eden to Foreign Office, April 24, 1954, FO 371/112056, DF 1071/314/G.

85. *Ibid.*

86. Eden to Foreign Office, April 24, 1954, 7:34 P.M., FO 371/112056, DF 1071/315/G.

87. Dulles to Department of State, April 24, 1954, *FR 1952–1954,* vol. 13, part 1, pp. 1391–93.

88. *Ibid.*

89. Dulles to Department of State, April 24, 1954, *ibid.,* pp. 1394–96.

90. *Ibid.*

91. Eden to Foreign Office, April 24, 1954, 7:34 P.M., FO 371/112056, DF 1071/315/G.
92. Hagerty Diary, Hagerty Papers.
93. Prados, *The Sky Would Fall*, p. 160.
94. Dillon to Department of State, April 25, 1954, with Bidault's reply enclosed, *FR, 1952–1954*, vol. 13, part 1, p. 1401. In earlier accounts, written before these documents became available, the Dulles-Bidault exchange fell victim to a British veto. While that was so, it is also absolutely certain that the American government would not have acted without a French agreement to internationalize the war. Philippe Devillers and Jean Lacouture are perfectly correct, for example, in stressing that Dulles hoped to use his letter to Bidault to bring pressure on the British. But it is misleading to argue, as they do, that the United States had agreed to intervene "provided only that the British would agree," for the other condition was equally crucial. See *End of a War: Indochina, 1954*, trans. by Alexander Lieven and Adam Roberts (New York: Praeger, 1969), p. 95 *et passim.*
95. Diary Entry, April 24, 1954, in Shuckburgh, *Descent to Suez*, p. 172.
96. *Ibid.*, 173.
97. Eden, *Full Circle*, p. 117.
98. The talking paper reproduced *ibid.*, p. 118, is not the same as that in Foreign Office archives, yet it appears this is the paper Eden was talking about in his memoirs. I have followed the Foreign Office version here, as prepared by Denis Allen, April 24, 1954, FO 371/112056, DF 1071/323, because it much more clearly reveals this pre-Geneva decision to accept partition.
99. Eden, *Full Circle*, p. 119, and Foreign Office to Paris, April 25, 1954, FO 371/112056, DF 1071/321/G.
100. Diary Entry, April 28, 1954, in Lord Moran, *Winston Churchill: The Struggle for Survival, 1940–1965* (Boston: Houghton Mifflin, 1966), p. 543.
101. Foreign Office to Geneva Delegation, April 27, 1954, FO 371/112057, DF 1071/344/G.
102. Herring and Immerman, "Eisenhower, Dulles, and Dienbienphu."
103. *Ibid.*
104. Except for the statements cited in the previous two notes, the material presented here is entirely from "Record of a Conversation at Dinner at Chequers, Monday, April 26, 1954," FO 371/112057, DF 1071/360/G.
105. Stephen Jurika, ed., *From Pearl Harbor to Vietnam: The Memoirs of Admiral Arthur W. Radford* (Stanford, Calif.: Hoover Institute Press, 1980), pp. 408–9. See also Radford to Dulles, April 26, 1954, Eisenhower Papers, Whitman Files.
106. Dulles to Walter Bedell Smith, April 25, 1954, *FR 1952–1954*, vol. 13, part 1, pp. 1404–5.
107. Shuckburgh, *Descent to Suez*, p. 176.
108. *Ibid.*; and see also Dillon to Department of State, April 25, 1954, *FR 1952–1954*, vol. 13, part 1, pp. 1402–3.
109. Diary Entries, April 24–26, 1954, Hagerty Diary, Hagerty Papers. Eisenhower also had the advice of one of his closest friends, General Al Gruenther, against military intervention to save Dienbienphu. Gruenther wrote on April 25, 1954, that he had talked with several people, including General Ely and Admiral Radford, both of whom were pushing for a decision to intervene. "Admiral Radford came to see me at 10:30 last night to tell me of Gen. Ely's urgent appeal for

U.S. intervention. I would not recommend U.S. *unilateral* intervention and I told him so. Of course Ely stressed the need for this intervention—not that it would save DBP but that will possibly save Indo China—and surely save Europe and NATO. That is a powerful argument, but I don't think it is valid. I think we can save NATO anyhow in spite of the setback we shall receive from an Indo China reverse. And the disadvantages of unilateral intervention are very very great." Eisenhower Papers, Whitman File, Administrative Series.
110. Robert Griffith, ed., *Ike's Letters to a Friend* (Lawrence: Univ. of Kansas Press, 1984), pp. 124–26.

CHAPTER EIGHT: THE "SETUP" IN GENEVA

1. U.S. Department of State, *Foreign Relations of the United States (FR) 1952–1954* (Washington, 1982), vol. 13, part 2, pp. 1419–21.
2. McCardle to Phillips, *FR 1952–1954* (Washington, 1981), 16:559–69.
3. Evelyn Shuckburgh, *Descent to Suez: Diaries, 1951–56* (New York: Norton, 1986), pp. 178–79.
4. Eisenhower to Dulles, May 1, 1954, *FR 1952–1954*, 16:640–41. In fact, Eisenhower had opened up the issue of partition. See note 23.
5. Anthony Eden confided to the American journalist Marquis Childs that the British were "very much disturbed and angered by Radford's coming over to London and trying to pressure the Cabinet and the Chiefs of Staff to come into Indo-China with sea and air power." Eden himself used the deprecating term "Radford's war against China." "Memorandum by the Assistant Secretary of State for Public Affairs . . .," April 30, 1954, *ibid.*, pp. 629–30.
6. The standard work on the Geneva Conference itself is Robert F. Randle, *Geneva 1954: The Settlement of the Indochinese War* (Princeton, N.J.: Princeton Univ. Press, 1969). Although published before most of the archival materials were available, it remains highly useful.
7. Devillers and Lacouture, *End of a War: Indochina, 1954*, trans. by Alexander Lieven and Adam Roberts (New York: Praeger, 1969), p. 122.
8. *FR 1952–1954*, 16:552–53.
9. Devillers and Lacouture, *End of a War*, p. 123.
10. *Washington Post*, April 29, 1954.
11. Eden to Foreign Office, April 26, 1954, Foreign Office (FO) 371/112055, DF 1071/309/G; "Memorandum of Conversation," April 25, 1954, *FR 1952–1954*, 16:553–57. Of the two accounts of this conversation, the American record is much fuller, especially concerning the discussion of partition.
12. Minister of State to Eden, April 26, 1954, FO 371/112055; Randle, *Geneva 1954*, pp. 127–28.
13. Minister of State to Eden, April 26, 1954, FO 371/112055.
14. Randle, *Geneva 1954*, p. 128.
15. *Washington Post*, May 3, 1954.
16. *Ibid.*, April 28, 1954.
17. "Minute of Conversation," April 27, 1954, FO 371/112057, DF 1071/361/G.
18. See Stephen Ambrose, *Eisenhower: The President* (New York: Simon and Schuster, 1984), pp. 157, 166–67.

19. See, for example, Randle, *Geneva 1954*, pp. 170–72.
20. Makins to Foreign Office, April 28, 1954, FO 371/112057, DF 1071/350. On this point, see also Melvin Gurtov, *The First Vietnam Crisis* (New York: Columbia Univ. Press, 1968), p. 145.
21. *New York Times*, May 17, 1954.
22. *Ibid.*, May 6, 1954.
23. National Archives, *Public Papers of the Presidents of the United States: Dwight D. Eisenhower, 1954* (Washington, 1960), p. 428.
24. Eden to Foreign Office, April 30, 1954, FO 371/112058, DF 1071/378. See also *FR 1952–1954* (Washington, 1985), 14:638–39.
25. Shuckburgh, *Descent to Suez*, p. 181.
26. Minute by R. L. Speaight, April 30, 1954, FO 371/112059, DF 1071/418/G.
27. Eisenhower to Dulles, May 1, 1954, *FR 1952–1954*, 16:640–41.
28. National Archives, *Public Papers of the Presidents, 1954*, p. 436.
29. FO 371/112056, DF 1071/316.
30. *Ibid.*, and Eden to Foreign Office, April 26, 1954, FO 371/112056, DF 1071/326/G. At least one report from Ambassador Makins indicated that the United States was thinking about going ahead with an alliance to defend Southeast Asia without British participation. See Makins to Foreign Office, April 29, 1954, FO 371/112057, DF 1071/366.
31. Louis L. Gerson, *John Foster Dulles* (New York: Cooper Square, 1967), was perhaps the first to suggest that Dulles entertained such thoughts. See, for example, the account of a Molotov/Bedell Smith conversation, pp. 178–79.
32. Dulles to Department of State, April 27, 1954, *FR 1952–1954*, 16:579–80.
33. Dulles to Eisenhower, April 29, 1954, *FR 1952–1954*, 16:605–7.
34. "Memorandum of Discussion . . .," April 29, 1954, *FR 1952–1954*, vol. 13, part 2, pp. 1431–45.
35. "Memorandum of Conversation with Mr. Eden," *FR 1952–1954*, 16:622–25.
36. Eden's remarks are called a "technical" point *ibid.*, without any elaboration; but in his own record of the conversation, the foreign secretary scores heavily with this comment: "I found it difficult to believe that it was unreasonable to ask of the South Koreans conditions which Dr. Adenauer had been perfectly willing to accept." Eden to Foreign Office, May 1, 1954, FO 371/112058, DF 1071/374/G.
37. Diary Entry, April 29, 1954, quoted in Robert Rhodes James, *Anthony Eden* (London: Weidenfeld and Nicolson, 1986), p. 378.
38. Eden to Foreign Office, May 1, 1954, FO 371/112058, DF 1071/374/G.
39. Eden to Foreign Office, May 2, 1954, FO 371/112058, DF 1071/379/G. See also the briefer account in Anthony Eden, *Full Circle: The Memoirs of Anthony Eden*, (Boston: Houghton Mifflin, 1960), pp. 125–27.
40. Eden to Foreign Office, May 2, 1954, FO 371/112058, DF 1071/379/G.
41. Shuckburgh, *Descent to Suez*, p. 187.
42. Dulles to Department of State, May 2, 1954, *FR 1952–1954*, 16:648–49. Dulles' account of the dinner conversation is so incomplete as to raise again the question of control of American policy, and especially the question of the recent interpretations of Eisenhower's complete grasp over both direction and detail.
43. Eden to Foreign Office, May 2, 1954, FO 371/112058, DF 1071/379/G.
44. Devillers and Lacouture, *End of a War*, p. 142 (emphasis in original). The authors also present a selection of current newspaper accounts of speculations about

partition. It seems clear that there was much talk about a possible "militarily defensible" line, if hardly any about the Inchon option.

45. James, *Anthony Eden*, p. 378.

46. *New York Times*, May 1, 1954.

47. Bidault, *Resistance: The Political Autobiography of Georges Bidault*, trans. by Marianne Sinclair (New York: Praeger, 1967), p. 200.

48. *Ibid.*, p. 201.

49. *Washington Post*, May 3, 1954. The Colombo nations were India, Pakistan, Indonesia, Burma, and Ceylon.

50. "RC's Summary of Principal Points Made by the President in Talking with Republican Leaders," May 3, 1954, Dulles Papers, Mudd Library, Princeton University, Princeton, New Jersey.

51. *Ibid.*

52. See David Eisenhower, *Eisenhower at War, 1943–1945* (New York: Random House, 1986), for descriptions of their relationship, e.g., pp. 376, 725, 797, *et passim.*

53. "I was encouraged by the prospect which his co-operation opened up," Eden, *Full Circle*, p. 125; Mendès-France, *Choisir: Conversations avec Jean Bothorel* (Paris: Stock Editions, 1974), p. 76.

54. Eden to Foreign Office, May 4, 1954, FO 371/112059, DF 1071/416/G.

55. *Ibid.* The next day Smith started off a conversation with Eden on a somewhat different plane, suggesting that American reluctance to intervene immediately could be changed overnight by Eisenhower because of the president's immense popularity. Eden argued in reply that the French were unable to continue by themselves, and that their native allies were unreliable. The best that could be hoped, therefore, was for a settlement that would leave Cambodia and Laos untouched, and at least part of Vietnam uncontrolled by Ho. "Mr. Bedell Smith admitted the truth of this and said that Mr. Dulles realized it. (I did not remark that he had never said anything of the kind to me.) I said that if we understood that this was the reality of the situation we ought to face it and then we should go to work with our French friends to get the very best terms we could. I think that this is now the American intention, here at least." This exchange is noteworthy as further evidence of the almost instantaneous change brought about by General Smith's arrival in Geneva. Eden to Foreign Office, May 5, 1954, FO 371/112062, DF 1071/431/G.

56. Shuckburgh, *Descent to Suez*, p. 192.

57. "Memorandum of Conference at the White House," May 5, 1954, *FR 1952–1954*, vol. 13, part 2, pp. 1466–70.

58. "Memorandum of Discussion . . .," May 6, 1954, *ibid.*, pp. 1481–93.

59. See, for example, Bernard Fall, *Hell in a Very Small Place* (Philadelphia: Lippincott, 1967), pp. 406–7, and Jules Roy, *The Battle of Dienbienphu* (New York: Carroll and Graf, 1984), pp. 282–83.

60. Both Fall, *Hell in a Very Small Place*, p. 410, and Roy, *Battle of Dienbienphu*, p. 283, report de Castries' supposed plea and offer other accounts and explanations. The Vietminh account was soon broadcast to the world. According to this latter, an order went out to all units on the afternoon of May 7. "Seize the opportunity to make a deep thrust into the heart of the enemy and capture alive Brigadier General de Castries." And when the Vietminh unit broke into his headquarters, shouting "Hands up!" the whole French company, with de Castries at its head,

stammered, "We surrender." *New York Times*, May 16, 1954. Obviously the symbolism of a French surrender and the capture alive of de Castries was not lost on either side.
61. Fall, *Hell in a Very Small Place*, p. 411.
62. *Washington Post*, May 9, 1954.
63. Devillers and Lacouture, *End of a War*, p. 156.
64. *Washington Post*, May 8, 1954.
65. "Memorandum of Conversation," by Livingston Merchant, May 9, 1954, Dulles Papers. Dulles also thought about trying to get a United Nations observer team into Laos, Cambodia, and Thailand, "rather than a call for troops, which, I fear, would be very difficult to obtain at the present juncture." This was a variation on the "plate glass theory." See Dulles to Henry Cabot Lodge, May 10, 1954, *ibid.*
66. Dillon to Dulles, May 10, 1954, *FR 1952–1954*, vol. 13, part 2, pp. 1522–24.
67. "Telephone Call to Adm. Radford," May 10, 1954, 3:00 P.M., Dulles Papers.
68. "Telephone Call from Adm. Radford," May 10, 1954, 4:22 P.M., *ibid.*
69. "Memorandum of Conversation," May 11, 1954, *FR 1952–1954*, vol. 13, part 2, pp. 1526–28.
70. "For Mtg. with the President," May 10, 1954, *ibid.*
71. "Memorandum of Conversation," May 11, 1954, *FR 1952–1954*, vol. 13, part 2, pp. 1526–28. See also a draft telegram to Dillon, dated 5/10/54, in Dulles Papers.
72. Marked "Copy, 5/10/54" and "Approved by President, May 11, 1954," Dulles Papers. The cable, with Eisenhower's brief amendment limiting any American intervention to "principally air and sea," is in *FR 1952–1954*, vol. 13, part 2, pp. 1534–36.
73. Memorandum of Conversation, May 11, 1954, *FR 1952–1954*, vol. 13, part 2, pp. 1532–33. For all of his efforts to convince the president on this point, it should not be assumed that Dulles was himself free from ambiguity. In a memo he carried with him to lunch at the White House, entitled "Points for Discussion," he repeatedly stressed the dangers of going ahead without the British. For one thing, any policy that risked war with China was sure to cause tension within the alliance, so much so, in fact, that it actually increased the risk of war, since the Chinese might anticipate a full-scale breach. If war came, the British might deny the United States use of military bases. Intervention would have to involve ground forces. It could not be done on the cheap by air and sea. And finally, "Any use of atomic weapons will raise very serious problems of Asian opinion and attitude of our allies." Dulles Papers.
74. Bidault, *Resistance*, p. 200; copies of State Department Press Releases in FO 371/112066; Devillers and Lacouture, *End of a War*, pp. 189–90.
75. See *FR 1952–1954*, vol. 13, part 2, p. 1536, and *FR 1952–1954*, 16:785–87. When Dulles was advised of the flap caused by his remarks, he tried to reemphasize that the United States was not giving up on Indochina. Yet, as he explained in greater detail to the Senate Foreign Relations Committee in Executive Session, he was preparing new defenses outside Indochina. "I am not willing to make Indochina the symbol for all of Southeast Asia. Southeast Asia has a population of 200 million, of which roughly 25 million are in Indochina. It has vast resources in the way of rubber, oil, tin, none of which are in Indochina. It has important strategic positions, and so forth, of which only one, Saigon, is in Indochina." United States

Senate, Committee on Foreign Relations, *Executive Sessions of the Senate Foreign Relations Committee, 1954 (Historical Series)* (Washington, 1977), 6:275.

76. Transcript in Dulles Papers.

77. Senate Foreign Relations Committee, *Executive Sessions, 1954*, 6:279.

78. *Ibid.*, pp. 279, 271, 267.

79. Dulles to Smith, May 12, 1954, *FR 1952–1954*, 16:778–79.

80. G. D. Anderson to Foreign Office, enclosing Pearson, "Interview with General Bedell Smith," May 13, 1954, FO 371/112067, DF 1071/579.

81. Memorandum of Conversation, May 8, 1954, *FR 1952–1954*, vol. 13, part 2, pp. 1512–15.

82. Eden, *Full Circle*, pp. 133–34.

83. *Ibid.*

84. Eden to Foreign Office, May 16, 1954, FO 371/112066, DF 1071/548/G. And see above, pp. 435–36.

85. Eden to Foreign Office, May 16, 1954, FO 371/112066, DF 1071/548/G. In *Full Circle*, p. 135, Eden says this portion of the cable, at least, was sent directly to the prime minister.

86. Diary Entries, May 4 and 5, 1954, in Shuckburgh, *Descent to Suez*, pp. 190–3.

87. Eden to Foreign Office, May 16, 1954, FO 371/112066, DF 1071/548/G. Smith's report to Washington concerning his conversation with Eden confirmed the exchange and the irritation expressed by the latter. He also downplayed the depth, however, of Eden's concern. He advocated taking the British into American confidence because "it will assist them in meeting political situations and will encourage them to move further in our direction if they believe we are giving them a considerable measure of confidence. There will be disagreements and we will be obliged at times to tell them that we are going ahead whether they agree or not, but I think they would infinitely prefer this than to be surprised with a press story." Smith to Department of State, May 16, 1954, *FR 1952–1954*, 16:815–16.

88. Minute by Kirkpatrick, May 17, 1954, FO 371/112067, DF 1071/565, and John Colville to A. A. S. Stark, May 17, 1954, FO 371/112067, DF 1071/565(a).

89. *New York Times*, May 17, 1954, and Eden to Churchill, May 17, 1954, FO 371/112067, DF 1071/561/G.

90. Eden to Churchill, May 17, 1954, FO 371/112067, DF 1071/561/G.

91. *New York Times*, May 17, 1954.

92. Eden to Churchill, May 17, 1954, FO 371/112067, DF 1071/561/G.

93. Dillon to Dulles, May 17, 1954, Eisenhower Papers, Whitman File, Dulles-Herter Series, Eisenhower Library, Abilene, Kansas.

94. Gerson, *Dulles*, p. 175.

95. *Ibid.*

96. McClintock to Department of State, May 22, 1954, *FR 1952–1954*, vol. 13, part 2, pp. 1599–1601.

97. McClintock to Department of State, May 19, 1954, *ibid.*, pp. 1582–83.

98. *Ibid.*

99. Smith to Department of State, May 17, 1954, *FR 1952–1954*, 16:827–28.

100. Dulles to Smith, May 20, 1954, *ibid.*, pp. 869–70; and for Churchill's declaration, see *ibid.*, pp. 834–35. Churchill recognized how well "Anthony's appeasement" (his phrase) went over in the Commons. "I like it up to a point, but only up to a point." The prime minister's conviction that intervention in Indochina was

folly never weakened, but he was not so sure that Eden's policy had the right tone to it. It had alienated the Americans, that was for sure. And perhaps it did leave the wrong impression. See Lord Moran, *Winston Churchill: The Struggle for Survival, 1940–1965* (Boston: Houghton Mifflin, 1966), pp. 549–52. Even in his speech to the Commons, the prime minister implied that the foreign secretary should return home to explain things in person. And whenever he started feeling this way, the prime minister thought about a trip to Washington to set things right.

101. Memorandum of Conversation with the President, May 19, 1954, *FR 1952–1954*, vol. 13, part 2, pp. 1583–84.

102. *FR 1952–1954*, 16:887.

103. For accounts of his conversations, see Dulles to Smith, May 22, 1954, *ibid.*, pp. 885–86, and Sir Leslie Munro, Interview, Dulles Oral History Project, Dulles Papers.

104. Munro Interview. Robert Randle, writing before many of the documents became available, stressed British resentment at being made the scapegoat. "They believed they had been made the scapegoat for an *American* decision not to intervene. (They had.)" *Geneva 1954*, p. 226. While certainly there was ample reason, given the divisions in the United States over Indochina policy, for the British to be suspicious along these lines, materials now available to the historian suggest that Dulles was not operating simply to make a record, and that, uncertain as he might be about immediate intervention or long-term collective defense, he was *very* serious about his efforts.

105. Memorandum of Discussion, May 20, 1954, *FR 1952–1954*, vol. 13, part 2, pp. 1586–90.

106. Dillon to Dulles, May 22, 1954, *ibid.*, pp. 1601–2.

107. Memorandum of Discussion, May 20, 1954, *ibid.*, pp. 1586–90.

108. Dulles to Dillon, May 21, 1954, *ibid.*, pp. 1594–95.

109. May 20, 1954, *ibid.*, pp. 1590–92.

110. Memorandum of Conversation with the President, May 25, 1954, Dulles Papers.

111. *Ibid.*; and see Stephen Jurika, ed., *From Pearl Harbor to Vietnam: The Memoirs of Admiral Arthur W. Radford* (Stanford, Calif.: Hoover Institute Press, 1980), pp. 425–26. Radford readily admitted that the JCS position was unlikely to find acceptance at the "political level" unless the Chinese intervened overtly. And he implies in these memoirs that the JCS were uninterested in any military action in Indochina itself, since that area was really devoid of the sorts of military targets that could make a difference, and since the Vietminh got most of its aid from outside Indochina. If his proposed air strikes against China did not suffice, he also admitted, "a highly selective atomic offensive" might be required.

112. Draft Memorandum to the President, May 28, 1954, Dulles Papers.

113. Dillon to Dulles, May 24, 1954, *FR 1952–1954*, vol. 13, part 2, pp. 1608–9.

CHAPTER NINE: MAKING PEACE ON A BED OF NAILS

1. Quoted in Denis Warner, *The Last Confucian* (New York: Macmillan, 1963), p. 74.

2. *Ibid.*
3. Eisenhower Papers, DDE Diaries, Whitman File, Eisenhower Library, Abilene, Kansas.
4. Quoted by Evan S. Connell, *Son of the Morning Star: Custer and the Little Bighorn* (San Francisco: North Point Press, 1984), p. 119.
5. Allan W. Cameron, ed., *Viet-Nam Crisis: A Documentary History*, 2 vols. (Ithaca, N.Y.: Cornell Univ. Press, 1971), 2:275–76.
6. David Carlton, *Anthony Eden: A Biography* (London: Allen Lane, 1981), pp. 347–51.
7. A very lively debate over this issue began with the Geneva Conference, and continues in historical accounts to this day. The issue is worth considering, for the matter of what was agreed on July 20, 1954, about the temporary nature or permanence of the line between North and South Vietnam is of obvious significance in talking about the origins of the second Indochina war. This is not the place to discuss the question fully, but Robert Randle, *Geneva 1954: The Settlement of the Indochinese War* (Princeton: Princeton Univ. Press, 1969), pp. 357–62, argues that the representatives from the Vietminh and Bao Dai's government never agreed that the settlement was permanent. At the same time, delegates of the Geneva "group" (Great Britain, France, Russia, China) appeared to hope for a permanent settlement, with the "observer" (the United States) reserving its position.

In recent years, the debate has become a departure point for discussions of American involvement in the war as, for example, expressed in Guenter Lewy's *America in Vietnam* (New York: Oxford Univ. Press, 1978). Lewy argues (p. 8) that the north accepted the partition at the time. The provisions providing for all Vietnamese elections, he adds, was an afterthought to save face for Ho Chi Minh. Furthermore, since South Vietnam did not sign the agreement, and really became independent after the conference, it was not bound by the imposed Geneva accords. In this interpretation (pp. 16–17), the north moved opportunistically to take advantage of ill will caused by Diem's anti-Communist efforts to start a war. For different reasons, Gabriel Kolko rejects the notion of a civil war, and sees the situation in *Anatomy of a War* (New York: Pantheon, 1986) as a war against a U.S.-supported army. "The primary origin of the Vietnam War was the American intervention and effort to establish and sustain an alternative to the Communist Party" (p. 8).
8. As reported in Philippe Devillers and Jean Lacouture, *End of a War: Indochina, 1954* (New York: Praeger, 1969), p. 222.
9. Jebb to Eden, May 29, 1954, Foreign Office (FO) 371/112069, DF 1071/635/G.
10. Eden to Foreign Office, June 1, 1954, FO 371/112069, DF 1071/620. Bidault also confided in Eden that if the talks failed, the Americans were ready to come in with three divisions. Eden replied that he could not complain of this "distant thunder" as the Frenchman had described the American moves, but warned again that London was not pledged to any joint action. *Full Circle: The Memoirs of Anthony Eden* (Boston: Houghton Mifflin 1960), p. 143. Eden now had to concern himself, obviously, with the possibility that since he had given pledges to consider joint action if the conference failed, the Americans would do everything they could to see that that happened.
11. Eden, *Full Circle*, p. 139.

12. Memorandum of Conversation with the President, June 2, 1954, quoted in Stephen E. Ambrose, *Eisenhower: The President* (New York: Simon and Schuster, 1984), pp. 206–7.
13. Washington to Foreign Office, June 8, 1954, FO 371/112070, DF 1071/653.
14. Eisenhower, *The White House Years: Mandate for Change, 1953–1956* (New York: Doubleday, 1963), pp. 362–63.
15. Smith to Dulles, June 7, 1954, with enclosures, U.S. Department of State, *Foreign Relations of the United States (FR) 1952–1954* (Washington, 1981), 16:-1054–55 (emphasis added).
16. Dulles to Smith, June 9, 1954, *ibid.*, pp. 1103–5.
17. *New York Times*, June 11 and 12, 1954.
18. Stanley Karnow, *Vietnam: A History* (New York: Viking, 1983), p. 202.
19. Eden to Foreign Office, May 20, 1954, FO 371/112067, DF 1071/574. Zhou passed along his concerns about Laos and Cambodia to Walter Bedell Smith via India's Krishna Menon, who had arrived in Geneva to push for Nehru's suggested solution of a military standstill. Menon told Smith that Zhou recognized that Laos and Cambodia were different, but under Western proposals for a truce and international supervision throughout Indochina, France and the United States would be able to build up their military strength in those areas. Smith to Dulles, June 5, 1954, *FR 1952–1954*, 16:1038–39.
20. *Ibid.* Eden would call his policy the search for a "protective pad." "Many countries had an interest in this and, if I could once get the conception established, the position might hold, perhaps for years." *Full Circle*, pp. 138–39.
21. If not Dulles, then Senator William F. Knowland and Congressman Walter F. Judd were extremely active at this time, passing around a "memorandum" that the Department of Defense was showing in confidence to various congressional committees. The memorandum purported to originate in Beijing, and it outlined the Chinese plan for world conquest. "Whether we can prevent the United States from starting the war [to preempt the Chinese program] depends upon how much success we have in isolating her and how effective is our peace offensive. If the war can be averted, the success of our plan of peaceful penetration for the other parts of Asia is assured." That would be a prelude to the collapse of Europe. It is significant that the Defense Department was showing this memorandum to the legislators as part of its presentation on behalf of a $3.5 billion appropriations request for foreign military aid. When it was made public, however, Congressman Judd added dramatically that he could not reveal the source, "but there is every reason to believe that it is authentic." *Washington Post*, May 31, 1954.
22. Alexander Werth, *Lost Statesman: The Strange Story of Pierre Mendès-France* (New York: Abeland-Schuman, 1958), pp. 88–89.
23. Jean Lacouture, *Pierre Mendès-France*, trans. by George Holoch (New York: Holmes and Meier, 1984), pp. 219–20.
24. Eisenhower, *Mandate for Change*, pp. 365–66.
25. Eden to Foreign Office, June 12, 1954, FO 371/112071, DF 1071/691.
26. Lacouture, *Mendès-France*, pp. 220–22.
27. Eisenhower, *Mandate for Change*, pp. 365–66.
28. Dillon to Department of State, June 20, 1954, *FR 1952–1954*, (Washington, 1982), vol. 13, part 2, pp. 1725–27.

29. Robert Randle, *Geneva 1954*, speculates that Bao Dai was induced to appoint Diem in the expectation of receiving greater aid from the United States in the first years of independence. He also notes shrewdly that one should pay more attention to the decline in French influence than to the maneuverings of American diplomats (p. 289). Most recently, George McT. Kahin, *Intervention: How America Became Involved in Vietnam* (New York: Knopf, 1986), pp. 79–80, repeats much of the same story, but notes that early in 1954, Walter Bedell Smith told Congress that the administration talked about providing "a certain religious leadership." It is also true, however, that Eisenhower was speaking about finding a Buddhist militant in this period. One reason, noted by Kahin and others, why the Eisenhower administration might not have embraced Diem right away was that most of his influential friends in America were Democrats!
30. Information in this and succeeding paragraphs is taken from Cooper's *The Lost Crusade: America in Vietnam* (New York: Dodd, Mead, 1970), pp. 120–28.
31. Cooper, *Lost Crusade*, p. 128.
32. Devillers and Lacouture, *End of a War*, p. 224.
33. Department of State, Press Release, June 11, 1954, Dulles Papers, Mudd Library, Princeton University, Princeton, New Jersey.
34. June 22, 1954, National Archives, *Public Papers of the Presidents: Dwight D. Eisenhower, 1954* (Washington, 1960), p. 587.
35. June 21, 1954, Eisenhower Papers, Whitman File, DDE Diaries.
36. National Archives, *Public Papers of the Presidents, 1954*, p. 587. An article in the June 25, 1954, *New York Times* noted that already Japanese trade was shifting to Asia, and that this development would "alleviate pressures" that had led to Pearl Harbor.
37. Edward Geary Lansdale, *In the Midst of Wars: An American's Mission to Southeast Asia* (New York: Harper and Row, 1972), chaps. 9 and 10.
38. *Ibid.*, p. 126.
39. *Ibid.*, p. 150.
40. *Ibid.*
41. Lansdale, *In the Midst of Wars*, p. 4. Two other accounts of the origins and nature of Lansdale's mission bear notice. First there is Richard Drinnon's scathing polemic *Facing Westward: The Metaphysics of Indian-Hating and Empire Building* (Minneapolis: Univ. of Minnesota Press, 1980), pp. 355–443, which traces them back to colonial attitudes toward the Indians, and the "obligations" of white men toward them. Then, of course, there is Graham Greene's famous novel *The Quiet American* (New York: Penguin, 1980), with its marvelously named hero, Alden Pyle, who champions the "Third Force" in Asia, and whose "innocence" leads to tragic results.
42. Memorandum for the Record, January 30, 1954, reproduced in the Senator Gravel Edition, *The Pentagon Papers*, 4 vols. (Boston: Beacon Press, 1971), 1:443–47. The discrepancy between Lansdale's account and the record in the Pentagon Papers was discovered by Drinnon, *Facing Westward*, pp. 404–5. Drinnon calls Lansdale Dulles' expert "native-handler."
43. Drinnon, *Facing Westward*, p. 406.
44. Devillers and Lacouture, *End of a War*, p. 224.

45. See *FR 1952–1954,* 16:1165, 1170–71, 1173–74; Lacouture, *Mendès-France,* pp. 220–21; and Anthony Eden, *Toward Peace in Indochina* (Boston: Houghton Mifflin, 1966), p. 5.

46. Lacouture, *Mendès-France,* p. 223.

47. *Ibid.*

48. Stanley Karnow interviewed Pham Van Dong in 1981, who revealed Vietminh distress on these issues with both Russia and China. When Molotov accepted a two-year interval before the elections, the Vietminh leader walked away from the last haggling session before the documents were agreed upon, complaining to Zhou, "He has double-crossed us." *Vietnam: A History* (New York: Viking, 1983), p. 204.

49. Lacouture, *Mendès-France,* p. 207.

50. Eisenhower Papers, Whitman Files.

51. See chapter 1. The administration succeeded in getting this interpretation into an editorial in the *New York Times* on June 30, 1954. "The new Declaration reiterates what the Atlantic Charter proclaimed—namely, that all nations capable of sustaining an independent existence are entitled to self-government and independence, and the two leaders pledge themselves to use every peaceful means to realize that aim."

52. Diary Entry, June 14, 1954, Hagerty Papers, Eisenhower Library, Abilene, Kansas.

53. For the full message, see Eisenhower Papers, Whitman File. Despite the impression many British political figures had—let alone the Americans—that Churchill was gaa-gaa (or approaching that state) when he talked about trade softening the heart of the Soviets, Eisenhower and Dulles occasionally touched on the same subject, in much the same way. They might not share the prime minister's newfound Quaker fantasies about the bear and the lion supping together under a spreading oak, but there were sound reasons of political economy for encouraging some East-West trade. Press secretary James Hagerty recorded the following White House discussion in his diary on June 23, 1954, when Churchill's letter had been read and Eisenhower and Dulles were thinking out loud. "We want the free world to be our friends," began the president, "but I get completely bewildered and it doesn't make sense to me when we try to cut off trade. I don't think the British are wrong on this, and we should be more liberal in our attitude." Trade could only weaken the Russian hold on the satellite countries, he went on. "I believe our military is scaring the hell out of us on a false premise on this one."

Dulles felt the same way about the Far East. "What we should do with Japan," he said, "is get them making things that the Chinese want so that the Chinese would have to turn to Japan for these materials." Hagerty Papers.

The problem always was how to develop such a sophisticated view with Congress, which time and again felt it necessary to ally-bash on the question of East-West trade. But while Eisenhower and his secretary of state occasionally talked this way, they held to the view that the flag followed trade, and Japan and Germany could be "lost" this way to the Sino-Soviet bloc.

54. *New York Times,* June 24, 1954.

55. *Ibid.,* June 25, 1954, and *Washington Post,* June 24, 1954.

56. Eden was in a feisty mood on the airplane to Washington, seemingly ready for a showdown. See Lord Moran, *Winston Churchill: The Struggle for Survival,*

1940–65 (Boston: Houghton Mifflin, 1966), p. 558. In Washington, meanwhile, Congressman Walter Judd, a leader in the China lobby, told Dulles that he thought Eden's purpose in making the speech was "to destroy and discredit you," and that the "British think they are moving into the dominant position in Asia." "Telephone Call from Congressman Judd," June 24, 1954, Dulles Papers.

57. The Eisenhower administration's efforts to eliminate a leftist regime in Guatemala, and the dubious interpretations they required of international law and treaty obligations, cannot be discussed in any detail here. An excellent short account is in Ambrose, *Eisenhower*, pp. 192–96, while the fullest is Richard Immerman, *The CIA in Guatemala: The Foreign Policy of Intervention* (Austin: Univ. of Texas Press, 1982).

58. "Telephone Call to Amb. Lodge," June 25, 1954, Dulles Papers.

59. Diary Entry, June 28, 1954, by John Colville, *The Fringes of Power: 10 Downing Street Diaries, 1939–1955* (New York: Norton, 1985), p. 694.

60. See the account in Eden's memoirs, *Full Circle*, pp. 150–55, and his comparison of the situation with Suez events in 1956, p. 634.

61. Hagerty Diary, June 24, 1954, Hagerty Papers.

62. *Ibid.*, June 23, 1954.

63. For comments on the impact of Australian influence in favor of SEATO, see *ibid.*, June 26, 1954. This had been long in coming, but Americans thought that the pressure on the British would now be "simply tremendous" to put aside their doubts. A good account of the Zhou-Nehru talks is Randle, *Geneva 1954*, pp. 306–10. Zhou's emulation of Lenin's tactics in appropriating the right of self-determination, a Wilsonian principle but hardly a Marxist one, should not go unnoticed.

64. Hagerty Diary, June 25, 1954, Hagerty Papers.

65. Moran, *Winston Churchill*, p. 564; untitled memorandum, June 25 and 26, 1954. Eisenhower Papers, Whitman File, International Series.

66. Aide-Mémoire, June 26, 1954, reprinted in *FR 1952–1954*, vol. 13, part 2, pp. 1755–57.

67. *Ibid.*

68. For an excellent account of the reactions to Mendès-France's aide-mémoire, see Stephen Jurika, Jr., ed., *From Pearl Harbor to Vietnam: The Memoirs of Admiral W. Radford* (Stanford, Calif.: Hoover Institute Press, 1980), pp. 438–41.

69. *FR 1952–1954*, vol. 13, part 2, pp. 1755–57.

70. Colville, *Fringes of Power*, p. 693; Eisenhower, *Mandate for Change*, p. 369. On this same page, moreover, Eisenhower contrasted Mendès-France's diplomatic success with the deteriorating military situation in central Vietnam, with the French outlook "increasingly desolate."

71. Eisenhower, *Mandate for Change*, p. 368. "On one aspect only did our viewpoints differ," wrote Eisenhower. "Churchill and Eden merely wished to state a 'hope' that the French would settle for nothing less than our 'seven points'; we wanted these as minimal."

72. The text was released by the White House on June 29, 1954. For comments on the end of the conference and the wording, see *New York Times*, June 30, 1954.

73. *FR 1952–1954*, vol. 13, part 2, pp. 1757–58.

74. *Ibid.*, pp. 1785–86, 1791–92. After seeing Mendès-France in person in mid- [illegible] Dulles felt absolutely comfortable with this strategy, as he told the Senate

Foreign Relations Committee in Executive Session on July 16, 1954. "We believe, the French believe, that by stipulating for election conditions and this supervisory machinery and agreement by both regimes that the conditions are ready for elections, that election can be postponed until conditions are more favorable for them [South Vietnam], and if by that time conditions are more favorable to them, then probably the other side won't want to have elections." United States Senate, Foreign Relations Committee, *Executive Sessions of the Senate Foreign Relations Committee, 1954 (Historical Series)* (Washington, 1977), 6:642–43.
75. *FR 1952–1954*, vol. 13, part 2, p. 1865.
76. Press Conference, June 28, 1954, Dulles Papers; Hagerty Diary, June 28, 1954, Hagerty Papers. For a somewhat different account of the Dulles presentation to legislative leaders, see *FR 1952–1954*, vol. 13, part 2, pp. 1754–55.
77. For the transcript of Churchill's remarks at his press conference, see *New York Times*, June 29, 1954.
78. Press Conference, June 30, 1954, National Archives, *Public Papers of the Presidents, 1954*, p. 605.
79. *Washington Post*, July 5, 1954.
80. Eisenhower Papers, Whitman File, DDE Diaries.
81. Churchill to Eisenhower, July 9, 1954, *ibid.*, International Series.
82. Draft, July 9, 1954, Dulles Papers.
83. *FR 1952–1954*, vol. 13, part 2, pp. 1797, 1803, 1812–13. Much thought was also given to the fate of the EDC. If Mendès-France could extricate himself from Vietnam successfully, he might also be the only man who could pull that off as well.
84. Memorandum of Conversation, July 13, 1954, *FR 1952–1954*, 16:1348–55.
85. "Telephone Call from Congressman Vorys," July 16, 1954, Dulles Papers.
86. *Washington Post*, July 19, 1954.
87. Lacouture, *Mendès-France*, p. 227.
88. *Ibid.*, pp. 227–28.
89. *Ibid.*, p. 236.
90. Eden, *Full Circle*, p. 161.
91. Eden to Foreign Office, July 17, 1954, FO 371/112079, DF 1071/884.
92. Lacouture, *Mendès-France*, pp. 235–36.
93. Eden to Foreign Office, July 17, 1954, FO 371/112078, DF 1071/880, and FO 371/112079, DF 1071/885.
94. Smith to Dulles, July 18, 1954, *FR 1952–1954*, 16:1428–29.
95. Eden to Foreign Office, July 19, 1954, FO 371/112080, DF 1071/880.
96. Devillers and Lacouture, *End of a War*, pp. 298–99.
97. Eden to Foreign Office, July 19, 1954, FO 371/112080, DF 1071/880.
98. Karnow, *Vietnam: A History*, p. 204.
99. For a good discussion of the Wallace mission, see Herbert Feis, *China Tangle* (New York: Atheneum, 1965), pp. 146–49.

CHAPTER TEN: NATION BUILDING

1. U.S. Department of State, *Foreign Relations of the United States (FR) 1952–1954* (Washington, 1982), vol. 13, part 2, p. 2085.

2. In 1957 the Valley Forge Freedom Foundation, protector of the Washington image, named Diem its man of the year. Another view of Diem was offered by Chester L. Cooper. "Small, round, glossy, he looked like a porcelain Buddha," noted the diplomat, "a porcelain Buddha in a white suit." *The Lost Crusade: America in Vietnam* (New York: Dodd, Mead, 1970), p. 116.
3. Oral History Interview, Dulles Papers, Mudd Library, Princeton University, Princeton, New Jersey.
4. Quoted in Ronald Spector, *United States Army in Vietnam, Advice and Support: The Early Years, 1941–1960* (Washington, 1983), p. 230.
5. Eisenhower, *The White House Years: Mandate for Change, 1953–1956* (New York: Doubleday, 1963), p. 372.
6. Dulles to Wilson, August 18, 1954, *FR 1952–1954*, vol. 13, part 2, pp. 1954–56. Given the post–Vietnam War criticisms of nation building as a liberal fixation in the Kennedy-Johnson years that worked against a successful military effort, it is well to take note of the Joint Chiefs of Staff position in August 1954, when terms of reference for a U.S. training mission were being formulated: "From the military point of view it is absolutely essential that there be a reasonably strong, stable civil government in control. It is hopeless to expect a U.S. military training mission to achieve success unless the nation concerned is able effectively to perform those governmental functions essential to the successful raising and maintenance of armed forces." Department of Defense, *United States–Vietnam Relations, 1945–1967*, 12 vols. (Washington, 1971), 10:701–2. To be sure, the Joint Chiefs were not calling for democracy, only effective government, but the Military Assistance Mission in Saigon knew only one way to achieve that: "Develop strong democratic state oriented toward West." MAAG, Saigon, to Defense Department, August 8, 1954, *ibid.*, pp. 703–4. What made this especially tricky was that American policy-makers had to pursue democratic methods for the south, while they built a state based on a denial of all-Vietnamese elections.
7. Richard Bissell Interview, Dulles Oral History Project, Dulles Papers.
8. *Ibid.*
9. Speech in Chicago, November 29, 1954, text in *New York Times*, November 30, 1954.
10. Eisenhower to Alfred Gruenther, November 30, 1954, Eisenhower Papers, Whitman File, Administrative Series, Eisenhower Library, Abilene, Kansas.
11. Department of Defense, *United States–Vietnam Relations*, 10:691–98.
12. Memorandum of Discussion, August 24, 1954, *FR 1952–1954* (Washington, 1971), vol. 12, part 1, pp. 724–33.
13. Phillip Devillers and Jean Lacouture, *End of a War: Indochina, 1954* (New York: Praeger, 1969), p. 312.
14. *Ibid.*, pp. 320–21. Maurice Couve de Murville, foreign minister in a later French government, argued a variation on this theme in an interview for the Dulles Oral History Project. What precipitated the second Vietnam War, he asserted, was not the failure to hold elections, but the American determination not to leave Cambodia, Laos, and South Vietnam as they were after Geneva: neutral, independent states. "The American government didn't reject these agreements, but they never accepted them. And from the moment they were concluded, they took possession of South Vietnam and tried to work it out the other way; that is, taking the place that we had held before while we were at war, trying to create South

Vietnam as a Western Country, and, therefore, establishing a sort of American protectorate under the Diem government." Dulles Papers.

15. Transcript in Dulles Papers.

16. An adviser to Mendès-France, Jean Chauvel, assumed, in the aftermath of the Geneva Conference, that what Dulles had said earlier still obtained. "The only purpose of the Geneva Agreements," he wrote the premier, as the Americans see them, "is to provide a cover for the political, economic and military preparations for the conquest. In May, Dulles thought the preparations would take two years. The reconquest must be achieved, if not through war, then at least by the threat of war; therefore, the pact [SEATO] must create an international force designed either to wage war or to make the threat of war effective." See Devillers and Lacouture, *End of a War*, pp. 322–23. Chauvel's report is logical, and presents an interpretation of what the Americans no doubt *would have liked to do.* But their hands were full. In the final days of the Geneva Conference, Secretary Dulles spoke several times on the telephone with his brother Allen, director of the CIA, about the possibilities of "covert" action in Vietnam, but these abbreviated discussions suggest that liberating the north was down the list. They were dealing with trauma emergency situations, and priority went to restoring vital signs in the south. See "Telephone Call to Mr. Allen Dulles," July 19, 1954, "Telephone Call from Mr. Allen Dulles," July 19, 1954, and "Telephone Call from Mr. Allen Dulles," July 22, 1954, all in Dulles Papers. The man in charge of covert activities, Colonel Edward Lansdale, produced a report in 1955 about the Special Military Mission that detailed many of its undertakings, including the "sabotage" efforts in Hanoi to disrupt things for Ho's entering forces. See undated report in Senator Gravel Edition, *The Pentagon Papers*, 4 vols. (Boston: Beacon Press, 1971), 1:572–83. Although detailed notes were taken of "potential targets for future paramilitary operations," the activities of the SMM appear to be of the nature, in the north, of rearguard action—and, quite possibly, with the political intention of creating a bad atmosphere to forestall a French rapprochement with the Vietminh.

17. Dulles to Dillon, *FR 1952–1954*, vol. 13, part 2, pp. 1957–59.

18. Dillon to Dulles, August 20, 1954, *ibid.*, pp. 1964–66.

19. *Washington Post*, July 27 and 29, 1954.

20. Korean-American Talks, July 27, 1954, Eisenhower Papers, Whitman File, DDE Diaries.

21. *Washington Post*, July 31, 1954.

22. It is not a little interesting in this regard that Eisenhower sent Dulles a clipping of an article by columnist James Reston on August 7 that argued there was a "new sound" in Washington. "After all the thunder-like percussion of its statements on Indochina," the administration seemed to have decided that there really was no alternative to coexistence except no existence. The president said that he did not know if Dulles felt as acrobatic as the Reston piece suggested, but that he had "*thought*" he was marching straight ahead, "with my purposes and even my demeanor fairly consistent and persistent." Dulles replied that he was not aware of any "gyrations" in policy. Eisenhower to Dulles, August 9, 1954, and Dulles to Eisenhower, August 9, 1954, Dulles Papers.

23. *New York Times*, August 9, 1954, and Department of State, *Bulletin*, August 23, 1954, p. 265.

24. See George Mct. Kahin, *Intervention: How America Became Involved in Vietnam* (New York: Knopf, 1986), pp. 100–3.
25. Dulles Papers.
26. Memorandum of Conversation with the President, August 17, 1954, Dulles Papers. And "Telephone Call to Mr. Merchant," August 30, 1954, *ibid.*
27. "Telephone Call to Mr. Merchant," *ibid; Washington Post,* September 4, 1954.
28. *FR 1952–1954,* vol. 13, part 2, pp. 1999–2001.
29. "Telephone Call from Walter Judd," September 14, 1954, Dulles Papers.
30. Department of State, *Bulletin,* September 20, 1954, pp. 391–93.
31. Verbatim Proceedings, September 7, 1954, *FR 1952–1954,* vol. 12, part 1, pp. 862–84.
32. Text in Dulles Papers.
33. *Ibid.*
34. Memorandum of Discussion, September 12, 1954, *FR 1952–1954,* vol. 12, part 1, pp. 903–8.
35. See, for example, *Washington Post,* August 11, 1954, the effective date of the Indochina ceasefire.
36. *FR 1952–1954,* vol. 12, part 1, pp. 903–8.
37. *New York Times,* September 8, 1954. For a very well-balanced account of the crisis, see Eisenhower, *Mandate for Change,* pp. 461–66.
38. Eisenhower to Walter Bedell Smith, September 7, 1954, Eisenhower Papers, Whitman File, DDE Diaries.
39. Dulles to Eisenhower, September 3, 1954, Eisenhower Papers, Whitman File, Dulles-Herter Series.
40. *FR 1952–1954,* vol. 13, part 2, pp. 2058–59.
41. Washington's ire at Mendès-France was particularly evident at this moment because of the defeat of the EDC in the National Assembly. Sinking to the status of second-rate power even in Europe, Paris appeared ready to take its partners down as well. If that was his game, Dulles would put a stop to it. "We must now restore full sovereignty to Germany," he declared, and rushed off to Bonn to sign a memorandum with Chancellor Konrad Adenauer promising that West Germany would have a full role in Atlantic defense. For an interpretation written essentially from Mendès-France's point of view, see Jean Lacouture, *Pierre Mendès-France,* trans. by George Holoch (New York: Holmes and Meier, 1984), pp. 278–80. The EDC defeat turned out to be only temporary. Within weeks of the vote in the National Assembly, a plan was reached essentially between France and Great Britain, whereby the British agreed for the first time to the stationing of forces on the continent on a permanent basis. Thus German rearmament was accomplished, but at a very high cost. See Anthony Eden, *Full Circle: The Memoirs of Anthony Eden* (Boston: Houghton Mifflin, 1960), pp. 168–94.
42. *FR 1952–1954,* vol. 13, part 2, pp. 2066–70.
43. The course of the talks can be followed *ibid.,* pp. 2080–96.
44. A copy of the communiqué of September 30, 1954, is in the Dulles Papers; for the press reports, see *Washington Post,* September 28, 29, 30, 1954.
45. Smith to Heath, October 1, 1954, *FR 1952–1954,* vol. 13, part 2, pp. 2109–10.
46. Memorandum of Conversation, October 3, 1954, *ibid.,* p. 2115.
47. "Summary Minute of a Meeting . . . ," October 8, 1954, *ibid.,* pp. 2122–26.

48. *Ibid;* and see Dulles to Defense Secretary Wilson, October 11, 1954, *ibid.*, pp. 2132–35, and Memorandum for the Record, October 19, 1954, *ibid.*, p. 2142.
49. Eisenhower Papers, Whitman File, Dulles-Herter Series.
50. *New York Times,* October 17, 1954.
51. Heath to Department of State, October 13, 1954, *FR 1952–1954,* vol. 13, part 2, pp. 2135–38; *New York Times,* October 19, 1954; *Washington Post,* editorial, October 30, 1954.
52. *FR 1952–1954,* vol. 13, part 2, pp. 2166–67. For text, see Appendix III.
53. Memorandum of Discussion, October 26, 1954, *ibid.*, pp. 2183–86. In fact it was no secret that the French wanted to open up contacts with Ho's government. With over 6,000 businessmen in Hanoi, it was hardly surprising that the French, sudden reversal though it may have been, were interested in a cultural and economic agreement. According to some sources, the United States quietly let it be known that it would blacklist firms doing business with the Vietminh. Whether that was a prime factor in the exodus of French businessmen remains problematical, but only 114 stayed. See Michael Maclear, *The Ten Thousand Day War* (New York: Avon, 1981), pp. 50–51.
54. *FR 1952–1954,* vol. 13, part 2, pp. 2166–67.
55. Memorandum of Conversation, October 30, 1954, *ibid.*, pp. 2194–95.
56. *Ibid.*, pp. 2205–7.
57. See Paul Ely, *Memoires: L'Indochine dans la tourmente* (Paris: Plon, 1964), pp. 299–300.
58. Spector, *Advice and Support,* pp. 236–38.
59. November 5, 1954, *FR 1952–1954,* vol. 13, part 2, pp. 2215–16.
60. Collins to Department of State, November 16, 1954, *ibid.*, pp. 2256–57.
61. Memorandum of Conversation, November 17, 1954, *ibid.*, pp. 2265–67.
62. Telephone Call, November 20, 1954, Dulles Papers.
63. *New York Times,* December 17, 1954.
64. *Ibid.*
65. Background Press Conferences, December 16 and 18, 1954, Dulles Papers.
66. Dillon to Department of State, December 17, 1954, *FR 1952–1954,* vol. 13, part 2, pp. 2387–90.
67. Collins to Department of State, December 16, 1954, *FR* 1952–1954, vol. 13, part 2, pp. 2379–82.
68. Dulles to Saigon, December 24, 1954, *ibid.*, pp. 2419–20.
69. Jackson to Dulles, February 26, 1954, Dulles Papers. The best study of Jackson in the Eisenhower administration is Blanche Wiesen Cook, *The Declassified Eisenhower* (New York: Doubleday, 1981), especially pp. 13–14, 298–99.

CHAPTER ELEVEN: THE CONTRADICTIONS OF LIBERAL EMPIRE

1. "Notes for Remarks at Closed Session," February 21, 1955, Dulles papers, Mudd Library, Princeton University, Princeton, New Jersey.
2. George McT. Kahin, *Intervention: How America Became Involved in Vietnam* (New York: Knopf, 1986), p. 83.
3. *Ibid.*, p. 85.

4. *Ibid.*, pp. 85–88.
5. *Ibid.*, pp. 96–101.
6. See United States Senate, Subcommittee of the Committee on Foreign Relations, *Hearings: The Situation in Vietnam*, 86th Cong., 1st sess. (Washington, 1959).
7. Press Conference, June 21, 1956, Dulles Papers.
8. Oral History Project, *ibid.*
9. Background Press Conference, May 12, 1955, *ibid.*
10. Interview, Dulles Oral History Project, *ibid.*
11. Press Conference, May 7, 1955, *ibid.*
12. Quoted in Kahin, *Intervention*, p. 169. And for the essentials of the issue of American responsibility, see *ibid.*, chap. 6.
13. Quoted in Nguyen Tien Hung and Jerrold L. Schecter, *The Palace File* (New York: Harper and Row, 1986), p. 135. This account provides the best information to date, using correspondence between Thieu and Presidents Nixon and Gerald Ford previously unavailable in complete form.
14. Dulles Papers.
15. "Draft, 2/9/55," marked "Read and approved by the President," *ibid.*
16. "Revised Draft Outline: Secretary's Presentation at Bangkok," February 17, 1955, *ibid.*
17. Quoted in David Carlton, *Anthony Eden: A Biography* (London: Allen Lane, 1981), p. 348.
18. "Far East Presentation," May 10, 1955, Dulles Papers.
19. Press Conference, February 25, 1955, *ibid.*
20. *Ibid.*
21. Press Conference, March 1, 1955, *ibid.*
22. *Ibid.*
23. Press Conference, March 2, 1955, *ibid.*
24. *Ibid.*
25. Background Press Conference, May 12, 1955, *ibid.*
26. "Memorandum of Discussion . . . ," April 28, 1955, U.S. Department of State, *Foreign Relations of the United States (FR) 1955–1957* (Washington, 1985), 1:307–12.
27. Dulles to Collins, April 20, 1955, Dulles Papers.
28. For a well-reasoned suggestion that Colonel Lansdale was acting under orders, or at least authorization, from a back channel in Washington instructing him to stimulate Diem to take action against the sects—a last-ditch effort to save his neck—see David L. Anderson, "J. Lawton Collins, John Foster Dulles, and the Eisenhower Administration's 'Point of No Return,' " paper delivered at the annual Society for the History of American Foreign Relations Conference, June 1986.
29. This summary is based on *FR 1955–1957*, 1:291–301, 337–39.
30. Dulles to Collins, May 1, 1955, *ibid.*, pp. 344–45.
31. Dulles to State Department, May 8, 1955, *ibid.*, pp. 372–77.
32. "Memorandum for Record," June 23, 1954, Eisenhower Papers, Whitman File, Legislative Meetings, Eisenhower Library, Abilene, Kansas.
33. "Meeting with Special Advisory Group," excerpts printed in William Appleman Williams et al., eds., *America in Vietnam: A Documentary History* (New York: Doubleday, 1985), pp. 270–72.

34. For a succinct summary of the arguments, see Guenter Lewy, *America in Vietnam* (New York: Oxford Univ. Press, 1978), p. 28.
35. Taylor, *Swords and Plowshares* (New York: Norton, 1972), pp. 339–40.
36. Senate Foreign Relations Committee, *Executive Sessions of the Senate Foreign Relations Committee, 1963 (Historical Series)* (Washington, 1987), 15:737.
37. See note 7, chapter 10.
38. Eisenhower to Diem, undated, *FR 1952–1954* (Washington, 1982), vol. 13, part 2, pp. 2166–67.
39. Harry S. Truman, *Years of Trial and Hope* (Garden City, N.Y.: Doubleday, 1956), pp. 61–62.
40. *Ibid.*, p. 735.
41. Senator Gravel Edition, *The Pentagon Papers,* 4 vols. (Boston: Beacon Press, 1971), 2:346.
42. Diary Entry, November 24, 1953, in C. L. Sulzberger, *A Long Row of Candles* (New York: Macmillan, 1969), pp. 926–28.
43. See note 1, Introduction.

Appendix

GENEVA DECLARATIONS

The final declarations of the Geneva Conference on July 21, 1954. (Source: Democratic Republic of Viet-nam, Ministry of Foreign Affairs, Press and Information Department, *Documents Related to the Implementation of the Geneva Agreements Concerning Viet-nam* [Hanoi, 1956], pp. 181–83.)

1. The Conference takes note of the Agreements ending hostilities in Cambodia, Laos, and Viet-nam and organizing international control and the supervision of the execution of the provisions of these agreements.

2. The Conference expresses satisfaction at the ending of hostilities in Cambodia, Laos and Viet-nam; the Conference expresses its conviction that the execution of the provisions set out in the present Declaration and in the Agreements on the cessation of hostilities will permit Cambodia, Laos, and Viet-nam henceforth to play their part, in full independence and sovereignty, in the peaceful community of nations.

3. The Conference takes note of the declarations made by the Governments of Cambodia and of Laos of their intention to adopt measures permitting all citizens to take their place in the national community, in particular by participating in the next general elections, which, in conformity with the constitution of each of these countries, shall take place in the course of the year 1955, by secret ballot and in conditions of respect for fundamental freedoms.

4. The Conference takes note of the clauses in the Agreement on the cessation of hostilities in Viet-nam prohibiting the introduction into Viet-nam of foreign troops and military personnel as well as all kinds of arms and munitions. The Conference also takes note of the declarations made by the Governments of Cambodia and Laos of their resolution not to request foreign aid, whether in war material, in personnel or in instructors except for the purpose of the effective defence of their territory and, in the case of Laos, to the extent defined by the Agreements on the cessation of hostilities in Laos.

5. The Conference takes note of the clauses in the Agreement on the cessation of hostilities in Viet-nam to the effect that no military base under the control of a foreign State may be established in the regrouping zones of the two parties, the latter having the obligation to see that the zones allotted to them shall not constitute part of any military alliance and shall not be utilized for the resumption of hostilities or in the service of an aggressive policy. The Conference also takes note of the declarations of the Governments of Cambodia and Laos to the effect that they will not join in any agreement with other States if this agreement includes the obligation to participate in a military alliance not in conformity with the principles of the Charter of the United Nations or, in the case of Laos, with the principles of

the Agreement on the cessation of hostilities in Laos or, so long as their security is not threatened, the obligation to establish bases on Cambodian or Laotian territory for the military forces of foreign powers.

6. The Conference recognizes that the essential purpose of the Agreement relating to Viet-nam is to settle military questions with a view to ending hostilities and that the military demarcation line is provisional and should not in any way be interpreted as constituting a political or territorial boundary. The Conference expresses its conviction that the execution of the provisions set out in the present Declaration and in the Agreement on the cessation of hostilities creates the necessary basis for the achievement in the near future of a political settlement in Viet-nam.

7. The Conference declares that, so far as Viet-nam is concerned, the settlement of political problems, effected on the basis of respect for principles of independence, unity and territorial integrity, shall permit the Vietnamese people to enjoy the fundamental freedoms, guaranteed by democratic institutions established as a result of free general elections by secret ballot. In order to ensure that sufficient progress in the restoration of peace has been made and that all the necessary conditions obtain for free expression of the national will, general elections shall be held in July 1956, under the supervision of an international commission composed of representatives of the Member States of the International Supervisory Commission, referred to in the Agreement on the cessation of hostilities. Consultations will be held on this subject between the competent representative authorities of the two zones from 20 July, 1955 onwards.

8. The provisions of the Agreements on the cessation of hostilities intended to ensure the protection of individuals and of property must be most strictly applied and must, in particular, allow everyone in Viet-nam to decide freely in which zone he wishes to live.

9. The competent representative authorities of the Northern and Southern zones of Viet-nam, as well as the authorities of Laos and Cambodia, must not permit any individual or collective reprisals against persons who have collaborated in any way with one of the parties during the war, or against members of such persons' families.

10. The Conference takes note of the declaration of the Government of the French Republic to the effect that it is ready to withdraw its troops from the territory of Cambodia, Laos and Viet-nam, at the request of the governments concerned and within periods which shall be fixed by agreement between the parties except in the cases where, by agreement between the two parties, a certain number of French troops shall remain at specified points and for a specified time.

11. The Conference takes note of the declaration of the French Government to the effect that for the settlement of all the problems connected with the re-establishment and consolidation of peace in Cambodia, Laos and Viet-nam, the French Government will proceed from the principle of respect for the independence and sovereignty, unity and territorial integrity of Cambodia, Laos and Viet-nam.

12. In their relations with Cambodia, Laos and Viet-nam, each member of the Geneva Conference undertakes to respect the sovereignty, the independence, the unity and the territorial integrity of the above-mentioned States, and to refrain from any interference in their internal affairs.

13. The members of the Conference agree to consult one another on any question which may be referred to them by the International Supervisory Commission, in

order to study such measures as may prove necessary to ensure that the Agreements on the cessation of hostilities in Cambodia, Laos and Viet-nam are respected.

THE AMERICAN RESPONSE

Under Secretary of State Walter Bedell Smith delivered the American response to the Geneva Declaration. (Source: United States Senate, Committee on Foreign Relations, *Background Information Relating to Southeast Asia and Vietnam*, 90th Cong., 1st sess., 1967, p. 83.)

As I stated on July 18, my Government is not prepared to join in a declaration by the Conference such as is submitted. However, the United States makes this unilateral declaration of its position in these matters: *Declaration*

The Government of the United States being resolved to devote its efforts to the strengthening of peace in accordance with the principles and purposes of the United Nations takes note of the agreements concluded at Geneva on July 20 and 21, 1954 between (a) the Franco-Laotian Command and the Command of the Peoples Army of Viet-Nam; (b) the Royal Khmer Army Command and the Command of the Peoples Army of Viet-Nam; (c) Franco-Vietnamese Command and the Command of the Peoples Army of Viet-Nam and of paragraphs 1 to 12 inclusive of the declaration presented to the Geneva Conference on July 21, 1954 declares with regard to the aforesaid agreements and paragraphs that (i) it will refrain from the threat or the use of force to disturb them, in accordance with Article 2(4) of the Charter of the United Nations dealing with the obligation of members to refrain in their international relations from the threat or use of force; and (ii) it would view any renewal of the aggression in violation of the aforesaid agreements with grave concern and as seriously threatening international peace and security.

In connection with the statement in the declaration concerning free elections in Viet-Nam my Government wishes to make clear its position which it has expressed in a declaration made in Washington on June 29, 1954, as follows:

> In the case of nations now divided against their will, we shall continue to seek to achieve unity through free elections supervised by the United Nations to insure that they are conducted fairly.

With respect to the statement made by the representative of the State of Viet-Nam, the United States reiterates its traditional position that peoples are entitled to determine their own future and that it will not join in an arrangement which would hinder this. Nothing in its declaration just made is intended to or does indicate any departure from this traditional position.

We share the hope that the agreements will permit Cambodia, Laos and Viet-Nam to play their part, in full independence and sovereignty, in the peaceful community of nations, and will enable the peoples of that area to determine their own future.

Bibliography

MANUSCRIPT COLLECTIONS

Dwight D. Eisenhower Library, Abilene, Kansas
  The Papers of Dwight D. Eisenhower
    Ann Whitman File: Dwight D. Eisenhower Diaries; Administrative Series; International Series; Dulles-Herter Series.
  The Papers of James C. Hagerty
Herbert Hoover Institution, Palo Alto, California
  The Papers of Joseph Stilwell
Houghton Library, Harvard University, Cambridge, Massachusetts
  The Papers of Joseph Grew
Seely Mudd Library, Princeton University, Princeton, New Jersey
  The Papers of Bernard Baruch
  The Papers of John Foster Dulles
  The Papers of Arthur Krock
  John Foster Dulles Oral History Project
    Oral History Interviews:

Elliot Bell	Walter F. Judd
Richard Bissell	Leslie Munro
W. Walton Butterworth	John Chang Myun
Mark Clark	Richard O'Connor
C. Douglas Dillon	Matthew B. Ridgway
Dwight D. Eisenhower	William Sebald
Joseph C. Harsch	Nathan B. Twining

National Archives of the United States, Washington, D.C.
  General Records of the Department of State
  The Papers of Charles Bohlen
  Record Groups: 84, 319, 331, 332
  Harley Notter Records
  Records of the Philippine and Southeast Asian Office
  Records of the Policy Planning Staff
Public Record Office, London, England
  General Records of the Foreign Office: General Correspondence
  The Papers of Ernest Bevin
  The Papers of Prime Minister Winston Churchill
Franklin D. Roosevelt Library, Hyde Park, New York
  The Papers of Harry L. Hopkins

The Papers of Franklin D. Roosevelt
The Papers of Charles Taussig
Harry S. Truman Library, Independence, Missouri
The Papers of Dean Acheson
The Papers of John Melby
The Papers of Harry S. Truman
"The Princeton Seminar"

PUBLISHED COLLECTIONS OF DOCUMENTS

Cameron, Allan W., ed. *Viet-Nam Crisis: A Documentary History.* 2 vols. Ithaca, N.Y.: Cornell University Press, 1971.

Griffith, Robert, ed. *Ike's Letters to a Friend, 1941–1958.* Lawrence, Kan.: University of Kansas Press, 1984.

Kimball, Warren F., ed. *Churchill and Roosevelt: The Complete Correspondence.* 3 vols. Princeton, N.J.: Princeton University Press, 1984.

The Pentagon Papers: Senator Gravel Edition. 4 vols. Boston: Beacon Press, 1974.

Rosenman, Samuel I., ed. *Public Papers and Addresses of Franklin D. Roosevelt.* 13 vols. New York: Harper, Macmillan, Random House, 1938–1950.

U.S. Department of Defense. *United States–Vietnam Relations, 1945–1967.* 12 vols. Washington, 1971.

U.S. Department of State. *American Foreign Policy, 1950–1955: Basic Documents.* 2 vols. Washington, 1957.

———. *Foreign Relations of the United States: Japan, 1931–1941.* Vol. 2. Washington, 1943.

———. *Foreign Relations of the United States: Diplomatic Papers: The Conferences at Malta and Yalta, 1945.* Washington, 1955.

———. *Foreign Relations of the United States: Diplomatic Papers, General: The United Nations, 1945.* Vol. 1. Washington, 1967.

———. *Foreign Relations of the United States: Diplomatic Papers: The Conference of Berlin, 1945.* Vol. 2. Washington, 1960.

———. *Foreign Relations of the United States: Diplomatic Papers: The British Commonwealth, the Far East, 1945.* Vol. 6. Washington, 1969.

———. *Foreign Relations of the United States: Diplomatic Papers: The Far East, China, 1945.* Vol. 7. Washington, 1969.

———. *Foreign Relations of the United States: The Far East, 1947.* Vol. 6. Washington, 1972.

———. *Foreign Relations of the United States: East Asia and the Pacific, 1950.* Vol. 6. Washington, 1976.

———. *Foreign Relations of the United States: Asia and the Pacific, 1951.* Vol. 6. Washington, 1977.

———. *Foreign Relations of the United States: National Security Affairs, 1952–1954.* Vol. 2. Washington, 1984.

———. *Foreign Relations of the United States: Western European Security, 1952–1954.* Vol. 5. Washington, 1983.

———. *Foreign Relations of the United States: East Asia and the Pacific, 1952–1954.* Vol. 12. Washington, 1984.

———. *Foreign Relations of the United States: Indochina, 1952–1954.* Vol. 13. Washington, 1982.

———. *Foreign Relations of the United States: The Geneva Conference, 1952–1954.* Vol. 16. Washington, 1981.

———. *Foreign Relations of the United States: Vietnam, 1955–1957.* Vol. 1. Washington, 1985.

U.S. National Archives. *Public Papers of the Presidents of the United States: Harry S. Truman, 1950.* Washington, 1965.

———. *Public Papers of the Presidents of the United States: Dwight D. Eisenhower, 1953.* Washington, 1960.

———. *Public Papers of the Presidents of the United States: Dwight D. Eisenhower, 1954.* Washington, 1960.

U.S. Senate. Committee on Armed Services and Committee on Foreign Relations. *Military Situation in the Far East: Hearings Before the Committee on Armed Services and the Committee on Foreign Relations.* 82nd Cong., 1st sess., 1951.

———. Committee on Foreign Relations. *Executive Sessions of the Senate Foreign Relations.* Vol. 5, 1953. 83rd Cong., 1st sess., 1977.

———. Committee on Foreign Relations. *Executive Sessions of the Senate Foreign Relations Committee.* Vol. 6, 1954. 83rd Cong., 2nd sess., 1977.

———. Committee on Foreign Relations. *Executive Sessions of the Senate Foreign Relations Committee.* Vol. 15, 1963. 1987.

———. Committee on Foreign Relations. *Hearings Held in Executive Session: Economic Assistance to China and Korea, 1949–1950.* 81st Cong., 1st and 2nd sess., 1974.

———. Committee on Foreign Relations. *Hearings Held in Executive Session: Legislative Origins of the Truman Doctrine.* 80th Cong., 1st sess., 1973.

———. Committee on Foreign Relations. *Hearings: Japanese Peace Treaty and Other Treaties Relating to Security in the Pacific.* 82nd Cong., 2nd sess., 1952.

———. Committee on Foreign Relations. *The United States and Vietnam: 1944–1947.* Staff study based on the Pentagon Papers, study no. 2. 92nd Cong., 2nd sess., 1972.

———. Subcommittee of the Committee on Foreign Relations. *Hearings: The Situation in Vietnam.* 86th Cong., 1st sess., 1959.

Williams, William Appleman, Thomas McCormick, Lloyd Gardner, and Walter LaFeber, eds. *America in Vietnam: A Documentary History.* New York: Doubleday, 1985.

MEMOIRS AND DIARIES

Acheson, Dean. *Present at the Creation: My Years at the State Department.* New York: Norton, 1969.

Adams, Sherman. *Firsthand Report.* New York: Popular Library, 1962.

Berle, Beatrice Bishop, and Travis Jacobs, eds. *Navigating the Rapids: From the Papers of Adolf A. Berle.* New York: Harcourt Brace Jovanovich, 1973.

Bidault, Georges. *Resistance: The Political Autobiography of George Bidault.* Trans. Marianne Sinclair. New York: Praeger, 1967.

Blum, John Morton, ed. *The Price of Vision: The Diary of Henry A. Wallace, 1942–1946.* Boston: Houghton Mifflin, 1973.
Campbell, Thomas M., and George C. Herring, eds. *The Diaries of Edward R. Stettinius, Jr., 1943–1946.* New York: New Viewpoints, 1975.
Churchill, Winston S. *The Second World War: The Gathering Storm.* Boston: Houghton Mifflin, 1948.
———. *The Second World War: The Grand Alliance.* Boston: Houghton Mifflin, 1951.
Colville, John. *Fringes of Power: 10 Downing Street Diaries, 1939–1955.* New York: Norton, 1985.
Eden, Anthony. *Full Circle: The Memoirs of Anthony Eden.* Boston: Houghton Mifflin, 1960.
Eisenhower, Dwight D. *The White House Years: Mandate for Change, 1953–1956.* Garden City, N.Y.: Doubleday, 1963–1965.
Ely, Paul. *Memoires: L'Indochine dans la tourmente.* Paris: Plon, 1964.
Ferrell, Robert H., ed. *The Eisenhower Diaries.* New York: Norton, 1981.
Hughes, John Emmet. *The Ordeal of Power: A Political Memoir of the Eisenhower Years.* New York: Atheneum, 1963.
Hull, Cordell. *The Memoirs of Cordell Hull.* 2 vols. New York: Macmillan, 1948.
Jurika, Stephen Jr., ed. *From Pearl Harbor to Vietnam: The Memoirs of Admiral Arthur W. Radford.* Stanford, Calif.: Hoover Institute Press, 1980.
Kennan, George F. *Memoirs: 1950–1963.* Boston: Atlantic–Little, Brown, 1972.
Landsdale, Edward Geary. *In the Midst of Wars: An American's Mission to Southeast Asia.* New York: Harper and Row, 1972.
Leahy, William D. *I Was There: The Personal Story of the Chief of Staff to Presidents Roosevelt and Truman.* New York: Whittlesey House, 1950.
Lodge, Henry Cabot. *As It Was: An Inside View of Politics and Power in the Fifties and Sixties.* New York: Norton, 1976.
Macmillan, Harold. *The Blast of War, 1939–1945.* New York: Macmillan, 1968.
———. *Tides of Fortune.* New York: Harper and Row, 1969.
———. *War Diaries: The Mediterranean, 1943–1945.* New York: St. Martin's Press, 1984.
Murphy, Robert. *Diplomat Among Warriors.* New York: Pyramid Books, 1964.
Ridgway, Matthew B. *Soldier: Memoirs of Matthew B. Ridgway.* New York: Harper, 1956.
Shuckburgh, Evelyn. *Descent to Suez: Diaries, 1951–56.* New York: Norton, 1986.
Sulzberger, C. L. *A Long Row of Candles: Memoirs and Diaries, 1934–1954.* New York: Macmillan, 1969.
Taylor, Maxwell Davenport. *Swords and Plowshares.* New York: Norton, 1972.
Truman, Harry S. *Memoirs: Year of Decisions.* Garden City, N.Y.: Doubleday, 1955.
———. *Memoirs: Years of Trial and Hope.* Garden City, N.Y.: Doubleday, 1956.

NEWSPAPERS, PERIODICALS, AND UNPUBLISHED PAPERS

Anderson, David L. "J. Lawton Collins, John Foster Dulles, and the Eisenhower Administration's 'Point of No Return.' " Paper delivered at the Annual

Society for the History of American Foreign Relations Conference, June 1986.

Dulles, John Foster. "Security in the Pacific." *Foreign Affairs* 30 (January 1952): 184–87.

Fall, Bernard B. "Tribulations of a Party Line." *Foreign Affairs* 33 (April 1955): 499–510.

Fish, M. Stephen. "After Stalin's Death: The Anglo-American Debate Over a New Cold War." *Diplomatic History* 10 (Fall 1986): 333–56.

Gaddis, John Lewis. "American Policy and Perspectives: The Sino-Soviet 'Wedge' Strategy, 1949–1955." Paper delivered at the Beijing Conference on Sino-American Relations, 1986.

———. "Was the Truman Doctrine a Turning Point?" *Foreign Affairs* 52 (January 1974): 386–402.

Gardner, Lloyd C. "45/85." *Journal of American History* 73 (December 1986): 833–34.

Griffith, Robert. "Dwight D. Eisenhower and the Corporate Commonwealth." *American Historical Review* 87 (February 1982): 87–122.

Herring, George C. "The Truman Administration and the Restoration of French Sovereignty in Indochina." *Diplomatic History* 1 (1977): 97–117.

Herring, George C., and Richard H. Immerman. "Eisenhower, Dulles, and Dienbienphu: 'The Day We Didn't Go to War' Revisited." *Journal of American History* 71 (September 1984): 343–63.

Hess, Gary R. "Franklin Roosevelt and Indochina." *Journal of American History* 59 (1972): 353–68.

Keefer, Edward C. "President Dwight D. Eisenhower and the End of the Korean War." *Diplomatic History* 10 (Summer 1986): 267–89.

Kennan, George F. "The Sources of Soviet Conduct." *Foreign Affairs* 25 (July 1947): 566–82.

Krog, Carl. "American Journals of Opinion and the Fall of Vietnam." *Asian Affairs* 6 (1979): 324–32.

LaFeber, Walter F. "Roosevelt, Churchill, and Indochina: 1942–1945." *American Historical Review* 80 (1975): 1277–95.

Leary, William M. "CAT at Dienbienphu." *Aerospace Historian* 31 (September 1984): 177–84.

Mayers, David. "Eisenhower's Containment Policy and the Major Communist Powers." *International History Review* 5 (February 1983): 60–83.

New York Times.

Ovendale, Ritchie. "Britain, the United States, and the Recognition of Communist China." *Historical Journal* 26 (1983): 139–57.

Rotter, Andrew J. "The Triangular Route to Vietnam: The United States, Great Britain, and Southeast Asia, 1945–1950." *International History Review* 6 (August 1984): 404–23.

Stueck, William. "The Limits of Influence: British Policy and American Expansion of the War in Korea." *Pacific Historical Review* 55 (February 1986): 65–95.

Thorne, Christopher. "Indochina and Anglo-American Relations, 1942–1945." *Pacific Historical Review* 45 (1976): 73–96.

Time, October 25, 1971, p.20.

Vital Speeches 11 (February 1945): 273–75.
Washington Post.

BOOKS: SECONDARY SOURCES

Ambrose, Stephen. *Eisenhower, the President.* New York: Simon and Schuster, 1984.

Barnet, Richard. *The Alliance: America-Europe-Japan, Makers of the Postwar World.* New York: Simon and Schuster, 1983.

Bator, Victor M. *Vietnam—a Diplomatic Tragedy.* Dobbs Ferry, N.Y.: Oceana Publications, 1965.

Blum, Robert. *Drawing the Line: The Origin of the American Containment Policy in East Asia.* New York: Norton, 1982.

Boettcher, Thomas D. *Vietnam: The Valor and the Sorrow.* Boston: Little, Brown, 1986.

Bonner, Raymond. *Waltzing with the Dictator: The Marcoses and the Making of American Policy.* New York: Times Books, 1987.

Borden, William S. *The Pacific Alliance: United States Economic Policy and Japanese Trade Recovery, 1947–1955.* Madison: University of Wisconsin Press, 1984.

Borg, Dorothy, and Waldo Heinrichs, eds. *Uncertain Years: Chinese-American Relations, 1947–1950.* New York: Columbia University Press, 1980.

Bullock, Alan. *Ernest Bevin: Foreign Secretary, 1945–1951.* London: Heinemann, 1983.

Calleo, David P., and Richard M. Rowland. *America and the World Political Economy: Atlantic Dreams and National Realities.* Bloomington: Indiana University Press, 1973.

Carlton, David. *Anthony Eden: A Biography.* London: Allen Lane, 1981.

Childs, Marquis. *Eisenhower: Captive Hero.* New York: Harcourt, Brace, 1958.

Connell, Evan S. *Son of the Morning Star: Custer and the Little Bighorn.* San Francisco: North Point Press, 1984.

Cook, Blanche Wiesen. *The Declassified Eisenhower: A Divided Legacy.* New York: Doubleday, 1981.

Cooper, Chester L. *The Lost Crusade: America in Vietnam.* New York: Dodd, Mead, 1970.

Dallek, Robert. *Franklin D. Roosevelt and American Foreign Policy, 1939–1945.* New York: Oxford University Press, 1979.

Davies, John Paton. *Dragon by the Tail.* New York: Norton, 1972.

De Carmoy, Guy. *The Foreign Policies of France, 1944–1968.* Trans. Elaine P. Halperin. Chicago: University of Chicago Press, 1970.

Devillers, Philippe, and Jean Lacouture. *End of a War: Indochina, 1954.* Trans. Alexander Lieven and Adam Roberts. New York: Praeger, 1969.

Divine, Robert. *Blowing on the Wind: The Nuclear Test Ban Debate, 1954–1960.* New York: Oxford University Press, 1978.

———. *Second Chance: The Triumph of Internationalism in America During World War II.* New York: Atheneum, 1967.

Dower, John. *War Without Mercy: Race and Power in the Pacific War.* New York: Pantheon, 1986.

Drinnon, Richard. *Facing Westward: The Metaphysics of Indian Hating and Empire Building.* Minneapolis: University of Minnesota Press, 1980.

Duncanson, Dennis J. *Government and Revolution in Vietnam.* London: Oxford University Press, 1968.

Dunn, Peter M. *The First Vietnam War.* New York: St. Martin's Press, 1985.

Eden, Anthony. *Toward a Peace in Indochina.* Boston: Houghton Mifflin, 1966.

Eisenhower, David. *Eisenhower at War, 1943–1945.* New York: Random House, 1986.

Fall, Bernard B. *Hell in a Very Small Place: The Siege of Dien Bien Phu.* Philadelphia: Lippincott, 1966.

———. *The Two Viet-Nams: A Political and Military Analysis.* New York: Praeger, 1963.

Feis, Herbert. *China Tangle.* New York: Atheneum, 1965.

Foot, Rosemary. *The Wrong War: American Policy and the Dimensions of the Korean Conflict, 1950–1953.* Ithaca, N.Y.: Cornell University Press, 1985.

Freedman, Lawrence. *The Evolution of Nuclear Strategy.* New York: St. Martin's Press, 1983.

Gardner, Lloyd C. *A Covenant with Power: America and World Order from Wilson to Reagan.* New York: Oxford University Press, 1984.

———. *Economic Aspects of New Deal Diplomacy.* Madison: University of Wisconsin Press, 1964.

———. *Safe for Democracy: The Anglo-American Response to Revolution, 1913–1923.* New York: Oxford University Press, 1984.

Gardner, Lloyd C., ed. *Redefining the Past: Essays in Diplomatic History in Honor of William Appleman Williams.* Corvallis: Oregon State University Press, 1986.

Gardner, Lloyd C., Walter F. LaFeber, and Thomas J. McCormick. *Creation of the American Empire: U.S. Diplomatic History.* Chicago: Rand McNally, 1973.

Gardner, Richard N. *Sterling-Dollar Diplomacy.* New York: McGraw-Hill, 1969.

Gerson, Louis L. *John Foster Dulles.* New York: Cooper Square, 1967.

Gopal, Sarvepalli. *Jawaharlal Nehru: A Biography.* Cambridge, Mass.: Harvard University Press, 1976.

Gowing, Margaret. *Independence and Deterence: Britain and Atomic Energy, 1945–1952.* 2 vols. London: Macmillan, 1974.

Graebner, Norman A. *The New Isolationism: A Study of Politics and Foreign Policy Since 1950.* New York: Ronald Press, 1956.

Graebner, Norman, ed. *The National Security: Its Theory and Practice, 1945–1960.* New York: Oxford University Press, 1986.

Greene, Graham. *The Quiet American.* New York: Penguin, 1980.

Gurtov, Melvin. *The First Vietnam Crisis.* New York: Columbia University Press, 1967.

Hammer, Ellen. *The Struggle for Indo-China, 1940–1954.* Stanford, Calif.: Stanford University Press, 1966.

Herring, George C. *America's Longest War: The United States and Vietnam, 1950–1975.* 2nd ed. New York: Knopf, 1985.

Holland, R. F. *European Decolonization, 1918–1981: An Introductory Survey.* New York: St. Martin's Press, 1985.

Immerman, Richard. *The CIA in Guatemala: The Foreign Policy of Intervention.* Austin: University of Texas Press, 1982.

Iriye, Akira. *The Cold War in Asia: A Historical Introduction.* Englewood Cliffs, N.J.: Prentice-Hall, 1974.

Irving, R. E. M. *The First Indochina War: French and American Policy, 1945–54.* London: C. Helm, 1975.

James, Robert Rhodes. *Anthony Eden.* London: Weidenfeld and Nicolson, 1986.

Kahin, George McTurnan. *Intervention: How America Became Involved in Vietnam.* New York: Knopf, 1986.

Karnow, Stanley. *Vietnam: A History.* New York: Viking Press, 1983.

Kaufman, Burton I. *The Korean War: The Challenges in Crisis, Credibility, and Command.* New York: Knopf, 1986.

Kolko, Gabriel. *Anatomy of a War.* New York: Pantheon, 1985.

Korn, Walter, ed. *Modern Chess Openings.* 9th ed. New York: McKay, 1962.

Lacouture, Jean. *Ho Chi Minh: A Political Biography.* Trans. Peter Wiles. New York: Random House, 1968.

———. *Pierre Mendès-France.* Trans. George Holoch. New York: Holmes and Mier, 1984.

LaFeber, Walter, ed. *America in the Cold War.* New York: Wiley, 1969.

———, ed. *The Origins of the Cold War.* New York: Wiley, 1971.

Lewy, Guenter. *America in Vietnam.* New York: Oxford University Press, 1978.

Louis, Wm. Roger. *Imperialism at Bay: The United States and the Decolonization of the British Empire, 1941–1945.* New York: Oxford University Press, 1978.

Maclear, Michael. *The Ten Thousand Day War: Vietnam, 1945–1975.* New York: Avon, 1981.

Marr, David G. *Vietnamese Tradition on Trial, 1920–1945.* Berkeley: University of California Press, 1984.

McAlister, John T., Jr. *Vietnam: The Origins of Revolution.* New York: Knopf, 1971.

McMahon, Robert J. *Colonialism and Cold War: The United States and the Struggle for Indonesian Independence, 1945–49.* Ithaca, N.Y.: Cornell University Press, 1981.

Mendès-France, Pierre. *Choisir: Conversations avec Jean Bothorel.* Paris: Stock, 1974.

Moran, Lord. *Churchill: The Struggle for Survival, 1940–65.* Boston: Houghton Mifflin, 1966.

Mus, Paul. *Viet Nam: Sociologie d'une guerre.* Paris: Editions du Seuil, 1952.

Nguyen Tien Hung and Jerrold L. Schecter. *The Palace File.* New York: Harper and Row, 1986.

Ovendale, Ritchie. *The English-Speaking Alliance: Britain, the United States, the Dominions, and the Cold War, 1945–51.* London: Allen Unwin, 1985.

Ovendale, Ritchie, and *The Foreign Policy of the British Labour Governments, 1945–1951.* Leicester, Eng.: Leicester University Press, 1984.

Patti, Achimedes L. A. *Why Viet Nam? Prelude to America's Albatross.* Berkeley: University of California Press, 1980.

Prados, John. *The Sky Would Fall: Operation Vulture: The U.S. Bombing Mission in Indochina.* New York: Dial Press, 1982.

Prouty, Fletcher. *The Secret Team: The CIA and Its Allies in Control of the United States.* Englewood Cliffs, N.J.: Prentice-Hall, 1973.

Pruessen, Ronald W. *John Foster Dulles: The Road to Power.* New York: Free Press, 1982.

BIBLIOGRAPHY

Randle, Robert. *Geneva 1954: The Settlement of the Indochinese War.* Princeton: Princeton University Press, 1969.

Rees, David. *Korea: The Limited War.* New York: St. Martin's Press, 1964.

Ridgway, Matthew B. *The Korean War.* New York: Doubleday, 1967.

Roosevelt, Elliott. *As He Saw It.* New York: Duell, Sloan, and Pearce, 1946.

Roy, Jules. *The Battle of Dienbienphu.* New York: Carroll and Graf, 1984.

Sainteny, Jean. *Histoire d'une paix manquée: Indochine, 1945–1947.* Paris: Amiot-Dumont, 1967.

Sherwood, Robert. *Roosevelt and Hopkins: An Intimate History.* New York: Harper and Row, 1950.

Smith, R. B. *An International History of the Vietnam War.* Vol. 1: *Revolution Versus Containment, 1955–1961.* London: St. Martin's Press, 1983.

Spector, Ronald. *The United States Army in Vietnam, Advice and Support: The Early Years.* Washington, D.C.: Center of Military History, 1983.

Stueck, William. *The Road to Confrontation: American Policy Toward China and Korea, 1947–1950.* Chapel Hill: University of North Carolina Press, 1981.

Summers, Harry G., Jr. *On Strategy.* San Francisco: Presidio Press, 1982.

Thomas, Hugh. *Armed Truce: The Beginnings of the Cold War, 1945–46.* New York: Atheneum, 1987.

Thorne, Christopher G. *Allies of a Kind: The United States, Britain, and the War Against Japan, 1941–1945.* New York: Oxford University Press, 1978.

———. *The Issue of War: States, Societies, and the Far Eastern Conflict of 1941–45.* New York: Oxford University Press, 1985.

———. *The Limits of Foreign Policy: The West, the League, and the Far Eastern Crisis of 1931–1933.* London: Hamilton, 1972.

Truong Chinh. *President Ho Chi Minh, Revered Leader of the Vietnamese People.* Hanoi: Foreign Languages Publication House, 1966.

Tucker, Nancy Bernkopf. *Patterns in the Dust: Chinese-American Relations and the Recognition Controversy, 1949–1950.* New York: Columbia University Press, 1983.

Vo Nguyen Giap. *People's War, People's Army.* New York: Praeger, 1962.

Warner, Denis. *The Last Confucian.* New York: Macmillan, 1963.

Werth, Alexander. *Lost Statesman: The Strange Story of Pierre Mendès-France.* New York: Abelard-Schuman, 1958.

Whiting, Allen S. *China Crosses the Yalu: The Decision to Enter the Korean War.* New York: Macmillan, 1960.

Williams, William Appleman, ed. *From Colony to Empire: Essays in the History of American Foreign Relations.* New York: Wiley, 1972.

Ziegler, Philip. *Mountbatten: The Official Biography.* New York: Harper and Row, 1985.

Index

INDEX

INDEX